Politeness

During the last fifteen years, existing models of linguistic politeness have generated a huge amount of empirical research. Using a wide range of data from real-life speech situations, this new introduction to politeness breaks away from the limitations of current models and argues that the proper object of study in politeness theory must be commonsense notions of what politeness and impoliteness are. From this, Watts argues, a more appropriate model, one based on Bourdieu's concept of social practice, is developed. The book aims to show that the terms 'polite' and 'impolite' can only be properly examined as they are contested discursively. In doing so, 'polite' and 'impolite' utterances inevitably involve their users in a struggle for power.

A radically new account of linguistic politeness, the book will appeal to students and researchers in a wide range of disciplines, in linguistics and the social sciences.

RICHARD J. WATTS is Full Professor of English Linguistics, University of Berne, Switzerland. His previous publications include *Standard English: the Widening Debate* (edited with Tony Bex) (1999), *Politeness in Language* (edited with Sachiko Ide and Konrad Ehlich) (1992), *Alternative Histories of English* (edited with Peter Trudgill) (2002) and *Power in Family Discourse* (1991).

KEY TOPICS IN SOCIOLINGUISTICS

This new series focuses on the main topics of study in sociolinguistics today. It consists of accessible yet challenging accounts of the most important issues to consider when examining the relationship between language and society. Some topics have been the subject of sociolinguistic study for many years, and are here re-examined in the light of new developments in the field; others are issues of growing importance that have not so far been given a sustained treatment. Written by leading experts, the books in the series are designed to be used on courses and in seminars, and include useful suggestions for futher reading and a helpful glossary.

Forthcoming titles:

World Englishes by Rakesh Bhatt and Raj Mesthrie

Language Policy by Bernard Spolsky

Analyzing Sociolinguistic Variation by Sali Tagliamonte

Critical Discourse Analysis by Jan Blommaert

Politeness

RICHARD J. WATTS

CAMBRIDGE
UNIVERSITY PRESS

PUBLISHED BY THE PRESS SYNDICATE OF THE UNIVERSITY OF CAMBRIDGE
The Pitt Building, Trumpington Street, Cambridge CB2 1RP, United Kingdom

CAMBRIDGE UNIVERSITY PRESS
The Edinburgh Building, Cambridge, CB2 2RU, UK
40 West 20th Street, New York, NY 10011–4211, USA
477 Williamstown Road, Port Melbourne, VIC 3207, Australia
Ruiz de Alarcón 13, 28014 Madrid, Spain
Dock House, The Waterfront, Cape Town 8001, South Africa

http://www.cambridge.org

First published 2003

Printed in the United Kingdom at the University Press, Cambridge

Typeface Swift 9.5/12 pt.   *System* LATEX 2$_\varepsilon$ [TB]

A catalogue record for this book is available from the British Library

Library of Congress Cataloguing in Publication data
Watts, Richard J.
Politeness / Richard J. Watts.
    p.   cm. – (Key topics in sociolinguistics)
Includes bibliographical references.
ISBN 0 521 79085 9 (hardback)   ISBN 0 521 79406 4 (paperback)
1. Sociolinguistics.   2. Etiquette.   3. Forms of address.   I. Title.   II. Series.
P40.5.E75W38   2003
306.44 – dc21   2003043599

ISBN 0 521 79085 9 hardback
ISBN 0 521 79406 4 paperback

To my granddaughter, Jenny, who appears in chapter 7

Contents

Preface

Writing an introduction to politeness is like being in mortal combat with a many-headed hydra. You've barely severed one head when a few more grow in its place. The first head I needed to sever was whether politeness should be taken to include all forms of polite behaviour or to focus on polite language usage. For a linguist it was not difficult to chop off that particular head. It was obvious that an introduction to politeness should focus on forms of social behaviour involving language. But the problem was that, once I had severed that head, a whole set of other heads promptly emerged. Should an introduction to politeness, understood now as linguistic politeness, focus on the canonical models of politeness in language currently on the market? What *is* polite language in any case? Should an introduction to politeness reveal to the reader the wide scope of empirical research on politeness in fields as far apart as legal language, second language acquisition, business studies, gender issues, developmental psychology, etc.? At present I already have a bibliography that contains roughly 1,200 titles, and it is growing steadily week by week. Should an introduction to politeness focus more solidly on the theoretical issues informing this empirical research? Or would it not have been easier to write about linguistic structures that have traditionally been considered in the literature to be 'polite', e.g. honorifics, terms of address, polite formulaic utterances, indirect speech acts, etc.? And what about the vexing issue of why so little has been written about impoliteness?

From this the reader may conclude that it has taken a little longer to write this book than I had originally planned. Faced with the hydra of politeness that I could not possibly defeat, I retired from the battle and laid aside my sword. I then started to ask myself the fundamental questions that had been spilling around in my own head for years. How could I write an introduction to politeness for readers entering the field for the first time without getting them hopelessly bogged down in a morass of problematic theoretical issues in current research? At the same time, however, how could I set out in as readable a way as possible what I consider to be a new approach to the field and, at the same time, carry the reader along with me?

One thing was immediately clear to me: a new approach to linguistic politeness must involve a break with the dominant research paradigm in the field, i.e. Brown and Levinson's long 1978 article published in book form in 1987 with the title *Politeness: Some Universals in Language Usage*. But it would also necessitate the introduction of technical terms with which the reader may not be familiar. To make the book as accessible as possible to the uninitiated reader, I have therefore provided a glossary of technical terms at the end of the book, and I have endeavoured to keep my explanations as straightforward as possible.

This preface already seems littered with negative metaphors like a battle with the hydra of politeness and readers getting bogged down in a morass of theoretical issues. (The previous sentence continues the trend by introducing the metaphor of metaphors littering the text!) So perhaps the reader will grant me one last negative metaphor. At one stage in writing this book I distinctly felt that I was alone and adrift in an ocean of Brown–Levinsonian empirical work on politeness and that I was desperately trying to find dry land and a friendly shore. I found the land I was looking for in 2001 when I read Gino Eelen's book *A Critique of Politeness Theories* and was relieved to see that my intellectual compass had not led me astray. A direct consequence of my reading it was the collaboration between Gino, myself and Jim O'Driscoll in organising a colloquium on what we call, taking Gino's lead, the *discursive* approach to linguistic politeness at the 'Sociolinguistics Symposium 14' held at the University of Ghent in April 2002. Working towards that colloquium set me back on track to finish off the writing of this book. Without the support and intellectual stimulation provided (perhaps not always consciously) by Gino and Jim, I might still be writing it now. At this point I should also like to extend my thanks to the other participants at the colloquium, Maria Sifianou, Juliane House, Derek Bousfield, Saeko Fukushima, Miriam Locher, Gudrun Held and, although he is not really 'into' politeness research, John Haviland, for making it such a memorable occasion and for giving me renewed confidence in presenting my ideas on linguistic politeness to readers new to the field.

I suppose the person responsible for getting me to fight the hydra in the first place, for allowing me to see whether I could cross the bog without sinking in and for casting me out on the Brown–Levinsonian sea (and also for causing me to leave behind quite remarkable quantities of litter) was Andrew Winnard at Cambridge University Press.

I would like to extend my warm thanks to him and the team at Cambridge for a magnificent job. Without a good publisher behind me, I would never have begun the work. I have never regretted having taken on the challenge, but without Andrew's remarkable restraint in not constantly badgering me to keep to the time limits that I set myself, it would not have been brought to fruition (yet another metaphor, but positive this time).

Teachers at universities should never forget the debt that they owe to their students. It was Noam Chomsky who once said that if you're still teaching at age 50 what you were teaching at age 25, you should think of giving up. But university teachers would not bridge that time gap creatively if they did not have innovative, keen young intellects urging them on to stay young in their own minds and to keep abreast of the latest movements in their field. I have tried out the ideas in this book on my own students in the English Department of the University of Berne and on students in the English Department of the University of Lausanne while I was teaching there during the academic year 2000–1. They were critical, sometimes harshly so, and many of the chapters have had to be changed dramatically on the basis of our discussions. I would like to take the opportunity of thanking them all for their constructive criticism and their unfailing support. It would be nice to think that I may have sown the seeds from which a future generation of politeness researchers will emerge.

I would also like to extend warm thanks to my assistant at the University of Berne, Adrian Pablé, for taking on the job of giving the first draft a good close reading. In particular my thanks go to Simon Hicks at the Department of English, who has been a good colleague of mine for several years now, for putting me through an amazingly critical reading of the second draft, including a couple of raps over the knuckles concerning comma placement! A further, very special vote of thanks goes to my very own graduate student guinea-pig, Kellie Gonçalves from the USA, for proving that the book *is* readable by graduates new to the field.

When university teachers write books, they tend to strain the patience of colleagues and co-workers. I should therefore like to thank all my colleagues in the English Department at the University of Berne for putting up with my frequent disappearances from the department during the process of writing. At least the book is evidence that the disappearances were not in vain. However, I would like to thank my research assistants, Peter Schärer, Dominique Kläy and, in particular, Miriam Locher, for fruitful discussions and heated arguments about linguistic politeness and for putting up with a frequently moody professor.

The warmest thanks are reserved for those who have to bear the major brunt of the ups and downs during the course of writing a book – one's family. Apart from me, my family consists of my wife Anne-Marie, my son Chris, my daughter-in-law Heike and my granddaughter Jenny, to whom this book is dedicated with love. When my wife learnt that I had been asked to write an introductory book on politeness, she could not resist making the following comment: 'It's ironic that just about the most impolite person I know has been asked to write about politeness.' She has since shown amazing tenacity in putting up with me throughout the writing process. My thanks also go to my son, my daughter-in-law and my granddaughter for coming round and lifting up my spirits whenever they were getting low.

1 Introducing linguistic politeness

CHARACTERISING POLITE BEHAVIOUR

Most of us are fairly sure we know what we mean when we describe someone's behaviour as 'polite'. To define the criteria with which we apply that description, however, is not quite as easy as we might think. When people are asked what they imagine polite behaviour to be, there is a surprising amount of disagreement. In an effort to find some kind of consensus we may of course take refuge in very general statements, but our usual way out of the dilemma is to resort to giving examples of behaviour which we, personally, would consider 'polite'. We might make statements like 'He always shows a lot of respect towards his superiors', or 'She's always very helpful and obliging', or 'She speaks really well', or 'He always opens doors for the ladies or helps them on with their coats', etc. Some people feel that polite behaviour is equivalent to socially 'correct' or appropriate behaviour; others consider it to be the hallmark of the cultivated man or woman. Some might characterise a polite person as always being considerate towards other people; others might suggest that a polite person is self-effacing. There are even people who classify polite behaviour negatively, characterising it with such terms as 'standoffish', 'haughty', 'insincere', etc.

Moving from evaluations of polite behaviour in general to the more specific case of polite language usage, i.e. 'polite' language, we encounter the same types of problem. To characterise polite language usage, we might resort to expressions like 'the language a person uses to avoid being too direct', or 'language which displays respect towards or consideration for others'. Once again, we might give examples such as 'language which contains respectful forms of address like *sir* or *madam*', 'language that displays certain "polite" formulaic utterances like *please, thank you, excuse me* or *sorry*', or even 'elegantly expressed

1

language'. And again we would encounter people who consider the polite use of language as 'hypocritical', 'dishonest', 'distant', 'unfeeling', etc. Talk about polite behaviour, linguistic or otherwise, is *metapragmatic* talk, i.e. it is talk about talk or talk about other people's general behaviour.

In addition to having our own personal assessments of what constitutes polite behaviour, we also have a tendency to opine on and thereby evaluate the behaviour of others, and sometimes – although much more rarely than might generally be expected – we classify that behaviour (or aspects of it) as 'polite' or 'impolite'. We might also use terms like 'respectful', 'courteous', 'offhand', 'rude', 'cringing', 'pusillanimous', etc. depending on what our own personal folk notions of polite behaviour happen to be. Personal assessments of polite or impolite behaviour can also be expected to vary quite considerably, and indeed they do.

We can best illustrate this by looking at a couple of real-life examples. Consider the following very short extract:[1]

(1)

[1]R:	supposing you say		
	to me <LOW BURP>	beg your pardon\	supposing you
B:	oo::	<@pardon me@>\ yes\<@@@>	
[2]R:	say to me ...		
B:			

Taken out of context, anyone commenting on R's behaviour here might evaluate his low burp as impolite. B seems to take it as a joke, though, since she laughingly repeats his apology and, after appealing for him to continue what he was saying (*yes*), bursts into another brief round of laughter. So any interpretation of the burp as impolite behaviour by a commentator on the interaction in (1) is at odds in that evaluation with the ongoing assessment of the participant to whom R is addressing his utterance. R's expression *beg your pardon* might be interpreted as an acceptable way to atone for 'bad' behaviour. Some might call it an expression of politeness, whereas others might suggest that it is simply the commonest way of overcoming what Goffman (1955) calls an 'incident' – although, of course, they probably would not use that terminology – and is therefore a ritualised rather than a polite expression.

I shall return to extract (1) a little later. For the moment, however, consider the next brief extract:

(2)

[1]S:	yes\ can I come back on Mandy's point\ because I think this is one aspect . of TVEI\ which has been
C:	

[2]S:	totally underemphasised tonight\ what TVEI is about is creating fresh opportunities\ it is creating
C:	

[3]S:	fresh initiatives – no let me finish\ it is a pilot scheme . where ...
C:	it's not\

Again, looked at out of context, C's intervention into S's turn at talk might be taken as impolite behaviour by some commentators, and, indeed, S is quick to capitalise on the possibility of this interpretation in his response to C. On the other hand, others might suggest that the extract seems to have been taken from an argument about the status of something called TVEI and that in an argument it is perfectly natural for one participant, generally an opponent, to intervene in her/his adversary's turn at talk. At the beginning of his turn S's *yes* is not obviously addressed to C, and he seems to be asking permission to return to 'Mandy's point' and elaborate on it. Some commentators might assess his expression *can I come back on Mandy's point . . .* as polite behaviour; others might suggest that he could just as easily have said *I'd like to come back on Mandy's point . . .* and that, far from being genuinely polite, he is only simulating politeness and is in reality currying favour with the person he is addressing or some other person or set of persons.

Contextualising both extracts might of course modify our evaluations of whether the participants are being 'rude', 'polite', 'hypocritical' or whatever. Extract (1) is taken from a family gathering in which all the participants are drinking home-made barley wine brewed by one of the participants. R is B's 41-year-old son and the general atmosphere is, to say the least, convivial. Extract (2) is taken from a television debate on TVEI (Technical and Vocational Education Initiative) during the 1980s. S is a Conservative Party politician and C is professor of education at a British university. Both of them are indeed opponents in this particular debate. S is addressing his turn at talk to the moderator of the programme as well as to the wider television audience viewing at home. But even enriching the extracts by contextualising them does not rule out different interpretations of (a) whether or not a participant's behaviour is 'polite' or 'impolite' or (b) whether the 'polite' behaviour is evaluated positively or negatively. 'Impolite' behaviour is, of course, hardly likely to receive other than a negative interpretation.

We can call the varied interpretations of politeness and impoliteness in ongoing verbal interaction 'folk interpretations' or 'lay interpretations'. They are clearly not of the same order as the terms 'politeness' and 'impoliteness' when these are used as technical concepts in sociolinguistic theorising about social interaction. Watts *et al.* (1992a) maintain that researchers into linguistic politeness frequently confuse 'folk', or 'lay', interpretations with the technical interpretation, and throughout this book I shall make a concerted effort to keep the two perspectives apart. I shall call 'folk' interpretations of (im)politeness 'first-order (im)politeness' (or, following Eelen 2001, (im)politeness$_1$) and (im)politeness as a concept in a sociolinguistic theory of (im)politeness 'second-order (im)politeness' (or (im)politeness$_2$).

Eelen refers to the kinds of metapragmatic evaluation of the nature and significance of politeness/impoliteness as *metapragmatic politeness$_1$*, and the comments made either by outsiders to the interaction or even by the participants themselves as *classificatory politeness$_1$*. He also suggests a third type of politeness$_1$, which he calls *expressive politeness$_1$*, in which participants aim at explicitly producing polite language. Expressive politeness$_1$ is in evidence when participants make use of formulaic language, presumably to adopt a respectful, or polite stance to the addressee. In extract (1) R's utterance *beg your pardon* could be called expressive politeness. Had he said nothing, he would have indicated either that in this group of people burping is a normal form of behaviour and does not need to be atoned for, or that he is hoping that no other participants will have noticed the 'incident'. Similarly, it is also possible to classify S's *can I come back on Mandy's point* in extract (2) as a formulaic utterance expressing concern for the moderator, although it's perhaps not quite so formulaic as R's utterance in (1). There is a difference in the two situations, however. In extract (1) R does not really have much choice but to use an instance of expressive politeness$_1$ if he does not want to be thought of as a boorish, ill-bred person. In extract (2), however, S *does* have a choice, and no one would think him impolite if he had used an utterance like *I'd like to come back on Mandy's point*. S's choice of language here appears to be strategic, whereas social constraints do not leave R any choice in extract (1). Both types of expressive politeness$_1$ (socially constrained utterances and strategically chosen utterances) have been the subject of theorising about politeness as a pragmatic, sociolinguistic concept. Before we go on to make a clearer distinction between (im)politeness$_1$ and (im)politeness$_2$, however, we first need to consider briefly the nature of the distinction between polite and impolite behaviour, remembering while we do so that we are still referring to politeness₁.

POLITE AND IMPOLITE BEHAVIOUR

Eelen (2001) points out, quite rightly, that theories of politeness have focused far more on polite behaviour than on impolite behaviour. This is all the more surprising since commentators on and participants in verbal interaction are more likely to comment on behaviour which they perceive to be 'impolite', 'rude', 'discourteous', 'obstreperous', 'bloody-minded', etc. than on 'polite' behaviour, and they tend to agree far more readily in their classification of the negative end of the scale than of the positive end. Fraser and Nolen (1981) and Fraser (1990), for instance, suggest that behaviour which indicates that the participants are abiding by what they call the Conversational Contract (CC) generally goes unnoticed. It's only when one of the participants violates the rights and obligations of the CC that her/his behaviour is classified as 'impolite'.

Kienpointner (1997) has written on various types of 'rude' utterance displaying impoliteness, and Austin (1990) has discussed forms of impolite behaviour in New Zealand. In a rarely quoted but fascinating article, Baumann (1981) examines what he calls the 'rhetoric of impoliteness' among the early quakers in America. A small set of researchers have examined the function of strategic or mock impoliteness, following on from Labov's work on ritual insults among black adolescents in the USA (1975). Kotthoff (1996) has examined impoliteness in conversational joke-telling and Culpeper (1996) discusses 'mock impoliteness' or 'banter' which is not intended to be understood as serious criticism. Baroni and Axia (1989) have examined how children learn to distinguish between polite and impolite ways of formulating requests. But apart from this work and one or two articles of a more specialised kind, this seems to be the extent of the literature on impolite behaviour.

If Fraser and Nolen (1981) and Fraser (1990) are correct, perceived impoliteness should constitute salient behaviour that is commented on in conversation. Extract (2) in the previous section did indeed contain an explicit comment by S on C's attempt to interrupt him – *no, let me finish* – which can be interpreted as an outright rejection of C's intervention – *no* – followed by a statement implying that S interprets C as not wanting S to complete his turn – *let me finish* – which, having been granted the conversational floor, he has a right to do. Extracts (3) and

(4) display clear evidence of participants expressing their disapproval of the other participants' behaviour, even though they do not directly use either of the lexemes 'impolite' and 'rude'.

(3)

^{1}E:	Peter Taylor reporting\ well with me in the studio watching the film \ is Mr Arthur Scargill\ president
S:	
^{2}E:	of the National Union of Mineworkers \ Mr Scargill\ .. the issue causing .. the breakdown was/ all
S:	
^{3}E:	last week the issue .. at the front of the news\ and in everybody's minds \ was the .. union's refusal
S:	
^{4}E:	to accept the closure of uneconomic pits \ are you now willing to discuss: uneconomic pits \
S:	... we're
^{5}E:	⇓ you're not/ sorry if I interrupt you .. there \
S:	not prepared to go along to the National Coal Board \ and start –
^{6}E:	y/ I- I/ let me just remind you that –
S:	⇑ er: (..) :er: (..) are you going to let me answer the question \ you put a- a
^{7}E:	
S:	question\ for God's sake let me answer

The extract is taken from an interview on the BBC television programme *Panorama* during the famous miners' strike in the early 1980s. Even allowing for the 'freedom' that programme moderators seem to have preempted for themselves these days, E's intervention at the first double-shafted arrow in score 5 can be classified as an example of blatant interruption (cf. Watts 1991). This is evidenced by his insertion of the formulaic utterance of expressive politeness$_1$ *sorry*. S's intervention at the second double-shafted arrow in score 6 contains a highly emotive comment on E's behaviour, which constitutes clear evidence of the way he has interpreted it, even though he does not use either the lexeme 'impolite' or the lexeme 'rude'.

In the following extract from a radio phone-in programme on the subject of snooker and billiards, in which the moderator is accompanied by an expert in the studio, one of the callers feels somewhat left out at one stage in her call and protests (good-naturedly). The behaviour of the moderator and the expert is openly criticised, and the moderator is the first to admit the mistake. As in the previous extract, the word *impolite* is not used explicitly as an evaluative comment on their behaviour (classificatory politeness$_1$) by any of the participants, although non-participants commenting on this extract might easily classify it as such:

(4)

¹M: I would like to ask please/ I'm not really/ but I love snooker – how do I get a ticket for Sheffield\
 J: < @@@ >
 C:

²M: I have written every year\ and no one is answering\ and I am desperate\
 J: < @ @ @ >   (1.3) I would say (..)
 C: < @ @ @ @ @ >

³M: I shall do so then\   uhuh
 J: write now\   write now\   1.2 tell them he/ tell them you've been .. on the
 C:

⁴M:
 J: programme\ and we've suggested you write now\ they might be kind\ I'm sure they will\
 C: how do

⁵M:
 J:
 C: they distribute the tickets\ you know what happens at Wimbledon\ and you know that the- there's

⁶M:
 J:
 C: a ballot\ is there any sort of balloting system\ or is it first come first served\ is there- is there some

⁷M:
 J: well I mean\
 C: sort of membership\.. or VIP people who get the tickets f- first\ what exactly is the system\

⁸M:
 J: I wouldn't ... :er: profess to be expert at/ on this phase\ but :erm: I think if you write early enough\
 C:

⁹M:
 J: I think you'll get tickets\ it's a question of .. booking .. booking a couple of seats or whatever\
 C:

¹⁰M:
 J: for a certain day\ ... and if you get there early enough you'll get them\ if you- if you wait and
 C:

¹¹M: ⇓ can I come back in now\
 J: wait and wait\ and go on the offchance\ well of course it's terribly difficult\
 C:

¹²M: ⇓ you've had your little tête-à-tête you pair\.. :er: can I just say thank you to all the players
 J: yes\
 C:

¹³M: for their marvellous entertainment\
 J:
 C:

¹⁴M: well they're all lovely people\ ... thank you very much indeed\   thank
 J:
 C: thank *you* very much indeed\

¹⁵M: you\   bye now\
 J:
 C: bye bye\   ... ⇓ felt she put me in my place there\ fair enough\ I think that's quite right\

M's utterance at the first double-shafted arrow in score 11 displays expressive politeness$_1$ in the formulaic indirect request *can I come back in now*, but it merely prefaces her critical remark at the second double-shafted arrow in score 12 in which she upbraids J and C for having left her out of the interaction. She has after all called to participate in the programme and is left hanging on the phone listening to J and C when *she* has the right to participate and *they* have the obligation to allow her to participate. There is also a clear change of footing immediately after this utterance. She inserts a pause and signals a shift to a further topic by using the pause filler *er*. After the exchange is completed, there is a significant pause of roughly one second after which the moderator C, at the third double-shafted arrow in score 15, assesses the significance of M's criticism – *felt she put me in my place there* – acknowledges his mistake – *fair enough* – and her right to intervene – *I think that's quite right*.

THE DISCURSIVE DISPUTE OVER POLITENESS$_1$

(Im)politeness$_1$, therefore, reveals a great deal of vacillation on how behaviour is evaluated as 'polite' at the positive end of the scale when compared with the negative end. It would also seem that whether or not a participant's behaviour is evaluated as polite or impolite is not merely a matter of the linguistic expressions that s/he uses, but rather depends on the interpretation of that behaviour in the overall social interaction. The interpretations are thus first-order evaluations which are often not expressed in terms of the cluster of adjectives associated with (im)politeness. If they are, it is far more likely to be impolite behaviour which is commented on. If the researcher wishes to locate polite behaviour, s/he must begin by examining very closely what happens in the flow of social interaction in order to identify the kinds of behaviour that seem to warrant the attribution of the term 'polite'.

At this point, however, we encounter a further difficulty, one which may at first sight seem insurmountable. The term 'politeness' itself is in dispute among lay members of society in that they appear to be engaged in a discursive struggle over the value of the term. We saw in the first section of this chapter that characterisations of politeness in English-speaking societies range from socially 'correct' or appropriate behaviour, through cultivated behaviour, considerateness displayed to others, self-effacing behaviour, to negative attributions such as standoffishness, haughtiness, insincerity, etc. This should not surprise us if we consider that other fairly commonly used lay terms such as 'good/bad taste', 'culture', 'beauty', 'art', 'democracy', etc. are also involved in discursive struggles. I shall therefore adopt the following position in this book: the very fact that (im)politeness is a term that is struggled over at present, has been struggled over in the past and will, in all probability, continue to be struggled over in the future should be the central focus of a theory of politeness. To put it another way, investigating first-order politeness is the only valid means of developing a social theory of politeness.

Does this then mean that a second-order theory of politeness, a theory of politeness$_2$, should only concern itself with lay notions of politeness? The answer to this question is equivocal: yes and no. Yes, in the sense that a scientific theory of a lay term must take that lay term in lay usage as its central focus, but no, in the sense that a theory of politeness should not attempt to 'create' a superordinate, universal term that can then be applied universally to any socio-cultural group at any point in time. If we were to do that – and I shall argue that this is exactly what has hitherto been done (by myself as well as others) – we would bring back and apply to the study of social behaviour a set of concepts revolving around a notion of politeness$_2$ that transcend the ongoing struggle over the term '(im)politeness'. We would then be studying something else in social behaviour which, although we might call it '(im)politeness', is not what lay members of the social group would label in the same way. We would fail to approach an understanding of how the term is used and the nature of the struggle over its use. To put it briefly, we would create a concept of '(im)politeness' which does not correspond to native speakers' everyday conceptualisations of the term.

POLITENESS$_1$ AND POLITENESS$_2$

A theory of politeness$_2$ should concern itself with the discursive struggle over politeness$_1$, i.e. over the ways in which (im)polite behaviour is evaluated and commented on by lay members and not with ways in which social scientists lift the term '(im)politeness' out of the realm of everyday discourse and elevate it to the status of a theoretical concept in what is frequently called Politeness Theory.

One thing at least is certain about polite behaviour, including polite language; it has to be acquired. Politeness is not something we are born with, but something we have to learn and be socialised into, and no generation has been short of teachers and handbooks on etiquette and 'correct behaviour' to help us acquire polite skills. So, given the everyday nature of politeness, it might seem surpising to learn not only that it occupies a central place in the social study of language, but also that it has been the subject of intensive debate in linguistic pragmatics, sociolinguistics and, to a lesser extent, social theory for several years now.

In that debate, the term 'politeness'[2] means something rather different from our everyday understanding of it and focuses almost uniquely on polite language in the study of verbal interaction. My aim in this book is to approach the technical term 'politeness' from a variety of perspectives, with respect to ways in which it is manifest in language usage, and to highlight some of the controversies focusing on it. At the outset, therefore, I should state unequivocally that my focus will be on what has been called *linguistic politeness*.

An enormous amount of empirical research into the phenomenon of linguistic politeness in a wide range of cultures has been amassed over the years, much of it helping inch by inch to carve a way through what is still a very complex jungle of related ideas concerning social interaction. The research has made use of a relatively narrow set of 'theories of politeness' put forward since the early 1970s. As is often the case, one of these models, outlined in detail in 1978 by Penelope Brown and Stephen Levinson in the form of an inordinately long contribution to a book on social interaction edited by Esther Goody, has dominated all other attempts to theorise about linguistic politeness. Brown and Levinson's work proved to be so influential during the 1980s that the original text was reprinted in book form in 1987 without any changes made to it but with an informative 54-page introduction addressing some of the problems in using the model that had arisen in the intervening nine years.

Clearly, Brown and Levinson (1978/1987) will figure very prominently in this book. Like all of the other theories of politeness[2] that have hitherto been proposed, however, hacking a path out of the jungle of ideas on social interaction has only served to make those ideas grow more quickly and become more rampant. Brown and Levinson's work will undoubtedly continue to exert as much influence on research into the subject in the coming years as it has in the past. But a number of crucial criticisms of Brown and Levinson's approach have emerged since the beginning of the 1990s, opening up broader perspectives from which to approach the phenomenon of linguistic politeness. In addition, the study of verbal forms of social interaction has now progressed so far that alternative methods of studying the phenomenon of politeness are available. Although none of them is completely able to invalidate Brown and Levinson's conceptualisation of politeness, all of them can help us to refine and elaborate on their original insights.

The present book, however, should be seen as a radical rejection of politeness$_2$ as a concept which has been lifted out of the realm of lay conceptualisations of what constitutes polite and impolite behaviour and how that behaviour should be evaluated. If there is a scientific concept which transcends our everyday notions of (im)polite behaviour, to call it 'politeness' is not only confusing, it is also misleading. The present book does not aim to present yet another theory of politeness$_2$, but rather to help us find our way back to what we should be doing in the study of social interaction, that is, showing how our lay notions of social behaviour, as they are struggled over discursively by participants in social interaction, are constitutive of that behaviour and of the habitus of a historically situated and socially located *homo interactionalis*, subject to change as the locus of the struggle itself changes. The struggle over politeness$_1$ thus represents the struggle over the reproduction and reconstruction of the values of socially acceptable and socially unacceptable behaviour.

In the years since 1987 an important collection of contributions on cross-cultural differences in the realisation of speech acts central to much research in linguistic politeness, requesting and apologising, was published in 1989 by Shoshana Blum-Kulka, Juliane House and Gabriele Kasper with the title *Cross-Cultural Pragmatics: Requests and Apologies*. In 1992 Richard Watts, Sachiko Ide and Konrad Ehlich edited a collection of essays on linguistic politeness entitled *Politeness in Language: Studies in its History, Theory and Practice*, which attempts to cover various historical, theoretical and practical approaches to linguistic politeness. Two books appeared in 1994 which lean heavily on Brown and Levinson's model of politeness, one by Hilkka Yli-Jokipii with the title *Requests in Professional Discourse*, which is an investigation into the business writing practices of American and Finnish firms, the other a volume of essays on facework with the title *The Challenge of Facework: Cross-Cultural and Interpersonal Issues* edited by Stella Ting-Toomey.

Maria Sifianou's doctoral dissertation was published in book form in 1992 with the title *Politeness Phenomena in England and Greece*, and in 1995 Janet Holmes published a book with the title *Women, Men and Politeness*. In the same year as Janet Holmes, Gudrun Held published her post-doctoral dissertation with the title *Verbale Höflichkeit* [Verbal Politeness], in which she studies ways of theorising about linguistic politeness and presents the results of empirical research carried out with

French and Italian youths. The book has not yet appeared in an English translation. Since Held's book only three book-length publications that specifically deal with linguistic politeness have been published, Song Mei Lee-Wong's doctoral dissertation in 1999 with the title *Politeness and Face in Chinese Culture* and Saeko Fukushima's doctoral dissertation in 2000 with the title *Requests and Culture*. Gino Eelen (2001) has recently published a book criticising Politeness Theory.

However, with the possible exception of Eelen (2001), none of these books lays claim to being a critical introduction to the field of linguistic politeness. The time thus appears ripe for a book of this kind, one which will introduce readers to the controversies in the field of linguistic politeness without itself being uncritical, one which will help the reader through the maze of research publications on the topic, but above all one which will tackle the fundamental questions head-on:

- What *is* linguistic politeness?
- Is politeness theory a theory about a concept of politeness$_2$, or can it be formulated in such a way that it can shed light on the struggle over politeness$_1$?

One of the central claims made in Brown and Levinson is that politeness$_2$ is a universal feature of language usage. In other words, all of the world's languages possess the means to express politeness. Their claim for universality, however, is made in relation to their conceptualisation of an idealised concept of politeness$_2$, not in relation to the ways in which groups of participants struggle over politeness$_1$ (or whatever terms are available to them in their own languages) in social interaction. Nor should their notion of universality be understood to refer to the linguistic means through which politeness is expressed. In the first place, these means differ quite radically in terms of the structural types that realise politeness across a range of different languages. Secondly, the claim that politeness is a universal phenomenon of social interaction, particularly of verbal interaction, necessitates a shift of attention away from a primary focus on linguistic realisations of politeness$_2$ towards a more detailed look at the complexity of social interaction itself and the role politeness$_1$ plays in it.

THE TERMS 'POLITE' AND 'POLITENESS'

The major problem for anyone entering the field of politeness research is the bewildering ambiguity in the use of the terms 'polite' and 'politeness' themselves. In Watts *et al.* (1992b) the problem of terminology is raised, but not solved (cf. Eelen 2001). Some researchers try to avoid the problem by suggesting other terms, e.g. 'emotive communication' (Arndt and Janney 1985a), 'tact' (Janney and Arndt 1992; Leech 1983), 'politic behaviour' (Watts 1989c, 1992), but 'politeness' always seems to creep back in.

In theories of politeness, the term is used almost exclusively to refer to the different ways of conceptualising politeness$_2$. But doing this only clouds the issue, since *polite* and *politeness* are lexemes in the English language whose meanings are open to negotiation by those interacting in English.[3] Their meanings are reproduced and renegotiated whenever and wherever they are used in verbal interaction, which of course means that related terms such as *rude, rudeness, (dis)courteous, impolite, impoliteness,* etc. are also struggled over. To use a lay concept in one language as a universal scientific concept for all languages and cultures is particularly inappropriate. Take the hypothetical example of a Japanese sociolinguist discussing politeness$_2$ as a social concept with a German colleague in English. In a situation such as this there is no way we can be sure that either of them is referring to the same set of ideas represented by that concept. In the first place, we cannot be sure that some lay concept that might (or might not) be roughly equivalent to English expressions referring to politeness$_1$ in Japanese or German does not lie at the base of their conceptualisations of politeness$_2$. Secondly, if an English-speaking colleague joins the discussion, there is no way in which s/he can dissociate her/himself from English expressions referring to politeness$_1$ when applying the concept politeness$_2$. Thirdly, and most importantly for the present discussion, those English expressions are at the heart of a discursive struggle over their values. Fourthly, the ways in which '(im)polite' and '(im)politeness' (i.e. politeness$_1$) were understood in previous centuries are very different from the ways in which they are understood today, indicating that the struggle over politeness is in a constant state of historical change and flux. Is it therefore possible for the English-speaking colleague to discard her/his position in that struggle from the scientific concept under discussion, namely politeness$_2$?

Scholars from non-English-speaking cultures tend to distance themselves from the first-order concepts that exist in their own languages and are the subject of struggle in their own cultures and tend to elevate the rough translation equivalents of *polite* and *politeness* into their understanding of politeness$_2$. It would therefore be useful to review some of the variability in terms for politeness$_1$ used in other languages. My aim is to underscore the difficulty in distinguishing clearly between politeness$_1$ and politeness$_2$ from a terminological perspective. I shall argue in this book that we should turn our attention away from setting up a notion of politeness$_2$ to investigating the discursive nature of the social struggle over the terms available to native speakers of other languages that refer to 'polished' behaviour, socially (in)appropriate behaviour, etc. If we do not want to give up the claim for universality, we will need to define politeness$_1$ in such a way that we can recognise it in verbal interaction in any language.

The first step is to assume that in all human cultures we will meet forms of social behaviour that members will classify as mutually shared consideration for others. Cooperative social interaction and displaying consideration for others seem to be universal characteristics of every socio-cultural group. By the same token, we will also meet forms of social behaviour that violate the principles of mutual cooperation and the display of consideration for others. Native speakers of any language will have individual ideas about what sort of behaviour is denoted by the lexical terms available to them, and very often they will disagree. In general, however, we must assume that there is likely to be a core of agreement about the rough outlines of what is meant.

As in the case of the English lexemes *polite* and *politeness*, terms in other languages – if indeed they exist at all – may vary in the meanings and connotations associated with them from one group of speakers (even from one individual speaker) to the next. Like the English terms, they are the locus of social struggle and are therefore open to semantic change through history. As a part of her research methodology Sifianou (1992a) conducted a survey of ways in which Greek and English subjects perceived first-order politeness in their respective cultures (i.e. she investigated metapragmatic politeness$_1$). In both cases 'consideration for the other person is seen as an integral part of politeness . . . but it seems that what is construed as consideration differs' (1992a: 92). And indeed this is the fundamental aspect of what is understood as 'polite' behaviour in all other cultures, even given the widely differing range of terms used to refer to it and the kinds of negative evaluation that may be assigned to it.

Greek informants stress the expression of concern and consideration for the addressee as the fundamental characteristic of politeness$_1$. Greek perceptions of politeness$_1$ (the rough translation equivalent of *politeness* in Greek being *evgenia*) stress the expression of intimacy and the display of warmth and friendliness. English conceptualisations of politeness$_1$, on the other hand, tend to be broader than those of the Greek subjects. Consideration towards others is stressed, but formality, a discrete maintenance of distance, a wish not to impose upon addressees, and expressions of 'altruism, generosity, morality, and self-abnegation' (Sifianou 1992a: 88) are more important for the English subjects.[4]

There may not always be a unique lexeme that is equivalent to *politeness* in every language but where there is none, there will always be conventionally periphrastic ways of expressing a similar conceptual content. Nwoye (1992), for example, maintains that there is no equivalent term in Igbo, but he argues that what is meant by politeness in European cultures is conveyed by an Igbo expression meaning roughly 'good behaviour'.

The understanding of politeness$_1$ in Russian society is expressed through the lexeme *vezhlivost'*, the root of which is the verb *vedat'* ('to know, to be expert in', etc.) (Rathmayr 1999: 76). Like Sifianou, Rathmayr carried out a survey among Russian informants to discover their metapragmatic evaluations of politeness$_1$ (Rathmayr 1996a, b). She discovered that for Russians *vezhlivost'* 'vient du coeur' (1999: 76) and that Russians defined a polite person as 'likeable, calm, harmonious, attentive, cultivated, well-wishing, amicable, warm, well brought up, reserved, disposed towards recognising her/his mistakes, not gross, not insolent, not rude, positive, someone who always answers letters and who is prepared to listen to the same thing several times'.[5] In general, then, the Russian conceptualisations of politeness$_1$, like those of Sifianou's Greek informants, tend to stress the expression of intimacy and the display of warmth and friendliness – apart from the term 'reserved' in Rathmayr's list of attributes.

But there is one significant difference between Greek and Igbo conceptualisations, on the one hand, and Russian conceptualisations on the other. Russians frequently maintain that a polite person should not use vulgar or coarse language. There is, in other words, a link between language and politeness in Russian metapragmatic politeness$_1$. Non-Russian commentators on the social behaviour of Russians, however, note the high degree of unmitigated directness in speech-act types, which contradicts the English tendency towards showing distance, reserve and formality.

Russian culture is certainly not exceptional in preferring more directness in speech-act types that may constitute face-threatening acts (for an explanation of this term see the glossary and chapters 4 and 5). For example, Gu (1990) suggests that in Chinese society the standing of an individual can only be inferred through his/her relation to the group. As a consequence, speech acts such as requests, offers and criticisms are not nearly as face-threatening or as imposing as they are in British, or even Greek, society. Both Gu and Lee-Wong (1999) stress the distinct Chinese preference for directness. The term that comes closest to politeness in Chinese is *limao*, which, Lee-Wong (1999: 24–5) suggests, is a compound of *li* ('ceremony', 'courtesy', 'etiquette') and *mao* ('appearance'). She defines it as 'a code of conduct which stipulates how one should conduct oneself not only in public but at all times'. Like Gu (1990) she rejects the conceptualisation of politeness$_2$ as a set of redressive measures, but she also suggests that there might be certain individual needs that transcend the socially determined code of behaviour represented by *limao*.[6]

Blum-Kulka (1992) maintains that there are two first-order terms in use in Modern Hebrew that are equivalent to 'politeness', *nimus*, which has acquired the denotation of politeness only in the twentieth century, and *adivut*, taken from Arabic. Blum-Kulka's informants did not make clear and consistent distinctions between the two terms, but *nimus* appears to be more in use for formal aspects of social etiquette, whereas *adivut* is used to express considerateness and the effort to accommodate to the addressee. We seem to have a duality of terms here similar to the Greek *evgenia* and *filotimo* (see note 4), although the latter term in Greek has a stronger implication of honour and selflessness. Nevertheless, as in Greek, it is also the case for Modern Hebrew that *nimus* is frequently evaluated more negatively and *adivut* more positively.

Blum-Kulka also makes an interesting distinction between politeness in the public and in the private sphere. She suggests that complaints about lack of consideration, deplorable public service and lack of individual restraint in public places indicate 'the lack of clear conventions for politeness as a socio-cultural code' (1992: 259). Within the sphere of the family, however, there is a cultural notion of *lefargen*, which means roughly 'to indulge, to support, not to begrudge' (1992: 260) and which is redolent of positive values such as the expression of love and gratitude. Thus while Israeli culture is similar to Russian culture in its insistence on directness, there are nevertheless group constraints on cooperative social behaviour similar to Chinese and Igbo culture although on the more localised level of close-knit groups such as the family.

A study carried out by Ide *et al.* (1992) aimed at assessing the extent to which the adjectives 'polite' and 'friendly' in a range of more or less polite situations do or do not correlate in Japanese and American society. A rough translation equivalent of 'polite' in Japanese is *teineina*, which, as has been pointed out by Ide elsewhere (1989, 1993) and by Matsumoto (1988, 1989), does not refer to individual attempts to mitigate or avoid face-threatening, but, as in Chinese, or even more so, is part of a complex code of socially appropriate behaviour.[7] It was found that the adjectives *teineina* and *sitasigena* ('friendly') were evaluated along completely different axes from *polite* and *friendly*. Whereas in American culture 'politeness' correlates reasonably well with 'friendliness', there is no apparent relationship between the two sets in Japanese. On the other hand, the two adjectives *keii no aru* ('respectful') and *tekisetuna* ('appropriate') are closely related to *teineina* from the positive to the negative side of the scale, whereas *respectful* is a little further away from *polite* than *keii no aru* from *teineina* and *appropriate* is positioned on a very different axis from *polite*. This is strong evidence that the Japanese notion of politeness₁ as expressed in the adjective *teineina* is very different from the American notion. Indeed, perhaps more than in any other language, politeness forms have been largely grammaticalised in Japanese, with the result that unless the speaker is able to discern the degree of politeness required in any given social situation in accordance with the Japanese term *wakimae* ('discernment'), it is virtually impossible for her/him to produce a 'grammatically' correct utterance.

It would of course be possible to go on listing the rough lexical equivalents to *polite* and *politeness* in other languages, but there is little point in doing so. By now it should have become clear that politeness₁, whatever terms are used in whatever language to refer to mutually cooperative behaviour, considerateness for others, polished behaviour, etc., is a locus of social struggle over discursive practices. As such it warrants much more detailed study than has hitherto been the case in the politeness literature. In saying that, however, I do not mean to imply that this book will range over a diverse set of languages. On the assumption that my readership is English-speaking, I will restrict myself to examples from English with the occasional example taken from elsewhere.

POLITIC BEHAVIOUR, (IM)POLITENESS AND RELATIONAL WORK

The reader could be forgiven for feeling that in the previous section I was slipping gears a little in defining polite behaviour as mutual cooperation in verbal interaction and as displaying consideration for other participants. After all, if there is a discursive dispute over the social values of the terms *(im)polite* and *(im)politeness*, whichever social group and language we look at, how can we then determine single-handedly what politeness is? At this point it is necessary to recall what was said about impoliteness in an earlier section of this chapter. On the one hand, I suggested that native speakers are much more likely to agree on the negative evaluation of forms of behaviour which they may consider 'rude', 'impolite', 'abrupt', 'offensive', etc. than they are on the positive evaluation of politeness. On the other hand, I also suggested that impoliteness is clearly a salient form of social behaviour in the sense that it appears to go against the canons of acceptable, appropriate behaviour operative for the ongoing social interaction. In extract (1) R's low burp immediately necessitated some form of verbal atonement for the offence, i.e. at least in this particular social group burping is salient, negatively evaluated social behaviour. In extract (2) S interpreted and commented on C's intervention as an illicit attempt to take the floor from him. In extract (3) S evaluated E's behaviour in not letting him answer the question he was asked as offensive behaviour and reacted accordingly. In extract (4) M gave a negative evaluation of J and C's behaviour, which was accepted as such by C after the exchange with M. In each case we have evidence on the part of a participant in the social interaction that s/he has interpreted a co-participant's behaviour as not being socially acceptable.

But what about polite behaviour? We also have evidence from the speaker's own utterances or from the ways in which we as commentators might evaluate what was said that some of the verbal behaviour produced in all four extracts was either necessary in the circumstances and therefore to be interpreted positively, e.g. R's *beg your pardon* after making his burp in extract (1), or was not necessary, e.g. in (2) S's *can I come back on Mandy's point*. R's utterance is socially constrained, and since it is expectable, we are unlikely to define it as polite. If he had not said it, however, we would be within our rights to evaluate it as impolite. S's utterance is interpretable as a strategic move since he could just as easily have stated directly what he wanted to say. It appears to be intended as an overt sign of deference towards the moderator and possibly also to the TV audience. If we interpret it as unnecessary but do not assign any further intention to S, the utterance can be viewed neutrally or negatively. If we do assign the intention to show deference, we are free to interpret it positively or negatively, depending on how we position ourselves with respect to the kind of behaviour which should be displayed on a TV debate programme.

In extract (3) E begins his interruptive turn, hesitates and adds *sorry if I interrupt you there* before continuing. In this case, E's formulaic utterance *sorry* prefacing an explicit statement of what he has just done is strategic. It is often classified as polite behaviour, but it cannot undo the threat to S represented in the fact that he has just interrupted him. So even if this is explicit polite behaviour, it is far more likely to be interpreted negatively by the TV audience, as it is by S himself.

Extract (4) contains a number of utterances that are open to interpretation as polite:

1. The beginning of M's first turn after she has been asked what question she wants to put to the expert: *I would like to ask please*
2. M's attempt to reenter the floor before protesting about J and C's behaviour: *can I come back in now?*
3. The introduction of M's fresh topic after her protest: *can I just say thank you to all the players for their marvellous entertainment . . .*
4. M's expression of thanks for being allowed to participate in the programme: *thank you very much indeed*
5. C's expression of thanks to her for having participated: *thank you very much indeed*

Points 1, 4 and 5 are realisations of the kind of verbal behaviour that those familiar with this type of phone-in programme would expect. They are in effect reproductions of discursive formats that have become institutionalised as expectable behaviour and as such they help to reestablish this part of the overall interaction as 'a call in a phone-in programme'. The linguistic expressions *please* and *thank you* are highly ritualised and do not, as such, constitute salient behaviour. On the other hand, M's utterances beginning with *can I* (the second of these hedged with the marker *just*) are salient, the first because she needs to reenter the floor in order to criticise J and C, the second because she is putting an explicit request to change the topic.

Hence, even from the meagre data we have looked at so far, it should be clear that there are linguistic structures in excess of what the speaker needs to utter which nevertheless go unnoticed, since they form part of the reproduction of institutionalised discursive formats. I have suggested elsewhere (Watts 1989c, 1992) that linguistic behaviour which is perceived to be appropriate to the social constraints of the ongoing interaction, i.e. as non-salient, should be called *politic behaviour*. As we shall see in chapter 3, this is not quite the same as Fraser and Nolen's Conversational Contract. Linguistic behaviour which is perceived to be beyond what is expectable, i.e. salient behaviour, should be called *polite* or *impolite* depending on whether the behaviour itself tends towards the negative or positive end of the spectrum of politeness.

Note that I am not suggesting that the politeness$_1$ that is observable in an interaction is automatically evaluated as positive behaviour, or even that it is evaluated as (im)polite at all. What a theory of politeness should be able to do is to locate possible realisations of polite or impolite behaviour and offer a way of assessing how the members themselves may have evaluated that behaviour. Nor am I suggesting that politic behaviour is some kind of Parsonian social reality, as Eelen (2001) has suggested. The very fact that we participate so frequently in a multitude of different kinds of verbal interaction but that we generally know or work out what sort of behaviour is expectable indicates that in entering and participating in those interactions we recreate them, we reproduce them. This in itself is evidence of the fact that most forms of social interaction have become institutionalised and that the appropriate discursive practices are known to us beforehand. *Politic behaviour* is that behaviour, linguistic and non-linguistic, which the participants construct as being appropriate to the ongoing social interaction. The construction may have been made prior to entering the interaction, but it is always negotiable during the interaction, despite the expectations that participants might bring to it. In Watts (1989c: 135) I defined politic behaviour as:

> socioculturally determined behaviour directed towards the goal of establishing and/or maintaining in a state of equilibrium the personal relationships between the individuals of a social group.

And it is this definition which has led Eelen, quite justifiably, to the imputation of a Parsonian interpretation of social facts which exist prior to engaging in communication. My original definition assumes:

1. that all social interaction is geared towards cooperation, an assumption which the literature on conflictual discourse and impoliteness has shown to be false;
2. that the behaviour patterns constituting a social interaction are in some sense determined prior to entering the interaction, a point which is not entirely without some substance when we recall that participants do tend to model new instances of social interaction on their previous experiences and that very many instances of social interaction are to a greater or lesser degree institutionalised;
3. that social interaction has the major goal of assuring the maintenance of some form of social equilibrium.

Point 1 can be dispensed with only if we are prepared to abandon the Gricean assumption of cooperation, and this is exactly what, in a later chapter, I shall argue we will have to do. Point 2 is neutralised if we accept that any new occasion of social interaction enacts and therefore reproduces earlier similar forms of interaction, but is at the same time always open to discursive negotiation that might help to reconstruct the interaction type. Hence, from the point of view of the social theory that I shall present in chapter 6, the interaction type is itself always a locus of struggle with respect to what constitutes that form of social interaction. Point 3 is in any case vacuous unless some definition of 'social equilibrium' can be offered, which, because of the radically different goals, settings, participants, etc., of any social interaction, remains impossible.

For these reasons I return to the definition of politic behaviour as given above: *Politic behaviour*: that behaviour, linguistic and non-linguistic, which the participants construct as being appropriate to the ongoing social interaction.

Polite behaviour will therefore be behaviour beyond what is perceived to be appropriate to the ongoing social interaction, which says nothing about how members evaluate it. At the same time, however, the definition implies that linguistic structures are not, *per definitionem*, inherently polite. Impolite behaviour will be behaviour that is perceived by participants to be inappropriate behaviour, which again says nothing about how individual members evaluate it. This needs to be illustrated with an example. Consider the following extract from my family discourse data:

(5)

¹R: is it that expensive to have a car in this country\
 B: well 'tis when you don't use it very much\ I mean
 D:

²R:
 B: it'll cost you – ...   ⇓ just to keep it on the road\ it's :er: well over a ten/ it- it- it's
 D: well yes\ it costs a <???>

³R:
 B: coming up to twenty pounds a week really ⇓ isn't it\   yes\ and the rest\ actually you see\
 D: never mind the rest\

⁴R:
 B: they haven't got a garage\ :erm: ... the thing was kept out in the open\ :uh: which/<CLEARS
 D:

⁵R:
 B: THROAT>it was deteriorating ⇓ wasn't it\ through being left out\ ...
 D: don't say that \ mine's out\

R's first turn questions whether owning cars in Britain is more expensive than where he lives (i.e. Switzerland). In this sense, it could be understood as containing a veiled criticism of the people being referred to, who have had to sell their car. B does not need to preface her response with *well*, so it is beyond what would be required for the politic behaviour of a family chat. However, to evaluate it as 'polite' depends entirely on whether she has inferred R's criticism and is responding to the challenge by mitigating the damage to the self-esteem of those selling the car, even though they are not physically present. It is much more likely that she would evaluate R's question as 'unfair', 'hypercritical', etc., i.e. as bordering on the impolite. Similarly the use of the discourse marker *I mean* in B's first turn (score 1) could be interpreted as a defensive strategy, justifying why the car was sold.

B's second turn at the first double-shafted arrow in the transcript (score 2) intervenes in D's explanation of how much it costs to keep a car on the road. It is done at a higher volume level, thus obliterating the completion of D's turn. It is at least open to interpretation as impolite behaviour. On the other hand, D has taken over the reply to R's question after a significant pause following B's first abortive attempt to explain the costs. Does he feel that he needs to make B's response a little more precise? If so, it is interpretable as an affront to B's ability to answer the question herself, and perhaps for this reason he also mitigates his response by using the discourse marker *well*.

B seems to be aware of the negative force of her interruption. She stutters quite considerably, modifies her own estimate of the costs from ten to twenty pounds a week, further relativises this with the discourse marker *really* and then finally defers to D's greater knowledge by inviting him to take the floor through the tag question *isn't it* (at the second double-shafted arrow in the transcript in score 3). Is she atoning for her non-politic behaviour in interrupting D, who in much of my family data constructs himself and is constructed by the other participants as the most knowledgeable resource person? Perhaps.

This is of course the researcher's, the outsider's evaluation, but it is supported by her next turn, in which she again defers to D by agreeing with his assessment and then refocussing on R's question. The discourse marker *actually* appears to signal that she is about to give the real reason why 'they' no longer own a car, and she appeals to R's understanding through the discourse marker *you see*. Later in her turn, in a renewed attempt to repair the possible damage of her interruption, she again appeals to D's shared knowledge concerning the reasons for the car having been sold by inserting the tag question *wasn't it* (the third double-shafted arrow in the transcript in score 5). D ends the extract by defusing the criticism implied by R's original question by making a joke out of B's final point.

All in all, then, D and B are concerned to defuse R's criticism without offending him in their turn. They are also concerned to protect the 'family image' of those selling the car. B is concerned to atone for her breach of politic behaviour in having interrupted D. The passage shows participants who are doing their best to be considerate towards one another whilst at the same time countering a potentially threatening question by R. They are therefore carrying out what I shall call *relational work*. But would it be correct to say that the participants are indulging in linguistic (im)politeness? It is in sequences of verbal interaction like this that we can see the struggle over (im)politeness, and it is a struggle which we the researchers are confronted with as much as the participants themselves in the ongoing interaction. The participants in extract (5) appear to be doing their best to restore the balance of potentially impolite acts such as directing criticism at someone, interrupting, etc. So it is politic verbal behaviour in which we can see relational work being carried out.

The passage also shows us how difficult it is to 'spot' instances of linguistic politeness, whereas participants themselves appear to react towards potentially impolite acts by carrying out forms of repair work. Any attempt to locate (im)politeness in naturally occurring discourse is confronted with four problems, which have hitherto been largely ignored in the politeness literature:

1. It is impossible to evaluate (im)polite behaviour out of the context of real, ongoing verbal interaction. Often the amount of contextual information needed can be considerable.
2. A theory of (im)polite behaviour needs to take the perspectives of the speakers and the hearers adequately into consideration, firstly, because speakers are also hearers, and vice versa, and secondly, because social interaction is negotiated on-line. This latter point implies that what may have been originally interpreted as '(im)polite' behaviour is always open to evaluative remodification as the interaction progresses.
3. As a direct corollary of the previous two points, it will never be possible to develop a predictive model of linguistic (im)politeness.
4. Consequently, there can be no idealised, universal scientific concept of (im)politeness (i.e. (im)politeness$_2$) which can be applied to instances of social interaction across cultures, subcultures and languages.

Should we as researchers into linguistic (im)politeness worry about these four points? I think not, although we should obviously take them very seriously. Indeed, the present book will be an attempt to show how they can enrich our understanding of what goes on in social

interaction. In the final section of this first chapter I shall summarise
how I shall go about doing this.

THE STRUCTURE OF THE BOOK

We began this chapter by commenting on the ways in which we
would try to characterise polite behaviour and polite language and
concluded that our everyday, lay interpretations of the terms 'polite',
'impolite', 'politeness' and 'impoliteness', what I have termed *first-order
(im)politeness* and Eelen (2001) calls *(im)politeness*$_1$, are those that should
be focused on by a model of linguistic (im)politeness. We then located
the word as a *terminus technicus* within the study of social interaction in
general, pointing out that '(im)politeness' has become a central term
in sociolinguistic and pragmatic approaches to the study of language.
The undesirability of elevating a lay concept to the status of a technical term in so-called 'Politeness Theory', however, was discussed at
length. The main problems discussed were the following:

(a) A theory of *second-order (im)politeness*, or *(im)politeness*$_2$ does not
     take adequate account of the evaluative moment in real verbal
     interaction, when participants display their awareness of salient
     social behaviour, which they may or may not designate as
     'impolite' or 'polite'.
(b) While impolite social behaviour is thought of in negative terms,
     lay members of a social group vacillate over whether polite social
     behaviour is to be thought of in positive, negative or neutral
     terms, thus displaying an inherent instability in the term and
     an ongoing struggle over its social value.
(c) If researchers do not build this fact into their theories, they will
     fail to take account of the chameleon-like nature of politeness
     in social interaction and their theories will end up by being
     theories of something else, but not of (im)politeness.
(d) The 'real' object of study in a theory of politeness is politeness$_1$
     (first-order politeness), which means that it will not be possible
     to define a universal scientific concept of (im)politeness which
     can be applied (with the requisite modifications) to all human
     societies.
(e) The 'real' universality of (im)politeness consists in the ways in
     which it and/or related terms are struggled over in every human
     society, thus making it a term in the close study of socio-
     communicative verbal interaction.

(f) Studying social interaction means that the researcher should be able somehow to transcend participation in the social interaction s/he is interpreting and to observe the participants *qua* participants, and not as either speakers or hearers.

(g) A theory of (im)politeness can therefore never be predictive, but it can help to open up and display social processes at work.

The major aim of this book is to review the literature on linguistic (im)politeness as a technical term and to suggest ways in which many of the false pathways that have been followed may be rectified. My first move in chapter 2 will be to present a number of ways in which our lay understandings of politeness have evolved over the centuries, displaying as I do so the inherently unstable nature of the term. My argument will be that the enormous amount of relativity, both historical and cultural, that can be found simply in the English terms 'polite', 'impolite', 'rude', 'courteous', 'polished', etc., are clear evidence of the need to take evaluations of politeness$_1$ seriously.

In chapter 3 I will present some of the most widely used models of linguistic politeness (or politeness$_2$) in the literature in a critical way, arguing that we have still not achieved a proper understanding of the second-order concept of politeness. Chapter 4 will continue this discussion, focusing more specifically on Brown and Levinson's model and criticisms of it.

Chapter 5 will focus on the term 'face', since the most commonly used model of politeness is still Brown and Levinson, a model which has given rise to the equation of Politeness Theory with Face Theory. I shall give examples of facework from naturally occurring data gathered in other discourse activity types. I shall argue that a more satisfactory model of linguistic politeness that is grounded in a theory of social interaction needs to return to Erving Goffman's notion of 'face' rather than continue with the dual notion of positive and negative face which forms the basis of Brown and Levinson's model.

Chapter 6 frames the study of (im)politeness$_1$ as an ongoing struggle over the differential values of appropriate social behaviour within a social-theoretic approach which owes a lot to the work of Pierre Bourdieu. I shall integrate my own concept of the emergent social network into this framework as a way of illustrating how participants in social interaction actually construct and/or reproduce and modify their evaluations of politic behaviour and relational work and the place that '(im)polite' behaviour has in this construction and reproduction.

In chapter 7 I will review some of the kinds of linguistic structure that have been categorised as realisations of linguistic politeness, and

I will argue that those very structures are as open to alternative interpretations, i.e. as 'polite' or not, as the term '(im)polite' itself. Indeed,
it will be my purpose to show that there is not only a struggle over
'(im)politeness', but also a struggle over how it is realised through language. This introductory chapter has already indicated that a great
deal of caution needs to be applied in making such categorisations.

Chapter 8 presents a criticism of the Gricean approach underlying
three of the major models of politeness, Lakoff, Leech and Brown and
Levinson, and replaces it with a Relevance Theoretic approach to social
interaction in which Eelen's demand that 'when speaker and hearer
are psychologically on a par, their interactional practices must also be
interpreted using the same criteria' (2001: 110) can be met. Relevance
Theory offers a more subtle and flexible method of deriving the kinds
of inferencing processes that participants in social interaction may be
using when evaluating one another's social behaviour. In this chapter
I also deal more explicitly with the relationship between power and
politeness. Chapter 9 offers a detailed analysis of naturally occurring
verbal interaction from the point of view of (im)politeness$_1$. Finally, in
chapter 10 I shall review the alternative way of looking at linguistic politeness presented in this book and highlight some residual problems
which still need to be addressed.

2 Politeness through time and across cultures

WHAT IS FIRST-ORDER (IM)POLITENESS?

A theory of linguistic (im)politeness should take as its focus the ways in which the members of a social group conceptualise (im)politeness as they participate in socio-communicative verbal interaction. In other words, it should concern itself with first-order politeness (or politeness$_1$) and should offer the researcher the means of recognising and interpreting the evaluative moments in which participants react to linguistic behaviour which is in excess of politic behaviour (see the definition of 'politic behaviour' given in chapter 1 and in the glossary). It should enable us to evaluate those moments as significant points in a social process in which institutionalised forms of discourse are reproduced and reconstructed, but it should also enable us to look for the universal aspects of (im)politeness within social interaction no matter what socio-cultural group is under consideration.

For this reason, it is useful to have a first, rough idea of what (im)polite behaviour entails in our own society. Some examples of perceptions of (im)politeness were looked at in chapter 1, and we saw that it is often easier to locate impolite behaviour than polite behaviour. I shall therefore begin with another situation, fictive this time, in which participants' evaluations of a member's behaviour are likely to be negative. Imagine yourself standing in a queue at the booking office of a coach station. It is your turn next, but before you can even begin to order your ticket, someone pushes in in front of you and asks the official behind the counter for a single ticket to Birmingham. Fortunately, this sort of thing is not a daily occurrence, but when it does happen, we are likely to feel somewhat annoyed. The least we could have expected is some kind of excuse on the part of the person for her/his action. We would also have expected the official to point out that there *is* a queue, that it is *not* that person's turn to be served, that newcomers to the queue should take their place at the back, etc. We would expect those behind us in the queue to start complaining, and

27

we would feel ourselves justified in voicing our own complaint to the 'offender'. If we were asked to comment on the incident afterwards, we would probably suggest that the pusher-in had behaved *impolitely*, even *rudely*, to those in the queue. We might not consider his behaviour to have been rude towards the official, but we would certainly have expected the official to point out the 'rules of the game' and to refuse to serve her/him.

This fictional situation is recognisable as a public service encounter in which none of the participants is expected to know any of the others (although, of course, they may). As a social activity type it is subject to a so-called *interaction order*, i.e. the politic behaviour of waiting to be served in a queue involves the participant in certain types of behaviour which take place at certain sequentially ordered points in the interaction. Our internalised understanding of this particular interaction order is that it is institutionalised and governed by a set of behavioural conventions. By standing in the queue and waiting for our turn to order a ticket we effectively reproduce and validate the politic behaviour characterising it.

There are at least three conditions that need to be fulfilled before we can categorise the social activity type as subject to an interaction order. Firstly, it would not be one if the other participants in the situation had not also internalised the same institutionalised conventions. Secondly, social activities are culturally relative. There are similar situations, even within Europe, in which members of the public, for example, do not form queues. Thirdly, exceptional features in this type of situation would override or neutralise our feelings of outrage and indignation. If the pusher-in had been in the uniform of the police, for example, or if he had been brandishing a Kalashnikov and wearing a stocking over his head – and of course if a single ticket to Birmingham had not been ordered, but some other speech activity had taken place, e.g. an order to the official behind the counter to hand over the monetary contents of the till – our reactions would have been predictably different.

The conventions regulating the politic behaviour of this institutionalised social activity type are determined by *mutually shared forms of consideration for others*,[1] and, although the specific forms of consideration might differ (sometimes greatly) from one culture or subculture to the next, they are still understood as governing all forms of social interaction. In the social activity type engaged in and reproduced by those in a queue at the booking office of a coach station forms of politeness, linguistic or otherwise, are most conspicuous by their absence. It is only when the politic behaviour of the activity type is violated that we actually become aware of the conventions. We might then classify the pusher-in as 'impolite', perhaps even as downright 'rude'. The very least we could have expected was an explanation from her/him for the offensive behaviour, whether or not s/he was in police uniform. Within a public social activity type like this we expect the participants to abide by the conventions of politic behaviour and, where necessary, to pay for any deviations from it with behaviour which goes beyond the politic and becomes polite. The pusher-in could, for example, have prefaced her/his action with linguistic behaviour such as the following:

(1)   I'm terribly sorry. I wonder if you would mind me jumping the queue. My coach leaves in five minutes and I desperately need to catch it. I got held up by traffic.

What about those types of social activity which we would probably not immediately classify as institutionalised, such as those in the family or in a close-knit circle of friends, or chance meetings between two individuals who may or may not know one another? We can of course make a case for saying that even this type of social interaction has become institutionalised and is subject to some kind of interaction order and the conventions of politic behaviour. Determining the politic behaviour appropriate to a social activity type, verbal or non-verbal, and explaining when and why certain forms of behaviour constitute social payment, i.e. when and why certain forms of behaviour can be called 'polite', is fundamental to explaining how human beings communicate with one another. Language and forms of language behaviour are at the heart of social communication and the reproduction of social structure. So the study of politic behaviour and linguistic politeness lies at the heart of socio-communicative verbal interaction.

In discussing the fictional situation in the coach station I suggested that the unspoken conventions regulating politic behaviour were *culturally specific*. To be more exact, readers might recognise a 'typically' British scene here in which queues are 'automatically' formed and people await their turn to be served. In other cultural settings there might not even be such places as coach stations, and if there were, customers might have to take a numbered ticket from a ticket dispenser and wait till the number on their ticket is called to be served at the counter. In still other cultural settings passengers might have to get their ticket from the driver of the coach. Hence the conventions for travelling by coach[2] and the forms of politic behaviour that are typical of the social interaction are *culturally relative*.

FIRST-ORDER AND SECOND-ORDER POLITENESS: A REPRISE

The first difficulty that confronts us in the field of linguistic politeness is to define the object of study. In chapter 1 I argued that our lay conceptualisations of politeness are frequently rather vague, since we tend to take forms of politeness for granted. I also suggested that we should call such lay conceptualisations 'first-order politeness'. As chapter 1 progressed, however, we rapidly encountered the term 'politeness' as a technical term used in the pragmatic and sociolinguistic study of socio-communicative verbal interaction, and I suggested that that use of the term should be referred to as 'second-order politeness' (politeness$_2$).

In the previous section of this chapter I maintained that politic behaviour consisted of 'mutually shared forms of consideration for others'. In all human cultures we will meet forms of social behaviour that we can classify as culturally specific forms of consideration for others. Cooperative social interaction and displaying consideration for others are universal characteristics of every socio-cultural group, so we might say that the theoretical second-order terms 'politic social behaviour', or simply 'politic behaviour', and 'politeness' can serve to refer universally to such social behaviour.

At the same time, as we saw in chapter 1, '(im)politeness' and '(im)polite' are also lexemes used in the English language and are subject to wide fluctuations in the ways they are interpreted by speakers of English in both their current usage and the ways they have been used in the past. For example, not every speaker of English would associate positive feelings with 'polite' or 'politeness', and the ways in which they were understood in previous centuries are very different from the ways in which they are understood today. Native speakers of any language will have different ideas about what sort of behaviour is denoted by the lexical terms available to them, and very often they will disagree. In general, however, we can still assume that there will be a core of agreement about the rough outlines of what is meant by (im)politeness$_1$, and this will include the perception that politic behaviour involves mutually shared forms of consideration for others in a given culture, that impoliteness is an observable violation of politic behaviour which is open to negative evaluation by the participants and the researcher, and that polite behaviour is an observable 'addition' to politic behaviour, which may be positively evaluated, but is equally open to negative evaluation.

As in the case of the English lexemes *impolite, polite, impoliteness* and *politeness*, terms in other languages – if indeed they exist at all – may vary in the meanings and connotations associated with them from one group of speakers (even from one individual speaker) to the next (see the discussion in chapter 1). They are therefore open to semantic change through history. In a later section I shall illustrate this historical relativity in (im)politeness$_1$ by looking at the development of the English lexemes *polite* and *politeness* over the past four centuries. From a historical point of view, at least in western Europe, the lexical realisations of (im)politeness$_1$ in different western European languages have undergone several semantic transformations since they were first used systematically by the Italian conduct writers in the sixteenth century, and prior to the emergence of *polite* from the Latin past participle *politus*, meaning 'polished', we can safely assume that there were other linguistic means to refer to violations of and additions to politic behaviour.

Some of the kinds of linguistic expression which could be classifed as realisations of (im)politeness$_1$ but might equally well form part of the politic behaviour of a social interaction, like saying *please* and *thank you* or prefacing a request made of a stranger with *excuse me* or apologising with *I'm so sorry* or *pardon me*, are highly routinised, ritualistic linguistic formulae (Ferguson 1976). Other forms of social behaviour like opening doors for others to enter or exit before oneself, not belching at mealtimes, holding one's hand in front of one's mouth and turning one's head away when coughing, offering one's seat in a tram or bus to an older person or an invalid, etc., are culturally specific and are also part of our first-order understanding of politeness.[3]

At the basis of all these examples of (im)politeness$_1$ are a consideration for others, often at the expense of one's own interests, and an almost instinctive feeling that the fabric of social relations relies on the reciprocal maintenance of those forms of behaviour. Generally, of course, impoliteness$_1$ is interpreted negatively and politeness$_1$ positively, although it is behaviour that has to be learnt: 'Politeness means learning to accommodate to others within a given social group' (France 1992: 5). However, even though the types of social situation in which politeness$_1$ is institutionally required fluctuate from one social group to another, from one culture to another, and from one period of time to another, it must still have some basis in a universal model of social interaction. For the rest of this chapter we shall be considering the cultural and historical relativity of politeness$_1$ in English, but in chapters 3 to 5 we shall turn our attention to the status of the second-order term in models of politeness (notably not models of impoliteness). I shall argue in this book that a notion of politeness$_2$ should not be abstracted away from politeness$_1$. To do so would represent an

inadequate way of examining those evaluative moments in social interaction which are interpreted as impolite or polite. This would then
prevent us from recognising important clues as to how we manage social interaction and how politic behaviour is constructed, reproduced
and modified in and through instances of socio-communicative verbal
interaction.

I have mentioned a number of times that politeness$_1$ is not always
interpreted positively. It may even arouse strong feelings of resentment
in some people. To call a person's behaviour 'polite' in English does
not necessarily imply a positive evaluation of that behaviour. If we accommodate towards other members of a social group, we might have
to relegate our own best interests in favour of theirs. The problem
is how do we know, if we temporarily put ourselves into the background, however symbolically, that others will at some stage also do
the same? At what point do self-abasing actions become necessary in
social interaction? How far can we go with these symbolic actions before *others* begin to take advantage of *us*? Would it not be easier to
do what is to our advantage and disregard others' feelings? In situations that provoke questions such as these 'politeness could be seen as
an oppressive force, taming the individual, imposing conformity and
deference' (France 1992: 4).

THE ETYMOLOGICAL ORIGINS OF THE TERMS 'POLITE' AND 'POLITENESS'

Etymologically, there is an interesting link between the four terms *polish*, *police*, *poli* (Greek 'city', 'polity') and *politizmos* (Greek 'civilisation')
(France 1992; Sifianou 1992a). The etymological roots of the English
lexeme *polite* lie in the Latin past-participle form *politus*, meaning 'polished'. The same is true for the French term *poli*, which is the past
participle of the verb *polir* 'to polish'. On the surface *polite* appears to
have little to do with the etymological roots of *police* or *politics* in the
Greek *poli* and *politizmos*. Norbert Elias (1939) has shown, however, that
civilisation (*politizmos*) is nothing but the long evolutionary process of
human beings learning how to control 'bodily function, speech and attitudes' (France 1992: 63) resulting in effective methods of self-control
and social control.

France (1992) illustrates that the ideology of politeness that lay at the
heart of court society, hence politics, in seventeenth- and eighteenth-
century France, enforced codes of behaviour on courtiers which led
them to subordinate themselves to 'an increasingly centralized political system' (1992: 63). The ideology of politeness (of being polished)
construed the courtier as hard, but polished and aesthetically pleasing

in contradistinction to other classes of society, who by implication were rough and in need of polishing. Politeness was thus instrumental in creating and maintaining a strictly hierarchical and elitist social structure, and it was used as a means of enforcing social differences. In this sense, it did indeed become a highly efficient way of 'policing' society. As we saw in the previous section Peter France (1992) considered that politeness was used 'as an oppressive force, taming the individual, imposing conformity and deference'. So it is hardly surprising that polite behaviour is frequently viewed with suspicion as being socially divisive and elitist.

France prefers to see first-order politeness 'in its broad eighteenth-century sense' as meaning 'not only polite manners but something akin to what we call civilization, in other words an interrelated set of values which together define a certain ideal of modern European society and culture' (1992: 2). Similarly, Carey McIntosh, whose focus is on the development of written style in English prose writing of the eighteenth century, considers that '[p]oliteness . . . meant something more than just etiquette, however important manners and ceremony may have been; it was a matter of civilization. It measured in part the distance a person or community had come from savagery' (1998: 160).

Thus, while the close association of politeness with civilisation and the fact that it is something more than just etiquette are mentioned by these authors, there is still an uneasy sense of ambivalence evident in remarks such as the following by France:

> What is true politeness? The crown of social values, or a convenient mask for the self-seeking individual? The cloak and agent of tyranny, or the promise, in an unequal society, of equal relations between citizens? (1992: 54)

> In moral terms, the essential notion of politeness is constant consideration for others, a desire not to shock and hurt them, but to gratify and please them . . . Altruism and egoism mingle here. The desire to please and to create a favourable impression can perhaps be satisfied by a mask better than by a real face. What if polish in politeness is merely a superficial and deceptive surface? (1992: 58–9)

The etymological roots of the terms *polite* and *politeness* in English are thus to be found in notions of cleanliness, a smooth surface and polished brightness which can reflect the image of the beholder. There is, of course, a danger that the smooth, polished brightness is 'merely . . . superficial and deceptive', hiding far less altruistic intentions. Native speakers of German sometimes use an aphorism taken from Goethe's *Faust* to express this other side of politeness, namely 'Im Deutschen lügt man, wenn man höflich ist' ('In German you lie when you're polite'). It is this kind of interpretation which links politeness to terms like *politics* and *police*. When it becomes a code of behaviour imposed socially from above, politeness takes on such functions as social control and social discrimination. We shall return to the 'negative' side of politeness later in this chapter and outline how it came to take on those functions in England from the sixteenth century on. But before embarking on a discussion of how the term 'politeness' developed, we first need to consider its historical relativity more generally in the following section.

THE HISTORICAL RELATIVITY OF FIRST-ORDER POLITENESS: POLITENESS IN WESTERN EUROPE FROM THE SIXTEENTH TO THE NINETEENTH CENTURY

There has been considerable fluctuation over the centuries in the ways in which the English first-order lexemes *polite* and *politeness* have been interpreted to refer to forms of mutually cooperative verbal and non-verbal behaviour. Conceptualisations of politeness are subject to historical relativity. Amongst the majority of people in English-speaking countries, current usage no longer bears the connotations of class-consciousness, social climbing, upper-class elitism, social discrimination, etc. which it had in the eighteenth and nineteenth centuries, although there may still be some who are wary of the terms.

In the sixteenth and seventeenth centuries the term 'politeness' in western Europe (and its translation equivalents in other languages) certainly referred to strategies for constructing, regulating and reproducing forms of cooperative social interaction, but it also became closely associated with forms of displaying respect, deference, even obedience, and with strategies aimed at currying favour, at increasing the opportunities for self-advancement, etc. Prestigious social hierarchies in the polities controlled by and from powerful aristocratic courts became dominant in defining forms of polite behaviour.

The philosophical interpretations assigned to politeness through the work of Descartes in France, its more general propagation through the French conduct writers and its adoption in England by Shaftesbury caused a subtle but significant shift in its semantic reference in eighteenth-century England. Politeness became the hallmark of the gentry and the values that it stood for became the socially desirable goal for the new and upwardly mobile middle classes of society. Langford (1989) admirably sums up this movement, which he even calls a 'revolution', as follows:

Nothing unified the middling orders so much as their passion for aping the manners and morals of the gentry more strictly defined, as soon as they possessed the material means to do so. This was a revolution by conjunction rather than confrontation, but it was a revolution none the less, transforming the pattern of social relations, and subtly reshaping the role of that governing class which was the object of imitation. The aspirants sought incorporation in the class above them, not collaboration with those below them . . . (1989: 63)

Commentators were as much intrigued by the impact of affluence on manners, as by its material consequences. In a word, they charted the progress of politeness. This was an ambiguous term. It was naturally associated with the possession of those goods which marked off the moderately wealthy from the poor, the trappings of propertied life. It also included the intellectual and aesthetic tastes which displayed the continuing advance of fashion in its broadest sense. But most of all it affected the everyday routine and rules of social life, from matters as trivial as the time at which one dined, and the way one ate one's dinner, to matters as important as the expectations and arrangements of partners in marriage. There was no shortage of manuals and advice on all such questions. The essence of politeness was often said to be that *je ne sais quoi* [that 'undefinable something', RJW] which distinguished the innate gentleman's understanding of what made for civilized conduct, but this did not inhibit others from seeking more artificial means of acquiring it. (1989: 71)

Politeness$_1$ in eighteenth-century Britain was thus part of an ideological discourse through which the British social class system came into being, as I shall briefly illustrate in the final section of this chapter.

Before doing so, however, let's look at the historical relativity of *polite* and *politeness* in English over the past four and a half centuries. Two terms have been in frequent use in English to categorise the kind of cooperative social behaviour outlined in the previous sections, namely 'polite/politeness' and 'courteous/courtesy', the former being more frequently used today than the latter. There are, of course, other terms that might be used to classify whether an individual's behaviour is polite, and these seem to cover various aspects of the first-order meaning of the term 'politeness' today. For example, we could consider someone's behaviour to be 'considerate' or 'thoughtful', or we could classify that person as 'well mannered'.

Since the middle of the sixteenth century, however, the meanings of 'polite' and 'courteous' have varied quite considerably, although they have always been used to define behaviour that displays considerateness towards others. At different periods of history one or the other term has acquired a set of negative, as well as positive connotations. They have even been used as the basis of models of philosophy, aesthetics, rhetoric, prose writing, diplomatic interaction, etc., so that we would not be incorrect in talking about 'ideologies of politeness'.

It is unclear precisely when the term 'polite' first entered the English language, but sporadic uses can be found in late medieval and early modern English texts. As we saw above, it is derived from the Latin *politus* 'polished'. Its more frequent use in the sixteenth century may have been due to the equivalent term *poli* in Renaissance French, but it did not gain popularity until towards the end of the seventeenth century. Like the Latin past participle *politus*, the French adjective *poli* is also the past participle of the verb *polir* meaning 'to polish, to clean, to brighten'.[4]

The English term *polished* is also sometimes used instead of *polite* in reference to forms of social behaviour, and politeness$_1$ takes on many of the connotations of that term. In contrast to *polir/poli*, however, the modern English lexeme *polite* can only be used in reference to a person's behaviour (or an aspect of her/his behaviour, and in particular to her/his use of language) and, by extension, to that person's character.

During the sixteenth century terms that were used in preference to 'polite/politeness' were 'good manners', 'civil', 'courtesy', 'virtue', 'good nurture', 'good conduct', etc., and the sections of society to which the terms were referred were 'gentlemen', 'courtiers', 'nobility', etc. We can infer from this list that socially cooperative behaviour in the sixteenth century consisted in the appropriate forms of behaviour to be displayed by male members of the nobility at court. Courtiers who successfully endeavoured to live up to the criteria of 'good manners' or 'courtesy' were classified as 'gentlemen'.

The origins of politeness in one of its modern first-order senses in western Europe are thus to be found as part of the courtesy and conduct literature of the late Italian Renaissance at the beginning of the sixteenth century (cf. Patrizi 1992; Magli 1992; Montandon 1992).[5] The first known publication of its kind is Baldassare Castiglione's *Il Cortegiano*, written at the court of the Duke of Urbino and first published in 1516. Judging by the number of translations made into French and English in the sixteenth and seventeenth centuries, the two most influential of these books were Giovanni Della Casa's *Galateo* (1558) and Stefano Guazzo's *La ciuil conuersatione* (1574).[6]

One of the most significant features in the Italian conduct books of the sixteenth century is that language behaviour is given a great deal of prominence, particularly in Guazzo and Della Casa, but also as early as in Castiglione. A certain amount of attention is given in Castiglione to questions of written style. One of the signs of a well-mannered courtier was the ability to carry out 'civil' or 'familiar' conversation. It was this ability, more than any other, that was focused on at the end of the seventeenth century and throughout the eighteenth century in England when the notion of the gentleman was extended beyond the nobility at court and applied to the rising class of the gentry.

During the seventeenth century the ideology of courtesy shifted to the court of the French monarchy, in particular to the court of Louis XIV, the Sun King. The hegemonic discourse was altered and extended by introducing Cicero's notion of the *honestus vir*, translated into French as the *honnête homme*, whose business it was at the court to please others (cf. Faret 1632). *Poli* came to refer to the quality of appropriate behaviour at court, such that civil and courteous behaviour had to show the qualities of *politesse*, of 'being polished'. Polished behaviour was a metaphorical extension from polished silver and brassware; it had to shine, it had to be brilliant, it had to reflect the person who looked at it (i.e. it had to concern itself with the needs of the 'other'), it had to be admired, it had to be aesthetically pleasing, etc.

During the long reign of the Sun King, the concept of politeness was refined and developed as the anchor-pin of a hegemonic discourse controlling behaviour (particularly language behaviour) at court. It was based on Descartes' metaphor of the moving machine, or automaton, and connected as it was to Cicero's concept of the *honestus vir* (*honnête homme*), it bore all the features of ideological discourse. French conduct writers in the last thirty years of the seventeenth century suggested a direct relationship between the mechanical functioning of the individual human body and the state of that person's soul. René Descartes postulated that human beings consisted of a body and a soul (or 'mind', depending on how one translates the French lexeme *âme*), and that it was the soul/mind that distinguished humans from animals. Descartes used the metaphor of the moving machine, or automaton to conceptualise the relationship between the body and the soul/mind more clearly. The body/machine referred to the movements, gestures and postures of the human body, and these were seen as being under the control of *passions intérieures* ('interior passions'). The major distinction between animals and humans, however, resided in the human capacity for thought and language. For Descartes this was the *âme*.

The 1717 English translation of the Abbé de Bellegarde's *Reflexions upon the Politeness of Manners* contains the following statement:

> . . . there's so great a Correspondence betwixt those Springs that move the Heart, and those that move the Countenance; that we may judge by this outward Dial-plate, how the Clock-work goes in the Soul. ([1698] 1717: 40)

The harmonious correspondence between the body and the mind/soul, i.e. the perfect union between an individual's outward behaviour (the body) and his character (the mind/soul), was termed 'politeness' or 'modesty' and the disharmony or disjunction of body and soul/mind was termed 'affectation', not 'impoliteness' (cf. Ketcham 1985: 50). Bellegarde defines 'affectation' in the following way:

> Affectation is the falsification of the whole Person, which deviates from all that is Natural, whereby it might please to put on an ascititious Ayre [sic!], wherewithal to become Ridiculous . . . People corrupted with this Vice, have nothing natural in their way of Talking, Walking, Dressing, turning their Eyes or Head, these are Motions unknown to other Men. ([1698] 1717: 58)

The ideological conceptualisation of politeness$_1$, therefore, represented it as a 'natural' quality and placed it in opposition to affectation. Both are revealed in an individual's actions and, above all else, in her/his words. So right from the outset language use, particularly civil conversation, is taken as an indicator of that harmony between body and soul known as 'politeness'.

There is, of course, a major problem with Bellegarde's definition of politeness$_1$. If politeness$_1$ is natural and is the harmonious union between the body and the soul, would we not have to say that a person with an evil soul, whose behaviour 'naturally' reflects his/her evil character, is also polite? Clearly, this is not what the conduct writers are trying to suggest. Instead, they posit that the perfect union between body and soul is a virtue, not a vice. Hence, only if an individual is 'naturally good' can we talk of 'politeness'.

Bellegarde goes one step further and posits that the virtue of politeness should 'have its Principle in the Soul, as being the Product of an accomplish'd Mind, centring on it self, and Master of its Thoughts and Words' ([1698] 1717: 2). In other words, in order to rescue the concept of politeness as one of the pillars of the ideological discourse, it is necessary to make a division between the soul and the mind. The soul (which we might correlate roughly here with the notion of character) is then taken to be the product of the mind, but only after the latter has been refined or polished, i.e. has become 'accomplish'd'.

Clearly, this contradicts the principle that politeness is natural. Polishing our minds, or having them polished for us, is a social process, a process of education and acculturation. The kind and degree of accomplishment which is the goal of the process is ideologically constructed, and since it is determined not by the individual her/himself but by repeated habitual interactions with others, it is socially reproduced and is therefore institutionalised.

In fact, Bellegarde contradicts his earlier assertions about the ideal harmony between the 'accomplished', self-possessed mind and exterior behaviour in the examples he gives, which display individuals almost wholly concerned to please others by carrying out actions (including modes of language usage) intended to influence them. He gives a second definition of the polite individual as one who 'puts on all Appearances, and transforms himself into all Shapes, the better to gain his Point' ([1698] 1717: 2), the purpose being to 'purchase the Esteem and Affection of Men' ([1698] 1717: 39).

In the conduct writers, and in particular in Bellegarde's work, we can identify the following self-contradictory and somewhat confusing aspects of the ideological conceptualisation of politeness₁ which still occupy us today:

1. Politeness is the ideal union between the character of an individual and his external actions (e.g. the language which that individual uses).
2. Politeness is the ability to please others through one's external actions (e.g. through one's language usage).
3. Politeness is the natural attribute of a 'good' character.
4. Politeness is a socially acquired state of mind that is adjudged to have reached a state of being 'polished' and of thereby being in conformity with a set of socially accepted forms of behaviour.

The contradictions evident here make it possible to argue that an individual is born polite, i.e. that there is a *natural* connection between his soul/mind and bodily actions (including language usage). But it is just as easy to argue that a person may acquire the ability to please and influence others whatever the circumstances of that person's birth. They also make it easy to argue that politeness can only be acquired if one is *socialised* into the 'correct' set of socially accepted norms, i.e. if one is born into the appropriate social class, and therefore that those who are born outside that class can never acquire politeness. The opposite notion of 'affectation' can always be used to categorise the behaviour of those who are not class members.

It was precisely the social interpretation of first-order politeness that was taken up by writers on language, morals, society and philosophy in eighteenth-century Britain. The claim that politeness is a natural attribute of certain individuals and not of others is used to exclude the latter from the ranks of the former. In addition, language behaviour was interpreted as one of the most significant markers, if not the most significant marker, of politeness. This was so pervasive that 'standard English' became almost synonymous with 'polite English' or 'the English of polite society', and even found its way into some of the prescriptive grammar books of the eighteenth century (cf. Watts 1999b, 2002).

During the eighteenth century in Britain the term 'polite', particularly when it was connected with language use, was manipulated in a socially selective way (cf. McIntosh 1998). The concept of politeness was appropriated as the basis of a hegemonic discourse in which the ability to control a specific language variety was interpreted as providing access to high social status from which power could be exercised. Determining who was a member of 'polite society', however, was in the hands of those who had already gained access.

This semantic shift only became possible through what we might call the 'gentrification of politeness'. After the accession to the throne of William III and Mary following the Glorious Revolution of 1688 the centre of power shifted perceptibly from the nobility at court to the rising class of the gentry, i.e. the lower echelons of the nobility and prosperous landowners with no hereditary titles, and away from the metropolis to the country. With the establishment of 'the dominance of gentlemen over English society and politics' (Klein 1994: 1) came a shift in the hegemonic discourse, ushering in 'an era of gentlemanly culture' (ibid.), in which politeness$_1$ came to be redefined to acquire a central significance. The most significant figure in creating the 'gentrification of politeness' was Anthony Ashley Cooper, the third Earl of Shaftesbury, for whom the creation of a philosophy of politeness became the major thrust of his work (cf. Watts 1999a).

Klein argues that Shaftesbury located the discourse of politeness in the social circles of the gentry for three reasons:

> First, 'politeness' was situated in 'company,' in the realm of social interaction and exchange, where it governed the relations of the self with others. While allowing for differences among selves, 'politeness' was concerned with coordinating, reconciling or integrating them. Second, it subjected this domain of social life to the norm of 'pleasing.' . . . Third, 'politeness' involved a grasp of form. (1994: 4)

Shaftesbury set the tone for others like Addison, Steele, Pope and, later in the century, Burke, Smith, Kames, Campbell, Blair and others to follow. Politeness$_1$ had in a sense become emancipated and with the rise of the middle classes in the eighteenth and nineteenth centuries became part and parcel of what we understand as cooperative social interaction at all levels of society. It did so at a cost, however. As Klein points out, 'the psychological dimension of "politeness" was laced with complexity. On the surface, politeness oriented individuals towards each other's needs and wishes: it seemed to arise in a generous concern for the comfort of others. In reality, the polite concern for others might be a secondary effect of a far more basic self-concern' (1994: 4). In other words even in the gentrification of politeness$_1$ and its subsequent expansion through all levels of society, the fundamental contradiction that we noted in the conduct writers was not overcome. I would even argue that it remains with us today. In the final section of this chapter we shall consider the effect that the ideology of politeness had on the development of the British class system and on the emergence of 'standard English' as the legitimate form of language of those in control of that system. I shall begin the discussion by referring to the term 'politeness' as it was represented in English-language teaching books in Switzerland in the last decade of the nineteenth century and the first decade of the twentieth.

POLITENESS$_1$ AND THE SOCIAL CLASS SYSTEM: POLITENESS$_1$ AND 'STANDARD ENGLISH'

The second part of a coursebook for learners of English as a foreign language in Switzerland, which went into its fourth edition in 1894, its seventh in 1908 and its eighth in 1914, provides a set of reading texts for the learners. Among the sections dealt with in the seventh edition is one that contains a set of texts on politeness, courtesy and chivalry. The author, Andreas Baumgartner, heads his section on politeness with the following quotation from H. E. Norton's *Courtesy Reader for Older Boys and Girls*:

> You know what is meant by Good Manners or Politeness. It is not Character; it only lies on the surface, and yet it is a very important thing. Success or failure often depends on whether our manners are good or bad.

Norton's understanding of politeness$_1$ is typical of one way of thinking about it in the final decades of the nineteenth century, and in some social circles today it still forms part of one of the first-order interpretations of the term. 'Politeness' is equivalent to 'good manners'; it does not reflect a person's character since it is only a superficial form of behaviour; yet it could be a crucial element in deciding on the success of a young person's career. A more significant concept than 'politeness' for Norton – and via Norton for foreign teachers of English at the turn of the twentieth century like Baumgartner – is 'courtesy':

> Courtesy is more than Politeness; it comes from the heart: it is kindly and thoughtful consideration for others. It does not always accompany politeness . . . (Baumgartner 1908: 100)

It would be hard to find many people who would still subscribe to this evaluation of the two terms today, even amongst those who associate politeness₁ with dishonesty. But it is interesting to see that by the time we reach British society in the late nineteenth century, writers like H. E. Norton saw politeness₁ as something purely superficial, denying any connection between a person's character and the degree of politeness s/he displayed towards others.

The claim that successful social interaction among human beings depends upon the will of the participants to cooperate in localised forms of social endeavour does not prevent certain forms of human social interaction from being confrontational and competitive, with the result that success and failure will then be measured by who wins and who loses. But the very fact that human beings are social animals ensures that cooperation will ultimately prevail over competition. The mutually shared forms of consideration for others that are the basis of social cooperation from culture to culture will obviously differ, since, as we have seen, politeness₁ is a culturally and historically relative term.

Systems of politeness₁, however, may be part of a discourse that discriminates against and excludes large groups of the population from highly valued symbolic and material resources. Well-developed first-order systems of politeness can even provide a means for those in possession of the relevant resources to discriminate between 'haves' and 'have-nots' linguistically, socially, genderwise and possibly also racially. They are thus used by those in positions of power to provide a justification for the construction of social classes, and they remain relatively stable over lengthy periods of time. During the course of time, some aspects of polite linguistic performance may become pragmaticalised or grammaticalised in the structure of the language.

To give a brief illustration of the elitist and socially exclusive nature of politeness₁ systems and the role that language plays in constructing and reproducing them, I shall, in this final section, consider the development of the British social class system and the role played by language and politeness in that development. To begin with, consider a sentence in the quotation from Langford (1989) given above: 'The essence of politeness was often said to be that *je ne sais quoi* which distinguished the innate gentleman's understanding of what made for civilized conduct . . .' The sentence is resonant with implied meanings which I will now attempt to unravel.

Firstly, those who talked about politeness₁ in the eighteenth century considered that the concept was formed around a meaningful core ('the essence of politeness'). But, secondly, those same people (whoever they were) professed themselves unable, unlike Shaftesbury, to define that core, except to say that it was a *je ne sais quoi* which they instinctively recognised.[7] This imbued the meaningful core of politeness$_1$ with a sense of the mysterious. We can infer that those who had the *je ne sais quoi* constituted a privileged in-group. With the benefit of historical hindsight, we know that the in-group was composed of groups of individuals with political, financial and moral power in the state. So it is hardly surprising that they did everything to uphold the mystique of politeness and to construct the knowledge of the *je ne sais quoi* as an elusive but, for outsiders, never to be attained goal.

Thirdly, the hegemonic groups were composed of 'innate gentlemen', from which we can infer that this is how they projected themselves publicly. In other words, for an upwardly mobile social climber, the goal could never be attained in any case; the only ones who held the key to the elusive *je ne sais quoi* were those who were born gentlemen. The definition of a gentleman entailed the notion of hereditary transference. Fourthly, politeness$_1$, whatever it was, was construed by those in power as the major component of 'civilized conduct'.[8]

Fifthly and finally – although this is not stated or probably even implicated in Langford's sentence – the whole argument deconstructs itself when we recall Shaftesbury's dictum that in order to be a gentleman, one needs to acquire politeness. We could of course argue that all the gentry were doing in the eighteenth century was extending the hereditary nature of politeness$_1$ downwards from the aristocracy. But this counter-argument does not work if we recall the contradictions in the definition of politeness in the writings of French seventeenth-century conduct writers like Bellegarde.

Notwithstanding the arguments provided above, the ideology of politeness in eighteenth-century Britain created a social revolution. For the members of the middle classes, who were rapidly becoming more affluent, more mobile and more self-confident, being 'incorporated' into polite society, i.e. the class above them, was the goal of their social aspirations. As Langford points out, collaboration with those less affluent and less fortunate than themselves was never their goal. It is therefore hardly surprising that they sought access to the prestigious ideological discourse of politeness. It is also hardly surprising that those in control of that discourse, paying lip-service to the aspirations of the middle classes, presented it as an attainable goal through which the members of the middle classes might gain access to valued symbolic resources. At the same time, of course, they did everything they could to thwart those ambitions.

In the first thirty years of the nineteenth century, after the Napoleonic Wars and the initial surge of the Industrial Revolution, it was no longer possible to deny power-sharing to the middle classes. But this also meant that British society, having been moulded through the social construction of class consciousness in which the ideological discourse of politeness played a major role, was faced with a very large, conveniently forgotten but not to be forgotten class of have-nots, i.e. the working classes.

Let us now briefly turn our attention to the connection between the ideology of politeness in eighteenth-century Britain and the development of standard English. It is an accepted principle in modern sociolinguistic research that the innovators and diffusers of linguistic change are likely to be those members of society who are least firmly embedded within a close-knit, sustaining social group, i.e. those who are socially mobile. The linguistic goals at which socially mobile speakers will aim are syntactic and phonological structures, lexemes, styles of speech and writing used by the socially prestigious groups they emulate. It stands to reason therefore that the upwardly mobile middle classes in eighteenth-century Britain took as their linguistic goal the forms of English used by the 'polite classes' of society, i.e. 'polite English'. As McIntosh (1998: 9) points out, '[i]n language, the age demanded elegance and politeness, not merely a school-masterly freedom from "errors"'. He goes on to quote Adam Potkay (1994: 1), who argues 'that "an emerging ideology of polite style" dominated mid-century discourse'.

On the other hand, I argued above that the social class of the gentry held out the ideology of politeness as a means of gaining access to valued symbolic resources, but at the same time did everything they could 'to thwart those ambitions'. In terms of language, this implies that 'polite language' became the equivalent of 'standard language', i.e. the standard in speech and writing which the middle classes should strive to attain. The enormous numbers of prescriptive grammars, books claiming to teach polite style, dictionaries and, later in the century, books on elocution and pronouncing dictionaries are testimony to the perceived needs of the middle classes and also to the burgeoning growth of literacy and print culture.

However, as McIntosh (1998: 23) points out, 'the presumption of a system of social rank is deeply implicated in the language itself' and in order to retain that presumption standards were constantly shifted as the century wore on. The prose style of the major writers changed perceptibly from being a reflection of oral modes of thought and expression, cf. Swift, Addison, even Shaftesbury, in the first twenty years of the century to becoming refined and imitative of classical Latin and Greek forms of written expression, i.e. writing that no longer reflects oral style. It should come as no surprise that these newly developed forms of style were classified as 'polite'.

In the last forty years of the century the efforts to retain an elite standard English were refocused on pronunciation and elocution.[9] By shifting ground in the specification of how standard or 'polite' English was to be understood, assimilation to the standard language remained always just out of reach of the middle classes (cf. Mugglestone 1995; Crowley 1989; Bex 1999). Thus, the acrimonious debate on what is and what is not standard English in present-day Britain can ultimately be traced back to the ideology of politeness in the eighteenth century.

We have spent this second chapter discussing politeness₁ in Europe and Britain, particularly in the period from the Renaissance to the nineteenth century. In the following chapter I shall switch my attention to politeness₂ and review the principal models referred to in the literature on linguistic politeness.

We have also seen in this chapter that for reasons of clarity it is important to make a distinction between lay notions of politeness (politeness₁) and theoretical notions (politeness₂). In the last resort, however, the focus of a model of politeness must be politeness₁ and the evaluative moments observable in ongoing social interaction in which a participant's behaviour is judged to be a violation of politic behaviour or an addition to it. The model cannot therefore be a model of language production, since such a model could only work linearly from a speaker's assessment of the possible effects on the hearer(s) in an effort to predict what that speaker is likely to say. A production model can only work with a concept of politeness₂ that has been abstracted away from interpretations of politeness₁. Politeness₂ would therefore not be equivalent to politeness₁, and any analysis of social interaction that claimed to predict or explain those instances of interaction would necessarily falsify what social members understand by politeness₁.

This chapter has shown that conceptualisations of politeness₁ and impoliteness₁ are highly variable, not only with respect to the way individual participants conceptualise (im)politeness, but also with respect to different interpretations of the display of mutual consideration for others across different cultures and through different periods of history. This would appear to be a fact about (im)politeness₁ which is conveniently ignored by scientific theories of politeness. To ignore the unstable nature of (im)politeness₁ and the great amount of relativity evident in non-scientific writings on it, however, is to overlook a fundamental fact with respect to the term, namely that it is the locus of struggle over its social value which makes it so intriguing in the analysis of social interaction. This will be the focus of our attention in chapters 6 to 9. As a term disputed over discursively, it is open to manipulation by those claiming to possess 'real' politeness and, as such, is the locus of ideological struggle and the exercise of power in discourse. In the following chapters, however, we need to discuss what is wrong with politeness$_2$ in the pragmatic and sociolinguistic literature.

3 Modelling linguistic politeness (I)

In the first two chapters I argued that the object of study for a theory of (im)politeness should be lay perceptions of (im)politeness, or first-order (im)politeness. The problem is that individual evaluations of what constitutes polite and impolite behaviour and the ways in which instantiations of (im)politeness are assessed are so varied that researchers have preferred to abstract away from the kinds of cultural, historical and social relativity inherent in first-order conceptualisations.[1] Second-order politeness, or politeness$_2$, then becomes an abstract term referring to a wide variety of social strategies for constructing and reproducing cooperative social interaction across cultures. The fact that the English lexeme *politeness* is used to denote this second-order concept is either merely an accident of science or, more probably, a consequence of the rapid spread of English as the *lingua franca* in the international research community.

As a technical term, then, the word 'politeness' does not always mean what native speakers of English in the here-and-now take it to mean. Instead, it has to be assigned a timeless, placeless existence as a non-value-laden term in a model of polite behaviour.[2] However, if, in using the term 'politeness', we attempt to rid ourselves of all the first-order connotations the word might have, (im)politeness$_1$ and the wide variety of evaluations of the terms 'politeness' and 'impoliteness' can no longer be the object of study for a theory of linguistic politeness. The attempt to exclude all first-order connotations of the word *(im)politeness* is, of course, an attempt to claim that the theory is non-normative and descriptive rather than normative and prescriptive, but it is an attempt which, I shall argue, must ultimately fail (cf. Eelen 2001: 174–86). The question that we shall address in this chapter and the next is whether it is at all possible to construct a second-order theory of (im)politeness while retaining the claim to non-normativity, i.e. the absence of norms and explicit rules, and description. Several theories have been proposed but, as Eelen (2001) shows, none has escaped the inevitable slippage into normative and prescriptive stances. The reason for this is relatively simple, but we first need to consider what we mean by the two terms 'theory' and 'model'.

A theory of X aims at giving a dispassionate, 'objective' account of X, i.e. at giving at least an adequate description of X and, if possible, an explanation for X's occurrence in the 'real', non-theoretical world. In order to do this, the scientist needs to construct a model of X. At this point we should bear in mind that a model is always a simulation of the real thing, never the real thing in itself. A model plane is not a real plane, and a fashion model models clothes to give potential buyers an impression of what the clothes might look like on them. In both cases we are dealing with the simulation of reality. For example, if we asked a group of ten people individually to make us a model of the Eiffel Tower in Paris, we would get ten different models. We might then ask someone to judge these models according to a set of criteria, and future modellers of the Eiffel Tower might decide to base their own models on one or another of them. But none of the models is the real Eiffel Tower; hence none of them can be totally 'correct'.

In constructing a theory of human language, the linguist needs a *model* of human language, and there are a large number of models on the market from which s/he can choose. Some of them are judged to be better than others, but none of them can ever be totally 'correct'. The problem with human language is that, however much the linguist might try to abstract away from the ways in which we use it, it remains the major means through which we construct our views of the world and the social worlds in which we exist. Its very essence is prescriptive and normative, and it is the locus of constant struggle over its relative social values.

This is not to say, however, that it is not possible to look at human language as an abstract system, i.e. to model language by temporarily detaching it from those who use it, and indeed spectacular successes have been achieved in theoretical linguistics by taking that step. The problem comes when we try to apply the theory to account for the ways in which language is *used* by human beings. Try as we might, we cannot avoid becoming embroiled in first-order conceptualisations of the value of language unless we buy into that prescriptive, evaluative struggle.

Politeness and impoliteness – and of course their rough equivalents in other languages – are terms referring to ways in which individuals use language socially, so the model of (im)politeness, politeness$_2$, can never be stripped of its evaluative clothing. The reason is simple:

(im)politeness *is* the clothing! As such it is open to changes in fashion, positive and negative assessments, approbation and abuse; it can be used to impress, to shock, to seduce, to deceive, etc. The model for (im)politeness cannot therefore divorce itself from these facts, which leads to the seemingly absurd conclusion that (im)politeness$_1$ is the model for (im)politeness$_1$. The way out of this obvious tautology is to suggest that studying how members evaluate and struggle over (im)politeness$_1$ is a way of describing and explaining how they construct their social worlds. There is, *per definitionem*, no way of lifting (im)politeness$_1$ out of the social world in which it realises various social values and reifying it as (im)politeness$_2$. But this is precisely what has been done in one model of politeness after another.

The present chapter is therefore devoted to a critical presentation of some of the models of (im)politeness$_2$ which are frequently referred to by researchers in the field. The major theory, Brown and Levinson's, and criticisms of that theory will be dealt with in the following chapter. To begin with, however, let us consider how definitions of politeness which can be found in the theoretical literature never escape from first-order evaluations.

DEFINITIONS OF SECOND-ORDER POLITENESS

Researchers into (im)politeness$_2$ are not always successful in escaping from the inherently evaluative nature of (im)politeness$_1$. Why is this the case? Firstly, if we wanted to set up a theoretical model of (im)politeness$_2$, the first thing we would have to do is to find ways of isolating across cultures all those strategies, verbal as well as non-verbal, that construct, regulate and reproduce forms of cooperative social interaction – an obviously impossible task.[3] Secondly, a theory of (im)politeness$_2$, or linguistic politeness, would be one in which it could be explained as a universal facet of human social interaction across cultures. It would be one in which forms of human interaction could be interpreted and described as instances of politeness and in which forms of linguistic usage in any language community could be observed and analysed as helping to construct and reproduce politeness. No theory of this kind at present exists, precisely because of the evaluative nature of (im)politeness$_1$, although the Brown and Levinson model, which we will look at in more detail in chapter 4, does attempt to explain politeness as a universal facet of social interaction.[4] The argument presented in the previous section, and throughout this whole book, is that no such theoretical model could ever be set up. Thirdly, in using language in different social activity types, including academic discourse on politeness itself, we are continually reproducing politeness.

Curiously enough, definitions of second-order politeness are largely absent from most theoretical work in the field (cf. Fraser 1990), and the reader often has to infer from the theoretical principles of each model how 'politeness' might be defined. Some writers *are* careful enough to define what they mean by the term and, in general, modern definitions agree on the basic substance of the notion, i.e. that it consists of mutually shared forms of consideration for others. What they do not take properly into consideration, however, is that what might be assessed by some as a 'mutually shared form of consideration for others' might easily be assessed differently by those others.

Let's take a brief look at a range of definitions given in the literature. These are presented by Sifianou (1992a: 82–3), and they are followed with a definition of her own. She begins by commenting on and quoting from a range of works on linguistic politeness, which I present briefly here (italics mine):

> a. Lakoff (1975a: 64): '. . . politeness is developed by *societies in order to reduce friction in personal interaction*'.

The assumption here is that friction in personal interaction is undesirable, a prescriptive stance, and that societies, in some mysterious way, develop strategies, i.e. politeness, to reduce that friction. Politeness$_2$ thus ends up being a set of norms for cooperative behaviour: it does not escape from the evaluative framework in which (im)politeness$_1$ is used.

> b. Leech (1980: 19) defines it as 'strategic conflict avoidance', which 'can be measured in terms of *the degree of effort put into the avoidance of a conflict situation*', and *the establishment and maintenance of comity*.

The same criticisms can be levelled at Leech's concept of politeness$_2$ as were levelled at Lakoff's. Here, however, the avoidance of conflict is represented as a conscious effort on the part of the person being polite, since it is 'strategic'. In addition, if politeness is behaviour which aims at the establishment and maintenance of comity, this must mean that people evaluate other forms of behaviour as subverting those aims, i.e. politeness$_2$ is evaluative.

> c. Brown and Levinson (1978) 'view politeness as *a complex system for softening face-threatening acts*'.

Brown and Levinson appear to present a definition of politeness$_2$ which avoids becoming embroiled in the evaluative struggle over (im)politeness. As we shall see in the next chapter, this is only superficial, since they, too, like Leech, present speakers who strategically evaluate how to avoid face-threatening. The aims in doing so, however, are frequently egoistic, rather than altruistic, and we cannot know how the hearer (who is conveniently forgotten in Brown and Levinson except insofar as s/he has a face which needs to be considered) will react. The reaction will in any case reveal the evaluative nature of politeness$_2$, making it once again (im)politeness$_1$.

d. Kasper (1990: 194) bases her work on Brown and Levinson's approach to politeness and maintains that 'communication is seen as a fundamentally dangerous and antagonistic endeavor'. Politeness is therefore a term to refer to *the strategies available to interactants to defuse the danger and to minimalise the antagonism.*

Kasper's definition contains explicitly evaluative terms such as 'fundamentally dangerous' and 'antagonistic'. Politeness$_2$ is given the job of 'defusing the danger' and minimising the antagonism', which of course implies that others involved in the interaction are not concerned to do this. The struggle continues!

e. Arndt and Janney (1985b: 282) see politeness as '*interpersonal supportiveness*'.

Here again, we note that politeness$_2$ is seen from a normative perspective, since normal behaviour implies that we give one another mutual support in social interaction. Quite apart from the fact that there are plenty of social interaction types in which 'interpersonal supportiveness' is not the aim of the interaction, what would Arndt and Janney do with an utterance like 'Excuse me, would you mind getting your elbow out of my stomach?', said by an exasperated member of the general public in an overcrowded tube train?

f. Hill *et al.* (1986: 349) define politeness as 'one of the constraints on human interaction, whose purpose is *to consider others' feelings, establish levels of mutual comfort, and promote rapport*'.

Hill *et al.*'s definition of politeness$_2$ sees it as a set of constraints, i.e. normative and prescriptive rules on how to interact with others, and, once again, the laudable goals are the establishment of mutual comfort and the promotion of rapport. Even mentioning these goals implies that there are others with other goals.

g. Ide (1989: 225) sees it as '*language usage associated with smooth communication*'. As Sifianou puts it, this 'is achieved through the speaker's use of intentional strategies and of expressions conforming to prescribed norms'.

Ide's definition uses the evaluative term 'smooth'. What is *smooth* communication? Is this not in itself prey to innumerably variable interpretations? Sifianou interprets Ide as presenting politeness₂ as 'strategic' and normative.

h. Fraser and Nolen (1981: 96) see politeness as '*a property associated with a voluntary action*'.

Fraser and Nolen present perhaps the most veiled definition of all. How are we to understand the expression 'voluntary action'? If we perform an involuntary action, does this then mean that politeness is excluded? The number of voluntary actions that can be produced in a social interaction by all the participants leaves the interpretation of those actions open to a wide choice of various evaluations. Hence the normative and implicitly prescriptive stance of other definitions is not avoided by Fraser and Nolen.

Sifianou then gives the following summary of these definitions:

> People tend to be considerate because this *repays* them with a pleasant feeling of satisfaction; furthermore, *they receive consideration in return* and at the same time satisfy the needs of others. It is a *multiple reward*. This obviously does not mean that they behave in the way that they do because they have any ulterior motives (although this may be true in a few cases), or that they expect any tangible *reward*. It simply means that they have internalized the fact that *in order to live in a harmonious society you give and take and thus participate in maintaining the necessary equilibrium of relationships*. (1992a: 83, italics mine)

The quotation openly displays the evaluative nature of definitions of politeness₂ (note, never of *im*politeness₂), but at least it recognises the 'give and take' of interaction. It is not focused entirely on speakers, but indicates that politeness₂ is a joint venture. As a joint social venture, however, it is implicitly open to dispute and discursive struggle. It is in fact politeness₁. What is interesting about Sifianou's own definition is her use of the expressions I have highlighted in the quotation, namely the verbs *repay, receive, give* and *take*, the nouns *consideration* and *reward*, and the phrases *in return* and *equilibrium of relationships*, all of which indicate a first-order relationship of some kind involving the exchange of metaphorical goods, payment and the desired effect of the payment, i.e. harmony and social equilibrium. As we shall see, these are notions that lie at the heart of politeness$_1$, and they do not always imply harmony and equilibrium.

Sifianou's definition becomes explicitly normative and prescriptive in the following quotation, which is strong evidence that what she is referring to is not politeness$_2$ at all, but politeness$_1$:

> I use the term 'politeness' in a more general sense, and see it *as the set of social values which instructs interactants to consider each other by satisfying shared expectations.* (1992a: 86, italics in the original)

The idea of second-order politeness 'instructing' interactants to produce socially harmonious interaction also introduces elements of morality and the social-psychological development of children, thus providing further evidence of the prescriptive nature of concepts of politeness. The result of this brief survey of definitions of politeness$_2$ is that it cannot possibly figure as a model of politeness$_1$ in a theory of politeness. It *is* politeness$_1$.

PREPRAGMATIC APPROACHES TO LINGUISTIC POLITENESS

Politeness in linguistic pragmatics and sociolinguistics is a relatively young subdiscipline in western Europe and North America, dating back to the late 1960s and early 1970s. As we shall see later in this section, however, politeness phenomena have been a feature of the study of the Chinese and Japanese languages for millennia.

The major reason for the late appearance of politeness in the west is that those linguists who were interested in politeness phenomena in language had little or no theoretical basis to fall back on until speech act theory appeared in the 1960s (cf. Austin 1962; Searle 1970, 1972). The insights of speech act theory were then enriched and elaborated by researchers putting to use Erving Goffman's notions of face and facework (cf. chapter 5), and work on conversational implicatures by the ordinary-language philosopher H. Paul Grice in the late 1960s and early 1970s.

Goffman's indirect contribution to politeness research consisted of significant concepts such as 'face' (or public self-image), 'ritual order' and 'the human individual as a sacred object', which found their way into politeness theory in the 1970s. Grice's ground-breaking work on non-natural meaning, the Cooperative Principle (and its maxims) and pragmatic implicatures had been known since the 1950s and 1960s, but it was not until his William James lectures came to be published individually after 1975, particularly 'Logic and conversation', that linguistic pragmatics began to shake off the need to distinguish itself from semantics and to release itself from the attempt to apply speech act theory to generative theories of language.

Despite the upsurge of interest in the phenomenon of linguistic politeness in the 1970s, however, we should not allow ouselves to imagine that prior to that decade there were no approaches to linguistic politeness worth considering. Gudrun Held (1992a, b, 1995) has written persuasively on what she calls 'prepragmatic linguistic politeness' within the framework of Romance and German linguistics, and I shall focus on her work here.[5] Held makes the point that the interest in second-order politeness reaches at least as far back as the early nineteenth century and thus coincides with the development of the historical study of Indo-European. As she says (1992a: 133):

> Incentives towards studying the problem reach as far back as the German Romantic movement and were taken up by the school of idealism to bolster theories about the relationship between psychological feeling, national character and verbal creativity (Spitzer 1922; Beinhauer 1930; Lerch 1934).

The 'school of idealism' in the 1920s and 1930s was an early attempt to link the study of language with such abstract notions as the psychology of emotions and national characteristics. It set itself the task of discovering links between forms of *emotive language* and *linguistic creativity*, Leo Spitzer's name being closely associated with an early version of literary stylistics. The major problem in this approach was the link posited between these two constructs, on the one hand, and so-called 'national character', on the other. The link between 'national character' and language goes back to the linguistic work of Wilhelm von Humboldt in the first quarter of the nineteenth century. Humboldt had suggested that the structures of a language, continually produced and reproduced by its speakers, were an outer reflection of an inner national character (or 'soul'). Humboldt's theory was in this sense an early version of linguistic relativity, although he postulated a link between language and nation rather than between language and culture. The re-emergence of this theory in the twentieth century opened it up to distortion and manipulation in the service of the fascist dictatorships that arose in Europe in the 1920s and 1930s.[6]

Linguists such as Spitzer, Beinhauer, Lerch and others believed that 'polite' utterances were at one and the same time creative linguistic acts that could not be repeated but were individual instantiations of a 'collective style, i.e. of the *Umgangssprache* "colloquial language" of a people, whose typical attitudes they reflect' (Held 1992a: 138–9).

Held suggests that this approach towards linguistic politeness robs the individual speaker of intentionality and turns her/him into a 'creative representative of a language community whose values and norms are anchored in the quasi-magical term *Wesen* or *Wesensart* "being" or "type of being"' (1992a: 138–9). The attempt to create a deterministic link between language and the 'character of a nation' is grounded in the assumption that language is a social product. But at the same time language is also a uniquely individual and creative system. Forms of linguistic politeness, therefore, are considered in this approach to politeness to be communal norms, to all intents and purposes lying beyond the control of the rational individual. Thus, even before the rise of modern studies on linguistic politeness, the normative nature of politeness was stressed.

This way of thinking about linguistic politeness phenomena was prefigured by the Saussurean and immediate post-Saussurean Genevan school of linguists, e.g. Bally, Gabelentz, Brunot, Dauzat and Kainz, who argued in favour of external influences on linguistic structure (Held 1992a: 138). Such external influences were mostly taken to be social, although Kainz argued, in a psychological vein, in favour of what he called 'secondary ethical functions'.[7] Social (and psychological, ethical) influences were said to have an effect on various levels of linguistic description, particularly the lexicon and morphosyntax. Seen in this light, therefore, politeness, far from being a 'set of strategies for constructing, regulating and reproducing forms of cooperative social interaction', is beyond the immediate control of the individual and is therefore not strategic. It consists of the social constraints that are taken to be part of the collective national character.

We can of course think of social constraints as being quite independent of 'national character'. After all, each of us is socialised over a relatively long period of time into the production of forms of language which are considered necessary to 'reduce friction', to 'avoid conflict', to 'establish comity', to 'minimalise antagonism', to 'establish interpersonal supportiveness', etc. If we filter out the nationalistic component from this view of politeness, it comes close to some of the ideas I shall present in chapter 6.

The impression that the reader might have gained from this brief outline of prepragmatic approaches to second-order politeness is, firstly, that such approaches are confined to movements in European linguistics and, secondly, that they do not appear much before the beginning of the nineteenth century. Impressions such as these are far from accurate. Two important cultures in the Far East, China and Japan, have a long history of studying linguistic politeness phenomena within the framework of theories of rhetoric (in the case of China) and theories of the national language (in the case of Japan). Lee-Wong (1999: 21–3), for example, criticises Ehlich (1992) for having omitted, in his discussion of the historicity of politeness, any discussion of politeness phenomena in China. She goes on to refer to Ancient Chinese theories of rhetoric in which politeness played a central role:

> 'Easing the jolts' was a major purpose of ancient Chinese rhetoric, so much so that their social processes had as one of their principal functions the avoidance of embarrassment – or 'saving face', as it came to be known. (1999: 21)

Shibamoto (1985) discusses two fields of academic interest with language in Japan which do not have equivalents in western countries, namely the study of the national language and what she calls 'language life studies'. The first of these reaches back over a period of more than two thousand years and includes at various points in its history detailed theoretical analysis of and reflection on structures of politeness in Japanese. Prepragmatic approaches to the study of politeness$_2$, therefore, are by no means restricted to Europe and have a much longer history than we tend to imagine.

Approaches to politeness earlier than the 1960s, whether they have been a current feature of theorising on language for millennia (cf. Japan and China) or whether they go back no further than the age of Romanticism (cf. western Europe), were developed before the rise of linguistic pragmatics. For that reason I have classified them as 'prepragmatic' approaches. Pragmatic and postpragmatic approaches are those which have been constructed on the principles of pragmatics. It is these approaches that have seemed to politeness researchers to offer the most promising insights into the universal phenomenon of politeness, and I shall discuss some of them in the following sections. I shall begin with a short résumé of the enormously influential work of Paul Grice in the field of linguistic pragmatics. Grice's work will be picked up again in chapter 8 and examined in more critical detail, but in this chapter the reader merely needs to be familiar with one of the most important foundation stones in models of linguistic politeness.

GRICE'S COOPERATIVE PRINCIPLE

The watershed between, on the one hand, speech act approaches to the study of intentional meaning and logico-pragmatic approaches to the study of presuppositions, and, on the other, the study of processes of inferencing and the negotiation of meaning is without doubt represented by the work of H. P. Grice. In the former type of approach to non-semantic meaning the theoretical focus was still on the role of the speaker. In the latter type of approach, frequently referred to as 'Gricean', the role of the hearer emerges more forcefully as a crucial factor in processes of inferring meaning.[8]

Grice's contribution to the 'pragmatic revolution', however, reaches back into the 1950s to the publication of the article 'Meaning' in 1957 and is developed in more detail in 'Utterer's meaning and intentions' (1969). 'Meaning' was reprinted in a collection of papers on semantics edited by Steinberg and Jakobovits in 1971, in which Grice's theory of meaning gets very short shrift indeed at the hands of logicians and semanticists (cf. Harman 1971; Ziff 1971).

Grice (1957) posits two levels of 'meaning' involved in any verbal utterance, which can be summarised as the conventional denotative (possibly also connotative) meanings represented by the semantics of the language in which the utterance is made, and the intention(s) of the speaker in making the utterance. The former type of meaning is close to what is often called truth-conditional meaning, or propositional meaning. The latter is closely related to speech act notions such as illocutionary act and illocutionary force. Speaker intentions, of course, were an important component in speech act analysis.

Grice's most significant contribution to the study of utterance meaning, however, was only made during the series of William James lectures that he delivered at Harvard University in 1969, one of which, 'Logic and conversation', embedded his original dual level of meaning interpretation into what he called a 'cooperative principle' for conversation (see Grice 1975).

Grice's Cooperative Principle (CP) consists of a limited set of conversational maxims to which, Grice maintains, interactants in a conversational exchange should, but frequently do not, adhere.[9] Violating any of the maxims leads the addressee to make what Grice calls 'implicatures' (or inferences) in order to ascertain the speaker's intended meaning and thereby reinstate the CP.

The following maxims are proposed by Grice:

a. the maxim of Quantity, in which interactants should keep their conversational contributions as informative as is required for the purposes of the conversational exchange, but not more informative;

b. the maxim of Quality, in which interactants should say only what they believe to be true or that for which they have adequate evidence;

c. the maxim of Relation, in which interactants should make their contributions relevant to the purposes of the overall conversation;

d. the maxim of Manner, in which interactants should avoid obscurity of expression and ambiguity, should not engage in unnecessary verbosity and should present their contributions in an orderly manner.

In addition, Grice also mentions, almost as a passing comment, that the CP may need to be augmented by the addition of further maxims, one of which, he suggests, might be a maxim of Politeness. We shall return to a more critical look at Grice's work in chapter 8. For the remainder of this chapter, however, we shall focus on this point since it was precisely this suggestion that prompted attempts by linguists, notably Robin Lakoff and Geoffrey Leech, to formulate the missing maxim.

POLITENESS AS CONFLICT AVOIDANCE: LAKOFF'S CONVERSATIONAL-MAXIM APPROACH

Both George and Robin Lakoff were associated in the late 1960s with the development of a semantics-based model of generative grammar commonly referred to as 'generative semantics' and with the possible integration of speech act theory into generative models of language (cf. Ross 1970). The positive impact of Grice's Cooperative Principle and the negative impact of Chomsky's attacks against generative semantics (1972) combined to shift Robin Lakoff's linguistic interests decisively in the direction of Gricean pragmatics. At the same time, she became increasingly involved in the American feminist movement of the late 1960s and 1970s and published a pioneering work on language and gender entitled *Language and Woman's Place*, first as an article, then as a monograph in 1975, in which politeness has a prominent place.

Robin Lakoff's work on politeness consists primarily of a number of relatively early articles (1973a, b, 1975b, 1977 and 1979), her monograph on gender differences in language (1975a) and a more empirically based article (1989) dealing with the language of the courtroom and the language of therapeutic discourse. The clearest expression of the way in which she conceptualises the phenomenon of politeness is contained in the 1973 article ('The logic of politeness; or minding your p's and q's') and I shall summarise her model of politeness from that work here.

Lakoff suggests setting up pragmatic rules to complement syntactic and semantic rules and adding a set of 'rules of politeness' to Grice's CP, which she redefines as the 'rules of conversation'. Grice's fleeting comment about the need for a politeness maxim was thus taken up seriously. Lakoff also makes the strong prediction for pragmatics that 'there is no reason why such rules couldn't, in the future, be made as rigorous as the syntactic rules in the transformational literature . . .' (1973a: 296).

Lakoff has always stressed the significance of her training as a generative linguist for her approach to the pragmatic and social study of language. It is therefore hardly surprising that the 1973 article represents an attempt to set up rules of pragmatic well-formedness as an extension to the rules of grammar:

> We should like to have some kind of pragmatic rules, dictating whether an utterance is pragmatically well-formed or not, and the extent to which it deviates if it does. (1973a: 296)

The principle of pragmatic well-formedness can only be applied to the realm of sentences, of course, and not to the realm of utterances. Utterances can be evaluated as *pragmatically appropriate*, but hardly as pragmatically well-formed. Nevertheless, Lakoff insists that the search for pragmatic 'rules' would have to be grounded in a notion of Pragmatic Competence, analogous to Chomsky's notion of grammatical competence.

Despite her insistence on pragmatic rules, however, Lakoff does not attempt to set up a production model of politeness (see the critical comments in Fraser 1990 and Watts *et al.* 1992b). She claims that 'if one causes something to happen by linguistic means, one is using a linguistic device' (1973a: 293) and that 'the *pragmatic* content of a speech act should be taken into account in determining its acceptability just as its syntactic material generally has been, and its semantic material recently has been' (1973a: 293–4). However, one does not gain the impression that she ever intended to set up anything more than a model that would account *post factum* for the acceptability or non-acceptability of polite utterances. Indeed, a closer look at her work during the 1970s and since leads us to reassess her wider aims, within which politeness does not figure quite so prominently as has often been assumed.

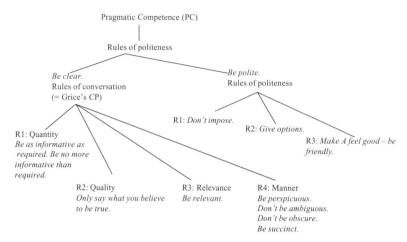

Figure 3.1   *Lakoff's rules of pragmatic competence*

Lakoff suggests two overarching rules of Pragmatic Competence, both composed of a set of subrules, namely 1. Be clear; and 2. Be polite. Rule 1 (Be clear) is really the Gricean CP, which she renames the 'rules of conversation'. Rule 2 (Be polite) consists of a subset of three rules, R1: Don't impose; R2: Give options; and R3: Make A(ddressee) feel good – be friendly. Lakoff's pragmatic competence can thus be represented schematically in figure 3.1 above.

I have inserted the Gricean maxims under 'Be clear', which is immediately dominated by the rules of politeness, as Lakoff argues that the rules of clarity are a 'subcase of the rules of politeness' (1973a: 305). Whichever way we look at the diagram, however, if a speaker follows the rules of politeness by not imposing, giving options and making A feel good, s/he will be certain at some stage or another in the interaction to violate the rules of conversation. As we shall see, this is one of the great weaknesses of models constructed along Gricean lines.

Lakoff is fully aware of this dilemma, and she suggests that by following the rules of conversation, the speaker/writer does everything in her/his power not to impose on the addressee(s) by requiring too many implicatures to be made in order to fully interpret the utterance. This leads her to the conclusion that 'when Clarity conflicts with Politeness, in most cases (but not . . . all) Politeness supersedes' (1973a: 297). But this still does not alter the fact that abiding by the rules of politeness means breaking the rules of conversation.

In accordance with the pragmatic well-formedness of utterances, Lakoff (1979) suggests a cline of politeness types ranging from *formal* (or *impersonal*) *politeness* (Don't Impose), through *informal politeness* (Give Options) to *intimate politeness* (Make A Feel Good). If a speaker were to preface an utterance with 'I'm sorry to disturb you, but . . .', that part of the utterance would constitute formal politeness. If s/he were to say 'Would you mind closing the window?', this would constitute an example of informal politeness. If a speaker were to preface a request for a loan with an utterance like 'Hey! That's a terrific suit you've got on there!', this would constitute an example of intimate politeness.

Fraser (1990) maintains that Lakoff fails to define what she understands politeness to be, but as we saw in an earlier section of this chapter, this is not entirely true. In the 1975 article she states that 'politeness is developed by societies in order to reduce friction in personal interaction' (1975b: 64). In any case, it is by no means the most important criticism of Lakoff's approach. There are a number of significant, more substantial objections to be made. For example, what is the nature of Pragmatic Competence? Will pragmatic well-formedness in language A exclude utterances which are pragmatically well-formed in language B if those same utterances in A are non-well-formed? Does the assumed existence of Pragmatic Competence not logically entail the assumption that certain utterances are inherently polite and others inherently impolite? What is the nature of the pragmatic rules (including of course the rules of politeness)? They surely cannot be algorithmic rules such as those in a generative grammar producing pragmatically well-formed utterances. Are they simply normative rules prescribing the ways in which individuals *should* behave rather than describing how they *do* behave? Lakoff's later work does not give us answers to these questions, although it does indicate that her insistence on pragmatic rules is applied less to questions of politeness than to questions of gender and culture differences in language behaviour. Even if they could be answered coherently, we might still argue that Lakoff's model hardly constitutes a model of politeness$_2$.

Her interest in issues of gender discrimination led to the publication of *Language and Woman's Place* (1975a), which had earlier appeared as a long journal article. *Language and Woman's Place* has been enormously influential and, needless to say, enormously controversial in the field of gender studies on language since the 1970s, and it still continues to generate argument and dissension. One of the features of women's language, says Lakoff, is that women use politer language than men, and they do so for reasons of insecurity. She takes up the position that the unmarked, dominant forms of linguistic behaviour are male, whereas the linguistic behaviour of women is marked and discriminated against. In accordance with a number of types of language structure and patterns of language behaviour that she discusses as being 'female' she makes the point that women are perceived to be more polite than men. Now, while one would normally expect this 'observation' to be assessed positively, Lakoff argues that, precisely *because* women's interactive behaviour is usually taken to be deferential (i.e. as expressing informal and intimate politeness), the more unmarked forms of politeness behaviour (formal, or impersonal, politeness) are classified as negatively marked – which brings us back to the struggle over the social values of politeness$_1$. Lakoff's conclusion is encapsulated in the aphorism 'You're damned if you do; you're damned if you don't.' At all events, her remarks on gender and politeness have sparked off a series of publications on this aspect of the subject alone.[10]

In a collection of essays on the subject of 'Language, sex, and gender' Lakoff (1979) contributes an article that elaborates on these ideas. Instead of talking about pragmatic rules, she now refers to 'rules of style', which women and men in American society have internalised as behavioural norms.[11] She suggests a range of styles from *clarity* (i.e. abiding strictly to the Gricean CP), through *distance* (in which formal/impersonal politeness strategies are used), *deference* (in which options are given to the addressee, i.e. informal politeness is in evidence) to *camaraderie* (where intimacy and intimate forms of politeness are displayed). Women's styles of interaction are said to vacillate between deference and camaraderie and men's between clarity and distance.

Her discussion is of course much richer than I can do justice to here but we can assume that certain utterances are taken to be, if not inherently, then at least more typically polite than others, and that the perceptions made by certain cultural and subcultural groups (in this latter category men vs women) concern the degree of politeness of other groups. Lakoff exemplifies this (albeit in very generalised terms) by pointing out that German culture is felt in America typically to practise strategies of distance whereas Japanese culture is classified according to strategies of deference.

In reviewing Lakoff's approach to politeness, it is unwise to think in terms of a theory of how speakers come to produce utterances that are classified as '(im)polite'. It is not, in other words, a theory of politeness production, despite all her talk about pragmatic rules and the need to make them as 'rigorous' as syntactic rules. The insistence on equating pragmatic competence with grammatical competence and attempting to set up rules through which polite behaviour can be explained will not lead to a theoretical model of politeness$_2$. In the following section we shall focus on a further attempt to elaborate a model of pragmatics along Gricean lines in which politeness plays a leading role, i.e. Leech's model of general pragmatics.

LEECH'S 'GRAND' SCHEME: A MODEL OF GENERAL PRAGMATICS

As a theoretical framework to carry out their empirical work on linguistic politeness phenomena, researchers tend to choose between either the Brown and Levinson approach, which I will present in the following chapter, or the approach proposed by Geoffrey Leech (1983). Other models, including Lakoff's, are rarely applied to data. Leech maintains that his model is descriptive, which it can be shown not to be (cf. the comments on his definition of politeness in an earlier section). It is certainly very taxonomic, and a number of researchers have found it particularly useful in accounting for linguistic politeness in their data.[12] The Brown and Levinson model is a production model, which has attracted a large amount of attention, mainly because it purports to explain the occurrence of specific forms of linguistic politeness in preference to others and to do so on the basis of claims for universality. The fact remains that only Leech and Brown and Levinson have elaborated their positions in sufficient detail to allow them to be tested through application to real-language data. In addition, only these two models have given extensive examples of the kinds of linguistic structures that are put to use to realise politeness strategies. Researchers are thus given data and analyses of these data that they can check against their own materials.[13]

As with Lakoff, Leech's approach to linguistic politeness phenomena forms part of an attempt to set up a model of what he calls 'general pragmatics', which he glosses as an account of 'how language is used in communication' (1983: 1). Unlike Lakoff, however, Leech does not aim at accounting for pragmatic competence (whatever might be understood by that term). In other words, he is not concerned to create highly precise formalised rules such as those in the syntactic or semantic components of a grammar. One of his postulates is: 'Semantics is rule-governed (= grammatical); general pragmatics is principle-controlled (= rhetorical)' (1983: 5).

Leech conceptualises 'general pragmatics' as 'the general conditions of the communicative use of language' (1983: 10). In addition to 'general pragmatics' Leech proposes two further pragmatic systems, 'pragmalinguistics', which accounts for the more linguistic end of pragmatics in which 'we consider the particular resources which a given language provides for conveying particular illocutions' (1983: 11), and 'socio-pragmatics', which studies 'the more specific "local" conditions on language use'.

The approach that Leech takes to the study of general pragmatics is 'rhetorical', by which he means 'the effective use of language in its most general sense, applying it primarily to everyday conversation, and only secondarily to more prepared and public uses of language' (1983: 15). Leech recognises two systems of rhetoric:

1. *Textual rhetoric*, which consists of the following sets of principles: the Processibility Principle, the Clarity Principle, the Economy Principle and the Expressivity Principle.
2. *Interpersonal rhetoric*, which, among others, consists of the following sets of principles: the Cooperative Principle (i.e. Grice's CP), the Politeness Principle (PP) and the Irony Principle.

Thus, whereas Lakoff considers the *rules* of conversation (Grice's CP) and the *rules* of politeness (Leech's PP) to constitute pragmatic competence, Leech considers the CP and the PP to constitute only the *principles* of interpersonal rhetoric. If Leech were attempting to set up a model of pragmatic competence – which he is definitely not concerned to do – it would have to be augmented by the principles of textual rhetoric and related to the principles of pragmalinguistics and socio-pragmatics. It is, in other words, a much more complex and finer grained attempt to elaborate on Gricean pragmatics than is Lakoff's. Fraser (1990: 224) calls it 'a grand elaboration of the Conversational Maxim approach to politeness', and, as we shall see, the 'grandness' of its scale certainly fits it as a method of describing and interpreting utterances. But it is not intended to serve as a model of how individual interactants come to frame their utterances 'politely'.

Leech sees the function of pragmatics as being 'problem-solving' in that it 'relates the sense (or grammatical meaning) of an utterance to its pragmatic force' (Postulate 4, p. 30) by means of inferencing processes made by the hearer. Indeed, because of its focus on processes of interpretation, Leech rightly maintains that his model is centred on the hearer rather than on the speaker.

The point that is never dwelt on either in Leech or in any of the other theories of politeness is that, since (im)politeness is the locus of social struggle, a focus on either the speaker or the hearer does not allow us to observe this struggle taking place. All speakers are also hearers and vice versa, and language behaviour is not a matter of an utterance followed by a response, but rather the utterance and the response taken together and over longer periods of interaction than researchers are willing to allow for.

The major purpose of the PP is, according to Leech, to establish and maintain feelings of comity within the social group. The PP regulates the 'social equilibrium and the friendly relations which enable us to assume that our interlocutors are being cooperative in the first place' (1983: 82) – which, again, is clear evidence of an evaluative, normative stance despite claims to the contrary. Leech has a further reason for setting up a PP in addition to a CP which is essentially the same as Lakoff's, namely that it helps to provide an interpretation of conversational data where the CP alone appears to break down. He gives the following two examples of this:

(1)   A: We'll all miss Bill and Agatha, won't we?
      B: Well, we'll all miss ^BILL.
(2)   A: Someone's eaten the icing off the cake.
      B: It wasn't ^ME.

While B in (1) appears to be flouting Grice's Maxim of Quantity, s/he can also be interpreted as not wishing to give offence by giving the full information, i.e. 'we won't miss Agatha'. In effect, doing so would create a pragmatically very awkward utterance – 'Yes, we'll all miss them'. By prefacing the utterance with the discourse marker *well* B indicates a constraint on her/his ability to uphold the CP by abiding by the PP. The CP and the PP thus appear to be in conflict in example (1). In (2) B reacts as if A were accusing her/him of having eaten the icing off the cake, i.e. B's reaction appears to flout Grice's Maxim of Relation. In effect, however, B realises that A has abided by the PP, since making a direct accusation would be tantamount to uttering a 'conflictual' illocutionary force (i.e. an accusation) which would definitely not constitute a polite act. At the same time, however, B still interprets A's utterance as containing the implicature of an indirect accusation.

The problem with Leech's analysis, however, is that it is relatively easy to imagine other interpretations. A in (1) might say what s/he says with a heavily ironic intonation. How would one then interpret B's response? If A had said what s/he says in (3) immediately prior to (2) and had received the response in (3) from B:

(3)   A: Oh good!
      B: What?

B's utterance in (2) would have to be interpreted as disappointment that it wasn't her/him that had eaten the icing.

The central concept in Leech's model is that of a cost–benefit scale of politeness related to both the speaker and the hearer. Politeness, according to Leech, involves minimising the cost and maximising the benefit to speaker/hearer. The PP thus consists of six maxims, all of which are related to the notion of cost and benefit, and related pairs of values:

1. The Tact Maxim (which is only applicable in illocutionary functions classified by Leech as 'impositive', e.g. ordering, requesting, commanding, advising, recommending, etc., and 'commissive', e.g. promising, vowing, offering, etc.): a. Minimise cost to *other* [b. Maximise benefit to *other*]

We can illustrate the Tact Maxim with example (4) for the illocutionary function of advising:

(4)   *You know, I really do think* you *ought* to sell that old car. It's costing more and more money in repairs and it uses up far too much fuel.

The Tact Maxim is adhered to by the speaker minimising the 'cost' to the addressee by using two discourse markers, one to appeal to solidarity, *you know*, and the other as a modifying hedge, *really*, one attitudinal predicate, *I do think*, and one modal verb, *ought*. On the other hand, the speaker maximises the benefit to the addressee in the second part of the turn by indicating that s/he could save a lot of time and money by selling the car.

2. The Generosity Maxim (which is only applicable in impositives and commissives): a. Minimise benefit to *self* [b. Maximise cost to *self*]

To illustrate the Generosity Maxim we can take the illocutionary function of recommending in example (5):

(5)   *It's none of my business really*, but you look so much nicer in the green hat than in the pink one. If I were you, I'd buy that one.

In the first part of the utterance the speaker reduces any concern of hers to a minimum but indicates in the second half that she would far prefer to see her friend in the green hat rather than the pink one.

3. The Approbation Maxim (which is only applicable in illocutionary functions classified by Leech as 'expressive', e.g. thanking, congratulating, pardoning, blaming, praising, condoling, etc., and 'assertive', e.g. stating, boasting, complaining, claiming, reporting, etc.): a. Minimise dispraise of *other* [b. Maximise praise of *other*]

Examples (6) and (7) will serve to illustrate the illocutionary functions of thanking and complaining, in which the speaker maximises praise of the addressee in (6) and minimises dispraise in (7):

(6) Dear Aunt Mabel, I want to thank you so much for the superb Christmas present this year. *It was so very thoughtful of you.*

(7) I wonder if you could keep the noise from your Saturday parties down a bit. *I'm finding it very hard to get enough sleep over the weekends.*

4. The Modesty Maxim (which is only applicable in expressives and assertives): a. Minimise praise of *self* [b. maximise praise of *other*]

In example (8), illustrating the illocutionary function of praising, the speaker belittles her/his own abilities in order to highlight the achievements of the addressee:

(8) Well done! What a wonderful performance! *I wish I could sing as well as that.*

5. The Agreement Maxim (which is only applicable in assertives): a. Minimise disagreement between *self* and *other* [b. maximise agreement between *self* and *other*]

In example (9) the speaker and the addressee are engaged in a political debate. The speaker wishes to make a claim about his political party but to minimise the disagreement with the interlocutor:

(9) *I know we haven't always agreed in the past and I don't want to claim that the government acted in any other way than we would have done in power*, but we believe the affair was essentially mismanaged from the outset.

6. The Sympathy Maxim (which is only applicable in assertives): a. Minimise antipathy between *self* and *other* [b. Maximise sympathy between *self* and *other*]

Example (10) illustrates the illocutionary function of reporting, in which the speaker makes an effort to minimise the antipathy between himself and the addressee:

(10) Despite very serious disagreements with you on a technical level, *we have done our best to coordinate our efforts* in reaching an agreement, but have so far not been able to find any common ground.

The second, b. principle in each case applies when the illocutionary function itself would require it. For example, if the speaker wishes to apply the Approbation Maxim, s/he should minimise dispraise of the addressee when blaming or complaining (cf. example (7)) but maximise praise when thanking (cf. example (6)) or reporting. If the speaker wishes to apply the Agreement Maxim, s/he should minimise disagreement between her/himself and the addressee when complaining, but might choose to minimise it (cf. example (9)) or maximise it when claiming. The Tact Maxim is also subject to a condition which Leech calls the Meta Maxim (Do not put others in a position where they have to break the Tact Maxim).

As in the case of Lakoff, a number of questions arise. How are we to define the parameters on the various scales of values, e.g. 'cost', 'benefit', 'praise', 'sympathy', etc.? Are they universally valid (or even valid from one individual to the next or from one interaction to the next)? How is it possible for the speaker to take all these maxims, as well as those of the CP and the Irony Principle (IP), into consideration when formulating an utterance?[14]

Leech then goes on to suggest that there are scales of delicacy along which each of the maxims of the PP must operate. The first of these scales is, as we have seen, the Cost–Benefit Scale according to which a speaker has to weigh the amount of cost to her/himself and the amount of benefit his utterance will bring the hearer. The Cost–Benefit Scale also involves other related scales ranging over values such as 'antipathy–sympathy', 'agreement–disagreement' and 'praise' (cf. the six maxims of the PP).

The Optionality Scale assesses the degree to which the illocutions performed by the speaker allow the addressee a degree of choice. In example (4) the addressee is still left with a wide degree of choice to accept or reject the advice. The amount of choice in example (9), however, is seriously limited, since the addressee is restricted to the claim that the affair was mismanaged.

The Indirectness Scale measures the amount of work incurred by the hearer in interpreting the speech acts produced by the speaker. In example (4) the speaker does quite a lot of work in giving advice whereas in example (8) this is not the case. The Authority Scale measures the degree to which the speaker has the right to impose on the hearer. In example (5) the speaker appears to lack the authority to advise the addressee on which hat to choose, whereas in example (10) the speaker clearly has the authority to give the report s/he does. The Social Distance Scale assesses the degree to which the speaker and the hearer are acquainted, i.e. what is the social distance between them. In example (6) social distance is minimal whereas in example (7) we can assume it to be greater.

Again, the question concerning the ability of individual speakers to recognise these scales, even if only intuitively, and then to act accordingly is of primary importance. Leech would maintain that since his model describes how a speaker (or a researcher) interprets utterances, we should not imagine that speakers have to go through this complex system of principles, maxims and scales of delicacy to produce a pragmatically acceptable utterance that will be classified as polite. But if the hearer has this amount of computing to do, why should the speaker not also have to do a similar amount of work to produce the utterance?

As we shall see in the following chapter, some of Leech's terms are strikingly similar to those suggested by Brown and Levinson (1978). Leech's notion of hearer authority, which plays a part in assessing the cost–benefit scale of the Tact Maxim, is suspiciously similar to the assessment of power in Brown and Levinson. The social distance scale is also strikingly reminiscent of the parameter of social distance suggested by them. Like Brown and Levinson, Leech also suggests that the degree of indirectness in the production of speech acts will increase relative to the increase in the cost to speaker and the decrease in the benefit to hearer. This suggestion immediately runs into trouble with utterances expressing ironic politeness, i.e. indirect utterances in which the degree of indirectness is inversely proportionate to the intended effect of being polite, e.g. 'Would you think it an imposition on my part if I were to ask you to take your big feet off my table?'.

Leech also uses the two terms 'negative' and 'positive' politeness, although they are defined somewhat differently from Brown and Levinson. Negative politeness with Leech consists of the minimisation of the impoliteness of impolite illocutions, and positive politeness consists of the maximisation of the politeness of polite illocutions (Fraser 1990: 226). This entails that certain kinds of speech act are inherently polite (e.g. congratulating, praising, etc.) and that others are inherently impolite (e.g. criticising, blaming, accusing, etc.) and will be in need of minimisation in the form of certain kinds of prefacing formulas (e.g. 'I'm sorry to have to say this, but . . .').

The principal criticism of Leech's model, then, is that it considers linguistic politeness from the point of view of speech act types, some of which appear to be inherently polite or impolite, but gives the researcher no clear idea of how an individual participating in an interaction can possibly know the degree and type of politeness required for the performance of a speech act. Since Leech maintains that his theory is not one of politeness production, this criticism is possibly vacuous, but the deficiency is only partially remedied in Brown and Levinson's approach as we shall see in the following chapter.

POLITENESS₂ AS A CULTURALLY CONSTRUCTED CONCEPT

During the 1980s an international group of researchers headed by Shoshana Blum-Kulka, Juliane House and Gabriele Kasper embarked on a project to determine the realisation patterns of two important speech acts, apologising and requesting, in a range of different languages, namely three varieties of English (British, Australian and American), Canadian French, Danish, German, Hebrew and Russian. The project was called Cross-Cultural Speech Act Realization Patterns (CCSARP for short) and the results were published in book form in 1989 under the title *Cross-Cultural Pragmatics: Requests and Apologies*.

One of the aims of the project was to determine the degree to which native speakers of the languages studied used direct or indirect realisations of requesting and apologising, and it was this aspect of the research which gave rise to a number of significant questions about the assumed high correlation between degree of indirectness and degree of politeness. Both Leech and Brown and Levinson, whose work we shall review in the following chapter, had assumed that an utterance realising a speech act directly, e.g. a request to do something realised by the imperative mode (*Open the window*) would be perceived as far less 'polite' than a hint (*It's hot in here*) or a conventionally indirect utterance (*Would you mind opening the window?*). Degree of indirectness, in other words was posited as a universal realisation of linguistic politeness.

The results from this part of the project do not bear out this hypothesis. On the one hand, it was found that the speakers of certain languages preferred to realise apologies and requests more directly (e.g. Hebrew and Russian), while in all speech communities the nature of the overall speech event determined whether certain kinds of speech act would be realised directly or indirectly, without any consequent attribution of impoliteness to direct realisations. On the other hand, all speech communities perceived conventionally indirect utterances such as *Would you mind opening the window?*, *Could you open the window?* as the politest form of request, whereas hints in some speech communities were ranked high on a scale of politeness, but in others were ranked lower. In addition, in speech communities which preferred direct realisations of the two speech acts in certain speech events, politeness could still be introduced by adding elements such as terms of endearment, highly formulaic utterances like *please*, hedges such as *just, I believe*, and certain types of discourse marker, e.g. *alright, OK*.

In a series of articles during the late 1980s Blum-Kulka and her colleagues developed the implications of their findings to politeness research (Blum-Kulka 1987, 1989, 1990; Blum-Kulka, Danet and Gerson 1985; Blum-Kulka and Olshtain 1984; Blum-Kulka and Weizmann 1988) but without explicitly developing a model of linguistic politeness. In 1992, however, Blum-Kulka finally sketched out what we might call the 'cultural constructivist' theory of politeness, or what Eelen (2001) calls 'politeness as a cultural script'.

Blum-Kulka does not question the validity of the assumption that every socio-cultural group in the world has a means of realising politeness. Politeness, in other words, is still assumed to be an objective concept in a theory of politeness$_2$, and in this sense it is universal. As we might expect, Brown and Levinson's equation of politeness with face-threat mitigation is accepted without question by Blum-Kulka, but its realisations are subject to a form of cultural filtering:

> On a theoretical level this means that systems of politeness manifest a culturally filtered interpretation of the interaction between four essential parameters: social motivations, expressive modes, social differentials and social meanings . . . Cultural notions interfere in determining the distinctive features of each of the four parameters and as a result significantly effect the social understanding of 'politeness' across societies in the world. (1992: 270)

There are a number of problems in this formulation, which I will subsume under the following set of questions:

- What does Blum-Kulka mean by 'culturally filtered' and 'cultural notions'?
- How does she define the four parameters?
- Why are there four parameters? Why not three, or five or more?
- How does the cultural filtering take place?
- Should we really be talking about politeness at all in this context?

I shall deal with each of these questions in turn, but before I do so, I need to focus briefly on the research methodology.

Data for the CCSARP project were gathered by means of a discourse completion test, in which subjects were asked to complete dialogues in accordance with a clearly defined contextual setting (Blum-Kulka and Olshtain 1984). The number of informants for each language totalled 400, half of whom were male and half female. Half of the informants for each language were native speakers and the other half non-native speakers. The major problem with the sample arises from the fact that all the informants were students. Discourse completion tasks are a familiar feature of empirical work in politeness, but they suffer from the following weaknesses. Firstly, they are administered in the form of written dialogues and require written responses. There is therefore no guarantee that the respondents would actually produce similar utterances if they were in a naturally occurring oral dialogue of that kind. Secondly, asking the respondents to complete the dialogues in written form allows them to think about what might seem to them to be the most appropriate form of response. Once again this need not conform to what might actually occur in real life. Thirdly, for the same reason, deliberate manipulation of the responses by the informants cannot be ruled out.

In addition to the data gathering for the project Blum-Kulka also controlled for perceptions of indirectness and politeness by getting four groups of Hebrew-speaking and English-speaking students to (a) rate 45 Hebrew request realisations on a scale from 1 to 9 with respect to degrees of indirectness (56 informants); (b) rate 45 parallel request realisations in English on the same scale of indirectness (24 informants); (c) rate the same Hebrew realisations in terms of a nine-point politeness scale (32 informants); (d) rate the same set of English realisations on the nine-point politeness scale (24 informants). Once again, this kind of evaluation problem is also common to empirical work in linguistic politeness, but it suffers from one major weakness. The researcher asks the informants to rate the utterances *as* polite or not. We simply cannot assume that, if utterances of this kind were produced in naturally occurring verbal interaction, the same informants would perceive them as being 'polite'. In the majority of cases they would simply not register them as being out of the ordinary in any way, i.e. they would *not* be perceived as 'polite'. In addition, we have no way of knowing how the informants evaluate what they might perceive as 'polite' in verbal interaction, i.e. is politeness something positive for them or something negative?

Blum-Kulka's research into politeness realisations also included a project on family discourse in which twelve families in the U.S. and twenty-three in Israel (including Israeli families and the families of Americans who had emigrated to Israel) were recorded. The data from this project are on a much stronger empirical footing than either the CCSARP project or the back-up project with Hebrew-speaking and non-Hebrew-speaking students at the Hebrew University in Jerusalem. It is the results of this project which are used to support the development of her theory. A word of caution still needs to be inserted at this point, however. The project was preceded by interviews with twenty-four Jewish families (eight Israeli, eight American and eight immigrant), all of whom were asked to state whether family discourse was 'amenable to judgements of politeness' (Blum-Kulka 1990: 260). Assessments ranged from 'politeness is irrelevant when it comes to the family' through 'one should be polite with strangers, not with friends and family' to 'all family members should be polite to each other'. This is a strong indication of the discursive struggle over politeness applied to the interactional frame of family discourse.

Let us now return to the set of questions posed earlier in this section. The first was: 'What does Blum-Kulka mean by "culturally filtered" and "cultural notions"?' In discussing the first of the four parameters (social motivations) she has recourse to such sweeping terms as 'two cultures as different as the Israeli and the Japanese'. But in her own research with the family data she would surely have to admit that immigrants to Israel form part of Israeli society. She frequently mentions Katriel's (1986) work on *dugriyut* 'straight talk', which characterises the interactional styles of younger members of Israeli society. Can we therefore talk of 'Israeli culture' as if it were a homogenous, monolithic entity? In addition, she refers to work by Ide and Matsumoto on Japanese society, but omits to mention that other studies on Japanese society show that it is as diverse in interactional styles and modes of living as any other society.[15] Does it therefore make much sense to talk of 'Japanese culture'? While accepting Blum-Kulka's conclusion that politeness is a culturally relative concept, we still need to know precisely what is understood by the term 'culture' in this context.

I will spare the reader a detailed discussion of the second question here: 'How does she define the four parameters?' Suffice it to say that, according to Blum-Kulka, the major, and apparently only, social motivation for politeness is the need to maintain face. But this is hardly surprising, since all social interaction is infused with face (cf. Goffman 1967). Certain forms of politeness, however, can be used to threaten rather than to maintain face. The category 'expressive modes' refers to the wide range of linguistic expressions available in any language to realise (im)politeness. 'Social differentials' is a term referring to such factors as social distance, power and the degree to which speech acts constitute an imposition on the addressee. They are, in other words, the D (social distance), P (power) and R (degree of imposition) factors that we will discuss in chapter 4 when Brown and Levinson's model is looked at in more detail. The most interesting parameter is the category of 'social meanings', which I will look at a little more closely after dealing with the third question: 'Why are there four parameters? Why not three, or five or more?' Defining the number of parameters according to which politeness can be defined always runs the risk of inflation or deflation.[16] We might, for instance, suggest that social

meanings can be conflated with social motivations or that other social categories such as power or control should be added to the list.
There is no answer to the question 'How does the cultural filtering
take place?' to be found in Blum-Kulka's work.

The final question: 'Should we really be talking about politeness at
all in this context?' is the crucial one. In discussing 'social meanings'
Blum-Kulka refers to 'the degree to which any linguistic expression is
deemed polite by members of a given culture in a specific situation'
(1992: 275). Is it not likely, or at least possible, that individual members
may differ in their assessments of politeness, i.e. that (im)politeness
is indeed struggled over discursively, regardless of whether or not the
assessors are members of the same 'culture'? If that is so – and the rest
of Blum-Kulka's discussion of social meanings indicates that it *is* so –
are we not then dealing with (im)politeness$_1$ rather than politeness$_2$?
On the following page (p. 276) she summarises the scale of social meanings from 'impolite' (i.e. rude, 'foreign') through 'polite' (appropriate,
tactful) to 'extensively polite' (strategic-manipulative, 'foreign'), and she
suggests that the zone of polite behaviour consists of the 'range of cultural expectations for what constitutes appropriate social behaviour
relative to changing social situations', thus bringing us back to my
term 'politic behaviour'. More than that, she suggests that 'polite behaviour is largely taken for granted' and that 'it is deviations from
the cultural norms which will arouse attention'. Hence maintaining
face is an all-pervasive concern of socio-communicative verbal interaction which goes largely unnoticed. Do we therefore need to use the
term 'politeness' to refer to this, or would we not do better to take
the bull by the horns and turn our attention to precisely those divergent perceptions of salient behaviour and why members of a social
group dispute discursively with regard to whether they are polite or
just plain normal?

Of all the approaches to politeness discussed in this chapter Blum-
Kulka's 'theory' comes closest to the view of (im)politeness$_1$ presented
in this book. The problem with her approach is the appeal to a notion
of 'culture', which is not explicated properly but simply treated as if
it were a self-evident objective entity. The cultural relativity of politeness can only be explained if we are prepared to focus our efforts on
explicating the discursive struggle over what is and what is not polite
in terms of lay members' perceptions of the term. Blum-Kulka comes
close to doing just that, but her adherence to Brown and Levinson's
model prevents her from taking that crucial step. In the following
section I shall deal with a further model of politeness, developed by

Horst Arndt and Richard Janney, which appears to come close to the approach presented in chapters 6 to 9, but which still tends to take as wide and sweeping a view of the term 'culture' as Blum-Kulka's approach.

SOCIAL POLITENESS, INTERPERSONAL POLITENESS AND TACT

Horst Arndt and Richard Janney have developed an approach towards politeness from the early 1980s on which appears to be embedded within the framework of the cross-cultural teachability of politeness strategies.[17] It is therefore difficult to say with any real confidence that they are proposing a 'model' of politeness. For example, Arndt and Janney (1985a) begin with the following sentence: 'Little in the way of an adequate approach to studying or teaching politeness in speech has come out of linguistics in recent decades' and they suggest that 'applied linguists have been forced to become arbiters of appropriacy, prescribing politeness forms intuitively and hoping by this means to produce polite non-native speakers' (1985a: 281). After more or less admitting that what they call 'intercultural tact' rather than 'politeness' cannot really be taught or learned Janney and Arndt (1992) end with a set of four 'guidelines for avoiding conflicts in intercultural situations', these being the maintenance of a 'positive-reference group frame of communication with the partner', the avoidance of a negative frame of communication with the partner, the abandonment of common territory with the partner if conflicts do arise (in order to avoid aggression and hostility) and, if all else fails, breaking off contact with the communicative partner altogether (1992: 41).

There is nevertheless enough consistency in their work from 1980 on to allow us to suggest that they are providing us with a model of politeness, and from the point of view of the perspective on linguistic politeness taken in this book it is at least a model which comes close to suggesting that politeness$_1$ should be the object of study (cf. Eelen's comments in Eelen 2001: 68). It also shares the perspective taken here (see chapter 6) that no rules can be set up to define what forms of behaviour count as 'polite' in what situations. Native speakers rely very much on the 'feel for the game' that they develop through many years of participation in a wide variety of interactions. The major reason for the ultimate unteachability of politeness is that the 'feel for the game' is culturally determined. The problem at this point is that,

like Blum-Kulka, they offer no definition of what they understand by
culture.

However, let us start at the beginning and spell out the principles
on which they develop their model of politeness before we return to
the question of culture later. In earlier works Arndt and Janney make
a distinction between 'social politeness' and 'interpersonal politeness'.
'Social politeness' is considered to consist of 'rules regulating appropriate and inappropriate ways of speaking' and the 'locus of these rules is
society, not language itself' (1985a: 283–4). All speech activity consists
of a set of verbal conventions

> of which politeness might be called a sub-set, [and which] are
> sometimes defined as speech regularities which the members of a
> group maintain because they mutually know they have maintained
> these in the past and they have solved for them certain recurring
> kinds of coordination problems . . . (1985a: 284)

This is fine, as far as it goes, except that we have a certain vacillation here between 'rules' and 'conventions'. What they appear to
be discussing is what I have called politic behaviour, but as I point
out in chapter 6, developing the feel for appropriateness in socio-
communicative verbal interaction is a function of the development
of a habitus. Politic behaviour can then be understood as the sum
of individual perceptions of what is appropriate in accordance with
the habitus of the participants. It is always open in social practice to
renegotiation.

Their focus is on what they call in earlier work 'interpersonal politeness' and in later work 'tact'. In Janney and Arndt (1992: 23) they dis-
pose of social politeness by saying that its main function is 'to provide
a framework of standardised strategies for getting gracefully into, and
back out of, recurring social situations', and they suggest that 'tact is
quite another phenomenon, with different functions in human interaction' (ibid.). Tact is equated with the mutual concern for maintaining
face during interaction. It is not therefore a question of behaving in
a socially appropriate way but rather in an interpersonally supportive
way. The problem here is that some of the 'standardised strategies' of
social politeness, e.g. changing topics, holding the floor, maintaining
conversation, requesting repetition or clarification involve participants
in facework, i.e. tact. Does it therefore make much sense to maintain
a dividing line between social and interpersonal politeness (or tact)?
Surely not, if we then discover that the two 'systems' – if systems they
are – overlap with each other and interlock.

Tact is said to have two basic roots, one psychological, the other cultural. The impulse to seek or avoid confrontations is seen as 'rooted in human biology' (1992: 25) and is shared with other animal species. Within this biological–psychological framework Janney and Arndt maintain that there are two kinds of communication, *emotional* and *emotive*. Emotional communication consists of 'affective displays [which] are simply spontaneous, unplanned physical externalisations of internal affective states'. Emotive communication, on the other hand, is seen as being more strategic in that it consists of 'affective displays [which] are produced consciously . . . to influence others' perceptions and interpretations of conversational events' (1992: 27). They then go on to maintain that emotive communication is dependent on 'cultural and social conventions regulating how this is done' (ibid.). So while they reject rules and/or conventions in accounting for social politeness, they then reintroduce conventions to 'explain' emotive communication.

The cultural basis of tact is directly derivable from, or more accurately controls, the psychological in that 'emotive communication . . . is guided by various assumptions that people accept unquestioningly as a natural consequence of growing up in a particular group' (1992: 30). This sounds more like Bourdieu's concept of the habitus (which we will look at more closely in chapter 6), but note that they had previously stated that emotive communication is subject to conventions, which must now be interpreted as cultural. The fact that they really are assuming cultural conventions is supported by the prerequisites for being tactful in one's own culture, which include 'basic human needs, drives, feelings, motives, intentions, etc.', assumptions about positive and negative groups and the ways of signalling intimacy and/or distance in different situations, 'the basic dynamics of interpersonal relationships in the culture, and how levels of power and affiliation may be signaled in different situations', and 'verbal, vocal, and kinesic communication in the culture'.

There is therefore a certain amount of vacillation on (a) whether social and interpersonal politeness (or tact) really are separable, as they wish to see things, (b) whether both types or either type of politeness are regulated by a set of conventions, (c) whether it is really necessary to link up interpersonal politeness with face concerns (although we should note that this may be the reason for their using the term 'tact'), and (d) how we are to understand the term 'culture'.

Janney and Arndt (1992: 38) conclude their discussion of 'intercultural tact' by saying that 'ultimately, it may well be that tact in the intracultural sense is simply impossible in many intercultural situations', indicating once again that their basic concern is to provide solutions for teaching politeness. But what are we meant to understand by the term 'culture'? As with Blum-Kulka, it appears that culture is a self-evident entity. But is it an objective entity that can be used to explain politeness, or anything else for that matter? The problem with the term is that it can be expanded and contracted at will. We can talk of Anglo-American culture as do Janney and Arndt, although I would find it extremely difficult to define what I meant by the term. Or we can talk of 'youth culture'. Does this then refer to modes of social behaviour that are assumed to be common to (and aspired to) by *all* young people? We can compare Greek culture with British culture or with Japanese culture. But do we then mean that *all* the Greeks share a set of beliefs and behaviour patterns which are different from those shared by *all* the British or *all* the Japanese? The use of the term culture without properly defining what is to be understood by the term allows us to explain everything, but ultimately to explain very little. The term itself is probably as discursively disputable as the term politeness, as we shall see in chapter 6. In the following section we consider what is probably the most enigmatic model of politeness on the market, the Conversational Contract model by Fraser and Nolen.

THE CONVERSATIONAL CONTRACT THEORY OF POLITENESS

In an article dealing with the linguistic realisations of the notion of deference Fraser and Nolen (1981) suggest an alternative way of approaching the concept of politeness. Their first step is to propose the notion of Conversational Contract.[18] Fraser and Nolen (1981: 93–4) define the CC in the following way:

> On entering into a given conversation, each party brings an understanding of some initial set of rights and obligations that will determine, at least for the preliminary stages, the limits of the interaction.

These rights and obligations (R + O) may, of course, be misjudged by participants in the interaction, which either leads to a renegotiation of the rights and obligations that the participants have or to the possible imputation of impolite behaviour. If the R + O set (rights and obligations set) is upheld, the participants can be said to be performing 'politely'; indeed, it is Fraser and Nolen's belief that politeness is not consciously noted until the R + O set is violated in some way.[19]

Fraser (1990: 233) states this explicitly when he says that '[p]oliteness is a state that one expects to exist in every conversation'. Impoliteness is then recognised as marked behaviour that does not fit into the CC in which the participants are currently involved.

The terms of the CC fall into two major types: 'general terms, which govern all ordinary conversations; and specific terms, which hold because of the particulars of the conversation' (Fraser and Nolen 1981: 94). The general terms of the CC concern culture-specific conventions regulating turn-taking, clarity of speech, which language(s) to use, etc. The specific terms, however, are far more significant, since they regulate the types of speech activities expected in the CC enacted during the conversation and the content of those speech activities ('The specific terms of a relationship influence what types of speech acts can be seen as appropriate', 1981: 94). In addition, several types of CC are regulated in advance of the interaction by virtue of their institutional nature. Withdrawing money at a bank, interviewing candidates for a job, giving academic lectures, etc., are all highly constrained forms of linguistic and social behaviour, which will form part of the participants' cultural knowledge with respect to the specific terms of the CC.

Fraser and Nolen take over Goffman's notion of deference (see chapter 5), which Goffman sees as that component of a social activity 'which is a symbolic means by which appreciation is regularly conveyed' (1971: 56), and define it as an aspect of that activity which may or may not, but of course generally does, involve the interactant in specific forms of speech act. The level of deference required by the CC in a conversation currently in operation depends on the institutionalised status differences between the individual participants. For example, if a student at a lecture has not understood a point made by the lecturer, s/he first has to draw the lecturer's attention to the fact that s/he wishes to make a point, e.g. by putting up a hand, and to utter a request for the point at issue to be clarified, e.g. 'I'm sorry. Could you explain that again?' Both the form of the utterance and the signal for attention are parts of the politic behaviour regulating the social activity type and show deference to the higher institutional status of the lecturer.

However, in the academic institution within which I work in Switzerland, even this form of behaviour would not normally be part of the institutionalised CC in the lecture situation, particularly not if the lecturer is a guest lecturer. The CC can of course be renegotiated to accommodate the request. On the other hand, we can perfectly well imagine a lecture situation in another educational framework in which the

student would be well within the R + O set of the CC if he were simply
to call out, 'Sorry, explain that again.'

The point of the example is this: ways of showing deference which
are acceptable to the current CC are not necessarily forms of polite
behaviour, although they clearly belong to the politic behaviour in
operation in the social activity. They are, in other words, part of social
practice. For Fraser and Nolen, however, they are polite by virtue of the
fact that they uphold the R + O set in operation during the interaction.
They will only be noticed *in absentia*, i.e. when the CC is broken, since
a violation of the CC is open to interpretation as impolite. In addition,
according to Fraser and Nolen, other forms of linguistic behaviour
which encode the R + O set of the CC which have little or nothing to do
with deference are equally polite. Hence, if I say to a close friend, 'Shut
the door, you great idiot!' and the CC ratifies this kind of apparently
face-threatening behaviour, then the CC is upheld, the behaviour is
'normal' and thus polite. On the other hand, if the CC ratifies this
kind of linguistic behaviour and I say, 'I wonder if you would mind
shutting the door, old boy?', my utterance is open to interpretation by
my friend as ironic, humorous or at least distinctly odd behaviour.

The advantage of the Conversational Contract approach to politeness is that it avoids the temptation, as we have seen in the other
approaches discussed so far in this chapter, to implicitly or explicitly classify types of speech act as being inherently polite. However,
it ignores the fact that certain languages have developed elaborate
forms of linguistic structure that are explicitly classified as polite by
the cultures in which those languages are spoken. In certain cases,
notably Japanese, it is impossible to make even the most objective
and banal assertions without indicating deference towards the other
participants through the system of honorifics (Matsumoto 1989). We
could of course still argue that honorifics, particularly those associated with deference and beautification, are simply part of all CCs into
which interactants can enter. Since politeness is not the same as deference or the beautification of speech, this would therefore mean that
Japanese honorifics do not signal politeness at all, but rather deference. I suggest that this would have been the argument that Fraser
and Nolen would have adopted if they had developed their model
further.

There is a further problem with the CC approach. It is true that
individuals have sets of rights and obligations when they enter a conversation and that during the conversation there might be a need for
a renegotiation of those rights and obligations (Fraser 1990: 232). But

what is the nature of those rights and obligations and under what social conditions may they be renegotiated? Does the social activity type serve to reproduce already existent social roles or is it part of a social process through which those roles and the concomitant rights and obligations become defined? Let us assume that politeness is looked at as an unmarked form of social behaviour which abides by the R + O set of the CC currently in operation. Could the strategic manipulation of politeness (in the form of potentially impolite violations in the R + O set) not then be a significant factor in structuring and restructuring relationships of power, social roles and the nature of social institutions? One of the weaknesses in the study of linguistic politeness is that this line of analysis has not been followed up, although it has been hinted at by certain sociolinguists (cf. Coupland *et al.* 1988).

In the final section of this chapter I shall examine the criticism directed at Brown and Levinson (which will be dealt with in more detail in the following chapter) by Hill *et al.* (1986), Ide (1989) and Ide *et al.* (1992), which led to positing two terms relating to the cultural differences in the perception of politeness, *volition* and *discernment*, the latter term being more adequately expressed through the Japanese lexeme *wakimae*.

DISCERNMENT VS VOLITION: THE JAPANESE NOTION OF WAKIMAE

We have now moved beyond attempts to modify the Gricean model of pragmatics to account for the phenomenon of politeness$_2$. Arndt and Janney's approach to politeness takes us into the area of social psychology, while Fraser and Nolen introduce the sociological concepts of rights and obligations into their theory of the CC. We seem to have gone far beyond reference to the Gricean CP, so that we would be justified in labelling these approaches 'postpragmatic'. In this final section I shall present Sachiko Ide's approach to second-order politeness. Since this, too, is more sociolinguistic in its orientation we might also label it postpragmatic.

As we shall see in chapter 4, the severest criticism of Brown and Levinson's use of the concept of face in explaining polite linguistic usage has come from Asian linguists, particularly Japanese sociolinguists such as Sachiko Ide and those who have worked with her. It is also voiced in the work of the Japanese pragmaticist Yoshiko Matsumoto.

Brown and Levinson effectively set up a production model of politeness$_2$ (although not impoliteness$_2$!) which relies on dividing the notion of face into *positive* and *negative* face. Both Ide and Matsumoto argue that this division is not appropriate to those cultures in which the individual *qua* individual is less significant than the social group to which s/he is affiliated.

Ide's major objection to Brown and Levinson's model is that it is *eurocentric*. In reviewing Lakoff, Fraser and Nolen and an article by Penelope Brown (1980), Ide *et al.* (1992: 281) conclude that the essence of second-order politeness in all these approaches is 'the idea of appropriate language use associated with smooth communication'. Hence, whether the researcher starts off from a linguistic, a pragmatic, a social, a social-psychological or an anthropological point of view, politeness will always be equivalent to socially appropriate forms of behaviour.

The individualistic approach to politeness that Ide sees as the principal feature of western politeness research is a consequence of what she calls the concept of 'volition', i.e. individuals can decide to be polite or not, as the case may be. Like Gu (1990), Ide considers that politeness which stems from the will to be polite is an instrumental way of understanding it rather than a description of normative behaviour. During this chapter we have seen that there is every reason to assume that politeness does not always have to do with rational, planned, instrumental behaviour in the effort to preserve face – often for non-altruistic reasons. Ide and Matsumoto maintain that the individual social person in Japanese culture only has individual status by virtue of belonging to a social group. Thus a person's first allegiance is to the well-being and maintenance of that group.

In such a situation – and Gu (1990), LuMing Mao (1992, 1994) and Lee-Wong (1999) indicate that a similar situation holds in Chinese culture – politeness behaviour is determined by *discerning* the appropriate features of the ongoing social interaction, i.e. those features of the interaction which determine politic behaviour, and choosing socially appropriate strategies of interaction. The Japanese word for the ability to discern the correct form of behaviour in the ongoing situation is *wakimae*. Ide posits that there are societies, particularly those in Asia, e.g. China, Japan, Thailand, Korea, etc., in which the appropriate levels of politeness are contingent on specific features of the social interaction being enacted and that this is always the case regardless of whether or not the interactants are of equal status and members of the same close-knit social network (cf. also Matsumoto 1988, 1989).

Figure 3.2   *The discernment–volition spectrum*

But this is equivalent to saying that enacting the features of linguistic politeness is an integral part of all social practice, which in turn means that the substance of Ide's theory is (im)politeness$_1$ and not politeness$_2$.

The type of second-order politeness common in western societies, on the other hand, is one which the speaker can decide to use regardless of the features of the social activity type in which the interactants are involved. Ide calls this type of politeness *volitional*. There are of course problems with this apparently neat breakdown into two kinds of politeness. One of these is the simple fact that it is all too easy to talk about 'western societies', meaning, one assumes, those of the USA and western Europe. But even within what would normally count as western Europe there is a great deal of variation between social situations in which politeness is mandatory and those in which it is not – not to mention other parts of Europe (cf. Wierzbicka 1985).

This immediately brings us to the second point, i.e. that the required polite behaviour appropriate to the features of the social interaction is not just something that characterises Asian societies. The negotiation of facework requires continual assessment of the lines expected in different types of social interaction and the kinds of face attributed to individuals by the interactants. This also demands a high degree of discernment. In certain situations, producing linguistic politeness markers becomes almost mandatory even in non-Asian societies or in what Ide calls 'volitional politeness cultures'. We are not faced with a dichotomous distinction here between volitional politeness and discernment politeness, but rather with a spectrum of possibilities ranging from the two extremes of discernment and volition along which societies might be ranged and within which individuals from those societies might show further individual variation. This can be represented diagrammatically as in figure 3.2 above.

The two main points of criticism in Ide's work are

a. that Brown and Levinson's negative face is not appropriate as a theoretical notion to account adequately for how the Japanese use politeness forms, and that the whole edifice of negative vs. positive face needs to be reexamined, and

b. that since native speakers of Japanese need to apply *wakimae* to derive the correct forms of language that will express appropriate levels of politeness, Brown and Levinson's notion of the Model Person, who rationalises whether or not to use a polite utterance and which type of utterance to use, is also inappropriate to account for Japanese politeness.

These criticisms will be dealt with more extensively in the following chapter.

4 Modelling linguistic politeness (II): Brown and Levinson and their critics

BROWN AND LEVINSON'S THEORY OF POLITENESS: POLITENESS AS THE MINIMISATION OF FACE-LOSS

Brown and Levinson's theory of linguistic politeness first appeared in 1978, although Penelope Brown had already published an article entitled 'Women and politeness: a new perspective on language and society' in *Review in Anthropology* in 1976. The theory is often referred to as the 'face-saving' theory of politeness, as it builds on – but, I shall argue, also significantly changes – Goffman's notion of face.[1] Like Lakoff and Leech it also builds on the Gricean model of the Cooperative Principle.

In the spirit of Grice, Brown and Levinson posit a Model Person (MP) with the ability to rationalise from communicative goals to the optimal means of achieving those goals. In doing so, the MP has to assess the dangers of threatening other participants' (and hence her/his own) face and to choose the appropriate strategies in order to minimise any face threats that might be involved in carrying out the goal-directed activity. In contrast to Leech's model, therefore, Brown and Levinson's model can be seen as an attempt to formulate a theory of how individuals produce linguistic politeness, i.e. it is a production model.

Face in Brown and Levinson's model is a theoretical construct which they claim they have taken from the work of Erving Goffman.[2] The MP, with the ability to rationalise from communicative goals to the optimal means of achieving those goals, seems to fit well with their redefinition of face, but it is questionable whether the phenomenon of politeness can be reduced to forms of rational means–goals behaviour.[3] The MP in Brown and Levinson's model refers to the 'speaker', and the only reason the addressee is brought into the picture is in order that the MP can assess which is the most appropriate politeness strategy to use in the circumstances. No mention is made of the ways in which the addressee may react to the politeness strategy produced. Focus in Brown and Levinson's model is thus on the speaker, whereas in Leech's model it is on the hearer.

Brown and Levinson assume that every individual has two types of face, positive and negative. Positive face is defined as the individual's desire that her/his wants be appreciated and approved of in social interaction, whereas negative face is the desire for freedom of action and freedom from imposition. In line with Goffman's postulate that facework involves the maintenance of every participant's face for the duration of the social interaction (as far as this is possible), it is therefore in the interests of all the participants to reduce face-threatening to a minimum. Politeness strategies will therefore be those which aim (a) at supporting or enhancing the addressee's positive face (positive politeness) and (b) at avoiding transgression of the addressee's freedom of action and freedom from imposition (negative face).

In making a contribution to the interaction the MP must therefore rationally assess the possible face-threatening nature of the move s/he is about to make and then decide either to avoid it entirely, or at least to soften (or minimise) it by choosing an appropriate linguistic strategy (or strategies). Brown and Levinson therefore postulate a set of five possibilities which are available to the speaker to do this, ranging from the best case (strategy type 5 'Don't do the face threatening act [FTA]') to the worst (strategy type 1 'Do the FTA and go on record as doing so baldly and without any redressive action', i.e. without atoning for the FTA in any way) (cf. figure 4.1 below). If the participant goes on record as doing the FTA, s/he can soften the blow by carrying out two types of redressive action, (a) by choosing a strategy aimed at enhancing the addressee's positive face (strategy type 2 in figure 4.1) or (b) by choosing a strategy which will soften the encroachment on the addressee's freedom of action or freedom from imposition (strategy type 3 in figure 4.1).

These two kinds of strategy are similar to Leech's 'minimisation' and 'maximisation' strategies, and they form the core of what Brown and Levinson classify as 'politeness', positive politeness being addressed to the addressee's positive face and negative politeness being addressed to her/his negative face. The fifth strategy open to the participant is to go off record and flout one of the Gricean maxims on the assumption that the addressee is in a position to infer the intended meaning (strategy type 4 in figure 4.1). Here we may speak of off-record politeness. Utterances realising this type of strategy and those realising strategies of negative politeness are frequently couched in the form of indirect speech acts (cf. chapter 7).

Brown and Levinson's strategy types are presented diagrammatically in figure 4.1. The scale given on the left is the degree to which these

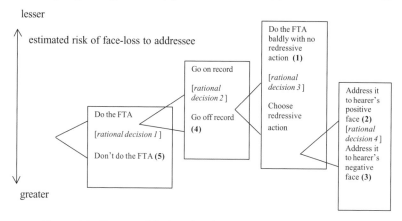

Figure 4.1 *Brown and Levinson's politeness strategies*

strategies are face-threatening to the addressee. To go on record baldly and commit the FTA without any redressive action clearly involves the greatest amount of face-threat and should therefore only be used as a strategy if there is a minimal risk of threatening the addressee's face. To avoid committing an FTA at all is obviously the least face-threatening of the strategies. In order of the degree of face-threat, strategy 1 is more likely to involve face-threat to the addressee than strategies 2 and 3. Strategy 4 is next on the scale followed by the least face-threatening action, strategy 5, i.e. do not carry it out at all. The boxes represent the rational decision that the MP has to make at each stage through the system, the first of these being 'Do I want to commit an FTA to the addressee or not?' If the speaker has no option but to risk the FTA, s/he is then confronted with the decision 'Do I want to go off record and hope that my addressee will be able to infer that my utterance would in any other circumstance be an FTA?' The risk of using this strategy is of course that the addressee might not be able to derive the inference, so that the effect of the intended FTA is lost.

At this point it should be noted that FTAs involve the performance of speech acts which aim either at inducing the addressee to carry out an action which would not under 'normal' circumstances be to her/his benefit or to accept an assessment of some aspect of the addressee's person or world which, again under 'normal' circumstances, would be evaluated as negative. The problem resides in deciding what constitutes normality in any form of social interaction. Committing FTAs is therefore in the speaker's rather than the addressee's interests and can be interpreted as an attempt to exercise power – even if the addressee is perceived to be institutionally invested with more power than the speaker. Brown and Levinson are perfectly aware of this aspect of their work, as we shall see a little lower down when we introduce the parameters of 'power', 'social distance' and 'strength of imposition of the action to be carried out or the evaluation to be accepted by the addressee'.

Returning to the boxes in figure 4.1, if the speaker decides to commit the FTA, s/he has to decide whether or not to do so with redressive action (rational decision 3: 'Do I just carry out the FTA openly and with no attempt to minimise the face-threat involved?'). Having decided to choose redressive action, the final decision is whether the FTA is addressed to the addressee's positive or negative face (rational decision 4: 'Is my FTA directed at the addressee's negative or positive face wants, and what kind of redressive action is appropriate in the circumstances?').

One of the major problems with Brown and Levinson's model is the degree of rational choice that speakers are expected to exercise in choosing an appropriate strategy. Setting out the choices open to speakers in the form of a binary system conveys the impression that they have to work their way through the whole system before they can arrive at the appropriate utterances in which to frame the FTA. It also excludes the possibility that two or more strategies might be chosen at the same time.

POSITIVE AND NEGATIVE POLITENESS STRATEGIES

Brown and Levinson give copious examples from three different languages, English, Tzeltal and Tamil, to illustrate the kinds of choices open to the speaker and to demonstrate that those structures are very similar across the three languages. They posit fifteen substrategies of politeness addressed to the hearer's positive face and ten addressed to the hearer's negative face. In this section I will list these strategies and give my own examples to illustrate them. Brown and Levinson's examples could have been used at this point, and the reader might wonder why I have not simply chosen to stick to them. Since my intention is to show that Brown and Levinson's strategies are addressed to facework, I need to demonstrate that their attempt to extrapolate from the minimisation of face-threats to a theory of linguistic politeness is misleading. It ignores the fact that the attribution of '(im)politeness$_1$' to the fictional turns I shall present, either by the participants themselves or by those outside the social interaction, is highly controversial for the following reasons:

a. For each example a context can easily be imagined in which the attribution of (im)politeness might lead to either positive or negative evaluation of the speaker's behaviour. This is equally the case for Brown and Levinson's examples.

b. Although it is relatively easy to see that facework of one kind or another is being carried out, facework is not necessarily coterminous with the attribution of politeness.

c. Since the examples are fictional, as are most of Brown and Levinson's, the context can be changed to display the struggle over politeness. Unless we give considerably more of the interactional context, i.e. more language usage, we can know neither how participants might have evaluated the utterances, nor how we, as researchers, might evaluate them.

d. In several examples more than one strategy is in evidence. This is particularly the case with positive politeness strategies, as we shall now see.

The following fifteen strategies are addressed to positive face and are thus examples of positive politeness;

(1) *Notice, attend to H (her/his interests, wants, needs, goods, etc.*:
(strategy 1) **Jim, you're really good at solving computer problems.** → (FTA) I wonder if you could just help me with a little formatting problem I've got.

(2) *Exaggerate (interest, approval, sympathy with H)*:
(strategy 2) **Good old Jim. Just the man I wanted to see. I knew I'd find you here.** →(FTA) Could you spare me a couple of minutes?

(3) *Intensify interest to the hearer in the speaker's contribution*:
(strategy 3) **You'll never guess what Fred told me last night. This is right up your street.** →(FTA) [begins a narrative]

(4) *Use in-group identity markers in speech*:
(strategy 4) **Here's my old mate Fred. How are you doing today, mate?** →(FTA) Could you give us a hand to get this car to start?

(5) *Seek agreement in safe topics*:
(strategy 5) **I agree. Right. Manchester United played really badly last night, didn't they?** →(FTA) D'you reckon you could give me a cigarette?

(6) *Avoid disagreement*:
(strategy 6) **Well, in a way, I suppose you're sort of right. But look at it like this.** →(FTA) Why don't you . . .?

(7) *Presuppose, raise, assert common ground*:
(strategy 7) **People like me and you, Bill, don't like being pushed around like that, do we?** →(FTA) Why don't you go and complain?

(8)   *Joke to put the hearer at ease*:
      A: (strategy 8) **Great summer we're having. It's only rained five times a week on average.**
      B: Yeah, terrible, isn't it?
      A: →(FTA) Could I ask you for a favour?
(9)   *Assert or presuppose knowledge of and concern for hearer's wants*:
      (strategy 9) **I know you like marshmallows, so I've brought you home a whole box of them.** →(FTA) I wonder if I could ask you for a favour . . .
(10) *Offer, promise*:
      (strategy 10) **I'll take you out to dinner on Saturday** →(FTA) if you'll cook the dinner this evening.
(11) *Be optimistic that the hearer wants what the speaker wants, i.e. that the FTA is slight*:
      (strategy 11) **I know you're always glad to get a tip or two on gardening, Fred,** →(FTA) so, if I were you, I wouldn't cut your lawn back so short.
(12) *Include both S and H in the activity*:
      (strategy 12) I'm feeling really hungry. **Let's stop for a bite.** (FTA = S wants to stop and have something to eat and wants to get H to agree to do this)
(13) *Give or ask for reasons*:
      (strategy 13) **I think you've had a bit too much to drink, Jim.** →(FTA) Why not stay at our place this evening?
(14) *Assert reciprocal exchange or tit for tat*:[4]
      Dad, →(FTA) if you help me with my maths homework, (strategy 14) **I'll mow the lawn after school tomorrow.**
(15) *Give gifts to H (goods, sympathy, understanding, cooperation)*:
      A: (strategy 15) **Have a glass of malt whisky, Dick.**
      B: Terrific! Thanks.
      A: Not at all. →(FTA) I wonder if I could confide in you for a minute or two.

In addition, there are ten substrategies addressed to the hearer's negative face:

(16) *Be conventionally indirect*:
      (strategy 1) **Could you tell me the time**, please?
(17) *Do not assume willingness to comply. Question, hedge*:
      (strategy 2) I wonder whether I could **just sort of** ask you a **little** question.
(18) *Be pessimistic about ability or willingness to comply. Use the subjunctive*:
      (strategy 3) **If** you **had a little** time to **spare** for me this afternoon, I'd like to talk about my paper.
(19) *Minimise the imposition*:
      (strategy 4) Could I talk to you **for just a minute**?
(20) *Give deference*: (strategy 5) (to a police constable) Excuse me, **officer**. I think I might have parked in the wrong place.
(21) *Apologise*: (strategy 6) **Sorry to bother you**, but . . .
(22) *Impersonalise the speaker and the hearer. Avoid the pronouns* I *and* you:
      (strategy 7)
      A: **That car's parked in a no-parking area.**
      B: It's mine, officer.
      A: **Well, it'll have to have a parking ticket.**
(23) *State the FTA as an instance of a general rule*:
      (strategy 8) **Parking on the double yellow lines is illegal**, so →(FTA) I'm going to have to give you a fine.

(24) *Nominalise to distance the actor and add formality*:
   (strategy 9) **Participation** in an illegal demonstration is punishable by law. →(FTA)
   Could I have your name and address, madam?[5]
(25) *Go on record as incurring a debt, or as not indebting H*:
   →(FTA) If you could just sort out a problem I've got with my formatting, (strategy 10)
   I'll buy you a beer at lunchtime.[6]

The fifteen strategies addressed to the hearer's positive face range over sets of structures that can only be interpreted as 'polite' in the presence of the face-threat itself. In addition to the prefacing strategies the FTAs also include structures which, in terms of (im)politeness₁, are often interpreted as 'polite', e.g. in example (15), positive politeness strategy 15, *I wonder if I could VP*, in example (13), strategy 13, *why don't you do X?* It's really only in the contextual environment of the FTA that the structures realising the strategy are interpretable as polite. In reality, participants in verbal interaction either do not necessarily classify the prefacing moves as polite, or they find them appropriate to what the speaker wants to do and may or may not agree that they are polite, or they may even disapprove of them.

For example, in example (1), strategy 1, the FTA resides in asking Jim to give up some of his valuable time and energy to help the speaker solve a formatting problem. But note that it would hardly have been appropriate for the speaker to have expressed this as an FTA (e.g. *Help me with a formatting problem I've got*) immediately after prefacing it with the indication that he is paying attention to Jim's interests, wants, needs, etc. So what do we do with the expression *I wonder if . . .*, the modal verb *could*, the hedging adverb *just* and the diminutive adjective *little*? If the utterances constituting (1) had really been produced, would Jim, the speaker, or anyone overhearing the conversation have evaluated this part of it as 'polite', or would they have focused on certain elements of the language used as expressing 'politeness'? And if they had, would they have felt positively or negatively towards the speaker, i.e. would politeness have been evaluated as a socially desirable or a reprehensible form of behaviour?

In example (2), strategy 2, it would hardly have been appropriate for the speaker to have uttered the FTA *Spare me a couple of minutes* after the prefacing strategy. In using this strategy, the speaker runs the obvious risk of being evaluated as insincere. S/he might intend the turn to be interpreted as polite. Jim might indeed recognise this intention, but he might not evaluate the speaker's politeness positively.

On the assumption that talking about football is a safe topic in example (5) and that the speaker is agreeing with the addressee's assumed evaluation of Manchester United's poor showing the previous evening, the change of topic involving the FTA is abrupt enough to lead the addressee to evaluate the preface as a tactical ploy to cadge a cigarette from her/him, but hardly as being polite.

Turning to the negative politeness strategies, it is a little more likely that participants will attribute politeness to the examples given, but this does not say anything about whether one participant evaluates this politeness positively while another might give a negative assessment. If we look at negative politeness strategy 1 (example (16)), asking somebody for the correct time might constitute an imposition for that person, but an indirect expression such as *Could you tell me the time?* is one of the conventionally normal ways to make the request. The linguistic expression that might be assessed as contributing towards the polite nature of the utterance is more likely to be *please* than the indirect form of the question. Negative politeness strategy 3 (example (18)) only makes sense if the utterance is contextualised as a student addressing a lecturer (*If you had a little time to spare for me this afternoon, I'd like to talk about my paper*). Using the subjunctive (*had*) gives the lecturer an out, i.e. s/he can simply say that s/he has no time. But what if the lecturer were to address the same utterance to the student, changing the expression *my paper* to *your paper*: *If you had a little time to spare for me this afternoon, I'd like to talk about your paper?* It's highly unlikely that the quality of politeness will be assigned to the lecturer's utterance. The utterance now gives rise to the somewhat ominous inference that there is something drastically wrong with the paper. It is highly unlikely to be interpreted as an instance of politeness.

In all these examples, we can once again see the discursive struggle over the social values of politeness, and it is precisely this struggle that Brown and Levinson do not take into account. They also give fifteen off-record strategies, three addressed to Grice's Maxim of Relation (Give hints; Give association clues; Presuppose), three to the Maxim of Quantity (Understate; Overstate; Use tautologies), four to the Maxim of Quality (Use contradictions; Be ironic; Use metaphors; Use rhetorical questions) and five to the Maxim of Manner (Be ambiguous; Be vague; Over-generalise; Displace H; Be incomplete, use ellipsis). There is little point in going through these strategies in detail, but they provide evidence that Brown and Levinson also take the Gricean CP as the basis of their conceptualisation of politeness$_2$. As we saw in chapter 3 and will deal with in more detail in chapter 8, this is not unproblematic.

CONTEXTUALISING FACEWORK STRATEGIES

This leaves us with the following problems:

a. Is it not the case that the strategies suggested by Brown and Levinson, whether they are addressed to so-called positive face or negative face, are *facework* strategies rather than politeness strategies? If so, the linguistic structures that realise these facework strategies are by no means always associated with linguistic politeness, although of course a large number of them may be.
b. Can negative face-threatening only be redressed by negative politeness strategies?
c. Will positive politeness always and only be addressed to positive face threats?

Some of the examples of Brown and Levinson's strategies seem to indicate that there is a good deal of vacillation and confusion on these issues. The local organisation of the discourse activity generally offers the clues to a polite interpretation. These clues indicate that the presence of politeness is often only interpretable through inferencing processes carried out when individual participants process the other participants' contributions to the verbal interaction.

We can illustrate these points with a further example. Imagine a situation in which the speaker wants to borrow the addressee's lawn-mower to mow her/his own lawn. S/he will immediately 'know' in some sense whether to go for strategy type (1) (bald on-record FTA), strategy type (2) (positive politeness), strategy type (3) (negative politeness), strategy type (4) (off-record politeness, in which the speaker will violate one or more of the Gricean maxims in the hope that the addressee will be able to work out the implicature – which is in effect an FTA) or strategy type (5) (not to do the FTA at all). The implicit presence of the other options certainly makes the choice easier, but the speaker will not have to go through the whole system represented diagrammatically in figure 4.1 in order to decide which strategy is the most appropriate.

If the speaker does not know her/his neighbour, s/he might decide to choose the negative pole of rational decision 1 (strategy 5), which would logically result in never borrowing the lawnmower at all! Of course, if the speaker is desperate, s/he could surreptitiously 'borrow' the lawnmower without asking and without the addressee knowing, but if this ever came to light, it would constitute a very serious face-threatening act.

S/he could decide to risk the FTA but to go off record. In this case s/he might say something like:

(26) S: Oh dear! My lawn's looking a real mess and my lawnmower's being repaired. It won't be back till the end of next week.

Certain social conditions in the relationship between speaker and addressee, however, direct the speaker towards making this choice. They might not know one another very well, so that the speaker is working on the off-chance assumption that the neighbour will be in a position to derive the correct set of inferences and spontaneously offer the use of the lawnmower.

The speaker could assess the situation in such a way that s/he can afford to go on record and decide to do so with redressive action. In this case s/he has an almost endless set of choices available, as we saw from the fifteen substrategies for positive politeness and ten for negative politeness. The action required of the neighbour is an encroachment on her/his territory; hence, according to Brown and Levinson it is a negative face-threat. Not all the possible utterances will be addressed uniquely to the negative FTA and expressed in the form of negative politeness strategies:

(27) S: **Lend me your lawnmower this afternoon, would you, Fred?**
[formulaic linguistic politeness marker in '. . . would you?': a very minimal example of the negative politeness strategy *Be conventionally polite*] **Mine's not back till the end of next week.**
[not normally an expression of linguistic politeness, but is it interpretable as such in this context?: an example of the positive politeness strategy *Give or ask for reasons: positive strategy 13*]

(28) S: **D'you reckon you could lend me your lawnmower this afternoon, Fred?**
[semi-formulaic linguistic politeness marker: an example of the negative politeness strategy *Do not assume willingness to comply. Question, hedge: negative strategy 7*] **Mine's not back till the end of next week.**
[not an expression of linguistic politeness, but is it interpretable as such in this context?: an example of the positive politeness strategy *Give reasons or ask for reasons: positive strategy 13*]

(29) S: **I say, Fred, old boy.**
[not an utterance explicitly realising linguistic politeness: an example of positive politeness strategy 2: *Exaggerate sympathy, approval*] **Would you mind me borrowing your lawnmower this afternoon?** [an example of the negative politeness strategy *Be conventionally indirect: negative strategy 1*] **Mine's in for repair at the moment.**
[see above]

The choice of all these structures can be classified as different means of expressing negative and positive politeness, e.g. use of the interrogative tag *would you?* after the imperative form, the choice of the lexeme *lend* rather than *borrow*, the use of the term of address *Fred* in

(27); questioning the feasibility of the action and use of the modal auxiliary *could* in (28); the choice of *borrow* rather than *lend*, use of the discourse marker *I say* to broach a topic, the familiar address form *old boy*, the use of the formulaic request structure *would you mind* in (29).

On the other hand, the neighbour might be so proud of his brand-new lawnmower that the action required of him can also be interpreted as more of a threat to positive face than to negative face, which would entail more explicit redressive action in the form of positive politeness, e.g.

(30) S: **That's a superb new lawnmower you've got there, Fred.**
         [an example of the positive politeness strategy *Notice admirable qualities, possessions, etc.*]
         I wonder if you'd mind me borrowing it for an hour this afternoon to do my lawn.
         [negative politeness strategy *Do not assume willingness to comply. Question*]
         Mine's in for repair at the moment.
         [see above]

It should be obvious that all utterances have to be appropriate to the politic verbal behaviour of the ongoing discourse activity and also to the knowledge of the social situation that the speaker has and can assume her/his addressee to have. This would appear not to be accounted for in Brown and Levinson. Many of the utterances in this type of interaction are not in themselves polite, but they are employed to carry out facework; for this reason they may be interpreted as polite within the context of the discourse activity. If Fred and the speaker have known one another for years and are frequently borrowing one another's gardening equipment, then the speech events in (29) and (30) are easily interpretable as unnecessarily polite, impolite, or just plain odd. Politeness also stretches over more than one speech event. It might even range over whole talk exchanges and contain examples of Brown and Levinson's 'positive' and 'negative' politeness. What therefore is the validity of making a distinction between these two kinds of face in the first place?

SOCIO-CULTURAL VARIABLES IN BROWN AND LEVINSON'S MODEL

The final part of Brown and Levinson's theory goes a certain way towards dealing with the social aspects of the situation as discussed in the previous section. They posit that the MP needs to assess three different socio-cultural variables of the FTA, the power that the addressee has over the speaker (although they make no effort to define precisely what they understand by 'power'), the social distance between the interactants, and the degree to which, according to some ranking of impositions in the culture concerned, the action required of the addressee or the evaluation of the addressee is rated as an imposition.[7] Is, for example, borrowing a lawnmower a serious imposition in culture A and a matter of course in culture B (and therefore not worth being classified as a social imposition at all)?

They suggest the following equation to compute the seriousness (or weightiness) of the FTA, since that will determine the appropriate type of strategy to be used:

$$W_X = D(S,H) + P(H,S) + R_X$$
Where x is the FTA

The weightiness of the intended FTA is a composite of the social distance D between S and H (the hearer), the power, P, that H wields over S and R, the degree to which x constitutes an imposition. The greater the value of W, the closer should be the utterance to strategy type 5 in figure 4.1. The smaller the value of W, the closer it should be to strategy type 1. Hence if borrowing lawnmowers from your neighbour is rated culturally as a serious imposition, if you do not know your neighbour, or if you know your neighbour is your local bank manager and you have a large overdraft, choose strategy 5, 'Don't do the FTA'.

Brown and Levinson have been criticised for not indicating the quantitative parameters in accordance with which W can be computed. In fact, their only intention in suggesting the formula was to indicate the reasons for choosing one strategy rather than another, and not to suggest that politeness strategies really could be measured in relation to a computed value for the variables P, D and R_X. But there are more serious criticisms relating to the suggestion itself. Watts, Ide and Ehlich (1992a: 9) point out that the degree to which the FTA is considered a serious imposition (R_X) depends on the power and social distance factors. For example, asking someone much higher than oneself in the social hierarchy or someone who is a complete stranger for a cigarette constitutes a more serious FTA than asking a close friend. In order for the MP to assess the value of R, s/he first has to know the values for D and P. Similarly, knowing the value for P may or may not depend on knowing the value for D.

It has also been shown that the social distance parameter is not a reliable way of characterising the relationship between S and H, and that a much more useful measure is the affective relationship between the MP and the addressee (cf. Holtgraves 1986; Holtgraves and Yang 1990; Brown and Gilman 1989). Fraser (1990) makes the valid point that, even if we were able to compute the value of W_x, we would not know whether high values in the D, P or R_x parameters contributed to the weightiness of the FTA, and surely this is of significance for the choice of strategy to be employed.

In addition to these flaws in the model there is a further problem which Brown and Levinson themselves raise in the 54-page introduction to the 1987 publication of their text in book form, and it concerns the validity of the politeness hierarchy itself (cf. figure 4.1). They suggest that not all aspects of the social interaction impinging on strategy selection, e.g. the influence of the presence in the interaction of third parties, were taken properly into account in the original 1978 text. Considering the fact that the 1987 text is the same as the 1978 text, it is regrettable that this sort of criticism should not have led them to carry out a revision of the model, since this now seems to be a necessary step to take. A revision of the hierarchy, as Coupland *et al.* (1988) point out, would once again have repercussions on the validity of their notion of face. Positive politeness may indeed be generally relevant to a participant's positive face – although, if we return to the Goffman notion of face as being socially attributable, we will need to revise our terminology somewhat – whereas negative politeness (again, if that term can be upheld at all) will be relative to the kind of FTA committed.

Coupland *et al.* (1988: 255) suggest that the best fallback position would be to abandon the search for a universal notion of politeness altogether and to 'be content with recognising overlapping sets of face-related strategies'. If Coupland *et al.* mean that the search for politeness$_2$ should be abandoned, then I find myself agreeing with them. What Brown and Levinson offer is indeed a theory of facework, rather than a theory of politeness. On the other hand, a theory of (im)politeness does not have to be abandoned altogether if we focus our attention on the divergent evaluations of politeness$_1$.

Brown and Levinson's model retains the dyadic structure of speaker–hearer utterances so common to speech act theory without considering the wider implications of the rest of the verbal interaction or even some of the significant aspects of the local context of discourse production. The impression that the reader constantly gains is that, because of the similarity in structure types in the examples used by Brown and Levinson to illustrate processes of face-threatening minimisation and the maximisation of the addressee's positive face, those structures are to be understood as being in some sense inherently polite. The argument presented in this book is that participants in verbal interaction are polite (or not, as the case may be), that they assess their own behaviour and the behaviour of others as (im)polite, and that (im)politeness does not reside in a language or in the individual structures of a language.

One can never be sure whether the structures in English, Tzeltal and Tamil used as examples of politeness by the authors have been chosen by a process of introspection precisely because they appear to support their argument of universality. If so, we would need to investigate examples of real verbal interaction in all three languages in great detail to see whether their claims hold up. Further to this, the claim for universality based on language data from just three languages is grossly overstated.

POST-BROWN AND LEVINSON (1987) RESEARCH INTO POLITENESS

Politeness research since the 1987 republication of Brown and Levinson in book form can be grouped, very roughly, into the following five categories:

1. *Work criticising aspects of Brown and Levinson's model* like the work I shall discuss in the next few sections. Some of this literature advocates a revision of Brown and Levinson and some of it opts for the Leech approach. Hardly any of the literature advocates a return to the Lakoff, Arndt and Janney or Fraser and Nolen approaches, although the CC is sometimes mentioned.

2. *Empirical work on particular types of speech activity* in a wide range of cultural and linguistic settings. The most commonly discussed speech activities are requests, apologies, compliments and thanks, with request situations far and away at the top of the list. Most of these make use of the Brown and Levinson framework on the grounds that, of the models available, it provides the most efficient tools for an analysis of those speech events, although some researchers prefer to use the Leech model.

3. *Cross-cultural work* assessing the ways in which two or more cultures differ in their realisations of politeness, either in general terms or in relation to specific speech activities. Once again the preferred model is Brown and Levinson.

4. *The application of politeness models,* mainly Brown and Levinson, to data in other disciplines, above all in developmental and

cognitive psychology, psychotherapy, business and management studies, language teaching, gender studies, law, etc.

5. *Sporadic attempts to suggest alternative lines of enquiry* (cf. most of the chapters in Watts *et al.* 1992b), Coupland *et al.* (1988), Culpeper (1996), some of the articles in Kienpointer (1999) such as Arundale (1999), Held (1999), etc. The most radical suggestions, however, have recently been made by Eelen (2001).

Work carried out under points 2, 3 and 4 tends to assume that one of the models available, generally Brown and Levinson, provides a sufficiently stable basis on which 'normal science' in the sense of Kuhn (1962) can be carried out. Work done under point 1 questions some of the fundamental theoretical assumptions of one or more of the models (mostly Brown and Levinson) but does not suggest that the model(s) as such is (are) inappropriate. Work carried out under point 5 does make this assumption, but either declines to take any major steps to remedy the situation, or appears unable to break away entirely from the grip of linguistic pragmatics, again with the exception of Eelen's recent critical book on politeness theory (2001). In chapter 6 I shall commit myself to an attempt to make this break more radically. In the following section I shall return briefly to the question of cultural relativity and universality.

CULTURAL RELATIVITY VERSUS UNIVERSALITY OF POLITENESS

In chapter 3 and the first part of this chapter I have presented some of the models of linguistic politeness on the market. A closer look at the extensive literature on the subject might lead to the conclusion that politeness researchers embed their notions of linguistic politeness within the cultural framework with which they are familiar, whether or not this is their intention. We have already seen examples of Asian scholars who have openly made this complaint about European and North American researchers (e.g. Ide 1989; Hill *et al.* 1986; Ide *et al.* 1992; Matsumoto 1988, 1989; Gu 1990). However, any restriction to a specific cultural viewpoint is likely to obfuscate rather than clarify the concept of 'politeness'. Indeed, the self-same critics seem just as firmly stuck in a cultural mould as those they are criticising.

At the heart of the controversy during the 1990s over the 'cultural relativity versus universality of politeness' question was Brown and Levinson's use of the term 'face' and the conceptualisation of politeness as a set of rational strategies to offset the potentially disruptive effects of face-threatening. The variables of 'social distance' (D) and 'power' (P) and the degree of seriousness of the imposition (R) have been a further bone of contention.

As early as 1980, Richard Schmidt published a review of Esther Goody's book *Questions and Politeness: Strategies in Social Interaction* (1978), in which Brown and Levinson's model first appeared. In it he comments on their conceptualisation of politeness as representing 'an overly pessimistic, rather paranoid view of human social interaction' (1980: 104). In a similar vein, Nwoye (1992: 311) suggests that if the Brown and Levinson account of politeness is accepted, then 'social interaction becomes an activity of continuous mutual monitoring of potential threats to the faces of the interactants, and of devising strategies for maintaining the interactants' faces – a view that if always true, could rob social interaction of all elements of pleasure'. Mao (1994: 459) concludes that Brown and Levinson's concept of face 'becomes, in the last analysis, a self-image'. Gu turns Brown and Levinson's argument on its head and says that the very fact that 'to be polite is to be face-caring means that all FTAs are not polite, since they do not care for but threaten face, hence they are impolite acts' (1990: 241).[8]

What these scholars implicitly realise is what Konrad Werkhofer (1992) states explicitly:

> the modern view [the view of politeness taken by Brown and
> Levinson: RJW] is biased towards a one-sided individualism, a bias
> that is not only due to the role ascribed to the speaker's initial
> face-threatening intention, but to other individualistic premises.
> (1992: 157)

Moving out from this central criticism Werkhofer then goes on to accuse Brown and Levinson of taking a static, narrow approach to social realities in the three variables of 'social distance', 'power' and 'rate of imposition':

> Being defined as static entities that determine polite meanings, these
> variables represent a narrow approach to social realities, an approach
> that neglects the dynamic aspects of social language use – aspects
> that may have no systematic status in the traditional view, but
> should be at the very heart of a modern one. (1992: 176)

If Werkhofer had suggested that the heart of a theory of politeness should be politeness$_1$, he would have come close to the crux of the matter. As it is, however, he can be interpreted as almost saying as much in the above quotation. For the moment, however, let's return to the notion of face.

CRITICISM OF BROWN AND LEVINSON'S DUALISTIC NOTION OF 'FACE'

Brown and Levinson (1978, 1987) postulate that the essence of politeness$_2$ resides in strategies employed by interlocutors in socio-communicative verbal interaction to guarantee

1. the universal need of individual human beings to be valued, respected, appreciated in social groups, i.e. that the self-image that an individual has constructed of her/himself should be accepted and supported by others, and
2. the universal right of individual human beings to relative freedom of thought and action, i.e. to perceived 'territory', in both the literal and metaphorical senses of the term.

The need to construct and maintain a self-image and the right to relative freedom of thought and action are claimed to be developments from Goffman's term 'face', but they are not what Goffman originally meant by the term. As we have seen, face is redefined in Brown and Levinson (1978, 1987) as *positive face* (self-image) and *negative face* (freedom of thought and action), and the relevant linguistic strategies chosen to address these reciprocal face needs are termed *positive politeness* and *negative politeness*.

Let's assume for the moment that Brown and Levinson's model is adequate for the interpretation of ongoing verbal interaction in which participants are reciprocally attending to one another's face needs. In that case, if it were possible to give an adequate definition of what is meant by culture, it would be entirely reasonable to suggest, as Brown and Levinson do, that the politeness strategies employed in one culture might be addressed more to the support of positive face than to the avoidance of threatening negative face in another culture, and to assume that there is a cultural spectrum of politeness types ranging from negative politeness cultures to positive politeness cultures.[9] The fact is, however, that in the politeness literature the term 'culture' ranges from national groupings, through languages, gender-specific differences, social classes, subcultures determined by interest groups, age groups, in-groups, etc. and back to broad, sweeping notions such as 'western European and North American culture', 'Asian culture'. The number of ways in which the term 'culture' is used in the literature, mostly without any attempt to define exactly what is meant by it, leads to the conclusion that it is a vacuous notion which appears to help the discussion of politeness$_2$ but clearly hinders any consideration of politeness$_1$.

One of the major criticisms of Brown and Levinson's work is that it assumes an individualistic concept of face,[10] which is not appropriate to 'cultures' in which the individual is defined by virtue of her/his membership in the social group. The criticism assumes that a theory of politeness$_2$ which stresses the choice of an individual to use a politeness strategy is appropriate only to individualistic societies but not to collectivist ones. If the individual's freedom of thought and action are constrained by collectivist societies and his/her freedom to what one might describe as 'metaphorical territory' is determined by the social status that the individual has in the group, the notion of negative face can have little or no meaning in those societies.[11]

Lee-Wong's evaluation of the Chinese notion of face, i.e. that 'face maintenance is essentially an act of balancing – the perception of self in relation to other' (1999: 24), is entirely in accord with both Gu (1990) and Mao (1994). Gu does refer to 'the Chinese negative face' but he modifies the term by suggesting that 'it is threatened when self cannot live up to what s/he has claimed, or when what self has done is likely to incur ill fame or reputation' (1990: 242). Mao maintains that 'Chinese face encodes a reputable image that individuals can claim for themselves as they interact with others in a given community; it is intimately linked to the views of the community and to the community's judgment and perception of the individual's character and behavior' (1994: 460). He also suggests that it 'depends upon, and is indeed determined by, the participation of others' (ibid.) and that, quoting Goffman, it 'is "on loan . . . from society"' (ibid.). All of this seems to have little to do with Brown and Levinson's concept of 'negative face'.

In a similar vein Matsumoto (1988), discussing the notion of 'face' in Japanese, suggests that 'preservation of face in Japanese culture is intimately bound up with showing recognition of one's relative position in the communicative context and with the maintenance of the social ranking order' (1988: 415). She argues that since Japanese interactants must always explicitly show in the language they use how they view the social relationship, it is possible to maintain that 'all utterances in Japanese can be considered face-threatening' (1988: 419). Her conclusion is similar to those of the Chinese researchers quoted above, i.e. that the concept of negative face is inappropriate for Japanese culture and that 'the Japanese politeness system places a higher value on recognition of the interpersonal relation than on mitigating impositions on freedom of action' (1988: 421).

The criticism of Brown and Levinson's notion of negative face is not restricted to Asian scholars. Nwoye (1992) discusses the notion of face in Nigerian Igbo society, which he categorises as 'egalitarian', and maintains that 'concern for group interests rather than atomistic individualism is the expected norm of behaviour' (1992: 310). His discussion of face in Igbo is remarkably similar to Gu's, Lee-Wong's and Mao's description of the face concept in Chinese.[12] Nwoye also argues in favour of what he calls 'group face', the group being taken as 'any social unit larger than the individual' (1992: 315). The justification for positing group face is that an Igbo must always be concerned with the 'collective' rather than the 'individual' self-image. Bayaktaroğlu (2000) makes similar points with respect to the inappropriateness of a notion of negative face for Turkish society, and Mursy and Wilson (2001) give yet more evidence from Egyptian Arabic society of its inapplicability.

As we can see from this selection of articles critical of Brown and Levinson's approach to politeness, it is always the validity of a concept of 'negative face' which is questioned.[13] What can we make of this fact and of the implied redundancy of Brown and Levinson's dual conceptualisation of face in general? Does Brown and Levinson's notion of face correspond to Goffman's and if it does not, should it simply be rejected out of hand? If it is rejected, we have taken the first step towards denying the universality of politeness$_2$. I will therefore return to Goffman's work in the following section and again in chapter 5 in an attempt to undo the Gordian knot.

GOFFMAN'S AND BROWN AND LEVINSON'S NOTIONS OF 'FACE'

Lakoff's and Leech's models of linguistic politeness are focused on the interpretation of pragmatic meaning, even when it is obvious that linguistic forms which would be classified by native speakers as polite either explicitly or implicitly encode social meaning. From this we might be led to conclude that certain forms of linguistic structure are 'inherently polite'. What is missing in Leech's and Lakoff's approaches is a conceptualisation of linguistic utterances (including those that are labelled polite) not just as actions, but, more importantly, as *social* actions.

Pragmatic 'rules' like 'Don't impose', 'Give options' and 'Make A feel good' (Lakoff 1973a) certainly show an awareness of the need for harmonious social interaction. But we still need to ask why that need is there in the first place. This is not a question that can be answered by referring to models of linguistic pragmatics. It is equally true that politeness is often (though not always) geared to the goal of achieving maximum benefits for the speaker and the hearer at a minimum cost

Table 4.1 *Goffman's and Brown and Levinson's notion of face compared*

Goffman	Brown and Levinson
• 'the positive social value a person effectively claims for himself by the line others assume he has taken during a particular contact' • 'an image of self delineated in terms of approved social attributes'	• 'the public self-image that every member wants to claim for himself, consisting in . . . negative face [and] . . . positive face' • 'negative face: the basic claim to non-distraction – i.e. freedom of action and freedom from imposition . . . positive face: the positive consistent self-image or "personality" (crucially including the desire that this self-image be appreciated and approved of) claimed by interactants'

to both parties and that politeness relates to the goal of 'establishing and maintaining comity' (Leech 1983: 104). But we still need to know why 'establishing and maintaining comity' in social groups is important in human society and why individuals within social groups need to achieve maximum benefits at minimum cost. We also need to explain why it is that not every social interaction is aimed at achieving comity and why interactants struggle over the social values attributed to (im)politeness.

The approaches to politeness proposed by Lakoff and Leech are not grounded (or are insufficiently grounded) in a social theory that might offer possible explanations for the vacillation in first-order notions of polite linguistic behaviour. The most ambitious attempt to correct this deficiency has been made by Brown and Levinson (1978, 1987), and, as we have seen, the social theory on which their model is based is Erving Goffman's. Goffman's notion of 'face' will be explained and illustrated with concrete examples from naturally occurring verbal interaction in the next chapter, so I shall restrict myself in this section to a comparison of his conceptualisation of the term and that of Brown and Levinson.[14] This can be done by briefly comparing the two notions, side by side, in table 4.1.

The Goffmanian 'member' makes a claim for a positive *social value* which is constrained by the 'line' others interpret him to be taking during the course of the interaction. That social value is dependent on the other 'members', and it can change from one moment to the next. It is an image of the self *constructed* in accordance with social attributes approved by others, and it may be unstable and changeable.

It is reproduced and modified in every instance of social interaction. The Brown–Levinsonian 'member', on the other hand, appears to have already constructed, prior to the interaction, a self-image that s/he *wants* to be upheld by society. So although a member's self-image might be changeable, it is far less so than Goffman's positive social value. One part of the Brown–Levinsonian member's wants consists in freedom of action and freedom from imposition (negative face) and the other part is to have an already constructed and 'consistent' self-image accepted and appreciated by the others.

In other words, Brown and Levinson work from the concept of wants based on what they call 'personality', which an individual has developed prior to the interaction, whereas Goffman works from a notion of the ongoing construction of the individual's self-image contingent on social factors. Brown and Levinson seem to be thinking of the self as a stable core of values lodged somewhere in the individual, whereas for Goffman self is far less 'real' and is constantly renegotiable. It is precisely this difference which we will need to take into consideration in assessing Brown and Levinson's model of politeness. If Goffman's notion is more appropriate, it can be put to use in the study of politeness₁ whereas Brown and Levinson's notion of face is linked to politeness as an abstract concept in a universal model of politeness (politeness₂).

For Goffman face is a socially attributed aspect of self that is on loan for the duration of the interaction in accordance with the line or lines that the individual has adopted for the purposes of that interaction. It does not reside in or on the individual. As a social attribution, it cannot be the image that an individual wishes to have accepted by the other participants. The self, however, can be transformed by social interaction from a social attribution to an individual attribution. Similarly, the line or lines we adopt in an interaction may involve us in the very opposite of the desire for freedom of action and freedom from imposition. So it is unclear how negative face, as conceived of by Brown and Levinson, should be understood in a 'culture' in which the individual's freedom of action is taken to be that of the community as a whole.

In his approach to the analysis of face-to-face behaviour between individuals Goffman uses two further concepts which frequently appear in the literature on linguistic politeness, *deference* and *demeanour*. We can say of an interactant that s/he defers to the higher social position or greater social status of the co-interactant. For Goffman deference is 'the appreciation an individual shows of another to that other, whether through avoidance rituals or presentational rituals' (1967 [1956]: 77; see chapter 5). We can also describe an interactant as demeaning himself before a person with higher social position, i.e. as denying positive attributes in the eyes of greater social status.

Presentational rituals involve *ego* in a concrete presentation of her/his appreciation of *alter* through observable behaviour, e.g. the forms of language s/he uses to *alter*. Goffman is well aware of the honorific nature of such behaviour and also of the strong possibility that the expressions of appreciation for *alter* might not be a reflection of the true feelings that *ego* holds:

> It appears that deference behavior on the whole tends to be honorific and politely toned, conveying appreciation of the recipient that is in many ways more complimentary than the actor's true sentiments might warrant. (1967 [1956]: 60)

By the same token, of course, *alter* might be perfectly aware of the gap between the expression of appreciation and the true value of *ego*'s feelings. This way of looking at deference and demeanour fits in perfectly with Goffman's notion of face as 'the positive social value a person effectively claims for himself by the line others assume he has taken during a particular contact'. The line that *ego* might be required to take in an interaction could lead him/her to adopt a face which effectively masks his true feelings.

Deference and demeanour can also be expressed through what Goffman calls 'avoidance rituals', which take the form of 'acts the actor must refrain from doing lest he violate the right of the recipient to keep him at a distance' (1967 [1956]: 73). Avoidance rituals are thus based on the right of *alter*, who is perceived for the purposes of the interaction to have a higher social status than *ego*, not to have his/her metaphorical territory impinged upon. At this point there is a clear connection with Brown and Levinson's notion of negative face. It is also clear that Goffman admits to a duality of concepts which are in a constant dialectical relationship throughout all social interaction. He expresses this duality as follows:

> There is an inescapable opposition between showing a desire to include an individual and showing respect for his privacy.
>   As an implication of this dilemma, we must see that social intercourse involves a constant dialectic between presentational rituals and avoidance rituals. (1967 [1956]: 76)

Hence, contrary to Brown and Levinson's dual notion of face, Goffman's duality resides in the dual concepts of deference and demeanour.

Demeanour also refers to the 'ceremonial' way in which *ego* presents her/himself to *alter*, e.g. through dress, comportment, bearing, style of interaction, command of forms of speech, etc. Again we might say that these factors form part of the behavioural mask which *ego* needs to adopt in order to interact successfully with *alter*, given that *alter* has greater social status. They are 'accoutrements', but they are nevertheless significant in conveying an overall impression of social skills.[15]

REINTERPRETING BROWN AND LEVINSON

Three researchers (Watts 1992; O'Driscoll 1996; and de Kadt 1998) have made suggestions as to how Brown and Levinson's model might be revised by carrying out a more literal interpretation of Goffman. Two have specifically addressed the notion of face (O'Driscoll and de Kadt), one has tackled the problem of universality (Watts).[16] Both O'Driscoll and de Kadt are in favour of maintaining the basic principles of Brown and Levinson's model, but they believe that the notion of 'face' is most in need of revision. De Kadt (1998: 174), for example, questions whether 'face' must be 'rejected out of hand' or whether it is not rather Brown and Levinson's interpretation of the original Goffman notion which is at fault. She examines 'face' in Zulu society and comes to the same conclusion as most other critics of the notion, i.e. 'the assumption underpinning their category of negative politeness, that S has a want that his action be unimpeded by others, is as questionable for Zulu as for the languages of the Far East' (1998: 175).

Her suggestion is that we take Goffman's definition of face seriously. In particular, for Goffman, face is not something that the individual somehow builds for her/himself, which then needs to be supported and respected in the course of interaction, but is rather 'public property', something which is only realised in social interaction and is dependent on others. It is, in other words, what de Kadt calls 'a mutual construct' (1998: 176).

Goffman's idea that face is 'on loan from society' fits perfectly into the ethos of 'collectively' organised societies in which an interactant is not only constrained to avoid certain kinds of behaviour which would arouse public criticism but also to produce other kinds of behaviour which would incur public appreciation. De Kadt interprets Goffman's concept of face as a 'mutual construct' such that '[a]n interactant will not merely need to avoid certain behaviours, but will be expected to produce certain other behaviours' (1998: 177). However, she also maintains that Goffman appears to pay scant attention to this requirement.

Goffman's notion of face certainly allows both the volitional and the discernment aspects of politeness (cf. Hill *et al.* 1986; Ide 1989) to play a role in the production of polite language since in Zulu society 'it is far more important to do what is socially correct than what one wants oneself' (de Kadt 1998: 183). Hence losing face is a public issue in Zulu social interaction, as Goffman's theory of face predicts.

Although de Kadt has made an effort to rescue the notion of face for politeness theory and to return to the Goffmanian interpretation rather than retain Brown and Levinson's individualistic dual notion of face, she does not actually provide us with a properly developed alternative to Brown and Levinson. It seems that for all those critics of the notion of negative face the Goffman approach is more helpful than Brown and Levinson's model, but de Kadt does not take issue with the interpretation of politeness as a set of strategies for the mitigation of face-threatening.

O'Driscoll (1996) goes one step further than de Kadt and attempts to salvage the model by arguing that, although Brown and Levinson have interpreted face differently from Goffman,[17] their approach can still be upheld if their concepts of positive and negative face are interpreted at a deeper level. O'Driscoll looks for universals 'in the existential characteristics of the human condition' (1996: 5). To do so, he first criticises Brown and Levinson, as others have done, for their formulation of face in terms of 'wants' and reminds the reader of Goffman's conceptualisation of face as 'bestowed from the outside and post factum' (1996: 6). Brown and Levinson, however, in stressing that face consists of 'wants', appear to be arguing that face is 'bestowed from the inside, and prefacto' (ibid.).

O'Driscoll then argues that human life, like that of the other primates, is predicated on the existential need to associate with others (i.e. 'for sexual and nurturing purposes') and that, because of the length of time taken up by nurturing, a primate society in which the social dimension was not of paramount importance would soon die out. At the same time, however, individual humans, again like other primates, have a physical need to separate themselves from the group, e.g. to hunt for food or to defecate. O'Driscoll suggests that one significant basic parameter along which all human interaction must take place is the duality between association and dissociation, belonging and independence, and merging and individuation.

If we reinterpret Brown and Levinson's concepts of positive face vs. negative face as a reflection of preconscious wants, then we can suggest that positive face is 'the background conscious (preconscious) desire that the universal need for proximity and belonging be given symbolic recognition in interaction' and negative face 'the background conscious (preconscious) desire that the universal need for distance and individuation be given symbolic recognition in interaction' (O'Driscoll 1996: 4).

Following Goffman, O'Driscoll also posits a third type of face, which he calls 'culture-specific face', defined as 'the foreground-conscious desire for a "good" face, the constituents of "good", because they are culturally determined, being culturally variable' (1996: 4). He equates the two terms 'background consciousness' and 'foreground consciousness' roughly with 'consciousness' and 'self-awareness' respectively. O'Driscoll's term 'symbolic recognition' in the definitions above is also crucial to his reinterpretation of Brown and Levinson, since he can argue that face dualism does not involve wants in any concrete sense, but rather that those wants should be recognised indirectly and symbolically in some way.

This reorganisation of terms from Goffman and Brown and Levinson leads O'Driscoll to suggest that the notion of a face-threatening act (FTA) need not be considered as intrinsic to the face dualism which he is suggesting. The weightiness of a face-threatening act in the Brown–Levinsonian equation should not be understood as the degree of face-threat that the speaker is likely to incur through the imposition on the addressee but rather as the amount of face-payment that the speaker considers it appropriate to remit. This is an ingenious way of retaining the hierarchy of politeness strategies but at the same time doing away with the apparent boundaries that are posited between the points on the politeness hierarchy. Smaller denominations of 'face-coinage' correspond to 'positively coloured' politeness and larger denominations to 'negatively coloured' politeness. It frees the individual from having to make conscious rational choices with respect to the politeness strategy to be used.

O'Driscoll deals with the criticisms levelled at Brown and Levinson by researchers who argue that western cultures tend to display an individualistic organisation of social structure whereas several Asian, African and Islamic cultures are more 'collectivist'. He does this by taking up a point made by Matsumoto (1988) and arguing for degrees of verticality or horizontality in social relationships. In societies with weak vertical ties higher social status does not entail much responsibility, so that the amount of face-payment can be decided on a more individualistic basis. In societies with strong vertical ties, on the other hand, higher-status persons have responsibility for those below them in the social scale and the amount of face-payment due will be socially determined.[18]

The awareness that we need to look more deeply for universal aspects of face is a step in the right direction. O'Driscoll and de Kadt are able to counter much of the criticism levelled at Brown and Levinson by advocating a reintroduction of Goffman's notion of face and by showing that politeness is not uniquely a question of mitigating FTAs.[19] But one thorny problem still remains. Brown and Levinson's model has been revised, corrected and extended, but its fundamental thrust stays the same. Its basis in Gricean pragmatics has not been properly addressed, and its status as a model is rather insecure. Is it a production model, i.e. given a set of social facts, how will the speaker rationally select the 'correct' politeness strategy? Or is it a means to interpret polite behaviour after the event, as it were? Or is Politeness Theory in effect Face Theory? The phenomenon of politeness has still not been adequately embedded in a viable social theory despite the progress made so far.

WERKHOFER'S CRITICISM OF BROWN AND LEVINSON

One of the severest criticisms of Brown and Levinson's model can be found in Werkhofer (1992). It is interesting because it makes an explicit connection between the symbolic value of politeness and money that was only hinted at by O'Driscoll. A critical assessment of Werkhofer's points will help us to look at the phenomenon of politeness in chapter 6 from the point of view of economic and social theory rather than from the standpoint of linguistic pragmatics.

Werkhofer begins his objection to Brown and Levinson's model by stating quite unequivocally that their 'Model Person' is an attempt to 'reconstruct systematically . . . the rationality that underlies polite talk', i.e. that the model is not an attempt to reconstruct what might be going on in a person's mind but rather a means to the end of solving a 'problem in linguistic pragmatics, and not in the psychology or sociology of language' (1992: 155). He also supports the view that politeness is an act (or set of acts, or stretch of behaviour) which is performed by individuals in social interaction. Politeness therefore mediates between the individual and the 'social, motivating and structuring courses of action' sanctioned by society and is a way of reproducing those courses of action.

He makes a distinction between a traditional view of politeness which suggests that the individual has no choice but to submit to polite forms of language since these form part of the 'collective' ethos of a people[20] and the modern, individualistic view of politeness that we see in most of the models sketched out in chapter 3 and in Brown and Levinson's model. The modern view 'is biased towards a one-sided individualism, a bias that is not only due to the role ascribed to the speaker's initial face-threatening intention, but to other individualistic premises' (1992: 157), and he suggests that the traditional view, despite its weaknesses, can still offer a great deal towards a more balanced assessment of politeness. On their own, both views imply a 'static universalism' that posits a small set of concepts or principles that are stable across cultures and across time.

Werkhofer's assumption is that Brown and Levinson's approach plays down its orientation to economics. He argues that it is precisely this element of politeness that should be foregrounded once again, and he goes even further than O'Driscoll in making an explicit comparison between the social power of money and that of politeness:

> In developed market economies . . . money may become a social force in itself, a force that, like politeness, playing the role of an active, 'powerful' medium, will feed back into the processes that had once given rise to it. (1992: 159)

He is therefore suggesting that we make a serious attempt to define the social power of politeness and to interpret it within the social processes that have given rise to it. It is, in other words, a factor mediating between the individual and the group.

Before presenting his comparison between politeness and money explicitly, he spends some time in taking Brown and Levinson's model to pieces. His first point is a criticism of Lakoff's and Brown and Levinson's handling of Grice. The modern view of politeness seeks to do the opposite of what Grice intended. Whereas Grice was seeking a means to explain how individuals successfully convey their intentions without literally expressing them, Brown and Levinson's Model Person seeks to obscure or hide those intentions. The Gricean model of pragmatics

a. does not adequately explain how addressees derive the implicatures they do;
b. does not account for other implicatures that might also be derived;
c. ignores the possibility that an addressee might infer more than one implicature and thus be faced with a potential dilemma in deciding which of them is most appropriate to the context of the utterance (see chapter 8 for a more extensive criticism of the Gricean CP).

Brown and Levinson's focus on Grice effectively leads to the assumption that politeness is in some sense less 'true' than the direct communication of one's intentions, and thus relegates the social force of politeness to a backseat.

Werkhofer's main counter-argument focuses on the notion of the FTA and the rational procedures that the speaker needs to go through in order to choose an appropriate politeness strategy from Brown and Levinson's hierarchy. He interprets Brown and Levinson as presenting a production model of polite utterances. Indeed, it is this aspect of the model that has attracted the bulk of empirical work carried out on linguistic politeness. If, after all, we are offered a set of operations which are said to be universal and which will 'generate' the appropriate politeness structures, then we have an ideal toolkit to compare and interpret the ways in which speakers handle a range of different speech events across a range of different cultures.

Werkhofer compares the rational decision-making which the individual needs to go through to produce a polite utterance with an internal dialogue taking place within the speaker's mind, i.e. it is quasi-mentalistic. The relationship between *ego* and *alter* thus becomes an antagonistic one:

> This antagonism takes the form of a dialogue, but of a strange kind of dialogue that only takes place within the speaker's mind: s/he *generates* as a first turn, what s/he intends to say. This move remains tacit so that the next move is not the addressee's answer to the first one, but is the speaker's anticipation of what the threat to her or his face would probably mean to the addressee. The polite utterance is then the third move or the speaker's second turn in this fictive dialogue. (1992: 166)

Werkhofer adds that there is no explanation for what happens if the face-threatening event has actually occurred.

The rational procedure leading from the intention to commit an FTA and the appropriate politeness strategy generated in the utterance is sequential, where the speaker must go from step 1 of the interior dialogue to step 2 and then on to step 3. There is no way in which a later step might feed back into earlier ones, and this indicates, as Werkhofer points out, that the whole process is unconstrained by social factors. The initial intention is 'confined to the limited subset of egocentric or face-threatening [communicative intentions]' and does not 'exploit the whole range' (1992: 166).

The variables determining the 'weightiness' of the FTA, P, D and R, are somewhat crude even though Brown and Levinson would have us believe that they should not be understood literally as sociological variables. On the other hand, Werkhofer maintains that such variables are perceived subjectively and then abstracted out as 'objective' variables in sociological theory. Surely both these aspects could and should be taken into account in the model. It is also reasonable to assume that interactants might perceive them to be interacting dynamically and possibly conflicting in the verbal exchange.

Werkhofer does not, however, stop there. He also adds the following points of criticism:

1. No mention is made of the role of the bystanders in the social interaction. Are we really just concerned with the speaker and the hearer? What, in other words, is the social context of the utterance and, I might add, of the locus in which it occurs?[21]

2. A polite interaction could stretch over a number of turns at talk involving alterations in initial communicative strategies in accordance with the reactions of the addressee(s), repair mechanisms, etc. It is not simply one utterance. To what extent, therefore, can we take politeness to be a socially constitutive factor in human interaction?

3. No distinction is made between 'a socially and historically prepatterned, highly conventionalised utterance and an individually or even idiosyncratically generated one' (1992: 168). Whether we like it or not, we still have to distinguish between 'quasi-automatic, well-established behaviour elicited by an external "stimulus"' on the one hand, and deliberately pre-planned and generated utterances, on the other. In other words, what is the distinction between formulaic, ritualised and semi-formulaic utterances expressing linguistic politeness and linguistic expressions that are neither formulaic nor semi-formulaic but are nevertheless interpreted as linguistic instantiations of politeness by virtue of the context in which they occur? Under what social conditions would one or the other type of utterance be performed in social interaction?

4. No provision is made for online processing such that, even while the speaker is producing her/his utterance, s/he will also be monitoring what is said and may want to go back to an earlier stage in order to 'correct' certain assumptions and cancel out certain aspects of the utterance.

5. Work by Clark and Schunk (1980, 1981) gives evidence that there is effectively no connection between the weightiness of the imposition implied by the utterance and the cultural ranking of the imposition being placed on the addressee by the speaker. 'Costly' favours do not always give rise to more polite utterances than

'cheap' favours and 'politeness may have more to do with what is considered just and right with regard to a particular social event or with the construction of social realities and with social order' (Werkhofer 1992: 172).

6. Brown and Levinson's 'sociological' variables are taken to be static social entities that determine the degree of politeness offered. In particular, power and social distance become reified, taking on an existence outside the social sphere of the interactants rather than being themselves constructed and/or reproduced through and in the interaction itself. They are not adequately defined, and Brown and Levinson do not consider the function that polite behaviour itself may have in reconstructing them. For example, if I say to a student who is in my office to discuss a paper with me:

(31)   Would you mind taking your feet off my desk?

the apparent politeness of my utterance allows me to reconstruct the social status differential which I perceive to hold between myself and the student in that location and within the social constraints of the situation ironically, affirming my power to make this demand more forcefully rather than his presumed power to treat my desk as if it were his own. Or if a barrister in a court of law asks the witness:

(32)   Would you be so kind as to tell us where you were on the night of the thirteenth
         of January last?

then this elaborate show of polite deference towards the witness will certainly not be interpreted as such. As in (31), the expression 'Would you be so kind as to tell us . . .' in (32) is an instance of ironic linguistic politeness and is used here to construct and reproduce relationships of power and authority. The witness will 'know' that s/he is required to answer the barrister's question and that there will be serious consequences if s/he does not comply. (32) is therefore being used as a form of social control rather than politeness.

7. In accordance with most of the above points, the scale of politeness strategies suggested by Brown and Levinson is at the very least questionable.

Werkhofer also criticises Brown and Levinson's notion of face in much the same way as other researchers have done.

What solutions to these dilemmas does Werkhofer propose? At one stage he talks about the need to 'revise' Brown and Levinson's model, but judging by the extent of his criticisms, this would be rather hard to do. What is needed is a radically new approach which takes stock of politeness as a mediating force between the individual and the 'social, motivating and structuring courses of action' sanctioned by society. His answer is to compare politeness with money. He goes back to Georg Simmel's *Philosophie des Geldes* ['The philosophy of money'] (1900), in which Simmel argues that money must be seen either as a private good or as a public good. As a private good, the key to understanding the nature of money is to consider the ways in which the individual maximises its utility as a symbolic resource in the exchange of goods, but as a symbolic resource it is 'a social institution and quite meaningless if restricted to one individual'. The analogy of politeness with money is summed up in the following way:

  (i) Politeness, like money, is a socially constituted medium.
 (ii) Again like money, it is a symbolic medium in the sense that its functions originally derive from an association with something else, namely with values.
(iii) Like money, too, politeness is historically constituted and reconstituted; its functions and the values it is associated with are essentially changeable ones (cf. the discussion in chapter 2).
(iv) During its history, the functions of politeness turn into a power of the medium in the sense that it may, rather than being only a means to the ends of an individual user, itself motivate and structure courses of action (cf. the discussion in chapter 2).
 (v) Correspondingly – and due to other forces, too – the chances of the user mastering the medium completely (which would mean being able to use it to his/her wishes) will be diminished. (1992: 190)

Werkhofer makes a point of stating that the social constitution of politeness does not imply that individuals do not have a role to play, but rather that politeness cannot be accounted for in individualistic terms alone. Like money, even though politeness is socially constituted, it can still 'itself motivate and structure courses of action, feeding into social processes and, thus, into the very conditions of its own existence or maintenance' (1992: 190). Just as money has a symbolic value which will fluctuate in accordance with the changes in the economic market, so too does politeness have social values which are derived from 'social order and social identity'. Politic behaviour consists in 'paying' with linguistic resources what is due in a socio-communicative verbal interaction. Politeness, I maintain, is used to 'pay' more than would normally be required in the ritual exchange of speech acts.

The implicit message throughout this chapter has been that the Gricean approach to conversational cooperation is inadequate as a basis for a model of linguistic politeness. Chapter 6 will thus aim to provide an alternative approach to linguistic politeness using the insights gained from the discussion of face and taking the comparison of politeness with money seriously by assessing other kinds of values it might incorporate. I will develop these ideas more explicitly in chapter 6 in the light of the theory of emergent social networks (Watts 1991) and the theory of social action (Bourdieu 1991).

5 Facework and linguistic politeness

THE SCOPE OF POLITENESS

Chapters 3 and 4 have outlined some of the major theoretical approaches to linguistic politeness in the literature and have discussed some of the criticisms of those approaches. The major criticism, centring on the dominant approach towards social structure evident in all the theories (an approach which Eelen (2001) calls Parsonian),[1] will be dealt with in chapter 6. Before taking on that challenge, however, we need to develop an argument briefly mentioned in chapter 4:

- Politeness Theory can never be fully equated with Face Theory.

I will develop my argument in this chapter using data from naturally occurring verbal interaction and/or personal experience.

For the moment, recall the fictive example of a situation at the booking office of a coach station discussed in chapter 2, which most readers, at least from the anglophone world, will have recognised as 'impolite' behaviour. The act of pushing in at the front of a queue is not in itself a verbal act, although it might provoke somewhat virulent verbal responses. The social activity of queuing would not be overtly classified by interactants as 'polite' behaviour (cf. the term *classificatory (im)politeness*₁ in chapter 1) unless the interaction order is violated in this way. Queuing is therefore a form of *politic behaviour* which is reproduced through every new realisation of 'queuing' (cf. my definition of politic behaviour in chapter 1). It has become a ritualised, institutionalised form of social behaviour.

Nevertheless, we tend to think that the appropriate forms of behaviour to display at, say, the ticket office of a coach station in some way 'exist' outside ourselves, perhaps in the form of social 'rules' of some kind. We think of these 'rules' as having been decided upon by 'others' rather than by ourselves and that we are socially constrained to abide by them. All we need to do to carry out the action of buying a ticket 'correctly' is to follow the rules. It is this way of thinking about

'social rules' or 'social norms' that Eelen calls 'Parsonian'. To a certain
extent, of course, it is not completely wrongheaded. After all, if we follow the 'rules', we are more likely to achieve our goals than if we don't.
But if we were not at that particular point in time standing in the
queue performing the activity type by following the interaction order,
or if, like the pusher-in, everyone in the queue decided to disregard
the 'rules', the social activity type itself would be called into question.

So by standing in the queue and doing what others (including ourselves) expect us to do, we actually help to reproduce that social activity. We are reproducing what the ethnomethodologist Harvey Sacks
might have called 'doing being in a queue'. The reproduction of the social activity relies on the tacit agreement of those participating to 'do
it all over again'. Anyone who falls out of line is likely to be evaluated
as 'rude' or 'impolite'.

How does this constructivist view of social activity fit Politeness Theory? The major premise on which the arguments in this book are based
is that the object of such a theory should be (im)politeness$_1$ and not
some notion of (im)politeness$_2$ abstracted away from ongoing social
action. As we saw in chapter 1, (im)politeness is a concept over which
social members struggle, like 'democracy', 'beauty', 'good taste', 'art',
etc. A theory of politeness which fails to take account of this discursive struggle will be a theory about something else, but not about
(im)politeness.

What might this 'something else' be? In chapter 3 we took a look at
some of the 'definitions' of politeness in the literature and discovered
that most of them avoid stating exactly what politeness *is* by listing
the *functions* it appears to fulfil. In this chapter I shall argue that these
functional definitions rely on the notion of 'face', i.e. on the mutual
respect for the feelings of others.

But we are still left with a fundamental definitional problem. Should
linguistic (im)politeness simply be defined as language usage which is
geared towards mutual face needs, as Brown and Levinson imply? Can
Politeness Theory be fully equated with Face Theory? If we adopt this
point of view, we find ourselves confronted with the following three
consequences:

a. The term 'linguistic politeness' runs the risk of becoming vacuous, since any linguistic expressions at all which are used in
face-maintenance would then be examples of 'linguistic politeness'.
b. Certain speech activities which 'look' and 'sound' polite in fact
aim to achieve the very opposite of face-maintenance.

c. The definition rests on the assumption that all social interaction is geared towards cooperative behaviour. The brief excerpt from a conflict-laden television interview from the BBC programme *Panorama* in chapter 1 disproves this assumption.

In this chapter we will take a closer look at what the object of study in linguistic politeness research has become, i.e. examples of facework, erroneously so, as I hope to show. Politeness is of course not restricted to language usage, and several forms of non-linguistic behaviour are also subject to metapragmatic, classificatory and expressive evaluation as (im)polite$_1$. For this reason there are two ways of approaching the study of politeness:

1. as general conditions on the conventions of social activity types and their interaction orders such as those outlined above, or
2. as the forms of linguistic behaviour that are produced in requirement of those conditions.

The first approach involves us in studying what is generally called *facework* by studying the politic behaviour of the social activity type. Some, but by no means all the social behaviour we call facework includes *linguistic politeness*. The second approach leads us into classifying a set of linguistic expressions in English as 'polite', i.e. as 'inherently polite'. Most of the linguistic structures used in the negotiation of facework, however, are not usually felt by participants in verbal interaction to be 'polite'.

These two points are pertinent to the study of linguistic politeness in the literature. As we saw in chapter 4, it is not always clear whether it is politeness or facework which is being analysed.[2] In addition, there is a great deal of confusion about whether the criticisms of current models of politeness, particularly those emanating from the non-European world, are valid. After all, their second-order conceptualisations of 'politeness' appear to be significantly different from those offered in the major models developed in Europe and North America. In the following section we shall outline in a little more detail the notion of 'face' itself.

THE NOTION OF 'FACE'

The notion of 'face' has been in use as a metaphor for individual qualities and/or abstract entities such as honour, respect, esteem, the self, etc. for a very long time. It was in use in ancient China and has surfaced in different cultures of the world at different points in their history, including of course Europe. In general, the term appears to have been of greater interest to anthropologists than to sociologists and linguists. One early article to appear in a western journal on Chinese face was published by Hsien Chin Hu (1944) in the journal *American Anthropologist*. In that article Hu traces the historical outlines of the development of the notion of 'face' from the two terms *lien* and *mien* to the modern Chinese term which is closest to *mien*, namely *miànzi* (roughly translatable as 'outer part', 'face', 'reputation' and 'prestige', cf. Lee-Wong 1999: 24).

Hu's article is referred to frequently by modern Chinese politeness researchers as providing evidence of the longevity of the term 'face' (cf., e.g., Lee-Wong 1999; Gu 1990; Mao 1994). Lee-Wong states that 'if one loves one's face, one should avoid face loss and attempt to maintain one's face; in looking after one's own face, it is imperative that one looks after *alter*'s face' and that 'face maintenance is essentially an act of balancing – the perception of self in relation to other' (1999: 24). The act of balancing here is that of individuals attempting to show mutually shared forms of consideration for others whilst not appearing to be uncooperative and losing the respect that they may have gained or they might wish to gain in the eyes of others.

I will illustrate this with an example from the interaction order of a Swiss social activity type. In Swiss shops, at least those in which one is still served over the counter, customers are asked by the person serving, 'Who's next?', at which the customers will generally look around at the other customers to verify whether or not it is their turn to be served. This seems to work reasonably well, although not always. The people serving behind the counter never take it upon themselves to keep a check on who came into the shop before whom, and in any case on a busy day with a shop full of customers why should they be expected to do so? They have enough work with the actual serving. So it is left up to the customers themselves.

To order out of turn is to lose one's self-respect, since to do so is looked upon by the other customers, in particular by the person whose turn it is, to be an offence, an infringement of that person's rights. Following Lee-Wong, 'if one loves one's face, one should avoid face loss and attempt to maintain one's face' and this can only be done by 'looking after *alter*'s face'. The act of ordering out of turn can therefore be an act that will incur 'face-loss' for both participants. The offending person damages the face of the person whose turn it is and, in the process, damages her/his own face in the eyes of the other participants.

But the situation is not always that simple. Imagine a butcher's shop in a small town on a Saturday morning in summer with local inhabitants and summer visitors waiting to be served. Imagine three people behind the counter serving. In Switzerland when you enter, you stand at the back of the shop and move towards the counter as people are served, ostensibly to look at the joints of meat, sausages, etc. on display behind the glass counter, but in actual fact to make sure that no one who entered after you is close enough to the counter to usurp your turn. At the same time it is also wise to estimate which of those serving behind the counter may be serving you when your turn comes.

The situation is further complicated by the fact that no queues are formed and no numbered tickets are taken by the customers on which the next person's turn, i.e. number, is called out by one of the servers. So it takes a lot of careful observation and the goodwill of the other customers to know when your turn has come. Imagine also that you are known to the locals as a newcomer to the town. If you put a foot wrong in 'doing being served next', there is quite a lot of self-esteem you could lose. On one occasion I forgot to look around at the other customers and simply assumed it was my turn. I was put very firmly in my place by a local woman and no amount of explaining on my part could mend her *and* my wounded pride (and face).

GOFFMAN'S CONCEPT OF FACE

The example of the butcher's shop will serve to show to some extent what facework involves. Before doing so, however, I will introduce a little more theory on the notion of face and facework, going back and forth between the theory and the butcher's shop example. The sociologist Erving Goffman developed a theory of social interaction in the 1950s and 1960s from the work of G. H. Mead (1934), in which he suggests that sociology and social anthropology in the 1950s had overstressed the search for the symbolic meanings of social practices and ignored the significance of the individual human being in those practices. In terms of the Swiss butcher's shop, therefore, Goffman would have criticised a symbolic interactionist for being interested in the symbolic significance of no queues or customer tickets, of the gradual movement of the customers towards the counter, of their looks at other customers when asked 'Who's next?', etc., rather than what individual members *do* to handle the situation themselves.

Goffman refers back to Durkheim, who suggests that 'the individual's personality can be seen as one apportionment of the collective *mana*', and he states that his purpose is 'to explore some of the senses in which the person in our urban secular world is allotted a kind of sacredness that is displayed and confirmed by symbolic acts'. Every customer in the butcher's shop thus has a kind of 'sacredness' which is confirmed by being considered by the other customers as the next customer to be served. Goffman's work thus focuses on the micro-level of human interaction rather than on a macro-level description of social processes; it considers what is said and done by the individuals involved in the social interaction, i.e. in our case the butcher's shop.

The conceptualisation of the individual as a sacred object implies the ritualised treatment of that object, and the ritualised treatment of the individual on the micro-level of social interaction involves 'stylised' prescribed actions with which all the participants are familiar. In other words, to perform adequately as a customer in a Swiss butcher's shop on a busy Saturday morning when one is known as a recently arrived local, one has

   a. to be prepared to enter into any local banter that might be indulged in while waiting to be served;
   b. to know that it is convenient to move closer to the counter after others have been served;
   c. to make a continual appraisal of which server will serve one;
   d. to know that one looks at others in the vicinity of the counter when the call comes 'Who's next?', etc.

Gluckmann (1962: 24–5) understands the term 'ritualization' to refer to 'a stylized ceremonial in which persons related in various ways to the central actors, as well as these themselves, perform prescribed actions according to their secular roles'. Gluckmann's focus here is on forms of religious ritual, but it is not too difficult to see how it can also be applied to the humdrum activity of conversational interaction, even to the example of the butcher's shop. Gluckmann also suggests that the participants in the ritual behaviour believe 'that these prescribed actions express and amend social relationships so as to secure general blessing, purification, protection, and prosperity for the persons involved in some mystical manner which is out of sensory control'. I submit that the interaction order in a Swiss butcher's shop on a summer Saturday morning serves to secure a secular 'general blessing'

from the other participants and a 'protection' of their rights just as
in the performance of religious rites.

Goffman implies that our knowledge of the world and the place
we occupy in that world is gained entirely through social interaction.
It is precisely the area of human interaction in which Goffman sees
forms of ritual behaviour being enacted. In his seminal article 'On
face work' (1955; republished in Goffman 1967) he makes the following
point:

> In any society, whenever the physical possibility of spoken
> interaction arises, it seems that a system of practices, conventions,
> and procedural rules comes into play which functions as a means of
> guiding and organizing the flow of messages. An understanding will
> prevail as to when and where it will be permissible to initiate talk,
> among whom, and by means of what topics of conversation. ([1955]
> 1967: 33–4)

That 'system of practices, conventions, and procedural rules' is in fact
the politic behaviour of the social activity type, and it is only 'there'
because it is continually reenacted through talk and has been judged
as 'correct', 'just' or 'good' by the participants, as we saw in chapter 2. Obviously, the continual reenactment of what is 'correct', 'just'
or 'good' in a social interaction order need not involve any talk at
all, as we have seen from the butcher's shop example. Most of the
time, however, it almost always does, as when one customer greets
another and chats to her/him, or when the butcher teases a customer or makes a joke, or in the simple act of placing an order. Certainly, however, the 'system of practices, conventions, and procedural rules' has no other basis in 'objective reality' than this continual
reenactment.

An individual's face is seen as an image 'pieced together from the
expressive implications of the full flow of events in an undertaking'
(i.e. a form of social interaction). Although it is never stated explicitly
by Goffman, we can assume this to be 'other' participants' construals
of an individual's self, which we learn to accept and to reproduce.
My 'self' at that moment of time in the butcher's shop, when I illicitly
placed my order before a local customer, suffered from the construal by
at least that customer of being 'non-local' whilst claiming to be 'local',
'arrogant', certainly 'rude' and possibly also 'non-Swiss' rather than
'Swiss', that is, if she knew of my identity. At the same time, however,
the conceptualisations we make of our 'selves' through the construals
of others imply that we are like players 'in a ritual game'. The ritual
orders in which the self is constructed consist of the 'system[s] of

practices, conventions, and procedural rules' that make up instances of verbal interaction.

The central concept developed by Goffman in 'On face work' is that of *face* itself, which is, as we have seen, a culturally widespread metaphorical concept existing in English in idiomatic expressions like 'to put on a good face', 'to lose face', 'to face up to X', etc. Goffman defines face as 'the positive social value a person effectively claims for himself [sic!] *by the line others assume he has taken during a particular contact*' (italics mine). In addition, it is 'an image of self *delineated in terms of approved social attributes . . .*' (italics mine). 'Face', therefore, is precisely the conceptualisation each of us makes of our 'self' through the construals of others in social interaction and particularly in verbal interaction, i.e. through talk. *Line* is defined as 'a pattern of verbal and nonverbal acts by which he expresses his view of the situation and through this his evaluation of the participants, especially himself'. The line I was expected to take in the butcher's shop constrained me to look at the other customers close to the counter to assess whether it really *was* my turn. By not doing so, I fell out of line. We can only lay claim to a positive social value in accordance with the way our actions are interpreted by the group, and on that particular Saturday morning such a tiny occurrence as 'wrongly' claiming a turn did not allow me to lay claim to a positive social value.

The number of possible lines we can take during a verbal interaction may be restricted, but we are still left with a choice. It follows from Goffman's definitions that a person's face – her/his claimed 'positive social image' – may differ from one interaction to the next, or from one part of the same interaction to the next, depending on the lines that have been chosen. This allows me now to look back on the incident dispassionately and to relate it here, confident in the assumption that I am not really an impolite oaf.

Looked at in this way, Goffman's notion of face is a highly change-able, almost unstable entity, but at the same time it helps us to form a relatively stable conceptualisation of the self.[3] It also follows from this that face is dependent on the interpretation of the other participants more than on ourselves. Goffman expresses this as follows:

> One's own face and the face of others are constructs of the same order; it is the rules of the group and the definition of the situation which determine how much feeling one is to have for face and how this feeling is to be distributed among the faces involved. ([1955] 1967: 6)

Face is therefore not a permanent aspect of our construction of the self. It is not 'lodged in or on [our] body' but is 'diffusely located in the flow of events in the encounter'. It is frequently the case that face is only visible 'when the events are read and interpreted for the appraisals expressed in them'. Goffman also makes it clear that, however important face might be for an individual, it is 'only on loan from society'. Any action that incurs the disapproval of the other participants might result in face being withdrawn. So although my face may have been temporarily withdrawn by at least one participant in the interaction, I am not now permanently stamped as 'trying illicitly to claim localness', 'being non-Swiss', 'being arrogant and rude', etc.

LINES, FACES AND FACEWORK

Face, then, is a socially attributed aspect of self that is temporarily on loan for the duration of the interaction in accordance with the line or lines that the individual has adopted. It is not our personal construction of the self, although the different faces we are required to adopt in different interactions do contribute towards that construction. In many cases face may coincide with *our* interpretation of the ritual role to be played in the ongoing interaction, but this is by no means always the case. If our constructed role remains relatively stable across interactions it will result in a form of institutionalisation of the self. However, if face is the 'condition of interaction, not its objective', it is equally clear that we have an obligation to maintain the faces of the other participants in the interaction, something which I omitted to do in the butcher's shop. From this we can derive Goffman's term *facework*, which is defined by him as 'the actions taken by a person to make whatever he is doing consistent with face. Face work serves to counteract "incidents" – that is, events whose effective symbolic implications threaten face.'

To illustrate the concepts of face, facework and line more exactly, let us consider the following extract taken from an open-line phone-in programme on BBC Radio Cornwall. The moderator is conversing with a blind man, by the name of Bill Bell, who has phoned in to talk about guide-dogs and his own guide-dog in particular. At this stage in the conversation the moderator changes the topic of the interaction:

(1)

¹Mod: and :er: what about your occupation\   long retired\
BB: oh :er: very long retired\   I used to be in
²Mod: in journalism\ right Bill\ very many thanks sir\
BB: journalism\   :er: on :er:/ I know how fastidious or
³Mod:
BB: meticulous you are about :er: the use of words\ a couple of days ago\ you talked about
⁴Mod: yes\   no\
BB: 'twopence halfpenny stampage'\   can I then understand it's from the dictionary\
⁵Mod: sheer self-indulgence\ guilty\   pure self-indulgence\
BB: after perhaps :er: Ted Wragg's talk\
⁶Mod: childlike faith\ Bill,
BB: you talked about childish faith\ and I think you meant childlike faith\
⁷Mod: thank you for being such a good listener\ and I plead guilty to the use of 'stampage'\
BB: < @I love to hear you David@\ >
⁸Mod: there was euphony in the word\ indulgence\ guilty\   thank you Bill\ bye bye\ that was
BB: bye\
⁹Mod: Mr Bill Bell of Carbis Bay\
BB:

This short extract of verbal interaction takes place on a local radio phone-in programme, so we can assume that the participants are not just Bill Bell and the moderator, but all those listening in and the studio staff, producer, switchboard operators, etc. The recording was made in the mid-1980s and does not seem to reflect much of the face-work, or lack of it, that is carried out in modern phone-in programmes today. But as with current audiences of local radio, we can also assume that many listeners will have tuned in to that same programme day after day. Some of them may even have been fairly regular active contributors, probably well-known to the studio staff, the producer of the programme and the moderator. It is clear from Bill's turn in score 7 that he is at least a regular listener when he compliments the moderator: 'I love to hear you David'.

The line that listeners can assume the moderator to be taking in this kind of phone-in programme is that of a friendly, sometimes jovial, sometimes serious but, apart from his voice, physically distant friend, giving sympathy and advice where it appears to be needed, joking with the participants and sometimes even teasing them. Because they listen regularly, the audience will feel that they 'know' the moderator. They also know that the programme is limited to a certain period of time during the afternoon and that the topics chosen, although perhaps interesting to *them*, will not be of national or international interest. So the face loaned to the moderator will have the following kinds of attribute. He should be friendly, humorous, helpful, sympathetic, not argumentative, although perhaps indulging in a little tease from time to time, knowledgeable about local events, issues and characters, etc. The face that is attributed by the audience to each individual caller will vary from case to case, and face attribution will take place during the ongoing interaction. The public face that the moderator will attribute to the caller, however, must be largely positive, although it may contain negative features.

When the moderator learns at the beginning of the call (which I have omitted here for reasons of space) that Bill is blind and has a guide-dog, he gives him the floor for extended turns at talk and only intervenes to support Bill and to display the behaviour of the sympathetic listener. Bill's topic is guide-dogs, and he has been motivated to ring in to offer some comfort to another blind caller who has just lost his guide-dog. The line expected of a caller on an open-line programme is of course much less well defined than if the programme were focused on a specific topic, but we can expect callers to raise problems of current interest or to refer to topics introduced in previous programmes or earlier in the same programme, as Bill does here.

Programme producers and moderators often expect callers not to be particularly articulate in stating their opinions, and they have a range of strategies which they can use to terminate the call quickly and, they hope, without losing face themselves if the conversation should lack general interest or might become boring for their listeners. But there is a slight problem here. Because the moderator and the producer are aware of these dangers, they must always try and keep one step ahead of the callers while not creating the impression that the callers might be losing face with the listening public. If they are not successful in upholding the positive image they seek to project, they and the local radio station might also lose face. Whether the callers are conscious of these facts or not, a great deal of facework has to be carried out by the moderator.

In the extract the moderator himself breaks out of line in his first turn in score 1 by opening up an additional topic of conversation after the topic of guide-dogs has been exhausted. Generally only one topic is dealt with per caller, but the moderator appears to go out of line because of a genuine desire to learn a little more about Bill. Bill is not particularly forthcoming although he admits in his second turn in scores 1 and 2 that he used to be in journalism. At this point the moderator realises that he has gone out of line, and he places his bid for a closing move – *right Bill* – and thanks the caller for ringing in. He also uses a deferential address form, 'sir', to the caller – *very many thanks, sir.*

At precisely this point Bill himself steps out of line by reopening the conversation in his third turn in score 2 after the preclosing move *right Bill* and the moderator's expression of thanks. Now, if the radio audience have accepted the moderator's attempted closure, Bill risks offending both him and them by trying to restart the interaction. But Bill goes even further. His initial *on*, which turns out to be a false start, was probably meant to locate the occasion on which the moderator used the term *twopence halfpenny stampage*, for which Bill is apparently criticising him now. That this is meant as a criticism and hence as a face-threat to the moderator is indicated by his prefacing utterance, which can be interpreted as an attempt to soften or mitigate his direct challenge – *I know how fastidious or meticulous you are about the use of words.*

The verbal interaction in scores 4 to 8 is a very good example of facework, given the line the moderator can be assumed to have taken and the kind of face he is assigned by the wider audience. The moderator admits that he did say *stampage*, but Bill tries to drive home his advantage by getting him to admit that he did not find the word in the dictionary. In other words he intensifies the face-threat. In his fifth turn in score 5 the moderator pleads guilty and admits that he used the word out of self-indulgence, thereby attempting to protect his own public face.

In the following turn in score 5 Bill, who by now has gained a distinct advantage over the moderator, asks whether he used the word after hearing a talk by Ted Wragg. The moderator repeats his excuse in score 5 that it was *pure self-indulgence* only to be accused of having committed another lexical blunder in talking about *childish* instead of *childlike faith*. The moderator handles this delicate situation with admirable expertise, thanking Bill *for being such a good listener* and once more pleading guilty to the use of the word *stampage*. He could have challenged Bill on both points. He could have denied using either of the words, or he could have argued with Bill, but doing any of these things would not have been in line with the face attribution given him by the wider audience. It would merely have contributed negatively towards his own self-image as a phone-in moderator.

POLITENESS IN FACEWORK

If we now consider which linguistic expressions in (1) might be classified as 'polite' or 'impolite' and whether we have evidence that one of
the participants may have perceived the other as having been 'polite'
or 'impolite', we run into difficulty. The two repetitions by the moderator in his second and third turns in scores 1 to 2 are supportive of
Bill's utterances, appearing to express interest on the moderator's part,
and although we might not always call them examples of politeness,
they certainly constitute positive facework on his part.

The moderator's use of the caller's first name *Bill* helps to create
a sense of comradeship between them, and it is responded to later
when Bill refers to the moderator by his first name, *David*. But this
is hardly 'polite', since it belongs to the politic behaviour expected in
an interaction of this kind. Ending the conversation in score 2 might
be interpreted by Bill as a face-threatening act, so the moderator uses
the deferential address form *sir* to place the caller, temporarily, on a
higher social plane than himself. The moderator precedes the address
term in his third turn (score 2) with *very many thanks*, which again
is interpretable as an example of politic behaviour. It is meant to be
heard as a preclosing move. The addition of the address term *sir* in
the same turn is of interest here. The politic behaviour of an open-line
radio phone-in programme does not require this degree of formality.
Since it is beyond what might be expected, it is open to interpretation
here as being a polite way of softening the blow. How might it have
been perceived by Bill and by the wider radio audience? If it is taken to
be a genuine expression of respect for Bill, the politeness expressed by
the address term *sir* could be evaluated positively, but it is just as open
to a negative evaluation on the grounds that it is *not* a genuine expression of respect for Bill Bell but merely an attempt to distance himself
from him with a view to closing off the conversation. Unfortunately,
Bill's third turn in score 2 overlaps precisely this term of address, thus
nullifying any evidence that Bill has taken it that way.

Bill knows in his third turn that he is about to carry out some
negative facework by threatening the moderator's face attribution, so
he deliberately prefaces that utterance with a positive evaluation of
the moderator. The compliment occurs immediately prior to the face-
threat in the same turn and is thus strategic. If compliments are taken
to be inherently polite behaviour, the radio audience listening in at
home are open to classify it as such, but there is no overt evidence to
support that interpretation.

In his seventh turn in score 6 Bill's third face-threatening act is softened by attributing, in a hedged way, the knowledge of the correct word to the moderator: *I think you meant childlike faith*. The moderator then gives back positive face to Bill: *Bill, thank you for being such a good listener*. Of the two utterances it is more likely that the latter, being a compliment from the moderator to Bill, will be classified as 'polite', but at the same time the moderator's compliment is open to interpretation as irony. He may be expressing (in obviously tactful terms) that he has perceived Bill's criticism as unnecessary, and therefore possibly 'rude'. Bill's laughter in his eighth turn in score 7 and his additional compliment *I love to hear you David* provides evidence that Bill may indeed have interpreted the previous turn by the moderator in that way.

The final closing sequence is highly routinised, but nevertheless necessary to terminate the interaction and remain in face. In this sense, the exchange of *Bye* and *Thank you Bill/bye bye* is part of the politic behaviour, although some commentators might classify it as polite.

Facework, in other words, consists partly, although by no means totally, of utterances that are open to interpretation as 'polite'. The problem is that the politeness, which, I shall argue, is equivalent to giving more than is required by the expected politic behaviour, may be evaluated positively or negatively. In the situation under discussion here (im)politeness is exclusively linguistic. As with the fictive situation at the coach station and my experience at the butcher's, we only notice politeness or its opposite when forms of behaviour or linguistic expressions in addition to or deviant from those necessary to abide by the politic behaviour of the social interaction are present. For example, we notice impoliteness when someone breaks out of line and does not abide by the interaction order of the social activity.

Politeness and impoliteness are part of the construction and management of everyday life. Possibly the most important part is the individual's development of a concept of self, which can only occur through the medium of socio-communicative interaction. Socio-communicative interaction primarily (but by no means always) takes place through the medium of language. As we have seen, this concept of self can be labelled 'face', and it can only be developed through repeated socio-communicative verbal interaction with others. The construction of our own concept of self and the work we do in social interaction to enable others to construct, reproduce and maintain their self-concepts can be called *facework*. All human social interaction consists of facework of one kind or another, and it may sometimes include linguistic politeness as one of its aspects.

I will summarise these ideas as follows, using the example from the local radio phone-in programme discussed above:

1. *Facework* involves the reciprocal social attribution of face to the participants in social interaction in accordance with the line or lines the participants can be assumed to be taking in the interaction. These lines constitute part of the politic behaviour associated with the social activity type. In the radio phone-in programme the lines defining the politic verbal behaviour of the discourse activity are the following:
   a. The moderator of an open-line phone-in programme takes calls from members of the general public and chats with them on a subject of the caller's choice.
   b. The moderator generally only deals with one topic per caller.
   c. The audience who have tuned in to the programme want to be 'entertained', not bored or intimidated.
   d. Callers expect to be addressed by their first names and expect to be able to address the moderator by hers/his.
   e. Callers and audience expect the moderator to be friendly, sympathetic and helpful, to be able to share a joke, to be in a sense 'one of them', etc.
   f. Callers must accept the completion of the conversation when the moderator signals the preclosing and closing conversational moves.

   In accordance with these lines moderators, callers and possibly also the wider audience, even though we can hardly have any direct evidence of this, attribute specific kinds of face to one another, and the interaction must be seen to construct, reproduce and maintain those faces.

2. Falling out of line constitutes a break in the politic behaviour which is interpretable by the interactants as an offence and as damage to the face of one or more of the interactants including the interactant who has fallen out of line. This kind of behaviour is often evaluated as *rude* or *impolite*. In the phone-in programme it is difficult, at least in the extract presented, to locate such behaviour, although I will show how this can happen in phone-in programmes in chapter 9. My behaviour in the butcher's shop, however, was a classical case of falling out of line, and I was seen as being rude.

3. Certain social interaction types have interaction orders with lines that *sanction or neutralise face-threatening* or *face-damaging acts*,

e.g. interaction between family members or among close friends, competitive forms of interaction such as political debate, rigidly hierarchised forms of interaction, e.g. in the military services. Expressive politeness₁ in this type of interaction can often lead to other kinds of interpretation than the maintenance of face attribution.

4. When one of the interactants is about to fall out of line, or immediately after s/he has fallen out of line, that interactant may take measures to indicate to the other participants that the overall attribution of face for the interaction is still valid. This is what can be called *supportive facework*, supportive because it contributes towards the overall facework of the interaction. It is frequently, but by no means always, signalled by highly conventionalised forms of linguistic structure. Whether or not it is classified as 'polite' or 'impolite', the *evaluation* of interpretations of politeness depends on a close analysis of the ongoing verbal interaction. In the extract given above, Bill carries out supportive facework by prefacing his criticism of the moderator's use of *stampage* by attributing positive qualities to him: *I know how fastidious or meticulous you are about the use of words*. This may or may not be interpreted as polite behaviour. When he continues his challenge, rather than say that *stampage* is not in the dictionary, he pretends that he does not know this fact and asks the moderator to put him right, i.e. if the moderator, being so meticulous about words, used *stampage*, then surely it must be in the dictionary: *Can I then understand it's from the dictionary?* In his second challenge to the moderator he hedges his statement pretending that he may be wrong in making the assumption he does, although of course he knows that this is not the case: *You talked about childish faith, and I think you meant childlike faith*. In his effort not to fall out of line, the moderator has no option but to compliment Bill: *Bill, thank you for being such a good listener*. And finally, in order to repair the possible damage done by challenging the moderator, Bill relieves the situation by reverting to laughter and by complimenting him in turn: *I love to hear you David*.

5. Most forms of politic behaviour contain highly routinised sequences whose purpose is to regulate the lines taken in the interaction order and to ensure overall face maintenance. This is the case with greeting sequences, leave-taking sequences (i.e. saying goodbye), request and acceptance sequences, apology sequences, addressing other interactants, etc. These sequences have a

regulatory force in facework, contributing to the reproduction of politic behaviour. Examples from the extract above are *Bill*, *very many thanks*, *bye*, and *bye bye*. However, certain of these expressions may exceed what is necessary, e.g. the use of the address term *sir*, and are interpretable as examples of politeness$_1$. As such they are frequently open to negative, rather than positive evaluation.

We can conclude from this discussion that a wide range of linguistic expressions are available to participants to carry out facework and thereby to reproduce the forms of politic behaviour associated with the social activity. However, this does not automatically mean that those expressions are interpretable by researchers or participants as (im)politeness$_1$. Even if such classifications are made, they are just as open to negative as to positive evaluation. Supportive facework aims at avoiding conflict and aggression and, if possible, at creating comity amongst the participants, but it does not automatically involve (im)politeness.

We now need to look at forms of social interaction which involve politic behaviour that sanctions or neutralises face-threatening or face-damaging acts (point 3 above). In this type of interaction linguistic evidence of supportive facework and attributions of politeness are not generally in evidence.

NON-SUPPORTIVE FACEWORK

There are several forms of socio-communicative verbal interaction in which facework is accomplished without participants resorting to structures which indicate that the facework is supportive. In most of these cases, the interaction takes place in social groups in which either the statuses of the participants are institutionally organised in a rigidly hierarchical manner prior to the interaction,[4] or in which the participants are interacting in a very close-knit social network where each member is intimately familiar with each other member,[5] or in which the interaction is staged in a public arena to generate discussion and possible conflict. Even without supportive facework, politic verbal behaviour that is open to interpretation as linguistic politeness may still be present. Social interaction in the military, for example, requires a whole range of correct forms of address and deferential means of saluting superiors as well as highly regularised forms of demeanour, e.g. correct dress, stance, etc. Even in intimate forms of social interaction such as family discourse, linguistic politeness may be invoked.

Extract (2) is taken from my own corpus of family discourse. Face-threatening certainly occurs in close-knit social networks such as the family, but unless the topic is known to be a highly sensitive one in which one of the participants is likely to be offended, it generally goes unnoticed. This is not the case here, however:

(2)

¹R: w- why then is the Civil Service able to (...) :er: pension you off\ or not pension you off as the
D:
A:
B:

²R: case may be\ at age sixty\ .. :er: retirement age is not reduced\ or is not being reduced from
D:
A:
B:

³R: sixty-five to sixty\ why- why that discrepancy\
D: ... the majority of people who (.) work in the
A:
B:

⁴R:
D: Civil Service\ have done their full ... time\ forty years or thereabouts\ .. and they get a
A: mm
B:

⁵R:
D: half-rate pension\ but you see, I've/???? I've done a????
A:
B: but even on a half-rate pension, David\ you couldn't really live without the

⁶R:
D: very likely not\no\
A:
B: retirement pension\   no\

The topic of the verbal interaction in (2) was the highly delicate question of my stepfather's imminent retirement from the Civil Service at age 60 and the fact that, given his late entry into the Civil Service, his retirement pension would be very low indeed.[6] All the participants know these facts, except for the details, which R (myself) is trying to clarify in his first turn.[7] The interaction is focused on finding possible solutions for what appears at this point in time to be a hopeless situation. Because this is the case, as the interaction progresses, a conflict develops between B and D, which results in efforts on my part at conflict management. The first sign of emergent conflict occurs in B's first turn in score 5, where she intervenes at a higher volume level than D, making the rest of his turn inaudible. She contradicts him with the discourse marker *but*, and her purpose is to force D to consider the pessimistic situation seriously. The intervention thus represents a serious face-threat to D, although nowhere in this extract is there evidence of linguistic structures that could be classified as 'polite'. But this does not mean that the participants are not carrying out facework. Quite clearly they are, and the kind of facework they are negotiating is very delicate indeed.

Socio-communicative verbal interaction which contains conflict and problematic facework can also occur in less close-knit groups, and it may, but need not, involve either supportive facework or linguistic politeness of a formulaic kind. It is frequently performed in institutionalised public settings in which the interaction order is perceived as given prior to the interaction. The two extracts presented in chapter 1, one from the television programme *Advocacy* and the other from the television programme *Panorama*, are excellent examples of the point I wish to make here, namely that face-threatening acts are not always accompanied by linguistic politeness. Such examples of conflict carried out in a public arena frequently contain examples of 'bald on-record face-threats' which are condoned by the kind of facework being negotiated in the interaction (cf. the discussion of a political interview in chapter 9).

The final extract in this section is taken from a television programme on AIDS involving a female moderator (M), two medical experts, Dr Jonathan Weber of St Mary's Hospital, Paddington (JW), and Richard Wells of the Royal School of Nursing (RW), and a representative of the Conservative government, the Junior Health Minister John Patten MP(P). The programme alternates between a live question–answer sequence in front of a studio audience and filmed sequences with, amongst others, sufferers from AIDS. The following extract is taken from the live studio sequence:

(3)

---

[1] Mod: Dr Weber briefly\ **can you explain** exactly what AIDS is\
JW: AIDS stands for the . Acquired
RW:
P:

---

[2] Mod:
JW: Immune Deficiency Syndrome\ and it's a new . viral disease\ . first recognized in 1981\
RW:
P:

3 Mod:
JW: ... and it ... / the virus itself attacks . cells in the blood which control the Immune System\
RW:
P:

4 Mod:
JW: ... and ... infected people can lose their ability . to fight off infection\ and some affected .
RW:
P:

5 Mod: so you don't **actually** die of AIDS\
JW: patients will die of the complications of the disease\   you
RW:
P:

6 Mod:
JW: don't die of AIDS itself\ you die of the complications/ through not having a functioning Immune
RW:
P:

7 Mod:
JW: System\ ... it's :er ...: a disease which is . present in the blood\ . and it's spread by .
RW:
P:

8 Mod: **I'm sure we'll come back to how- how it is spread a little**
JW: blood and . by sexual contact\
RW:
P:

9 Mod: **later on**\ Richard Wells\ now, the Royal College of Nursing is highly respected both in and out
JW:
RW:
P:

10 Mod: of the medical profession\ . and yet you have come up with figures\ . you estimate that one
JW:
RW:
P:

11 Mod: million AIDS victims could . exist in Britain in 1991\ now the DHSS said\ 'now come on\
JW:
RW:
P:

12 Mod: this is ludicrous!'\ . because on those figures\ . by 93\ (.) we would all be dead\ whether
JW:
RW:
P:

13 Mod: we're gay . pink, white . female . or what ´ev`er\ now why do you come out with these
JW:
RW:
P:

¹⁴ Mod: figures\
JW:
RW: **well**\ ... you've answered the question yourself\ because . the government actually
P:

¹⁵ Mod:
JW:
RW: stood up and said something\ . which was :er ... : one of our main thrusts in i- issuing those
P:

¹⁶ Mod:
JW:
RW: figures\ ... :er: we d- didn't estimate that that would happen\ we said that if the disease
P:

¹⁷ Mod:
JW:
RW: carried on doubling . at its present . rate\ . unchecked\ . that's what would happen\
P:

¹⁸ Mod:
JW:
RW: and that's/ is in fact what will happen if it goes on\ nobody believes it will\ but the most
P:

¹⁹ Mod:
JW:
RW: important thing\ ... is that it's actually opened up a proper debate\ ... :er: with the
P:

²⁰ Mod: **are you saying the**
JW:
RW: government\ about what we're going to do about this vile disease\
P:

²¹ Mod: **government is not doing enough** or???\
JW:
RW: I don't think it's done enough in the past\ . nearly enough\
P:

²² Mod:
JW:
RW: *I mean* . we had two years advance warning of this disease\ it began in America in 1979 ... ???
P:

²³ Mod: t- two years advance warning\ are you doing enough\
JW:
RW:
P: we're doing a very great deal\ we didn't go

²⁴ Mod:
JW:
RW:
P: so fast as the . advances in medical science about this disease will actually permit us to go\ we're

²⁵ Mod:
JW:
RW:
P: going very fast indeed\ we've/ what we've also got to do of course\ is not just to back the

²⁶ Mod:
JW:
RW:
P: discoveries which will help us to screen for\ and to test for the presence of AIDS\ ... and also

²⁷ Mod:
JW:
RW:
P: God willing one day have a cure for it\ but what we've also got to do is to work with . volunteer

²⁸ Mod:
JW:
RW:
P: organisations\ and others\ to try and do what we can to . get as much of an attitude of

²⁹ Mod:
JW:
RW:
P: responsibility as we can\ . in those people who are in the most <???> groups\ because prevention

³⁰ Mod: **thank you very much indeed**\ . well in a
JW:
RW:
P: is critically important to stop it growing any faster <???> years\

³¹ Mod: moment we'll be looking at other aspects of AIDS\ ......
JW:
RW:
P:

The only points in extract (3) at which politeness might possibly be
attributed to the participants are the utterances *can you explain exactly
what AIDS is?* in score 1 (the moderator could simply have asked *What
exactly is AIDS?*) and *Are you saying the government isn't doing enough?* in
scores 20 to 21 (the moderator could have asked *So the government isn't
doing enough?*), the two hedges *actually* (in score 5) and *well* (in score 4),
the mitigated refusal to deal at this point in the programme with the
question of how AIDS is spread in scores 8 to 9 (*I'm sure we'll come back
to how it's spread a little later on*), and the formulaic utterance in score
30 (*Thank you very much indeed*), all produced by the moderator.

Instead of saying . . . *can you explain exactly what AIDS is?* in score 1, the
moderator could have put the question in the following way: . . . *what
exactly is AIDS?* Obviously Dr Weber can explain what the disease is,
otherwise he would not have been invited to participate as an expert

on the programme. So to whom is the utterance directed, at Dr Weber, at the studio audience or even at the wider viewing audience? If it is directed at Dr Weber, it certainly would not constitute an offence to invite him onto the programme and then to ask him directly to explain AIDS. The use of the modal verb *can* is not necessary here, and the utterance constitutes linguistic behaviour in excess of the politic behaviour necessary for this form of social interaction. As such, it is open to evaluation as 'polite', even though there is no evidence from the behaviour of the other participants that it has been interpreted this way. It appears to be directed at the maintenance of the face which she has been attributed by the line she is expected to take in the programme. It is facework within the context of how the studio audience and the wider viewing audience expect her to behave. Could this be because she is a woman? Possibly, but it might simply be that the nature of this programme is less conflictual than, for example, the *Advocacy* programme from which an extract was taken in chapter 1.

The situation in score 8, however, borders on the conflictual. Her unwillingness to discuss at this point in the programme how AIDS is spread constitutes a face-threat to Dr Weber. To allow him to give an explanation would run counter to her conception of how the programme should progress. The facework here is thus rather more delicate. The question in scores 20 to 21 is rather different. She could simply accuse RW of saying that the government are not doing enough. By putting the accusation as a question (*Are you saying the government is not doing enough?*) she offers RW the option of disputing that this is in fact what he is saying, without appearing to share this opinion herself. She allows another participant to make the critical comment for her.

On the other hand, she intervenes at the end of RW's turn to pass the question of whether the government is doing enough to the Junior Health Minister. Neither her intervention nor her question can in any way be seen as examples of politeness, but they might be interpretable by the participants as impoliteness. In score 30 the moderator's formulaic utterance *Thank you very much indeed* is once again neutralised by her intervening in P's turn before he has quite finished what he was saying.

Extract (3) thus contains a great deal of facework, but because it is dealing with a topic of current interest, it is also liable to generate potential conflict. From this point of view the linguistic expressions used appear to be directed at the moderator's own public image and the image of the programme itself rather than at any of the co-participants. If any of the moderator's linguistic expressions are evaluated as realisations of politeness, they must ultimately be evaluated in the light of these facts.

In social interaction interactants are always involved in some form of facework, but the politic behaviour of many social interaction types does not demand that facework is directed at the maintenance of the faces assigned to the participants for the duration of the interaction. So it is not correct to say that facework *is* politeness. The most we can say is that any utterances classified as linguistic (im)politeness₁ may be used in carrying out facework.

In addition, some of the language used in performing supportive facework is not, on the surface at least, what would automatically be classified as 'polite'. Taken out of context, an utterance such as *I know how fastidious or meticulous you are about the use of words*, used by Bill Bell in extract (1) to preface a face-threat, is not inherently polite. But within the context of what he is about to say, it may be interpretable in this way.

On the other hand, an utterance like *I love to hear you, David*, even taken out of its proper context, would generally be interpreted as a compliment. Compliments tend to be classified as 'polite' behaviour, but this does not automatically imply that all compliments will therefore be evaluated as positive, supportive behaviour. Compliments are not 'inherently' polite, and I shall argue in chapter 7 that no linguistic expressions are inherently polite.

In addition, there are formulaic and semi-formulaic utterances which are likely to be classified as 'polite' but which, by being expressed explicitly as 'polite' utterances, can be used to enhance rather than soften a face-threat. Imagine the fictive situation of someone standing on your foot in a packed rush-hour underground train. If you were to say:

(4)   Excuse me. Would you mind not standing on my foot?

in which one formulaic expression is used – *Excuse me* – and one semi-formulaic expression –*Would you mind not Ving X* – the addressee would probably evaluate your politeness as potentially aggressive behaviour, since it is meant, and would be understood, as irony. You would, after all, be within your rights to use a bald, on-record face threat as in (5):

(5)   Hey. Get off my foot!

From this chapter it should have become apparent that no linguistic structures can be classified as inherently polite. In chapter 7, I will tackle this point in more detail. In doing so I will look more closely at linguistic structures that have been dealt with in the literature as realising politeness. I shall argue that, although the structures themselves carry out facework, they are not inherently polite. This raises the major question of how politeness$_1$ is best understood and whether a model of politeness$_1$, rather than politeness$_2$, can be formulated without making the connection between politeness and face which most researchers rigidly adhere to at present. Chapter 6 will make the attempt to break out of the 'politeness$_2$ = facework' deadlock. It draws heavily on Werkhofer's comparison of politeness with money (cf. chapter 4) and on two theories of social structure, Bourdieu's theory of practice and Watts's theory of socio-communicative verbal interaction as the production and reproduction of emergent networks.

I shall argue that the politic behaviour 'expected' of participants in the social activity in which they are involved needs to be differentiated from (im)politeness$_1$. What is 'polite' or 'impolite' language can only be assessed as such by analysing the context of real social practice. (Im)politeness$_1$, in other words, *emerges* contextually from instances of socio-communicative verbal interaction and is salient linguistic behaviour *beyond* the structures used in facework and politic behaviour. To classify as linguistic politeness all those structures which are used in positive and negative facework is to empty the terms 'polite' and 'impolite' of the meanings we attribute to these, and similar, lexemes in social practice and to deny that there is a discursive struggle over their use.

6 A social model of politeness

POLITENESS AND MONEY

The purpose of this chapter is to work towards an alternative model of politeness that does not have as its aim the explanation of how native speakers produce polite language. In other words, the model that I shall outline here does not aim at being a production model of linguistic politeness, as Brown and Levinson's model has frequently been understood. Nor does it aim to provide a blueprint for interpreting certain linguistic expressions, but not others, as realisations of politeness. Both the explanatory and the descriptive approaches to polite verbal behaviour make the same mistake in abstracting away from real data and creating a concept of politeness for which they claim universal validity, i.e. politeness$_2$. The claim is then made that those approaches are equipped to predict where instances of verbal politeness should occur in interaction. Politeness$_2$ in all the models discussed in chapters 3 and 4 has thus become a social given, a social 'fact'. It is assumed that politeness is present in all human societies, but all too often that which the theory predicts as polite behaviour is not classified as such by lay members.

Equating politeness$_2$ with strategies for mitigating face-threats has been the most feasible step in creating this particular social 'fact' and, despite all the criticism of Brown and Levinson's model (see chapter 4), it has led to the equation of Politeness Theory with Face Theory. Chapter 5 has shown that the equation is not always valid. So we now need to ask not only what is wrong with postulating a set of social facts that we then call 'politeness', but also whether it is feasible to build an entirely different kind of model centred on the discursive struggle over (im)politeness$_1$.

We first need to assess different approaches to the terms 'society' and 'culture' and see whether another approach might be more successful. The model I wish to develop does not claim *that* a particular utterance is a realisation of polite behaviour nor to explain *why*. It tries to offer ways of recognising *when* a linguistic utterance *might* be open to interpretation by interlocutors as '(im)polite'. It does not evaluate politeness in terms of social harmony, mutual consideration for others, comity, etc. Instead, it aims to provide the means of assessing how lay participants in ongoing verbal interaction assess social behaviour that they have classified as (im)polite utterances as positive or negative. It does not, in other words, try to define politeness as a term in a model of society, but it allows us to see how social members themselves define the term. This entails a return to a serious consideration of (im)politeness₁, or whatever terms are used in whatever linguistic communities we are looking at.

In order to do this, I shall use Bourdieu's theory of practice and my own theory of emergent networks, in which the notions of *capital* and *symbolic resource* are linked to ways of understanding politic behaviour. It is also at this point that we can reintroduce Werkhofer's novel idea of comparing linguistic politeness with money.[1]

Werkhofer argues for a radically new approach to linguistic politeness which sees it – like money – as a mediating force between the individual and courses of action that appear to be sanctioned by social structures. Human beings are social animals, and the ways in which we see ourselves and the world are constructed through social interaction with others. Ongoing interaction constitutes *social practice*, but that practice is determined by previous experiences of similar practice and by objectified social structures. Just as the individual only exists by virtue of her/his own specific history, so too does society only 'exist' by virtue of the history of previous social interaction, which lends those forms of behaviour the impression of objective validity. Throughout the social history of an invidual s/he constructs the idea of an objectified 'society' with objectified social structures that sanction the ways in which s/he behaves in ongoing interaction. In this sense, types of social interaction are sanctioned not by ourselves as individuals but by society as a whole. Politeness, like money, is one of the means by which we are able to adapt our behaviour to that which is appropriate to the social interaction type in which we are involved. The notion of 'appropriateness', or 'expectability', is an important notion to be considered later.

The key to understanding the nature of politeness is to consider the ways in which the individual maximises its utility as a symbolic resource. The five points in Werkhofer's analogy of politeness with money bear repeating here:

(i) 'Politeness, like money, is a socially constituted medium.'

(ii) Politeness, like money, is 'a symbolic medium in the sense that its functions originally derive from an association to something else, namely to values'.

(iii) Politeness, like money, is 'historically constituted and reconstituted; its functions and the values it is associated with are essentially changeable ones'.

(iv) 'During its history, the functions of politeness turn into a power of the medium in the sense that it may, rather than being only a means to the ends of an individual user, itself motivate and structure courses of action.'

(v) The chances of the user being able 'to master the medium completely . . . will be diminished'. (Werkhofer 1992: 190)[2]

If politeness, like money, is a socially constituted medium, it must form part of the linguistic resources that determine the discourse practices of all social interaction types. As a symbolic medium, like money, it must derive its functions from an association with something else, so that we need to investigate the nature of its symbolism and the values from which it is derived. If, like money, politeness is also historically constituted, then the values it represents and the functions it plays in discursive practices will be in a continual state of flux and change. There will, in other words, always be a struggle over the values of politeness. Werkhofer suggests that 'the functions of politeness turn into a power of the medium in the sense that it may, rather than being only a means to the ends of an individual user, itself motivate and structure courses of action' (1992: 190). If this is so, then there will be many cases in which the use of politeness will be a central factor in the social construction and reproduction not only of discourse practices but also of social institutions themselves. This relates directly to the notion of politic behaviour.

Let us now focus our attention on this term, which was defined in chapter 1 as follows:

- *Politic behaviour*: that behaviour, linguistic and non-linguistic, which the participants construct as being appropriate to the ongoing social interaction.

Participants enter verbal interaction in a specific social situation with a knowledge gained from previous experiences about what forms of social behaviour are appropriate and inappropriate to that type of situation. Their knowledge is constructed through their own personal history and the way it has been linked in the past with objectified social structures. Bourdieu calls the set of dispositions to behave appropriately the *habitus*, a term which we will deal with in more detail in the following sections of this chapter. During the ongoing interaction, however, individual members not only reproduce the appropriate behaviour through the habitus but they may even change and reconstruct what is appropriate. So politic behaviour is behaviour which is consistent with the dispositions of the habitus in accordance with the social features of the situational context.

To illustrate my argument I shall consider in some detail the opening turns from an interaction in another open-line phone-in programme. The moderator begins as follows:

(1)

```
¹H:   welcome Mrs George\
 G:                    hello Mr ˈHatch
```

The moderator, Dick Hatch, has spent quite a lot of time at the beginning of the programme 'priming the pump', i.e. giving potential callers ideas about what they might like to discuss. Finally, a Mrs George is put through to the moderator. Part of the politic behaviour in a radio phone-in programme is that the moderator greets the caller, and the caller returns the greeting. After listening to phone-in programmes on her local radio we can reasonably assume Mrs George will have acquired the knowledge that this sequence is part of the habitus of both the moderator and the caller, and she acts accordingly. The address terms *Mrs George* and *Mr Hatch* can also be considered as part of the required politic behaviour, as are the formulaic utterances *welcome* and *hello*.

The greeting formula *welcome*, however, is a little too effusive, and the rising intonation at the end of Mrs George's turn is evidence of some insecurity on her part. It's not that *welcome* is not a perfectly adequate greeting formula. Clearly it is, but it gives a little more to Mrs George than she was expecting. The address terms and Mrs George's greeting formula are part of the politic behaviour of the social situation. So, too, is Hatch's greeting formula, but *because* it is a little more than merely politic, it is also potentially open to a polite interpretation. Could it be that Mrs George's momentary insecurity is a sign that she recognises this?

The fact that Hatch has used *welcome*, rather than *hello*, or *good afternoon*, is a clue to what happens next:

(2)

²H:	how do you do madam\ don't be formal\ Dick's the name\
G:	

Hatch carries out a move expected of him in saying *how do you do*, but he adds the highly formal address term *madam*. He then proceeds to subvert this level of formality and the politic verbal behaviour expected of him in the greeting sequence by encouraging the caller not to be formal, but to call him by his nickname *Dick*.

The crass difference in formality between *madam* and *Dick* demands some form of interpretation. How will Mrs George react? Hatch has, after all, not threatened her face. On the contrary, he is demeaning himself whilst continuing to pay deference to her and thereby putting her in a position in which she has to infer relevance from what he has said. The most relevant inference she can make is <Hatch is teasing me>. If she derives this inference, she is free to interpret the tease as a face-threat. On the other hand, part of the line Hatch can be expected to take, i.e. part of the politic behaviour of an open-line phone-in programme, is to tease a caller. The face attributed to him allows him to create humour and to provide entertainment for the audience listening in.

Hatch appears to be reconstructing the politic behaviour appropriate to this particular call, and the success of the strategy will depend entirely on Mrs George's next turn:

(3)

³H:	oh\ right\ <@well you c- you call me Richard@>\
G:	yes\ I know\ and I prefer Richard\ <@I think when you've got a nice name like
⁴H:	
G:	Richard\ why they call you Dick I'll never know\

She pretends that she has not registered the tease and that Hatch seriously intended to suggest that she did not know his first name. She acknowledges the fact that she does know this and then proceeds to tease him in return by saying that she prefers the name *Richard*. Mrs George appears to have adapted herself rather quickly to the change in politic behaviour initiated by the moderator.

Hatch's response displays a certain amount of insecurity. He signals uptake of Mrs George's point with the discourse marker *oh* and agrees with her (*right*). The insecurity evidenced by the slight stuttering (*well you c- you call* . . .) shows that he has realised that the joke is on him. This is indicated by their laughter. The slight stuttering during the production of his utterance might also have been caused by Mrs George's next turn in which she interrupts what he is saying to stress her advantage (*I think when you've got a nice name like Richard, why they call you Dick I'll never know*).

Participants in verbal interaction are thus quite capable of temporarily changing the nature of the politic behaviour and adapting their habitus in accordance with the exigencies of the ongoing interaction. What is now essential is to explore the relationship between the habitus and politic behaviour.

BOURDIEU'S 'THEORY OF PRACTICE'

Over the years Bourdieu has developed a processual way of looking at social structure in which he denies the dichotomy between objective and subjective approaches to the study of society. The objective approach to social structure is often attributed to the work of Talcott Parsons (see Eelen 2001), and the Parsonian perspective of society and culture views those phenomena from the top down rather than from the bottom up. Society is conceptualised as consisting of a hierarchical structure of 'behavioral control' which Parsons calls a 'cybernetic hierarchy' (Parsons 1966: 9, 44, in Eelen 2001: 189). At the top of the hierarchy is the cultural system which controls the social system and thereby also personality systems in the individual and behavioural systems in social groups. In other words, the structure of social systems is under the control of cultural values, myths, beliefs, etc. and the behaviour of the individual or of the social group is under the control of the social structures. The mechanisms of cybernetic control in the hierarchy are not only top-down, but also bottom-up, although bottom-up control is conditional on the prior existence of the social and the cultural systems. Eelen (2001: 189) sums up the 'objective' approach of Parsonian sociology as follows:

> In combination with the distinctive nature of each system, this leads to a view where social reality is not only a reality *sui generis*, independent of the individual level (Parsons 1971: 7), but also takes precedence over the individual – because the latter occupies a lower position.

The Parsonian view of society thus consists of 'regularised' constraints on 'normal' or 'acceptable' social behaviour and sets of institutions (first and foremost of these being the state). These determine the structuring of social groups and the roles which individuals are 'expected' to play in those groups. According to Parsons, society thus regulates individual instances of social interaction. Social structure is seen as consisting of a set of 'givens' which need to be discovered empirically before they can be manipulated in different ways. The individual human being is thus reduced to the status of a pawn in the hierarchical chess game of 'society'.

The subjective approach to social structure, on the other hand, takes society to be part of the natural world, which can be neither acted upon nor changed by individuals. In a subjective view of society individuals see themselves as powerless to reflect upon the conditions of their own existence. Although subjective and objective approaches to social structure start their theorising from different ends of the spectrum of objectivity, both approaches reify the social world as a 'given', functionalist–structuralist sociology seeing it as a culturally determined, institutionalised entity and existentialist–phenomenological and ethnomethodological sociology seeing it as a natural entity.[3]

Bourdieu's solution is to synthesise the objective and subjective approaches by proposing a third option, which he calls the 'theory of practice':

> The theory of practice as practice insists, contrary to positivist materialism, that the objects of knowledge are constructed, not passively recorded, and, contrary to intellectual idealism, that the principle of this construction is the system of structured, structuring dispositions, the habitus, which is constituted in practice and is always oriented towards practical functions. (Bourdieu 1990: 52)

Practice is observable in instances of ongoing social interaction amongst individuals, which most often involves language, but it is important to note that any instance of ongoing social interaction is what Bourdieu calls 'the site of the dialectic of the *modus operatum* and the *modus operandi*' (1990: 53). The *modus operatum* consists of objectified structures, products, modes of behaviour which individuals have gained through previous interaction (not always involving themselves). So objectified social structures have been incorporated through prior interaction and determine the structure of ongoing practice. They are part of the 'history' of an individual, thus making historicity a crucial concept in Bourdieu's work as it helps to shape the process of structuring of social interaction (which Bourdieu calls the *modus operandi*). The logic of practice controls the determination of ongoing interaction subconsciously by means of continual improvisation, rather like the anticipation of teammates' next moves in a game of football, baseball or ice-hockey on the basis of a 'feel for the game'.

The central concept in Bourdieu's theory of practice is the *habitus*, and it is this term that is most closely related to the concept of politic behaviour outlined in the previous section. The *habitus*, in Latin 'a state of being', 'a demeanour, manner or bearing', or the 'style of dress or toilet',[4] is the set of dispositions to act in certain ways, which generates cognitive and bodily practices in the individual. The set of dispositions is acquired through socialisation. In typical Bourdieuan fashion there are two aspects to the habitus just as there are to the theory of practice in general. The first is that the habitus shapes the ways in which the individual internalises objectivised social structures in order to use them in dealing with ongoing interaction. In other words, the habitus actually constructs out of those objectivised structures forms of politic behaviour. So the product of both collective and individualised history gives the individual in ongoing social interaction the 'feel for the game'. The other aspect of the habitus is that, in instances of ongoing interaction, it generates practices and actions. The habitus is therefore responsible for both the reproduction and the change of social structure as we saw from the example taken from the beginning of the interaction between the moderator and a caller in a radio phone-in programme in the previous section.

Social practice is carried out within *social fields*, and individuals and groups are defined by their relative positions in them. Fields are thus arbitrary social organisations of space and time, and they are the sites of constant struggles over capital. Capital can thus be seen as an *incorporation* of resources, which become part of the individual's habitus. They can be loosely grouped into material, cultural or social 'marketplaces', in which three kinds of capital are at stake, material capital, cultural capital and social capital. Material capital consists of money, property, goods, stocks, profit, etc., and the fields in which material marketplaces will be found include all social activity in which goods are exchanged for other goods (including, of course, money). Cultural capital consists of educational qualifications, skills, cultural acquisitions, knowledge, etc. Hence a field in a cultural marketplace will be one in which this cultural capital can be acquired, e.g. its locus could be a school, a university, a training centre, a sports club, etc. Social capital consists of the network of relationships and the quality of those relationships which an individual has. Hence social marketplaces will include fields that are located in the family, friendship groups, political organisations, clubs of different kinds, etc. However, marketplaces are never uniquely material, cultural or social. In a field in which individuals are largely concerned with material capital, e.g. the workplace, cultural capital in the form of qualifications, skills, abilities, etc. are as much a fundamental aspect of the proper functioning of that field as are social relationships, i.e. social networks, among the employees.

Bourdieu represents his model with the following equation:

$$[(\text{habitus})(\text{capital})] + \text{field} = \text{practice}$$

Social practice is thus equivalent to the ways in which the product of the subjective structures internalised by the individual as her/his habitus multiplied by the capital the individual has gained in the marketplace is combined with the objectified social structures of the field. Fundamental to all human social action is language, which in itself is a form of cultural capital, but because language is at the core of social action, regardless of what field and in what marketplace interaction takes place, it constitutes a social resource in all those marketplaces (Watts 1991). We are therefore justified in conceptualising all situated linguistic utterances as linguistic practice and defining the latter with a revised version of the equation:

$$[(\text{linguistic habitus})(\text{linguistic capital})] + \text{linguistic marketplace}$$
$$= \text{linguistic practice}^5$$

Linguistic practice is equivalent to the ways in which the linguistic dispositions internalised by the individual as her/his linguistic habitus multiplied by the linguistic capital the individual has gained in the marketplace is combined with the objectified linguistic structures of the field.

The final two terms which are necessary to my discussion of Bourdieu's theory of practice are *doxa* (and the related terms *orthodoxy* and *heterodoxy*) and *symbolic power*. The doxa of a field is the 'undisputed, pre-reflexive, naïve, native compliance with the fundamental presuppositions of the field' (Bourdieu 1990: 68). It is, in other words, the social order of the field in question and is specific to that field. A challenge to the structure of the field in which the habitus tries to break with the doxic experience constitutes *heterodoxy*, i.e. it is subversive behaviour. The attempt to restore the old order, to 'restore the silence of the doxa' (Bourdieu 1991: 131), is termed *orthodoxy*. Those with the greatest amount of capital in the field (i.e. those with power) can also use heterodoxy to change the social order of the field deliberately, and in doing so they exercise what Bourdieu calls symbolic violence. We might therefore argue that, in Bourdieuan terms the moderator's restructuring of the politic behaviour of an open-line phone-in programme discussed in the previous section was an instance of mild 'symbolic violence'.

Bourdieu and Passeron (1990: 4) define symbolic power as 'every power which manages to impose meanings and to impose them as legitimate by concealing the power relations which are the basis of its force'. It can, in other words, only be effective either if it successfully manages to conceal its true nature through the silent orthodoxy of the doxa or by exercising symbolic violence. At this point Werkhofer's comparison of politeness with money becomes useful.

LINGUISTIC RESOURCES AS A FORM OF CAPITAL

In Werkhofer's comparison of politeness with money the focus must be on four central terms, *value, exchange, currency* and *conversion*. The exchange of goods between individuals or groups of individuals has always been predicated on roughly equivalent values placed by each individual or each group on the goods received and given. A surrogate good, i.e. money, can thus be assumed to 'represent' symbolically the value of one part of the exchange, but it has the advantage of allowing the possessor to tender it in exchange for goods that might represent a higher value for the buyer.[6] The surrogate good, money or, in our case, linguistic politeness, can be called *currency*, and one form of currency can be converted into another in a different market.

The institutionalised setting in which exchanges can be made and currency can be converted is equivalent to the Bourdieuan *marketplace*, in which the respective values are negotiated by the participants in the exchange. Some goods will have a relatively low value in the market while the value of others will be relatively high, and the values that are symbolically placed on those goods (including money) can fluctuate considerably over time.

As we saw in the previous section forms of material, cultural and social capital are produced and exchanged in three interlocking kinds of 'marketplace', but precisely because of the interlocking nature of the marketplaces symbolic currency acquired in one marketplace may easily be converted into other forms of currency in other markets. Bourdieu's discussion of language allows the presence of a fourth kind of capital, *linguistic capital*, which functions in all three marketplaces. To acquire forms of capital, different kinds of resource are necessary, and with reference to linguistic capital – whichever market we are considering – the resource is *language*. Language resources include control over language varieties (e.g. dialect, sociolect, regional standard, national standard, etc.) and/or skilled use in a variety of communicative media (e.g. various forms of written media such as handwriting, typewriting, writing by computer, etc., or forms of oral media such as face-to-face interaction, telephonic communication, etc.). As such, they allow the possessor of those resources to function in a range of communicative genres and discourse activity types, and they can be used as capital to bargain for 'goods' in other markets. Acquiring the habitus to function optimally in a social field and to manipulate forms of capital in different marketplaces entails the development of an understanding of politic behaviour, including linguistic behaviour, appropriate to an ongoing social interaction in which the individual is involved. Practice thus entails linguistic practice.

The argument put forward in this book is that what has often been thought of as politeness$_2$ is in effect the deployment of the linguistic structures of politic behaviour in ongoing social practice. Linguistic (im)politeness, on the other hand, is the *potentiality* of a linguistic structure for use and interpretation by individuals as a linguistic resource absent from or in excess of the linguistic structures of politic behaviour. In other words, utterances are open to characterisation and evaluation as linguistic (im)politeness$_1$, which does not imply, of course, that they are automatically *realisations* of linguistic (im)politeness$_1$. To use Werkhofer's terminology, politeness$_1$ is *payment*, but it is payment *in excess of* what is ordinarily required by the politic behaviour of the social interaction. The central role played by human language in social interaction means that conversion from one form of currency into another must take place discursively, and this enhances the significance of linguistic capital in the relevant market. Linguistic capital includes the ability to use linguistic politeness as a form of extra 'linguistic payment'.[7]

What role does politeness play in this model? Bearing in mind Werkhofer's comparison of linguistic politeness with money, if the symbolic value of money is operative in the economic market, then the symbolic value of linguistic politeness must be operative in the 'linguistic' market, and since linguistic capital is involved in cultural, social and economic markets, the linguistic market must overlap with all of these. As we know, politeness is not restricted to forms of language usage. Its value is not only realisable in linguistic capital but it can also be converted into different forms of cultural capital, e.g. acquired competences, behavioural skills, etc. As we have seen, Bourdieu's theory of practice can be put to use in accounting for linguistic (im)politeness as part of that theory because we can justify Werkhofer's comparison of linguistic politeness with money. The next section will illustrate this.

THE CONCEPT OF 'EMERGENT NETWORK'

At the beginning of the 1990s I was engaged in developing an extension of social network theory that would allow us to assess how social networks actually emerge in ongoing social interaction (Watts 1991, 1992, 1994, 1997a). Although I was not totally aware of this at the time, the relationship that I proposed between what I called the *latent network* and the *emergent network* corresponds quite neatly to the distinction Bourdieu makes between the *modus operatum* and the *modus operandi* (see above). Just as the *modus operatum* for Bourdieu consists of 'the objectified products and the incorporated products of historical practice' and the *modus operandi* the reproduction and reconstruction of those products in ongoing social practice, so too is the system of latent networks in which an individual is situated a set of objectified social structures produced by 'historical practice' and the emergent network is a 'dynamic process' in which 'participants also form a network for the duration of the interaction' (Watts 1991: 9, 155). The relationship between latent and emergent networks is historical, and emergent networks can only develop in social practice, i.e. in ongoing social interaction, on the basis of previously determined latent networks. So part of the habitus that an individual needs to develop in order to function in a social field is the way in which s/he has created latent network links and puts these to use in recreating old links and creating new ones.

All verbal interaction in whatever medium and however situated spatio-temporally is dialogic, i.e. social and communicative in the sense that the participants share something together. In verbal interaction speakers and addressees work together to create some form of common understanding among themselves, even if it is the common understanding that they do not and can never agree. So, to borrow a term from Relevance Theory (Sperber and Wilson 1995), a verbal utterance is an ostensive, informative act. The utterer is giving something to the addressee on the justified assumption that the addressee will give something back either in the way of a linguistic utterance or in some other way, even in a situation of conflict (see chapter 9), thus creating and sharing a common understanding. Every verbal interaction is therefore an exchange of utterances, which the interactants can assume to be in some sense meaningful. As I shall argue more extensively in chapter 7, every utterance either expresses at least one semantic proposition or directs attention to some semantic proposition(s) or, alternatively, does both these things at the same time.

At this point we can bring in the comparison with money by suggesting that each utterance has a certain value for both (or all) interactants, although the values may not be the same for each of them. The three 'sentence moods' *assertive, interrogative* and *imperative* can be interpreted, very broadly of course, as follows:

(i) Assertives *give* a value and can therefore expect the *payment* of some other equivalent value.
(ii) Interrogatives *request* a value but cannot automatically expect the payment of that value. If the value is given, however, some form of *return payment* can be expected by the giver.
(iii) Imperatives *request* a value, which may or may not be in the form of a linguistic utterance, and generally *do* expect the payment of that value.

So in any utterance an interactant gives or requests as many values as the propositions contained in that utterance. Since giving something of value is equivalent to carrying out an action and always implies exchange, speaking is always *inter*action.

The exchange of objects between givers and receivers creates social links between them and binds them in networks of reciprocal responsibilities. By the same token, the exchange of abstract values in the form of utterances also creates social networks, in which the links between the members of the network also take on values. Looked at in this way, socio-communicative verbal interaction entails the establishment, reestablishment and reproduction of social links between the interactants, which emerge during the interaction. It is these networks of social links set up during ongoing verbal interaction that I wish to call *emergent networks*. As participants in verbal interaction we can directly experience the construction of emergent networks and can effect the ways in which they are constructed. As researchers we can observe how the networks have emerged in social interaction and relate them to the social networks that have already been constructed as part of the *modus operatum*, i.e. of the objectified structures and modes of behaviour which individuals have gained through previous interaction. Social networks as objectified structures can be called *latent networks*, precisely because they are not 'real', but rather 'imagined' networks which may (or may not) influence the construction of emergent networks (see Watts 1991).

Every link in a social network, whether emergent or latent, carries at least one value (i.e. it is at least *uniplex*) but may have more than one value (i.e. it is possibly *multiplex*) (see Milroy 1980; Watts 1991). In addition, the link may be forged with one participant (i.e. it is *unidirectional*) and may be taken up by that participant (i.e. it is *ambidirectional*), or it may be directed at more than one participant (i.e. it is *multidirectional*). In the case of emergent social networks, it's the *process* of network formation which is the focus of attention for participants, and after an emergent network has been completed, it may or may not significantly effect already existent latent networks. One problem that still needs to be solved in the theory of emergent networks is when an emergent network can be said to have terminated, i.e. what is its duration, but as that question has little or no effect on my argument here, I shall leave it on one side for the moment.

At this point I want to introduce the notion of *equilibrium*, which Eelen (2001) has criticised as being a quasi-objective notion in his critique of politeness theories. Part of the habitus of an individual will be knowledge of the latent networks in which s/he functions (or could potentially function). The mode of functioning in those networks is equivalent to the polite behaviour characterising an interaction in a specific social field whenever the latent network is reactivated in new emergent networks. Clearly, an individual's habitus is built on the basis of the reciprocal construction of politic behaviour in all members of the network. I shall argue that there is always a tendency to construct the politic behaviour of social interaction in *latent* networks as being in a state of *equilibrium*.

The notion of equilibrium is, of course, an idealised state that it is necessary for an individual to adopt as part of her/his habitus. So preexisting social relationships *imply* an equilibrium of those relationships which can be expected to be reproduced in emergent networks. However, members may change the structure and content of the network links during an emergent network and thus disturb the equilibrium. In doing so, they are engaged in reconstructing the politic behaviour of the interaction, as we saw in the short extract from the radio phone-in programme presented in the first section of this chapter.

Changing the value and/or structure of network links in an emergent network is thus equivalent to the exercise of power by a member of the network and is what Bourdieu meant by the term 'symbolic violence'. Participants in verbal interaction will always be involved in a struggle over the right to exercise power over others. How do Bourdieu's theory of practice and Watts's theory of the emergent network help us to unravel the terms *politic behaviour, (im)politeness* and *facework*? This will be the topic of the following section, in which I shall illustrate the argument with a closer look at the data extract between Mrs George and Dick Hatch, the moderator of the Radio Manchester phone-in programme.

POLITIC BEHAVIOUR, FACEWORK AND (IM)POLITENESS

Establishing an equilibrium is *always* carried out in ongoing social practice and it *always* entails the construction and reproduction of emergent networks. It involves the struggle to exercise power in socio-communicative verbal interaction. It entails attempts at symbolic violence by individual participants which are designed to acquire power, however fleetingly. It is essentially what Ng and Bradac (1993) have called *power-to*. In highly institutionalised forms of social interaction (e.g. at a university lecture, in a committee meeting, buying a ticket at a coach station, etc.) part of the objectified structures that an individual has internalised as her/his habitus is that certain participants also have power over others, i.e. they have potential *power-over*, which will determine the politic behaviour characterising the social interaction, and power-over generally includes power-to. In such situations routinised forms of language will form part of the politic behaviour of the social interaction reciprocally shared by the participants, e.g. forms of deferential language such as terms of address, greetings and leave-taking. Such routinised forms of linguistic expression, I shall argue, are *not* instantiations of linguistic politeness. They form part of the politic behaviour expected in the social situation.

Let's see how this works by taking another look at the data extract presented in the first section enriched with the final three turns which, I suggest, make up the first emergent network in the interaction between Hatch and Mrs George:

(4)

¹H: welcome Mrs George\	how do you do madam\ don't be formal\ Dick's the name\
G:	hello Mr 'Hatch
²H:	oh\ right\ <@well you c- you call me 'Richard'@>
G: yes\ I know\ and I prefer Richard\	<@@@> I think when you've got a nice
³H:	well\ d'you know\ privately I entirely
G: name like Richard\ why they call you Dick I'll never know\	
⁴H: agree with you\ but when you've been Dick as long as I have because your family started it\	
G:	
⁵H: there's no point in arguing really\	however\ you carry on\
G:	no\ quite\

The value of Hatch's first utterance can be encapsulated in the formula <I bid you welcome to the programme> + <I refer this welcome to you, Mrs George>. Hatch sets up the first link in the emergent network.

The addressee, Mrs George, must now repay the speaker in kind, so turn 2 has the values <I hereby greet you> + <I refer this greeting to you, Mr Hatch>. *Welcome*, however, is more than is required by the politic behaviour of an open-line phone-in programme on local radio, whereas *Mrs George, hello* and *Mr Hatch* are within the bounds of what is politic. If the utterance pays attention to the addressee's face, the politic behaviour entails supportive facework.

What about the situation we are faced with here? Hatch does not appear to damage Mrs George's face with the expression *welcome*, but he does unsettle her for a brief instant, as is evident from her rising intonation on the term of address *Mr Hatch*. So at this early point in the emergent network Mrs George might interpret Hatch as attempting to upset the equilibrium that she has constructed as part of her habitus for performing in this type of social interaction. Hatch's utterance is open to interpretation as an attempt to acquire power to himself although it is not negative facework nor is it far from the politic behaviour that might be expected.

This is intensified in turn 3 (score 1), in which Hatch directs three utterances at Mrs George, the first of which has the following values <I hereby enquire after your well-being> + <I refer this enquiry to you madam>, the second of which contradicts the formal expression *madam* and has the following value: <I require the following value from you: that you are not formal, and I expect payment with that value>, and the third has the value <I hereby state that my name is Dick>. The second stage in the emergent network is thus an attempt by Hatch to amass power for himself. The hitch in the argument resides in the term of address *madam*, which is more than is required of an address term in the politic behaviour of a phone-in programme and clearly contradicts the value he expects from her, i.e. that she should give up the level of formality in addressing him.

At this point the following two questions arise:

1. Are the expressions *welcome* and *madam* polite, since they exceed what is expected at the level of politic behaviour?
2. Do we have a case of face-threat mitigation here by which we can explain the 'politeness' of those expressions?

Taking the second question first, the discussion of face in chapter 5, in which I opted for Goffman's definition, suggests very strongly that face-threatening is *not* being carried out here. Hatch is behaving absolutely in accordance with the lines expected of him, one of which is that the moderator of an open-line phone-in programme may be expected to tease a caller from time to time. And this is exactly how Mrs George takes it. The first question is put wrongly: I am not proposing that linguistic expressions *are* polite, but only that they are *open* to interpretation in this way. If Mrs George has interpreted Hatch's two expressions *welcome* and *madam* as 'polite', she will know that the 'politeness' is meant ironically.

However, this does not yet explain how the emergent network develops. In turn 4 (score 2) Mrs George does the following:

- Her first utterance is a response to Hatch's whole turn, since responding to the utterance *Dick's the name* only requires her to render the value <I know that Dick is your name>. The value of *yes* could be <I acknowledge your turn as a leg-pull>.
- Her second utterance has been dealt with above.
- Her third utterance gives the following value to Hatch <I prefer the name Richard>.

In doing this, Mrs George has effectively countered the advantage in terms of power-to which Hatch has gained in his first two turns by accepting the request to be informal but rejecting the nickname *Dick* and preferring the full name *Richard*. What we see being enacted here is relational work in which Mrs George has successfully adjusted to the slight alteration in politic behaviour introduced by Hatch's tease.

The emergent network is continued by Hatch responding to Mrs George's proposition in turn 4 (score 2), which the politic behaviour of the interaction type demands. The values of his first two utterances are *oh* <I have registered the point you have just made> + *right* <I accept that point>. The third utterance gives Mrs George the following values: *well* <I acquiesce in the point you have made> + <I hereby accept that you will call me 'Richard'>. What Hatch is acquiescing to here is that Mrs George is adept enough to counter his attempt to exercise power by immediately doing the same. The fact that he uses three non-propositional discourse markers and stammers a little in saying what he has to say is evidence of a certain amount of insecurity on his part. *Well* is often felt in the politeness literature to be a polite linguistic structure since it has been interpreted as minimising the force of face-threatening (Watts 1987, 1989b; Lakoff 1973b). But that is clearly not the force of *well* in the interaction under discussion. The laughter engaged in by both participants at this point in the emergent network shows that they have eliminated the cause of possible tension between them, i.e. that they have come to an understanding that the politic behaviour of this interaction type can include teasing.

What, then, are we to make of turn 6 (scores 2–3) in which Mrs George intervenes in Hatch's unfinished utterance? Her utterance gives Hatch the following values <you have a nice name like 'Richard'> + <I do not know why people call you 'Dick'> + <that is my opinion>

(*I think*). As we shall see in the next chapter, expressions like *I think* can either be understood as *referential*, hence propositional, indicating that the embedded clause is indeed what the speaker believes, or as a *hedge*, i.e. as a way of declining responsibility for the truth value of the proposition embedded (see Holmes 1995). The canonical interpretation of expressions such as *I think*, *I believe*, etc. in the politeness literature when they are used as hedges is that they are instantiations of linguistic politeness. The point I have made during this chapter is that they may be open to interpretation in this way, but they are not inherently 'polite'. In any case, Mrs George's use of *I think* in turn 6 is referential. Her utterance is therefore a possible face threat to Hatch in that she states it as her opinion that those who call Hatch 'Dick' rather than 'Richard' should be criticised. But she prefaces her criticism with *when you've got a nice name like 'Richard'*. Can we then maintain that the compliment is a realisation of politeness which is meant to neutralise a face-threat? The problem is this: if Mrs George had left out the compliment, she would have been openly criticising Hatch's friends and relations, and that would have run counter to the expectable politic behaviour. So the compliment is part of politic behaviour and constitutes supportive facework, but not politeness.

On the other hand, it is still a challenge to Hatch, who, if he wants to reestablish the social equilibrium, is constrained to carry out further relational work before the closure of the emergent network. He does this by returning the following values to Mrs George <I accept your point of view but suggest that there are extenuating circumstances> (*well*) + <I appeal to your understanding of the matter> (*d'you know*). + <I agree with you in private> + <here are the extenuating circumstances which contrast with your opinion> (*but*) + <my family started calling me 'Dick'> + <I've been called 'Dick' for a long time> + <it's useless to argue against people who call me 'Dick'>. Again, discourse markers like *well*, *d'you know* and *but* have been interpreted as instantiations of linguistic politeness, and, indeed, if Hatch had left them out and simply said *when you've been Dick as long as I have because your family started it, there's no point in arguing really*, he would still have been within the range of politic behaviour. In this case, the three utterances *well*, *d'you know* and *privately I agree with you* are open to a polite interpretation by being in excess of what is required here. What they do in this part of the interaction is to reestablish the social equilibrium so that the emergent network can reach closure. Mrs George appears to have interpreted them in precisely this way, as her final two utterances return the values that Hatch is hoping to acquire <I agree that there is no point in arguing> (*no*) + <I am entirely in agreement with you> (*quite*). This then allows Hatch to close the network (or this part of the network) by dismissing the topic of names – *however* – and inviting Mrs George to continue with her call – *you carry on.*

(IM)POLITENESS₁ AS AN ASPECT OF THE THEORY OF PRACTICE

At the beginning of this chapter I stressed that it should not be the aim of a theory of (im)politeness to set up a model with which we can either predict when and how speakers of a language will produce linguistic politeness or describe linguistic expressions which have been produced as examples of linguistic politeness. The models available in the politeness literature are of these two types, and they lay themselves open to the charge of abstracting out of interactive data a universal concept which is then called 'politeness' and is assumed to be valid in all ages for all languages, societies and cultures. In doing so scholars have manoeuvred themselves into the impasse of equating 'politeness' with something else, e.g. facework, and they have taken a stance on social structure which sees culture and society as being a set of timeless structures controlling the social behaviour of individuals and social groups. This kind of model may be appropriate to the description and explanation of the structures of the physical universe but it will not help us to understand how human beings cope with that universe in time and space.

The model that I am proposing here makes no claim to describe and/or explain what types of human social behaviour *are* polite, but rather to offer ways in which we as researchers can show when and perhaps why individual users of language in socio-communicative verbal interaction *classify* utterances as polite or even *express* utterances politely, and to allow both politeness and impoliteness to be evaluated by individual users. The theory must therefore be processual and, to borrow a Bourdieuan term, always 'oriented towards practical functions' (Bourdieu 1990: 52). It must allow us to account for why individuals agree or disagree on what is and what is not '(im)polite' language.

The two models that I have presented in this chapter allow us to do just that. Bourdieu's theory of practice suggests that what is interpretable as (im)polite depends on the linguistic habitus of the individual and the linguistic capital that s/he is able to manipulate. When these are combined with the objectified structures of social reality, they allow us to orient ourselves towards the practical functions of linguistic social action, or, as I have suggested, *inter*action. The amount of relativity in this kind of model is admittedly great, but it reflects the kinds of relativity that we discussed in chapter 2 and it allows for individuals to struggle over what they mean by the terms 'polite' and 'impolite'.

When combined with the theory of emergent and latent networks, it gives us an efficient set of tools to carry out a fine-grained analysis of verbal interaction in which we can posit certain structures as being open to classification and use as '(im)polite', thereby allowing us to focus on (im)politeness₁. The model of (im)politeness presented here consists of the following two major concepts:

    a. *Politic behaviour*: this is related to the habitus in Bourdieu's theory of practice in that it accounts for the knowledge of which linguistic structures are expectable in a specific type of interaction in a specific social field. It encompasses the objectified structures pertaining to expectable behaviour as well as the incorporation of those structures into an individual habitus. Behaviour which is not part of the politic behaviour of an interaction type is 'inappropriate' and open to classification as 'impolite'.

    b. *Linguistic politeness*: any linguistic behaviour which goes beyond the bounds of politic behaviour is open to potential classification as 'polite', which includes potential irony, aggressiveness, abuse, etc. It is thus open to dispute. The imputation of politeness to a linguistic structure, however, does not automatically mean that it will be given a positive evaluation. The opposite might easily occur. For this reason, utterances perceived as 'polite' play a role in the acquisition and exercise of power in the development of emergent networks in verbal interaction. The theory of emergent networks posits that every utterance conveys a value of some kind and must be responded to by other kinds of value. As long as the exchange proceeds within the framework of politic behaviour, the 'payment' will go largely unnoticed, but if it is not 'paid' it will almost certainly be noticed. Linguistic 'payment' in excess of what is required is open to interpretation as 'polite'.

RECOGNISING POLITIC AND POLITE BEHAVIOUR

Before we move on in chapter 7 to a discussion of linguistic structures frequently classified in the politeness literature as 'polite', we still need to answer two important questions: how are participants able to recognise when instances of extra 'linguistic payment' are made in the linguistic practice in which they are engaged and how may outsiders to the interaction still classify those instances as 'polite' after the event? Defining politic behaviour[8] as part of the habitus in Bourdieu's theory of practice and arguing that it includes the objectified linguistic structures relating to appropriate social behaviour leaves us with a definition of linguistic politeness$_1$ as linguistic behaviour that carries a value in an emergent network in excess of what is required by the politic behaviour of the overall interaction. This might seem an extreme step to take. Does it not merely empty 'politeness', as it has hitherto been understood in the literature, of most of its descriptive and explanatory power? For those who believe that there is a universal notion of politeness$_2$ this is the only conclusion that can be reached here. But if we reject this kind of reification of politeness as the object of study in a universally valid theory of human behaviour, which, following Eelen (2001), I have done consistently throughout this book, it is an entirely logical step.

As we shall see in chapter 7, the major consequence of taking this step is that linguistic expressions that are frequently said to instantiate politeness$_2$ in the research literature in fact turn out to be realisations of politic behaviour. Structures that convey a social value in excess of politic behaviour, as long as they are consciously produced *as* realisations of an extra value, can then be considered as *expressive politeness$_1$*. Those which are classified 'after the event' as having an extra value are examples of *classificatory politeness$_1$*.

Embedding a theory of (im)politeness within the theory of practice simply means redefining (im)politeness$_2$ as politic behaviour *and* potential (im)politeness$_1$. A theory of (im)politeness$_1$ must therefore be able to account for why and how participants classify certain linguistic structures as 'polite' and others as 'impolite'. It must also be able to account for the effects of any structure open to interpretation as 'polite' on the social equilibrium of the interaction. In other words, (im)politeness$_1$ must be linked to the exercise of power in emergent social networks. In addition to this, an integral part of a theory of (im)politeness$_1$ must be an account of the ability of individual participants to recognise the appropriate politic behaviour in the first place.

The questions that I shall deal with in this section are the following:

a. How does an interactant recognise the linguistic structures of politic behaviour, i.e. how does s/he 'know' what linguistic behaviour is or is not socially appropriate?

b. How does an interactant 'know' when some social value in excess of what is required is expressed by a linguistic structure, i.e. how does s/he know when that structure is open to interpretation as (im)politeness$_1$?

There are two additional questions, the first of which will be dealt with in chapter 7 and the second in chapter 9:

  c. What linguistic structures have been suggested in the literature as potential realisations of politeness$_2$?
  d. What is the effect on the development of emergent networks of instances of expressive and classificatory (im)politeness$_1$?

To answer questions (a) and (b) let us take a look at two examples which do not conform with the politic behaviour expected in the social interaction concerned. The examples are email messages sent to me by the Department of English at an Iranian university (example (5)) and by a Chinese post-graduate student (example (6)).^{9} It is significant, in the case of (5), that the request is being made from one academic institution to another. So we can assume that the anonymity of the request would not ratify informal expressions of familiarity that might characterise other forms of e-mailing. On the other hand, we would indeed expect a certain level of formality, but since a request is being made, we would also expect a more indirect formulation of the request than the one given. In example (6), a Chinese graduate student is requesting a favour from a higher-ranking academic in another country (in this case me) and again a certain level of formality and deference might be expected.

(5) Dear
      Islamic Azad University (L*** Branch) intends to be subscribed to your journal.
→   Please send the necessary forms and required information to the following address:
      Dr. J*** H***
      English Department
      Islamic Azad University (L*** Branch)
      L*** Iran

(6) Dear Watts, Richards J.,
→   How are you? I am a Chinese postgraduate student. My major is pragmatics. Now I am writing my dissertation concerned with politeness. I read the abstract of your article 'Language and politeness in early eighteenth century Britain' (in *Pragmatics* 1999) in *Linguistics and Language Behavior Abstracts*. I am very interested in it. Because we do not have the magazine *Pragmatics* here, I am wondering whether you could send me a copy of your article. Thank you very much. My address is 10# Z*** Normal University Z*** China. My name is M** M***.

Example (5) is a straightforward request for information on how to subscribe to a journal which I edit. The arrow in the text extract indicates the point at which I would have expected a little more than just *please send* . . . , although the email is efficient, to the point and otherwise in conformity with what a native speaker might expect.^{10} My personal habitus would lead me to expect something like *would you please send* . . . or *could you please send* . . . as a little more appropriate.

But I am still unable to give any *objectively* logical reason for why the email does not quite fit the expected politic behaviour, except to say that it forms part of the habitus I have internalised for this kind of interaction. It is a part of my previous experience in communicating via e-mail, and it's a habitus that I expect to share with others – at least to a certain extent. This is what Bourdieu calls the 'logic' of social practice. We should, of course, bear in mind that not everyone *will* share that habitus, and that this might also lead to potential struggle over how to e-mail requests of this kind appropriately.

Example (6) is easier to analyse. The term of address is odd, belying a lack of experience in how to address unknown professors appropriately. Having said that, however, it is still a little closer to what I would have expected than *Dear Sir* or *Esteemed Sir*. The arrow in the extract again indicates the point at which the politic behaviour is broken, and it focuses on the question *how are you?* in which the graduate student is apparently asking after my wellbeing. In a Chinese social situation equivalent to this one, it may indeed be appropriate to ask after the addressee's health, but in a native English-speaking environment M** M*** seems to be assuming some familiarity with me. My 'feel for the game', my habitus, tells me that this is not expected of someone making a request of a person s/he does not know. Once again, however, there is no objective reason for this being so beyond the logic of practice. In a native-speaker situation the question would be in excess of what is required. It would be extra payment for the request, thus opening up the possibility that *how are you?* will be interpreted as an expression of linguistic politeness$_1$ and may even be evaluated negatively.

Interactants can only 'know' what the appropriate behaviour in a particular social situation is by virtue of the interplay between the objectified structures of the social field (e.g. communicating requests by e-mail in examples (5) and (6)) and the habitus that the individual has internalised by virtue of the capital s/he has acquired in that field. There is simply no *objective* means to measure our feel for politic behaviour, which of course makes it as open to discursive struggle as the term '(im)polite' itself. In effect, there are only two ways in which one can become consciously aware of the appropriate politic behaviour: 1. when the values it symbolises are withdrawn in an instance of social practice (cf. example (5)), or 2. when more values are provided than are felt to be necessary (example (6)). The evaluation remains individual and can at best become interpersonal and intersubjective, but can never be objectively verifiable.

Let us take a look at question (b) What can we say about the value that is ascribed to verbal behaviour exceeding what is expected? How does an individual 'know' that a linguistic structure conveys more value than is required and is therefore open to interpretation as politeness$_1$? The answer must be the same as above, except to say that the habitus here is the *structuring* agent rather than the *structured* agent. The exigencies of the ongoing social practice will lead to interpretations being made and, possibly, to a temporary restructuring of the politic behaviour and the habitus (cf. the example between Dick Hatch and Mrs George). But, once again, there are no objective criteria with which we can 'measure' politeness, and the interpretations are always open to discursive struggle.

Very often, long sequences of verbal interaction need to be examined to locate where participants are being ousted into positions of powerlessness in an emergent network, thus invoking interpretations of the others' behaviour as 'impolite', 'inconsiderate', perhaps even downright 'rude' and why other participants revert consciously to expressive politeness$_1$. The following extract, taken from my family data, occurs after one of the participants, my stepfather (D in the extract), had attempted to display his gardening expertise on the subject of potatoes. He had virtually been invited by my mother (B in the extract) to take up the topic but was frequently prevented by her from developing it fully. I shall focus here on my uncle's (W in the extract) attempt to distract the participants' attention from the topic that D was trying to develop. W's offer of wine to his guests is a side sequence in the interaction, and is interpretable as an extraneous emergent network:

(7)

```
¹D:  the one I chose\ p. and c.\ is a waxy potato\ ... cos I prefer waxy pota/ I can't stand floury
 M:
 B:
 W:

²D:  potatoes\                                           without –
 M:        can't you\ <???>                                         no thank you
 B:              ⇑ you're a floury potato yourself\ <@@@>   ⇑ no\ never mind\
 W:

³D:        when you make <???> chips –
 M:  dear\ I haven't eaten anything like that anyway\
 B:                                    half a/ just a/. half an inch will do me
 W:              ⇑ ˆbea\ may I ask you to accept –

⁴D:
 M:                          did you say they make better chips
 B:  that's enough\ that's/ <@ woo woo @> thank you dear\
 W:  <???>
```

The data extract is a little confusing unless the reader bears in mind that D is trying to inform the others of the quality of different kinds of potato. The only person who appears to be interested in this topic is M (my aunt). D's wife B, who had earlier introduced the topic of potatoes and virtually invited D to take the floor, now makes a joke at his expense (at the first double-shafted arrow in score 2). This is interpretable either as a tease or as a direct face-threat. The participants are eating dinner together and W and M are the hosts. At this point in the conversation, W is concurrently offering M and B a little more wine. At the second double-shafted arrow in score 2 she intervenes in D's attempt to continue the topic by addressing the word *no* to W, who is poised to pour some more wine into her glass. Immediately after this she tries to mitigate the effect of her joke – *never mind*. Since she was the one who offered D the floor in the first place, preventing him from continuing with the topic at this point is not politic behaviour and is open to interpretation as an act of impoliteness.

At the third double-shafted arrow in score 3 W intervenes in yet another attempt by D to continue with the topic of potatoes and follows it with an explicit offer of more wine, again directed at B (despite her earlier refusal) (fifth arrow). In doing so, he pays with an ironic and overly formal expression *may I ask you to accept*, which is so far in excess of what is required by the politic behaviour of an informal family interaction that it is interpretable as expressive politeness. B evaluates this ironic politeness positively by being amused (note her laughter in score 4 after trying to prevent him from giving her more wine than she can take). We have no way of knowing what D's reactions were, but we can assume that he was not particularly pleased at W's intervention in what he was saying. After all, it has effectively brought to an end his display of gardening knowledge, even though M tries to revive the topic in score 4. W's expressive politeness in *may I ask you to accept* helps him to exercise power over D.

We are therefore forced to conclude this chapter on an ambivalent note. We recognise politic behaviour when engaging in social practice because it conforms to the objectified structures of the social field of the interaction and the forms of habitus we have developed to cope with the exigencies of social practice. But there are no objective criteria for determining politic behaviour even though we could say what is and what is not appropriate behaviour. There are also no purely subjective criteria, since social practice is always and only *inter*active. This corresponds to Bourdieu's understanding of the theory of practice as neither a subjective nor an objective theory of social structure, but rather an intersubjective and historically determined theory. In such a social theory there can be no objective criteria for deciding on what is or is not politic behaviour except for the past experiences of the individual and the perception of similar experiences in the interactive partners. But this is precisely why notions like (im)politeness are subject to dispute and can never be axiomatic concepts in a universal theory of human behaviour!

In chapter 7, we will turn our attention to linguistic structures which have been classified as polite in the literature. I will endeavour to show that those structures are frequently examples of politic behaviour rather than linguistic politeness. Part of the aim of the present chapter has been to show that linguistic politeness can only be recognised in instances of ongoing interaction, i.e. within actual social practice. Most of the structures listed in the literature are taken out of context, or if they are situated within a social context, that context is not rich enough to justify their classification as 'polite'.

In chapter 8 I shall deal in more detail with the exercise of power and introduce Relevance Theory as a means of accessing how interactants infer politeness. This will pave the way for an analysis of sets of real data in chapter 9.

7 Structures of linguistic politeness

FORMULAIC AND SEMI-FORMULAIC EXPRESSIONS OF LINGUISTIC POLITENESS

Chapter 6 presented a new approach to the study of (im)politeness₁ that focuses more on the perceptions of politeness made by interactants in social practice than on (im)politeness₂ as a theoretical term in a universal model of (im)politeness. In the latter type of model a range of linguistic expressions have routinely been put forward in the literature as examples of linguistic politeness. However, if the approach outlined in chapter 6 adequately accounts for the discursive struggle over (im)politeness, it follows that no linguistic structures can be taken to be inherently polite. In the present chapter I will focus on this problem. My aim will be to demonstrate that, at least in English, linguistic structures do not in themselves denote politeness, but rather that they lend themselves to individual interpretation as 'polite' in instances of ongoing verbal interaction.

In order to show that no linguistic structures are inherently polite, I will need to introduce a number of new terms. These will be explained as the chapter progresses, but definitions may also be found in the glossary. I shall begin by making a distinction between what I call *formulaic, ritualised utterances* and *semi-formulaic utterances*. I define *formulaic, ritualised utterances* as follows:

- highly conventionalised utterances, containing linguistic expressions that are used in ritualised forms of verbal interaction and have been reduced from fully grammatical structures to the status of extra-sentential markers of politic behaviour. They have little or no internal syntactico-semantic structure.

A wide range of examples of this type of structure will be given later in this chapter. For the moment, however, consider the following examples taken from the extracts in chapter 5:

(1) terms of address including first names (*Bill*, *David* (extract (1)), *David* (extract (2));
deferential titles (*sir* (extract (1)); first name + surname (*Richard Wells* (extract (3));
title + surname (*Dr Weber* (extract (4)))

(2) formulaic expressions of specific speech act types like thanking (*very many thanks*,
thank you (extract (1)), *thank you very much indeed* (extract (3)) or apologising *excuse
me* (extract (4)))

(3) ritualised expressions of leave-taking (*bye*, *bye bye* (extract (1)).

In the context of an interaction, linguistic expressions are also open
to potential interpretation as 'polite', i.e. as being in excess of politic
behaviour. While some of them may be formulaic, ritualised utterances, the majority are what I shall call *semi-formulaic utterances*. These
can be defined as follows:

- conventionalised utterances containing linguistic expressions
  that carry out indirect speech acts appropriate to the politic behaviour of a social situation. They may also be used, in certain
  circumstances, as propositional structures in their own right.

Examples from chapters 5 and 6 are:

(4) hedges of different kinds, i.e. linguistic expressions which weaken the illocutionary
force of a statement: by means of attitudinal predicates (*I think* (chapter 5, extract (1)),
I don't think (chapter 5, extract (3)), *I mean* (chapter 5, extract (3)) or by means of
adverbs such as *actually* (chapter 5, extract (3)), etc.

(5) solidarity markers, i.e. linguistic expressions which appeal to mutual knowledge shared
by the participants, or support and solidarity from participants, e.g. *you know*.

(6) boosters, i.e. linguistic expressions enhancing the force of the illocution in some way,
e.g. *of course*, *clearly*, etc.

(7) sentential structures containing specific modal verbs, e.g. *may I ask you to accept*
(chapter 6, extract (7)).

In the flow of conversation, structures such as these are generally
not perceived by participants as overt expressions of politeness, even
though they all make supportive contributions towards the facework
being negotiated among the participants and thus contribute towards
the politic behaviour of the interaction. On the other hand, if they are
missing, they tend to lead to an evaluation of a participant's behaviour
as 'impolite', 'brash', 'inconsiderate', 'abrupt', 'rude', etc. Because of
their frequent lack of salience for the participants, they are structures
that form part of the politic behaviour of the social interaction rather
than expressions of politeness. However, if they are used in excess of
what is necessary to maintain the politic behaviour of an interaction,
they are open to evaluation as 'polite'. The problem for the researcher
is to know when these expressions are salient enough in social interaction to attract participants' attention and to evoke a classification as

'polite'. When, in other words, can we say that we have – potentially, at least – examples of politeness$_1$?

There is at least one method by which linguistic expressions can be classified as open to interpretation as 'polite'. The researcher (or participant) first needs to assess, within the context of the ongoing social interaction, what would be the minimum set of linguistic structures required to carry out the necessary politic behaviour. What, in other words, is that participant's 'feel' for the situation and what has s/he internalised as part of her/his linguistic habitus in that situation? Linguistic structures that go beyond this politic behaviour may then be salient and open to interpretation as 'polite'. However, in order to reach such a decision, the researcher needs to carry out a fine-grained, sensitive analysis of verbal interaction relying heavily on features of the context. If (im)politeness$_1$ is a discursively disputed term in social practice, the model of (im)politeness$_1$ as social practice should emerge from every new instance of verbal interaction.

This point can be illustrated by looking at three examples of the moderator's behaviour in extract (3) from chapter 5. Remember that extract (3) is taken from a television programme on AIDS consisting (a) of sequences in which the female moderator questions a panel of 'experts' on various aspects of the disease in the studio before a live audience and (b) of sequences showing pre-filmed interviews with AIDS sufferers. So the studio sequences have two audiences, the studio audience and the viewing audience at home. The moderator has a number of different faces to uphold, a face assigned to her by the production team, one assigned to her by the studio audience, one that is assumed to be assigned to her by the viewing audience, and one assigned to her by the interviewees in the studio.

At the beginning of the extract she invites a medical expert on AIDS to explain the disease to the studio and the viewing audience:

(8)   M: Dr Weber briefly\ **can you explain** exactly what AIDS is\

The term of address (*Dr Weber*) is a formulaic, ritualised utterance and forms part of the expected politic behaviour in this type of verbal interaction. The adverb *briefly*, however, can be interpreted as an injunction to Dr Weber to make what he says brief before she actually tells him precisely what she wants him to do (*can you explain exactly what AIDS is?*). As we saw in chapter 5, this can be interpreted as an FTA (face-threatening act) not only to Dr Weber's face but also to almost every face she has been assigned. The reason for this interpretation is that, in the situation of a television programme on AIDS, she could simply have said to Dr Weber *Explain to us exactly what AIDS is*. Her indirect request, which makes use of the semi-formulaic utterance *Can you explain* . . . , is thus in excess of the required polite behaviour of the interaction and is open to an interpretation as 'polite'. On the other hand, telling Dr Weber to be brief before saying what she wants him to do is face-threatening. What looks like polite behaviour becomes corrective facework and is part of the politic behaviour being constructed in this stretch of verbal practice.

At the end of Dr Weber's 'brief' explanation he starts to explain how the disease is spread. Shifting to that aspect of the topic, however, would run the risk of excluding the other participants. The moderator prevents this from happening:

(9)

M:	
JW:	it's:er(...): a disease which is present . in the blood\. and it's spread by . blood and . by sexual
M:	**I'm sure we'll come back to how- how it is spread a little later on**
JW:	contact\

Her method of carrying out this potential FTA, i.e. preventing him from continuing with his turn at talk, consists of ensuring him personally that they will return to the question of how the disease is spread (*I'm sure*) and using an inclusive first-person-plural pronoun (*we'll come back* . . .). These are facework strategies ratified by the social interaction in which the participants are involved, but the fact that she only needs to use the second strategy to mitigate the FTA opens up *I'm sure* to a potentially polite interpretation.

At a later stage in the interaction the moderator addresses a potential FTA to Richard Wells of the Royal School of Nursing to the effect that the figures they have issued on the number of people who would be infected if AIDS is not checked are vastly exaggerated. To carry out this FTA – and the politic behaviour of a publicly held debate on a controversial issue like AIDS can expect a certain amount of face-threatening – she compliments the Royal College of Nursing for being 'highly respected both in and out of the medical profession' and attributes the criticism that the figures are ludicrous to the Department of Health and Social Security. Within this instance of social interaction, therefore, the compliment is not open to interpretation as 'polite' but is simply part of the facework being negotiated, i.e. as part of the politic behaviour being constructed in the ongoing interaction.

We can conclude from this brief analysis that establishing the linguistic structures that are open to classification as 'polite' depends on being able to determine what constraints the politic behaviour of a social interaction places on language usage. This is the case whether or not the linguistic expressions used are formulaic, ritualised utterances or semi-formulaic utterances. We can conclude from this that no linguistic expression can be automatically considered an example of politeness. Before we consider the taxonomies of 'polite language' that have nevertheless been suggested in the literature, we first need to consider the terms *propositional* and *procedural meaning*.

IDEATIONAL AND INTERPERSONAL MEANING: PROPOSITIONAL AND PROCEDURAL MEANING

In this chapter I shall suggest that expressions of politeness are always expressions of procedural rather than propositional meaning. But how are we to understand these two terms? We first need to make a distinction between *ideational* and *interpersonal* meaning and then relate these terms to *propositional* and *procedural* meaning. Let us begin by returning to the connection between language and social reality.

Language is at the heart of how we construct social reality. What we take as social reality, i.e. the ways in which we see ourselves and interpret the world around us, is constructed through repeated social practice with others and the different forms of habitus that we internalise in doing so (see chapter 6). The major means through which interaction amongst human beings is carried out is through language, i.e. by engaging in forms of linguistic practice. It is also in instances of linguistic practice that the structures of language are negotiated, and the meanings that these structures encode are the constant object of social negotiation. In the process, knowledge acquired by the individual is repeatedly constructed, changed, updated, reconstructed and reproduced. On the one hand, this is made possible by the objectified structures of the social field and the different types of habitus internalised by the individual. On the other hand, it depends on cognitive–communicative processes of inferencing, as we shall see in more detail in chapter 8.

Verbal interaction entails at least two interlocutors, which makes language inherently social. At the same time, from a structural point of view, human language is a complex semiotic system in which meanings can be encoded. It would, however, be a mistake to imagine that we merely transfer information by means of language; at the same time, we also, and more importantly, use it to construct our view of the world and our place in it. We construct, reproduce and sometimes destroy interpersonal relationships, and we create ideologies, art, myths, etc.

Just as important as what we do with language is how we do it, since that will always depend upon the personal relationships that have been constructed between individuals and social groups and the ways in which we perceive the social field in which we are interacting. From a linguistic rather than a social theoretical point of view, Halliday (1978) deals with these two sides of human language, the semiotic and the social, by suggesting that every utterance conveys *ideational* meaning and *interpersonal* meaning. The ideational structure of language is the way in which messages are put together for transmission, their logical structure. It's the meaning conveyed conventionally by the structures of the utterance.[1] Hence if I say to my neighbour:

(10) Nice day today.

the value that I give to her/him (cf. the discussion in chapter 6) is carried by the proposition <today is a nice day>. Halliday would call this the *ideational meaning* of the utterance. At the same time, however, my neighbour will interpret this as being my personal opinion on the state of the weather, i.e. <I think <today is a nice day>> and will also interpret me as making a statement, i.e. <I state here and now <today is a nice day>>. S/he will therefore derive inferences in excess of the propositions that make up the ideational meaning of the utterance, and those inferences are directly derivable from the linguistic form.

But saying something to my neighbour is also an interpersonal act creating a social link between her/him and me, and if this is the first time I have seen my neighbour on this particular day, the interpersonal meaning of my utterance can be inferred roughly as having the value of (11):

(11) <I am greeting you>

Since a greeting is an interpersonal act which routinely requires some form of greeting as a response, we can say that it is the first part of at least two utterances, one by me and one by my neighbour, which Sacks calls an *adjacency pair*. We are dealing here with interpersonal, or social meaning, and if we assess which of the two meanings is more important on a bright summer morning, then we would probably opt for the interpersonal meaning. We can both, after all, access the information that it really *is* a fine morning. Politeness payment is concerned with interpersonal rather than ideational meanings. It is less what we say than the way that we say it, or even simply the fact that we say it, that counts.

Ideational meaning is concerned with propositions, and propositions are assigned truth values. Either what I say is true or false in
a possible world (assertive mood), or I wish my interlocutor to give me
the truth value of what I say in a possible world (interrogative mood),
or I wish my interlocutor to carry out something so that the resulting
state of affairs has a truth value in a possible world (imperative mood).
Ideational meanings are also conveyed in the form of propositions in
which a state, action, process or event is predicated of an argument
or of arguments. Hence, if I say:

(12)   The door is locked.

I am predicating the state of being locked of the argument, 'the door'.
The *argument* is what is being talked about. The utterance (12) is either
true or false in the world that is being referred to. Because of the
presence of a truth value in expressing *ideational meaning*, I propose
that ideational meaning is equivalent to *propositional meaning*.

Individual words may also have truth values and may therefore be assigned propositional meaning. If my eighteen-month-old granddaughter says to me:

(13)   Wow wow.

her single lexeme, inasmuch as I can tell what it refers to, has propositional meaning. I can say:

(14)   No, that's a cat.

and deny the truth value of her utterance.

Utterances may also have more than propositional meaning. In fact,
they generally do, as they function on the interpersonal as well as the
ideational level. What, for example, is the meaning of *no* in (14)? We
could say that it is propositional in that I am indexing a truth value
to what she has said. But it could also be used as a signal to her that I
disagree with her classification of the object and that she should have
another go (i.e. by trying to utter the word *cat*), etc. Certain parts of
an overall utterance, like *no* in (14), indicate to the addressee how the
propositions contained in the utterance are to be interpreted. Some
relate a proposition to an earlier proposition, some point forward to
an upcoming proposition, and others are pertinent to the relationship
between the speakers and/or between the speakers and the context of
the utterance. They indicate sets of procedures through which propositional meaning can be derived, and we can call this kind of meaning
procedural meaning. In (14) what I am doing is giving my granddaughter some kind of procedure for evaluating her utterance. As we shall

see during this chapter, those parts of an utterance that open up the whole utterance to a 'polite' interpretation, i.e. as being in excess of the politic behaviour, always realise procedural meaning.

Most linguistic expressions potentially have both propositional and procedural meaning. Some, however, are used almost exclusively to convey propositional meaning and others to convey procedural meaning. I could have given my granddaughter the following response:[2]

(15) Well no, that's a cat.

The discourse marker *well* has been the central topic of a large body of linguistic, pragmatic and sociolinguistic literature,[3] and so far it has successfully avoided all attempts to locate its ideational (propositional) meaning in an utterance like (15). The reason is clear: *well* has procedural but very little, if any, propositional meaning.[4] It has become what I shall call in the next section *pragmaticalised*.

To see how a linguistic expression might have either propositional meaning or procedural meaning, consider an utterance taken from Janet Holmes's corpus of New Zealand English. It was produced by a teacher who wanted to tell her pupil that the solution to a problem was wrong:

(16) You've got that wrong, I think.

The expression *I think* has both propositional (<I think that p>) and procedural meaning, and it is the procedural meaning that is most interesting in (16). To say to an interlocutor that something s/he has done is wrong constitutes a face-threat. The interpersonal meaning of the utterance *you've got that wrong* is confrontational, since it places the speaker in a superior position in terms of the values of the cultural marketplace. The pupil has not yet acquired the skills that the teacher possesses. But is the expression *I think* aimed at supporting the pupil's face, i.e. is it politic behaviour, or is it a form of politeness payment for the negative assessment of the pupil's work? In other words, does the teacher intend the pupil to derive the inference that, although s/he *thinks* the solution is wrong, it might just be right? I submit that the latter interpretation is more likely. Had the teacher prefaced her assessment with *I think*, the propositional meaning would have been more salient and the politeness payment would either have been considerably reduced or completely effaced:

(17) I think you've got that wrong.

Linguistic politeness involves the use of linguistic expressions whose interpersonal meaning is foregrounded, so the procedural meaning of an expression is interpretable as giving politeness payment. This is the reason why several discourse markers in English, or, as Holmes prefers to call them, pragmatic particles, are used to convey politeness payment even though their principal procedural meaning might not always be focused on the need for politeness. Before dealing with the kinds of expression that convey procedural meaning, I first need to discuss the processes of *grammaticalisation* and *pragmaticalisation* in the following section, since it is these processes which give rise to them as language changes over time.

The important point about grammaticalisation and pragmaticalisation is that the sources of the two processes always lie in instances of socio-communicative verbal interaction and involve processes of pragmatic inferencing. Canonical instances of grammaticalisation/pragmaticalisation in the study of linguistic politeness (e.g. honorifics, pronominal second-person forms indicating familiarity, deference, formality, etc., terms of address) are only learnt by the child acquiring the language through a process of socialisation into their correct usage, i.e. socialisation into the acquisition of politic behaviour. This then reinforces the hypothesis that linguistic structures are not inherently polite.

GRAMMATICALISATION AND PRAGMATICALISATION

Grammaticalisation can be understood as both a framework for the study of language change and as the study of the individual instances of such change (Hopper and Traugott 1993: 1–2). It is understood as a process through which lexical, denotationally meaningful elements in a language are transformed by successive generations of speakers into morphologically dependent linguistic elements in the grammatical system of that language, often with a noticeably reduced phonological structure. The lexical expressions – which can even cross syntactic phrase structure boundaries – are sometimes so reduced by processes of semantic bleaching, cliticisation, levelling, analogy, etc. that they are lost altogether. Grammaticalisation always has its origins in language usage, i.e. in commonly occurring forms of socio-communicative verbal interaction.

Pragmaticalisation is more or less the reverse process of grammaticalisation but has frequently been dealt with as part of grammaticalisation.[5] The effect of pragmaticalisation is to bleach the propositional content of linguistic expressions to such an extent that they no longer function as expressions contributing to the truth value of a proposition but begin to function as markers indicating procedural meaning in verbal interaction. As such they often stand outside the sentential structure of the proposition to which they are attached (see *well*, *no* and *I think* in the previous section).[6]

Both grammaticalisation and pragmaticalisation are oriented towards our communicative goals as individuals in social interaction. As we shall see in chapter 8, we try to achieve those goals by carrying out processes of pragmatic inferencing and, in doing so, linguistic forms become so conventionalised that they begin to lose their flexibility of reference. Some become fixed as structural elements in the language system itself (grammaticalisation), while others lose most or all of their propositional content and begin to function as metapragmatic 'signposts' or 'instructions' to the addressee on how to process propositions (pragmaticalisation).

Four examples from English will help to illustrate this process, the grammaticalisation of the Old English preterite present verb *agan* giving two verbs in modern English (*owe* and *ought*), the ongoing grammaticalisation of *going to* as a quasi-modal verb, the pragmaticalisation of the discourse marker *you know* and the pragmaticalisation of the leave-taking marker *goodbye*.

In Old English the verb *agan* meant 'own, possess' or 'cause someone to own, possess'. It was a preterite present verb, i.e. at some stage in the prehistoric development of the Germanic languages its past tense had been used so frequently with a present-tense meaning that the original past-tense structure became the present-tense and a 'new' weak past-tense form developed.[7] In the case of *agan* this new past-tense form was *ahte*.

Studying Old English texts in which *agan* appears, particularly prose texts, leads to the conclusion that the second causative meaning ('cause someone to own, possess') triggered an inference through which the agent of the causative verb was reinterpreted as 'owing' the object referred to. When this meaning had become conventionalised, a process of metaphorisation set in, reinterpreting the 'object' owed as an abstract entity and leading to the meaning of 'obligation':

(18)   S ['cause to own'] *agan* O [concrete object]
                           ⇒[abstract object]
       ⇒ S ['owe', locus of responsibility, theme] *agan* O [abstract]

Preterite present verbs in Old English are the source of the system of modal verbs in modern English, so we might expect to see *owe/ought* alongside *can/could*, *may/might*, etc. But this did not happen. The semantic space occupied by *owe* became restricted to the meaning that the verb now has in modern English, the reason being that other modal verbs like *shall* and *must* began to 'occupy' the 'obligation' area of that space. The fact that the meanings of these verbs clearly overlap with the sense of obligation and also that the metaphorical meaning of *owe* was in any case an extension from its (later) prototypical meaning helped this process of change to develop.

The past tense *ahte*, however, was maintained alongside the other modal verbs as a verbal morpheme denoting obligation. In other words, it had become grammaticalised. In the meantime, of course, the verb *owe* had, by a process of analogy and levelling, developed a new weak past tense form *owed*.[8] It is interesting to see what is now happening to the 'modal verb' *ought*. In modern colloquial usage the negative, interrogative and tagged forms of *ought* give rise to such structures as *didn't ought/did . . . ought*, in which, curiously enough, the old past tense *ahte* is reflected in the use of *did* rather than *do*, even though *ought* is never used to refer to obligation in past time:[9]

(19) You oughtn't to lend him your car. vs. You *did*n't ought to lend him your car.
(20) Ought we to write and tell him? vs. *Did* we ought to write and tell him?
(21) He ought to phone us up, oughtn't he? vs. He ought to phone us up, *did*n't he?

Now let's turn to the second example. In its progressive form in sentences like (22):

(22) I'm going to buy some milk.

the lexical item *go* still retains its semantic denotation of movement away from the speaker, and the infinitive clause following it is still interpretable as the expression of purpose.[10] But if we extend the prototypical meaning of *go* by metaphorising it and using it in a sentence like (23):

(23) I'm going to see you this evening.

the purposive meaning in the infinitive clause virtually disappears.

If we extend the use of the structure to a sentence like (24):

(24) It's going to rain this afternoon.

no notion of movement (except in a very abstract sense) and no sense of purpose are expressed. The speaker is merely making a prediction about the state of the weather at a point in the future. In oral usage *going to* becomes a single phonological unit *gonna* or [gənə] indicating that it is undergoing grammaticalisation as a new modal verb. In some varieties of English this even leads to the disappearance of the verb *be* in affirmative statements, e.g. (25):

(25) You [gənə] get a real shock.

The examples show not only that the historical development of English is replete with examples of grammaticalisation, but also that it is an ongoing process that can be observed happening around us in real time.

The direction of the process of grammaticalisation is from *lexical item* to *syntactic structure* to *morphological unit* (Hopper and Traugott 1993: chapter 5). Pragmaticalisation works in the opposite direction showing a development from fully morphosyntactic structures to reduced structures with procedural rather than propositional meaning, as we shall see in the following section. These then tend to shift outside the propositional structure of the utterance and function as what are often called *discourse markers* (cf. Schiffrin 1987), i.e. elements that mark the discourse in specific ways and create continuity between different utterances in the discourse. Two examples of pragmaticalisation producing 'discourse markers' of different kinds will be discussed here: the development of *you know* and *goodbye*.

You know contains a second-person pronoun indexing the addressee(s) and the cognitive verb *know*. As with other structures that indicate the state of mind or attitude of the speaker to what s/he says, like *I think*, *I hope*, etc., the verb can take a finite sentential object with or without the complementiser *that*, and this is still the case with *you know*. Hence we can have:

(26) You know (that) you shouldn't say that.

Such prefacing elements, however, are easily detachable from the sentence-initial position and may be inserted parenthetically or sentence finally, as in (27):[11]

(27) You shouldn't say that, you know.

In these positions *you know* has become pragmaticalised. It has lost its original referential meaning and has taken on the discourse function of a solidarity marker, signalling that the addressee is expected to process the proposition as the speaker has. It has, in other words, now acquired procedural meaning, and it frequently functions as an appeal for support, as in (28):

(28) . . . and I can't, you know, go along with that decision any more.

The second example of pragmaticalisation concerns the leave-taking marker *goodbye* (*bye*, or *bye bye*). The original propositional structure from which *goodbye* developed was the invocation *God be with you*, which was used either as a greeting or a leave-taking formula. Evidence of the full pragmaticalisation of this structure in modern

English is the tendency for speakers to reduce it to *bye* or to redu-
plicate this shorter form as *bye bye*.

Having discussed how the processes of grammaticalisation and pragmaticalisation give rise to linguistic expressions that realise procedural
meaning, we can now return to the question of what an *expression of
procedural meaning* is in the following section.

EXPRESSIONS OF PROCEDURAL MEANING

In any language there are a number of linguistic expressions that
have become pragmaticalised to signal procedural meaning. I shall
call such structures *expressions of procedural meaning* (EPMs for short). I
shall begin the discussion of this term by considering the following
decontextualised utterance:

(29) Would you mind answering the phone?

The structure 'Would you mind Ving X?' is frequently felt to denote
a 'polite' request in English. Let us first consider the lexical meaning
of the verb *mind* a little more closely. In example (29), whether we
interpret it out of context as polite or not, *mind* is roughly synonymous
with *have something against* or *object to*, at least in the standard varieties
of English. The following examples show this meaning very plainly:

(30) I don't *mind* if you turn up late just as long as you let me know beforehand.
(31) I'm going to have one last beer. Do you *mind*?
(32) I wouldn't *mind* owning a car like that myself.

The verb *mind* is cognate with the noun *mind* and denotes some
form of mental process. In other non-standard varieties of English it
is roughly synonymous with the verbs *recall* and *remember*, as in (33) or
(34):

(33) I *mind* the time when I was young.
(34) D'you *mind* when we gatecrashed that party?

And it is from this meaning that the expression *mind you* is derived:

(35) He didn't even buy me a birthday present. *Mind you*, he knows so many people he
      probably just forgot it was my birthday.

So there's nothing *intrinsically* polite in a question like (36):

(36) Would you *mind* closing the window? There's an awful draught.

We could of course argue that the presence of the modal verb *would*
is what signals a 'polite' interpretation, but even this is not the case.

Example (37), with no modal verb, is certainly more direct than (36), but in certain circumstances it is also open to interpretation as 'polite':

(37) Do you mind closing the window? There's an awful draught.

There are two different prosodic patterns that can be used in uttering the questions in (29), (36) and (37), one in which there is a pitch movement upwards on the verb *mind*, the pitch level for the rest of the sentence remaining relatively high, with a second rising movement at the end of the question. This is a standard way of indicating prosodically that the utterance should be processed as a proper *yes–no* question asking the addressee whether s/he has anything against carrying out the action:

(38) Would you ˆmind ˉanswering the ′phone?
(39) Would you ˆmind ˉclosing the win′dow?
(40) Do you ˆmind ˉclosing the win′dow?

The prosodic structure of (38)–(40) does not usually lead to the interpretation of politeness. If, on the other hand, the pitch is kept low and the tempo fast throughout the utterance until we reach a nuclear stress at the end in which the voice rises in pitch and then falls on the word *phone*, or rises on the first syllable of *window* and drops on the second, the utterance is not interpretable as a genuine *yes–no* question:

(41) Would you ˍmind ˍanswering the ˆphone?
(42) Would you ˍmind ˍclosing the ′winˋdow?
(43) Do you ˍmind ˍclosing the ′winˋdow?

The prosody of these utterances is an expression of procedural meaning, since it is focused on instructing the addressee how to process the propositional content of the utterance. It indicates either that the utterance is open to interpretation as an example of linguistic politeness (and if not, is part of the politic behaviour expectable in the social situation),[12] or that the speaker intends his utterance to be processed as a genuine *yes–no* question. It is equivalent to a metapragmatic instruction to the addressee. The prosody of (41)–(43) 'instructs' the addressee to focus on the verb phrase of the non-finite embedded clause *answering the phone* or *closing the window*, rather than on the possible truth value of the question with *mind*, and to interpret it as the requests in (44) and (45):

(44) Answer the phone.
(45) Close the window.

The prosodic features of the *Would/Do you mind Ving X?* structure in English (low pitch, fast tempo, ending at a higher pitch in a rise–fall nucleus) perform the same procedural function as *I think* in (27). Both indicate that the utterance is either within the scope of the politic behaviour expected in the social situation or that it is in excess of it and interpretable as 'polite'. They are thus procedural rather than propositional and can be interpreted as *expressions of procedural meaning* (EPMs).

EPMs are an indispensable feature of linguistic practice since they are largely responsible for triggering inferences in the addressee that bear on interpersonal meaning (greetings, terms of address, leave-taking, etc.) or they instruct the addressee where and how to derive inferences from propositional values. In the first function they tend to be formulaic, ritualised utterances, and in the second function they are drawn from a range of utterance types that have become pragmaticalised. Examples of this type of EPM in English are non-linguistic utterances like *er, oh, mm, hmm*, etc. (which function conventionally to fill pauses, signal uptake and/or surprise, to signal continued attention on the part of the addressee to what is being said (minimal listener responses)); discourse markers like *you know, well, like, anyway, now*, etc.; ritualised expressions such as *please, thanks, excuse me, pardon*, etc.; formulaic clause structures like *The thing is . . .* , *What I was going to say was . . .* , etc.; and indirect but highly conventionalised and thus semi-formulaic structures like *would you mind Ving?, can you do X?*, etc. whose prosodic structure is identifiable as the EPM. EPMs are therefore part of the politic behaviour of different forms of linguistic practice. When they are missing, their absence is easily interpretable as impoliteness₁, and when they are in excess of what is required by the situation, they are easily interpretable as politeness₁.

In the following section I shall consider one of the taxonomies of structures of linguistic politeness offered in the literature. As I do so, it should become clear to the reader that those structures are all EPMs.

TAXONOMIES OF POLITENESS STRUCTURES

House and Kasper (1981) provide an interesting typology of linguistic expressions that are frequently used to signal politeness (or impoliteness) in English and German. A number of researchers have used this typology in their own work (e.g. Trosborg 1987), and there are alternative expressions for several of the structures discussed.

The following structural categories are suggested by House and Kasper:

- *Politeness markers,* by which they mean expressions added to the utterance to 'show deference to the addressee and to bid for cooperative behaviour'. The most obvious example of a politeness marker in English is *please,* but there are others, e.g. *if you wouldn't/don't mind,* tag questions with the modal verb *will/would* following an imperative structure (*Close the door, will you/would you?*), etc.

- *Play-downs,* by which they understand syntactic devices which 'tone down the perlocutionary effect an utterance is likely to have on the addressee'. These are then subdivided into five subcategories which in fact boil down to the following four: use of the past tense (*I wondered if . . . , I thought you might . . .*), progressive aspect together with past tense (*I was wondering whether . . . , I was thinking you might . . .*), an interrogative containing a modal verb (*would it be a good idea . . . , could we . . .*), a negative interrogative containing a modal verb (*wouldn't it be a good idea if . . . , couldn't you . . .*).

- *Consultative devices,* by which they understand structures which seek to involve the addressee and bid for her/his cooperation, e.g. *Would you mind . . . , Could you . . .*

- *Hedges,* by which they understand the avoidance of giving a precise propositional content and leaving an option open to the addressee to impose her/his own intent, e.g. *kind of, sort of, somehow, more or less, rather, and what have you.*

- *Understaters,* which is a means of underrepresenting the propositional content of the utterance by a phrase functioning as an adverbial modifier or also by an adverb itself, e.g. *a bit, a little bit, a second, a moment, briefly.*

- *Downtoners,* which 'modulate the impact' of the speaker's utterance, e.g. *just, simply, possibly, perhaps, really.*

- *Committers,* which lower the degree to which the speaker commits her/himself to the propositional content of the utterance, e.g. *I think, I believe, I guess, in my opinion.*

- *Forewarning,* which is a strategy that could be realised by a wide range of different structures in which the speaker makes some kind of metacomment on an FTA (e.g. pays a compliment, as did Bill Bell in the Radio Cornwall phone-in analysed in chapter 5) or invokes a generally accepted principle which s/he is about to flout, etc. (e.g. *far be it from me to criticise, but . . . , you may find this a bit boring, but . . . , you're good at solving computer problems*).

- *Hesitators,* which are pauses filled with non-lexical phonetic material, e.g. *er, uhh, ah,* or are instances of stuttering.

- *Scope-staters*, which express a subjective opinion about the state of affairs referred to in the proposition, e.g. *I'm afraid you're in my seat, I'm disappointed that you couldn't . . .* , *it was a shame you didn't . . .*
- *Agent avoiders*, which refer to propositional utterances in which the agent is suppressed or impersonalised, thereby deflecting the criticism from the addressee to some generalised agent, e.g. passive structures or utterances such as *people don't do X.*

Edmondson (1977) has suggested that what he calls *gambits* also help to downgrade the impact of an utterance, and he lists two types of gambit, *cajolers* and *appealers*. Cajolers are linguistic expressions which 'help to increase, establish or restore harmony between the interlocutors' (House and Kasper 1981: 168), and are represented by EPMs such as *I mean, you see, you know, actually, basically, really.* Appealers try to elicit some hearer confirmation and are characterised by rising intonation patterns, e.g. *ok´ay, ´right, ´yeah.* Further supportive moves may also be made to downgrade the force of an utterance, and these are categorised by House and Kasper as *steers*, i.e. utterances which try to steer the addressee towards fulfilling the interests of the speaker, e.g. *Would you mind making a pot of tea?*; grounders, i.e. utterances which give reasons for the FTA, e.g. *I'm thirsty. Get me a coca cola, will you?*; and preparators, i.e. a meta-statement expressing what the speaker wants the hearer to do, e.g. *I'm going to test your knowledge now. What is . . .?*

House and Kasper then go on to suggest a set of what they call *upgraders* in which the speaker uses so-called 'modality markers' to increase the impact of the utterance on the addressee, some of which act more like face-threatening utterances. Those which may lead to the 'polite' interpretation of an utterance are given below:

- *Overstaters*, which are adverbial modifiers through which the propositional content of the utterance is 'overrepresented', e.g. *absolutely, purely, terribly, awfully,* etc.
- *Intensifiers*, which are markers intensifying the degree to which an element of the propositional utterance holds good, e.g. *very, so, quite, really, just, indeed,* etc.
- *Committers*, by which the speaker can indicate a heightened degree of commitment to the propositional content of the utterance, e.g. *I'm sure, certainly, obviously,* etc.

The heterogeneity of this taxonomy of such expressions is immediately apparent, as is the fact that most of them do not have to be used in the pragmatic functions listed by House and Kasper. Holmes (1995) simplifies the taxonomy rather radically and classifies the linguistic expressions that she maintains are realisations of politeness into *hedges* and *boosters*. Hedges comprise the structures listed as downgraders by House and Kasper, although House and Kasper suggest that they only make up one subcategory within the overall class of downgraders. Hence committers, downtoners, understaters and hedges are all hedges for Holmes. She fails to indicate where she would place House and Kasper's consultative devices, play-downs and politeness markers. Boosters are what House and Kasper call upgraders, although many of the upgraders can hardly be said to contribute to politeness in an interaction (cf. e.g. aggressive interrogatives and lexical intensifiers). For this reason they were omitted in the list given above. The only real agreement between House and Kasper and Holmes is that boosters, hedges, upgraders and downgraders all have an effect on the illocutionary force of the proposition in which they are used. Hedges (downgraders) typically weaken the force of the utterance while boosters (upgraders) strengthen it. James (1983) calls downgraders/hedges 'compromisers', while Quirk *et al.* (1985) call them 'downtoners', Brown and Levinson (1987) call them 'weakeners' and Crystal and Davy (1975) call them 'softeners'. What Holmes calls 'boosters' are called 'intensifiers' by Quirk *et al.*, and 'strengtheners' by Brown and Levinson.

So the terminology used to define expressions of politeness is not only as heterogeneous as the expressions themselves; it's also confusing and in need of clarification. House and Kasper do at least lump most of the polite expressions they discuss into an overall category that they call 'modality markers'. But the major problem still remains: what is it about these linguistic structures which allows them to be used beyond the verbal expression of politic behaviour, and how do participants in verbal interaction come to classify them as 'polite' language – if in fact they do?

We have so far established that linguistic expressions that are used for the purposes of politeness are only interpretable as such by virtue of the context of their use. They may often simply provide supportive facework and as such be examples of politic behaviour. It has nevertheless been necessary to survey the set of expressions that have traditionally been called 'polite' in the literature. The real problem with them lies in their heterogeneity. Any attempt to categorise them in an ordered fashion is doomed to failure. The attempt to do so is made even more difficult by the fact that most of the expressions can be used as a form of polite payment, but may equally well be used in other ways.

In the following section, I will use the insights we have gained by considering the process of pragmaticalisation and the distinction between procedural and propositional meaning to find a way out of the taxonomic maze. My major hypotheses are (a) that so-called structures of linguistic politeness are always pragmaticalised EPMs encoding procedural meaning, and (b) that, while the range of EPMs to be discussed certainly form part of the politic behaviour in a social situation, they do not inherently encode politeness$_1$.

FORMULAIC, RITUALISED EPMs

We have by now established that the most productive process giving rise to both formulaic, ritualised EPMs and other highly conventionalised EPMs in English (as in many other languages) is pragmaticalisation. In languages with honorific forms and complex styles of politeness, e.g. Japanese, Korean and Thai, the development appears to have been one of grammaticalisation.[13]

A number of articles have appeared in the literature researching into how children acquire formulaic, ritualised utterances such as *hi, hello, bye bye, thanks, thank you, please*, etc. and, more generally, how they are socialised into using 'politeness' formulas appropriately.[14] The structures referred to are not all easily acquired and are sometimes quite late in appearing in a child's linguistic repertoire. In some unfortunate cases they may never appear at all. They are all formulaic, ritualised utterances that function as EPMs as we can see from the following examples:

(46) A: Would you like some more coffee?
      B: Yes, *please*.
(47) Put the dustbin out for me, *please*.
(48) Could I *please* have another piece of cake?
(49) May I *please* get down from the table?
(50) A: Have another piece of cake.
      B: No *thank you*.
(51) *Thanks* for letting us use your holiday flat in Mallorca.
(52) M: *Hello*, Mr Smith. *How are you?*
      S: *Hello* David. Fine *thanks*. *How are you?*
(53) *Hi* Fred. *How are things today?*
(54) M: *Bye*, Mr Smith. *Thanks* for calling in.
      S: *Bye bye*.
(55) *Sorry*, but could you say that again *please*.
(56) *Sorry*, would you mind not smoking in here?
(57) *Sorry to bother you*, but could I borrow your pen for a minute?
(58) *Excuse me*, is this the way to the station?

(59) *Excuse me*, could I just squeeze past you?
(60) *Excuse me* for butting in, but might I just ask a question?
(61) A: Could you give me your phone number, *sir*, and we'll ring you back.
     B: ???? [unclear]
     A: *Pardon?*
(62) A: The present government has proceeded to make a mess-up of the whole situation.
     B: *Pardon?*
(63) *I do beg your pardon*. I didn't quite hear what you said.
(64) A: *Sorry*, would you mind moving along a bit?
     B: Of course. *No trouble at all.*
(65) A: *Sorry* to bother you.
     B: *No worries.*
(66) A: *Thanks* for the lift, Bill.
     B: *A pleasure.*

Examples (46)–(66) illustrate an arbitrary range of formulaic, ritualised EPMs in English that have all arisen through processes of pragmaticalisation. The list could of course be extended, but it is at least sufficient to develop the argument presented here. Some of them, like *bye bye* and *please*, have already travelled a long way down the path of pragmaticalisation. Others, like *sorry*, *no trouble at all* or *a pleasure*, also occur in semi-formulaic structures (e.g. *I'm sorry to keep you waiting*; *It's a pleasure to help you, madam*) and thus appear to have not yet completed the pragmaticalisation cycle. Although *please* is still just recognisable as a descendant of the clause *if it please you*, *bye bye* in (54) is the reduplicated second element in the expression *goodbye*, whose forebear is hardly recognisable today as *God be with you*. Others appear to be rather recent developments, e.g. *How are things today?* (53), and still others have developed from other varieties of English than standard British or American English, e.g. *No worries* (65), which may have originated in Australia.

Apart from the adverbial placement of *please* in (48) and (49)[15] all of these formulaic expressions stand outside the propositional utterances to which they are attached, if indeed they are attached to propositions at all. Some of them have fully sentential structure, but are largely emptied of the propositional content that they must originally have expressed, e.g. *How are you?* (52) and *How are things today?* (53) even though the addressee is constrained to give some kind of response to the question.

The formulaic EPM *please* is always attached to a request or an offer. In (46) the first participant, A, uses a semi-formulaic EPM, with a prosodic contour signalling that the addressee should process the question not as a genuine *yes–no* question but as a 'polite' offer. Once A has framed this part of the social interaction as one in which s/he uses a ritualised EPM either within the framework of the politic behaviour or in excess of that behaviour, a similar token should be repaid by the addressee. In the event that the offer is accepted, the formulaic EPM common in English is *please*. If the offer is declined, as in (50), the appropriate formulaic EPM is *thanks, thank you, thanks a lot, thank you very much*, etc., depending on the amount of payment required by the politic behaviour of the interaction.[16] In (47) the speaker softens the force of her/his request by uttering the minimum token of politic behaviour *please*.

In (48) and (49) semi-formulaic EPMs are in evidence in the indirect speech acts (*Could I have . . .?, May I get down . . .?*) and are given supplementary force through the insertion of *please* into precisely the verb phrase which will be omitted by the addressee when s/he processes the utterances as requests and not questions. In this situation, *please* is interpretable as being in excess of the required politic behaviour and therefore open to interpretation as 'polite'.

Some of the formulaic EPMs, notably *sorry, thanks/thank you* and *excuse me*, have not quite lost the ability to take sentential and nominal complements. They may also occur as fully pragmaticalised markers immediately preceding or following a propositional utterance (cf. *thanks* in (52); *sorry* in (55), (56) and (64); *excuse me* in (58) and (59)), or as quasi propositional utterances followed by a complement (cf. *thanks **for letting us use your holiday flat*** in (51), *thanks **for calling in*** in (54), *thanks **for the lift*** in (66), *sorry **to bother you*** in (57) and (65) and *excuse me **for butting in*** in (60)).

Greeting formulas as in (52) and (53) display a high degree of pragmaticalisation. Although *how are you?* or *how are things?* should be responded to, it is not generally acceptable to use the opportunity to give an extended description of one's health or one's mental or affective state. A brief positive response is normal, but a brief negative response may often be used to open up the first topic of the conversation. A formulaic utterance such as *how do you do?*, however, has become fully pragmaticalised and may only be responded to in kind or with another greeting formula. The presence of the temporal expression *today* in example (53) is evidence of the fact that some greeting formulas are still open to a certain amount of propositional modification, i.e. they have not yet become fully pragmaticalised.

The formulaic EPMs in examples (64)–(66) – *no trouble at all, no worries* and *a pleasure* – function to minimise the sense of debt or obligation expressed by the first speaker. Speech acts of thanking and apologising are frequently followed by this kind of EPM. Of the three expressions selected here, *no worries* is the most fully pragmaticalised since, at least as far as I am aware, it is not possible to modify it in any way. It is still marginally possible to modify *no trouble (at all)* by inserting it as a predicative structure after the verb *be* (*It was no trouble at all*), and *a pleasure* can be used in a restricted number of fully or partially propositional utterances, e.g. *It was a pleasure, It was my pleasure, a pleasure to help you*, etc. The remaining EPM, *pardon*, occurs in a restricted number of highly formulaic utterances such as *beg your pardon, I beg your pardon, I do beg your pardon, pardon me*, etc., and has thus attained a high degree of pragmaticalisation.

In general, the number of linguistic expressions functioning as formulaic, ritualised EPMs in English is relatively restricted and shows evidence of varying degrees of pragmaticalisation. One reason has been put forward to account for this fact: English-speaking cultures are often said to stress what Brown and Levinson call 'negative politeness strategies'. Both Sifianou (1992a) and Bentahila and Davies (1989) maintain that Greek culture and Moroccan Arabic culture differ from British English culture in placing more value on positive politeness strategies that address the needs of the hearer's positive face. In chapter 4 I discussed criticisms of Brown and Levinson's model in detail, in particular their concept of 'negative face'. I argued that we need to be cautious about making such sweeping assumptions.[17]

The following section deals with semi-formulaic utterances in which the use of indirect speech acts in English (and in several other languages) are frequently interpreted in the literature as instances of 'negative politeness'.

SEMI-FORMULAIC EPMs: FORMS OF INDIRECTNESS

If one avoids committing an FTA by expressing it indirectly, this in no way means that one has avoided the FTA itself, as any native speaker of English will know. The addressee will simply register the fact that the speaker is 'paying' for the FTA by producing linguistic expressions that are open to interpretation as 'polite'. Directly expressed speech events such as requesting, ordering, warning, criticising, forbidding, etc. may restrict the addressee's freedom of choice of action, but only inasmuch as they represent a threat to her/his own self-assessment that s/he has that freedom of choice in the first place.

In many languages of the world indirect utterances, which are often questions in lieu of requests, are the canonical form of utterance taken to indicate politeness. For this reason speech act theory has frequently been used to explain the polite interpretation of such utterances.[18] An indirect speech act is one in which the illocutionary force of the speaker's utterance does not correspond in a one-to-one fashion with the illocutionary act. A speaker who utters (67), for example, will generally not be heard to be asking a question even if the actual illocution is formulated as such:

(67) Can you tell me the time?:   Illocutionary Act – question
                                      Illocutionary Force – request

Similarly a speaker who utters (68) will generally not be heard to be making a statement of her/his wishes, but to be making an indirect request:

(68) I'd like you to take out that dustbin sometime this morning: Ill. Act – statement
                                                                     Ill. Force – request

On Brown and Levinson's reading of politeness as the mitigation or avoidance of face-threatening acts, we might expect that indirect speech acts that would represent an imposition on the addressee if expressed directly constitute polite utterances. However, as we saw in examples (38) and (41) (repeated here for the sake of convenience):

(38) Would you ˇmind ˉanswering the ʹphone?
(41) Would you ˍmind ˍanswering the ˆphone?

the intonation contour of an utterance can supply the clue as to whether a question is to be interpreted as genuine or as an indirect request. Prosody, rather than syntax or the lexicon, has the function of instructing the addressee to filter out the extraneous linguistic material and focus on the request or order lying in the non-finite embedded clause of the utterance.

Is this the case with other indirect speech acts that are often said to express politeness in English? Are there alternative, non-polite interpretations for them? Consider the following example utterances:

(69) Close the door, will you?
      Structural type: 'Do X, will you?'
(70) Close the door, would you?
      Structural type: 'Do X, would you?'
(71) Would you be so kind as to move over a little?
      Structural type: 'Would you be so kind as to do X?'
(72) Could I have a look at that book some time?
      Structural type: 'Could I do X?'
(73) Can I have another piece of cake?
      Structural type: 'Can I do X?'
(74) May I remind you that there's no smoking in this room?
      Structural type: 'May I remind you that X?/May I remind you to do/not to do X?'

(75) I couldn't borrow your car for an hour this afternoon, could I?
      Structural type: 'I couldn't do X, could I?'
(76) I was wondering whether I could borrow £50 till the end of the week.
      Structural type: 'I was wondering whether I could do X.'
(77) I should like to ask you not to say that again.
      Structural type: 'I should like to ask you not to do X.'
(78) You couldn't do me a favour and look after my dog for a bit, could you?
      Structural type: 'You couldn't do me a favour and do X, could you?'
(79) I want you to listen to me carefully.
      Structural type: 'I want you to do X.'
(80) Might I bother you for a moment?
      Structural type: 'Might I do X?'
(81) Let me help you with those bags.
      Structural type: 'Let me do X.'
(82) Allow/permit me to disagree with you on that point.
      Structural type: 'Allow/permit me to do X.'

For the present analysis all we need to know is that addressees must assume that what their interlocutors have just uttered is meant to be interpreted as maximally relevant to the context of the social interaction. We must also assume that addressees will process utterances so as to produce what appears to them to be a maximally relevant propositional assumption in that context (cf. the discussion of Relevance Theory in chapter 8). All things being equal, the addressee of utterance (41), for example, is likely to construct a maximally relevant interpretation by inferring the following assumptions (83) and either (84a) or (84b):

(83)   <The speaker is asking me to answer the phone>
(84)a. <The speaker is using a structure which is appropriate to the polite behaviour of the situation>
    b. <The speaker is using a structure which is in excess of the polite behaviour of the situation and which I may therefore interpret as 'polite'>

If (84b) is inferred, the speaker is interpreted as 'paying more than is necessary' with a polite utterance, but the addressee will always interpret (41) as the realisation of a request. Since this is so, s/he will have little option but to answer the phone even though the speaker appears to be giving the addressee a possible way out of doing so.

The acid test for examples (69)–(82) is how many of them could be understood literally, but before we work our way through them, a number of important points need to be made. All of the examples contain the modal verbs, *can/could*, *may/might* and *will/would*, or quasi-modal structures such as *would like to*, *want to*, *let*, *allow* and *permit*, expressing the deontic modalities of 'will', 'permission' and 'desire'.[19] In most of the examples, although not all of them, the illocutionary act is that of a *yes–no* question whereas the underlying illocutionary force is that of an order, a request or an enquiry. If the utterance is not in the interrogative form, it is either an imperative with a tag question formed with the modal verbs *will/would* as in (69) and (70), an imperative using the verbs *let, allow* or *permit* as in (81) and (82), a statement followed by a tag question containing the modal verbs *can/could* as in (75) and (78),[20] an indirect question in which the verb in the matrix sentence is in the past tense indicating speaker-distancing as in (76), or a statement of wish or desire directed at the addressee as in (77) and (79). In each structure either the first- or the second-person pronouns or both are in evidence.

Examples (69) and (70), *Close the door, will you?* and *Close the door, would you?*, are what Brown and Levinson would call a bald on-record FTA (face-threatening act) with a minimum of redressive action, i.e. an explicit face-threatening act with no effort at softening the effects on the addressee. The only indicator of politeness here is the tag question *will you?* in (69) and *would you?* in (70), both of which follow the bald on-record request. The tag question with *will* is used to check whether the addressee is willing to carry out the request, so if the utterance is interpretable as 'polite', the degree of politeness is minimal. The use of the past-tense *would* distances the speaker from asking the addressee about her/his willingness to close the door. It is, in other words, a little more tentative than in (69). Since *will* could have been used given the constraints of the polite behaviour for the social situation, the tag question *would you* is open to potential interpretation as 'polite'. In an anonymous situation in which personal identities are not at issue, the appropriate EPM to use would be *please*, and this can also be combined with *will you?/would you?* Even the straight imperative can represent the polite behaviour of certain interaction types. If someone taps on your door, you are most likely to say *Come in* rather than something like *Would you mind coming in*? If you want to offer a second cup of tea to a guest, you are more likely to say *Have another cup of tea* than *Have another cup of tea, will you?*

If we test whether (69) or (70) can have a 'non-polite' meaning in another context, they both fail, indicating that the tag questions attached to bald on-record requests are *formulaic* and are almost automatically associated with the polite behaviour of the ongoing interaction. This is what we would expect of a tag question, which, I argue, is a form of EPM.

Moving on to examples (71)–(73), *Would you be so kind as to move over a little?*, *Could I have a look at that book some time?*, *Can I have another piece of cake?*, all three perform the illocutionary acts of questioning, but only in the case of (72) can we say that this still corresponds closely to the illocutionary force. (72) would generally be uttered with a rising intonation contour on the lexeme *time*, indicating its status as a *yes–no* question. The principal indication that it is a politic request to borrow the book is the past-tense form of the modal verb *could*, which again distances the speaker from being able to look at it, if only temporarily. The owner of the book would have to go through a series of inferences to reach the assumption that the speaker is requesting the future loan of the book, were it not for the highly conventionalised prefacing modal *Could I . . .?* If (72) really were a *yes–no* question, the speaker would be asking the addressee whether, in a situation relating to her/his physical or mental abilities, the addressee believes it is within the potential scope of the actor to carry out the action, as in (85):

(85) A: Could I swim twenty lengths of this bath?
      B: I'm sure you could.

whereas the response to (72) might be something like (86), but is highly unlikely to be (87):

(86) B: Yes, of course you can.
(87) B: ?Yes, of course you could.

So while there are not two different prosodic contours to choose from here, as in the case of *Would you mind . . .?*, there are certainly situations in which the *yes–no* question can only be interpreted literally, indicating that structural types 'Can I/you do X?' and 'Could I/you do X?' are not inherently polite and are therefore semi-formulaic EPMs lying within the scope of politic behaviour. As in the second prosodic structure in the *Would you mind . . .?* example, we are confronted with a process of pragmaticalisation which has not yet run full cycle.

But if this is the case, why are the 'Can I/you do X?' and 'Could I/you do X?' structural types so often interpreted as instantiations of politeness without the addressee having to pick her/his way through a chain of inferred assumptions? I submit that their frequency of occurrence is so much higher than the genuine *yes–no* questions asking the addressee to assess the speaker's ability that they are by now the unmarked forms within the scope of politic behaviour for a very wide range of verbal interaction types. I submit that no one would automatically classify them as 'polite'.

What about example (71): *Would you be so kind as to move over a little?* Is the structural type 'Would you be so kind as to do X?' not always interpreted as an expression of linguistic politeness? It is indeed difficult to imagine a context in which (71) would be interpreted as a genuine *yes–no* question, and we seem to be confronted here with a fully pragmaticalised politeness structure. But note that it is not completely formulaic. It is still productive in that it allows any infinitival clause to be interpreted as a genuine request. It is still the matrix syntactic structure of the utterance into which this clause must be slotted. I shall therefore argue that, while the structural type 'Would you be so kind as to do X?' is more or less fully pragmaticalised, it is still a semi-formulaic utterance. It is interesting to note that whereas in earlier forms of modern English it might have qualified as lying within the scope of politic behaviour for a restricted number of verbal interaction types, it is almost always interpretable today as a form of extra payment, i.e. as 'polite'. As such, however, it is also open to a negative evaluation.

The case is very similar to genuine questions of the structural type 'Can I do X?/Can you do X?' (cf. the examples with 'Would you mind doing X?' above). Requests expressed as questions beginning with 'Can I do X?/Can you do X?' like *Can I have another piece of cake?*[21] (e.g. in (72) and (73)) are by now so unmarked that the only option open to the addressee is to bypass all of the inferred assumptions (88a–e) and access the final two assumptions (88f, g):

(88)a. <The speaker requests me to tell her/him whether or not s/he has the ability to have another piece of cake.>
   b. <I have the authority to distribute pieces of cake.>
   c. <By virtue of b., the speaker requests me to tell her/him whether or not I grant her/him the permission to have another piece of cake.>
   d. <The speaker wants another piece of cake.>
   e. <The speaker knows b–d and knows that I know it.>
   f. <The speaker is requesting that I give her/him another piece of cake.>
   g. <The speaker is paying for the request by using a form that is compatible with politic behaviour.>

We can conclude from this brief discussion that while it might be the case that these uses of the structural type 'Can/could I do X?//Can/could you do X?' are on their way to becoming fully pragmaticalised, this does not mean that they are inherently polite. In point of fact, as we have seen, fully pragmaticalised EPMs are not usually open to a 'polite' interpretation although they form part of the politic behaviour in operation in the verbal interaction type. However, the interpretation of a genuine *yes–no* question is still possible.

Let us turn now to the structures contained in examples (74)–(76), *May I remind you that there's no smoking in this room, I couldn't borrow your car for an hour this afternoon, could I?, I was wondering whether I could borrow £50 till the end of the week.* Example (74) performs the illocutionary act of a question but its illocutionary force is that of a warning. The payment is, however, in excess of what is required by the politic behaviour and is thus open to a polite interpretation that is likely to be evaluated negatively by the addressee, e.g. as irony. There is absolutely no way in which it can be replied to with *Yes, you may* or *No, you may not* after which the addressee goes on smoking – unless, of course, s/he is deliberately subverting the politeness payment being offered by the speaker. In a situation such as this, it would be handy to suggest that we have a pragmaticalised structure inherently encoding politeness, were it not for the ability of the addressee to subvert the speaker's intention.[22] In addition, the structure is still productive in that I can insert virtually any infinitival clause into the frame 'May I ask you to . . .' and generate what amounts to a potentially polite reading. But note that, exactly as in the case of (71), the greater formulaic nature of the structure leads to its interpretation as unnecessary or ironic politeness. Just as the speaker could have produced (89) or (90) in place of (71):

(89) I wonder whether you could move over a little.
(90) Would you mind moving over a little?

so too could s/he have produced (91) or (92) in place of (74):

(91) I wonder whether you could stop smoking.
(92) Would you mind not smoking?

Examples (89)–(92) theoretically leave the addressee with the option of interpreting the utterances as genuine statements or questions concerning whether the addressee objects to the action of moving over a little or of stopping smoking. This is probably the reason why they would almost automatically be prefaced with the formulaic EPM *sorry*.

In (75) the speaker has performed the illocutionary act of a statement with an utterance containing the negative modal *couldn't*, and s/he has accompanied it with a tag question *could I?* modifying the force of that statement and creating a request out of it. Without the tag question, the addressee is absolutely unable to interpret the statement as a request, but the tag question in itself is not a realisation of politeness. The addressee will have to go through a set of inferred assumptions to come to the relevant information that the speaker is tentatively asking for the loan of her/his car. Hence the indirectness in (75) does not automatically realise politeness, since none of the structures, including the tag question *could I?*, are inherent denotations of politeness. However, the tag question contains an instruction to the addressee to reassess the speaker's statement with a view to correcting the negation expressed in it. The only person who has the power to do this is, of course, the addressee, the owner of the car. In addition, the speaker uses the lexeme *borrow*, which would not occur in the bald on-record request to borrow the car:

(93) Lend me your car this afternoon.

So the structural type represented in (75), in which the speaker makes a negative statement with *can* or *could* and invites the addressee with a tag question to annul that negation and access a request, represents a semi-formulaic EPM that abides by the constraints of the politic behaviour operative in the social situation.

Example (78) is exactly parallel to (75) except that it also contains an added indication of the obligation of the speaker to the addressee in the expression 'do me a favour' in the formulaic part of the utterance. As above with examples (75) and (78), the addressee will ignore the set of assumptions leading up to the conclusion of the interpretation of the utterance and access only the following in (94) for (75) and those in (95) for (78):

(94) <The speaker is requesting that I lend him my car.>
      <The speaker is paying for the request with politeness.>
(95) <The speaker is requesting that I look after his dog for a bit.>
      <The speaker is paying for the request with politeness.>

Example (76), *I was wondering whether I could borrow £50 till the end of the week*, is again indirect, expressing the illocutionary act of a statement but containing the illocutionary force of a request. The expression *I was wondering wh– . . .* is not in itself an indication that the statement should be reinterpreted as a request, as we can see from example (96) below:

(96) I was wondering yesterday how I might contact you again, and then I thought of phoning up your mother.

The reason for this is that the past tense in *I was wondering* does indeed refer to a point in time that is distant from the present, i.e. in past time. In (76), however, *I was wondering* refers to another kind of distance, hypothetical rather than temporal distance, since we can assume that the speaker is still wondering when he produces the utterance. This is strengthened by the presence of the hypothetical past-tense form of the modal *could* in the embedded clause. The presence of the temporal prepositional phrase *till the end of this week* helps the addressee to cancel out the alternative past-time variant of *I was wondering* and to focus on the hypothetical nature of the overall statement. The inferential pathway to the interpretation of payment of politeness by the speaker is open for the addressee, but this does not alter the fact that the structural type 'I was wondering whether I/you could do X' is not inherently polite, but is a semi-formulaic EPM.

Examples (77) and (79), like (76), are statements containing the quasi-modal expressions 'I should like' and 'I want'. The difference between the two, however, is that (77) expresses the illocutionary force of a warning ('do not say that again'), while (79) expresses that of a request ('listen to me carefully'). The degree of politic behaviour that must be shown by the speaker in (77) is therefore higher than in (79) since the face-damaging potential of a warning is always greater than that of a request. It is also more readily open to interpretation as 'polite'. For this reason the locutionary verb *ask* is also explicitly produced in the utterance. It would have been possible for the speaker to have used a less 'valuable' structure as in (97) or even one in which the formulaic EPM *please* is the only concession made to politic behaviour, as in (98):

(97) Would you mind not saying that again?
(98) Don't say that again, please.

The structural type 'I should like to ask you to do/not to do X' constitutes a partially pragmaticalised realisation of politeness payment, i.e. a semi-formulaic expression of linguistic politeness, since it is in excess of what would ordinarily be required of the politic behaviour allowing the addressee to derive the following inferences:

(99) <The speaker is warning me not to say that again.>
      <The speaker is paying for the warning with politeness.>

An analagous explanation can be given for example (79), except that the structural type 'I want/should like you to do/not to do X' does not necessarily require the addition of the verb *ask*.

The final two examples in the corpus given in this section introduce the verbs *let*, *allow* and *permit*. There is nothing about the syntactic or lexical structure of either of the example utterances to suggest that they are semi-formulaic expressions of linguistic politeness. The illocutionary force of (81), however, is that of an offer, and an offer to help the addressee that displays concern for the addressee's face and is at the very least politic behaviour. The illocutionary force of (82) is that of disagreement, which in itself represents a face threat to the addressee. Hence the structure requesting permission to make that statement is in excess of what would generally be required of the politic behaviour in a situation in which two people are in disagreement and helps us to classify (82) as a potentially polite utterance. If the syntax and lexis of the two examples are not in themselves indications of politeness, what about their prosodic structure? As with the structural type 'Would you mind doing X?', there are two distinct patterns possible, one which is interpretable in the case of (81) as a genuine request to the addressee to allow the speaker to help her, in which the speaker starts by rising to a high pitch level on *let*, maintaining high pitch throughout the utterance and ends with a fall–rise on *bags*, and the other a polite offer, in which the speaker maintains a low pitch throughout the utterance with a rise–fall on the final syllable *bags* and an increased tempo throughout:

(100)   'Let me ‿help you with those ˇbags.
(101)   ‿Let me ‿help you with those ˆbags.

The same pitch patterns are in evidence for (82) except that in this case the fall–rise in the first variant and the rise–fall in the second is on the final syllable of the lexeme *disagree*. So, as with the structural type 'Would you mind doing X?' different prosodies distinguish between a non-polite and a semi-formulaic polite reading of the structural types with *let*, *allow* and *permit*, and the structures in themselves cannot be said to be inherently polite.

The corpus of utterances analysed in this section is a small subset of structures in English which are often said to express politeness. I have interpreted them as *semi-formulaic expressions of procedural meaning*, some of which contribute to the politic behaviour expected in a specific social situation, while others clearly exceed what would be required. What, therefore, can we conclude from this brief analysis?

Firstly, in most cases we need much more than just the realisation of a speech act to assess whether politeness$_1$ is interpretable. In this section and the previous section I presented my argument with decontextualised utterances. But we need to know something about the situation in which linguistic structures occur in order to evaluate whether or not they are part of the politic behaviour of a situation or are beyond what can be reasonably expected of it and are thus potentially open to interpretation by participants and commentators as 'polite'.[23] But even given this potential weakness in the discussion, it should have become clear that we are dealing with highly conventionalised, formulaic and semi-formulaic utterances which are the result of or in the process of pragmaticalisation. I have called these utterances *formulaic, ritualised utterances* and *semi-formulaic utterances* both of which are realised by EPMs. They lie outside the propositional meanings conveyed by the language used and provide the addressee with clues as to how to derive relevant inferences. To call them structures of linguistic politeness is to misrepresent them. In virtually every case they are not 'inherently polite' although they may contribute to the smooth functioning of verbal interaction, i.e. they may be part of whatever politic behaviour is valid for the interaction.

There were, of course, certain utterances which went so far beyond what in any reasonable circumstances can be expected of the appropriate politic behaviour for a social interaction that they could be designated as 'polite', e.g. *May I remind you that there's no smoking in this room?* and *Allow/permit me to disagree with you on that point*, but these tend to be highly stylised and heavily laden with ironic intent.

Secondly, and leading on from this last point, although, according to our definition of semi-formulaic linguistic utterances, certain structures are still productive, they do not have non-polite, neutral equivalents. In such cases, e.g. 'May I ask you to do X?', 'Would you be so kind as to do X', we are left to conclude that the speaker intends his utterance to be understood as polite, perhaps even ironically polite.

Thirdly, it is not always possible to fit the underlying proposition of an utterance in one social interaction into the carrier of politic behaviour in another without creating some very odd effects. If, for example, our speaker were to have said *You couldn't close the door, could you?* instead of *Close the door, would you?* it would not represent part of the politic behaviour in the social situation of a teacher asking a student to do something in a classroom. The student would have almost no option but to interpret it as a case of insincere politeness. But if the speaker had said *May I remind you that I'd like another piece of cake?* instead of *Can I have another piece of cake?* the excessive politeness would probably be interpreted as an insult.

Fourthly, several structures involving the modal verbs *can/could* and *may/might* can be interpreted as unmarked structures encoding levels of politic behaviour, but because they may also be used in their literal sense, they cannot be called inherently polite, while still others, like *May I remind you that/of . . .* and *Would you be so kind as to . . .* seem to have fossilised as realisations of politeness that often go beyond the limits of what can be reasonably expected in a verbal interaction. Indeed, they are often interpreted as expressing insincere or ironic politeness.

Fifthly, most of the means of expressing politeness are not a priori politeness structures but are produced in combination with other utterances or parts of the same utterance which help the addressee to overlook several of the inferential steps s/he might need to make and to derive a politeness assumption almost automatically.

Sixthly, certain structures that are not produced within the propositional core of the utterance such as *please*, or the tag questions *will you?* and *would you?* to imperatives are pragmaticalised EPMs produced automatically in response to the demands of politic behaviour.

In this chapter it was not my intention to review all of the tax-onomies of linguistic politeness structures that have been set up in the literature, but rather to demonstrate that most of those structures may or may not appear in a social and linguistic context in which they go beyond what can be expected of the linguistic practice of the interaction. If they can be interpreted in this way, then they are open to interpretation as politeness$_1$. If they are missing, they will almost inevitably lead to an interpretation as impoliteness$_1$. Ultimately, what is or is not taken to be a polite utterance depends entirely on the mo-ment of utterance in linguistic practice and relies on the participants' habitus in the verbal interaction. Thus, with the exception of certain structures that are clearly interpretable as ironic, insincere politeness, there can be no inherent structures of linguistic politeness. There may, of course, be structures that are typical of the politic behaviour of a socio-communicative verbal interaction. (Im)politeness$_1$ is a disputed concept and is located in the divergent interpretations made by partic-ipants in instances of ongoing linguistic practice. In chapter 8 I shall show how the notion of relevance plays a role in interpreting 'polite' utterances and demonstrate how politeness can be used to exercise power in certain situations.

8 Relevance Theory and concepts of power

POLITENESS AND THE STRUGGLE FOR POWER

The alternative model of (im)politeness presented in chapter 6 places the onus of deciding what linguistic behaviour is 'polite' or 'impolite' squarely on the shoulders of members of a speech community in which these attributions or similar, related ones are made. It is therefore a model of (im)politeness$_1$ rather than politeness$_2$, and it makes no claim to be cross-culturally universal, even though we can expect other speech communities to apply roughly equivalent attributions in other languages or language varieties. It also makes no claim to be able to predict when language-specific attributions will be made by members.

The model of (im)politeness$_1$ is based on the theory of practice and the related theory of emergent networks, both of which draw on members' past experiences of previous interaction and the institutionalised, objectified structures of social reality that have been internalised in the process. In this sense the model of (im)politeness$_1$ presented in this book is dynamic, flexible and emergent. It deals with ongoing evaluations and characterisations of (im)polite behaviour in social practice, and it allows for discursive dispute over the resources of (im)politeness. These concerns are largely absent from all the models of politeness$_2$ presented in chapters 3 and 4.

Since social practice always involves relational work between the participants, it embodies a latent struggle for power in which perceptions of politeness play a significant role. The struggle for power, however, can only be perceived and engaged in by members against the background of previous preconceptions about what forms of linguistic behaviour are appropriate to the social practice being carried out. I have called social behaviour resulting from these preconceptions *politic behaviour*. I have also suggested that a failure to abide by members' expectations of what constitutes politic behaviour frequently leads to the attribution of impoliteness. Behaviour in excess of expected politic behaviour is open to interpretation as polite, which may then result in positive or negative evaluations by other participants in the interaction. Conceptualisations of politeness in the literature as ways to achieve comity, mutual concern for others, concern to uphold individuals' face needs, etc. are directed fundamentally to relational work and as such are aspects of politic behaviour.

The predictability of politic behaviour is derived from each interactant's habitus and the types of face attributed by the social group to the individual for the purposes of the interaction. So while the kinds of linguistic structure discussed in chapter 7 are not inherently polite, they are certainly open to interpretation as such if they represent 'extra payment' in terms of the value of an utterance. As a brief illustration of this principle consider again part of the extract from the BBC programme *Panorama* dealt with in chapter 1:

(1)

¹E: are you now willing to discuss uneconomic pits\
S: ... we're not prepared to go along to the National
²E: you're not/ **sorry** if I interrupt you .. there\ y/ I- I/ let me just remind you that–
S: Coal Board\ and start –   :er: .. :er:
³E:
S: .. are you going to let me answer the question\ you put a question\ for god's sake let me answer\

Emery's *sorry* in score 2 is a formulaic, ritualised EPM which is not inherently polite, but represents requisite politic behaviour in a wide range of social interactions. It can be interpreted here as an attempt by Emery to atone for his violation of the politic behaviour by interrupting Scargill. However, to say *sorry if I interrupt you there* after having committed the offence and then to follow it up with a reminder to Scargill is evidence that it has been deliberately uttered to justify the interruption. Emery has attempted to reconstruct the politic behaviour of a political television interview, thus making *sorry* an insincere form of payment for his violation, since it is in excess of what he seems to consider necessary here. It is immediately taken up by Scargill, who interrupts him in score 2 in order to remonstrate with the apparent resetting of the politic behaviour. What we see in this emergent network is a struggle by one participant to exercise power over the other, and attributions of (im)politeness lie at the heart of the struggle. In the final section of this chapter I shall return to this extract in order to illustrate how Emery and Scargill are engaged in a struggle over the exercise of power.

In this chapter I shall firstly reconsider the Gricean basis of the majority of pragmatically inspired politeness models critically and then discuss an alternative way of looking at communication and cognition as offered in Relevance Theory (RT). I shall follow this with a brief discussion of the notion of power and the term 'the exercise of power', since these two approaches to ongoing social practice will form a central part of the analysis of naturally occurring verbal interaction in chapter 9. To begin with, however, I need to make it clear that RT cannot be understood to be the theoretical basis of a model of (im)politeness$_1$ as social practice. The concept of an EPM as presented in chapter 7 has been developed from RT, and RT provides an excellent means to assess how potential violations of politic behaviour can be recognised and inference processes can be postulated that result in the interpretation of (im)polite behaviour. It can never substitute for a model of (im)politeness$_1$; it can only supplement it. Before discussing the usefulness of Relevance Theory, however, I will briefly return to Grice's theory of the CP and the criticisms of it.

THE GRICEAN BASIS OF LAKOFF, LEECH AND BROWN AND LEVINSON

In chapters 3 and 4 we saw that the Lakoff, Leech and Brown and Levinson models of politeness were all based in one way or another on the default assumption that interactants aim at establishing communicative cooperation. From the point of view of these researchers, working as they were in the 1970s and early 1980s, it comes as no surprise that Grice's Cooperative Principle was the cornerstone of models that explain polite utterances as one way of achieving mutual cooperation or contributing towards the establishment and maintenance of mutual face. At the same time these models also recognise that such utterances appear to violate one or more of the Gricean maxims. So there's an inherent contradiction in their work; polite language is a form of cooperative behaviour but does not seem to abide by Grice's Cooperative Principle.

In order to correct this apparent anomaly, Lakoff adopts Grice's lukewarm suggestion that a Politeness Principle might be added to the CP and even suggests that the maxims of the CP are subordinated to those of the PP. Leech, on the other hand, is not concerned to set up a model of pragmatic competence. On the contrary, as we saw in chapter 3, he divides pragmatics up into three different systems, pragmalinguistics, socio-pragmatics and general pragmatics and lumps the Gricean CP and his own PP together (plus other principles which do not immediately concern us here) as constituting general pragmatics. He subsumes all of this under the heading of 'interpersonal rhetoric'.

Brown and Levinson accept the basic tenets of the Gricean CP and attempt to resolve the anomaly by introducing Goffman's notion of 'face', although in a suitably altered form. Where Lakoff and Leech somehow recognise the significance of politeness for what is generally known as 'facework',[1] they seem unwilling to leave the safe harbour of Gricean pragmatics, which had been integrated into linguistic pragmatics by the end of the 1970s. Facework, however, is social work and therefore has to be looked at not only from the point of view of pragmatics, but also from the point of view of conversation analysis and social theory.

All three models must therefore be judged on whether Gricean pragmatics can still be upheld in its original form, and I shall argue that, given the present state of our knowledge of the processes of social interaction and communication, this is highly questionable. Grice conceived of the CP as a universally valid matrix of principles governing the cooperation of participants in social interaction. The term he chose to refer to social interaction was 'conversation', indicating that he was primarily concerned with the ways in which interactants negotiated meaning (both conventional and intentional) in everyday verbal exchanges. His approach to pragmatics predates the era of postmodernist theorising, as do the three major models of politeness, but it still represents an important break with code theories of meaning. At the same time it remains tied to the ideology of language as a semiotic code.

Pragmaticists working with the Gricean model claim that the CP has universal validity. If that is so, it should somehow *include* politeness and obviate the need to introduce supplementary maxims. After all, Grice was not so naïve as to believe that interactants always stick to the maxims; indeed, the whole *raison d'être* of the CP is that it would be impossible to stick to them, even if we tried. The central insight provided by Grice is that we repeatedly violate the CP and that we do so for different reasons. One of the maxims might clash with another, such that the interactant, in choosing which maxim to adhere to, has no option but to violate one of the others. Sometimes the interactant would prefer not to stick to a maxim, for reasons of her/his own. But frequently interactants will deliberately 'flout' a maxim, on the well-founded assumption that the co-interactant(s) will be able to spot the violation and fill in the communicative 'gap' for themselves. It is this type of violation which is interesting for Grice. In order for the co-interactants to reinstate the CP, i.e. to credit the speaker with cooperative intentions, they must be able to generate what Grice calls an 'implicature', an inference by means of which the CP may be restored.[2]

Grice's theory of meaning consists of natural and non-natural meaning. The generation of conversational and conventional implicatures is responsible for the non-natural meaning in an utterance, but non-natural meaning would make no sense at all if there were no theory of natural meaning. Grice's theory of natural meaning is grounded within the traditions of intensional/extensional and truth-conditional semantics, which amounts to saying that 'natural meaning' is in some sense encoded by the linguistic structure of the utterance and therefore that language 'contains' meaning(s). So despite the revolutionary nature of his Cooperative Principle – revolutionary in terms of the field of pragmatics in the late 1960s and early 1970s – it remains firmly anchored in the conduit metaphor of language (cf. Reddy 1979), in which language is a container with which a speaker can transfer meaning to a hearer.

Grice's departure from standard approaches to meaning, then, was to posit that when the maxims of the CP are violated, as they often are, the addressee is called upon to derive what he calls an 'implicature' to reinstate it. This can be illustrated as follows. If someone asks me a question such as

(2) Are you coming to the departmental party this evening?

and I reply

(3) I've got too much work to do.

the propositional (or truth-conditional) content of my utterance in (3) does not seem to relate to anything in the propositional content of (2). It thus violates the Gricean Maxim of Relation. However, within the linguistic, social and cognitive context of the interaction, I can expect the person who has asked me the question to recognise the violation as a case of flouting and to resolve the apparent lack of relation between the two utterances by deriving an implicature to the effect that I will not be coming to the departmental party *because* I have too much work to do. This is then a *conversational implicature*.

Grice also posits a second kind of implicature which he calls a *conventional implicature*. To illustrate this, let us take the following example. Assume that at the departmental party, that same person asks me

(4) Where's Margaret this evening?

and I answer

(5) She's either at a committee meeting or she's at home in Geneva.

Now, here I have flouted the Maxim of Quality, since, in effect, I do not know exactly where she is. If that is the case, I should have simply said 'I don't know'. But this response might be open to an interpretation of lack of cooperation. By putting my response as I do in (5), I at least give the person who has asked me the question explicit linguistic evidence of the flouting (through the use of the *either . . . or* construction) from which s/he is able to derive the following implicatures:

    a. that I don't know where Margaret is, but
    b. that I do know that there are only two possible answers.

Grice calls implicatures which can be derived on the basis of explicit linguistic evidence *conventional implicatures*.

The problem in all of this is that Grice does not tell us how the addressee goes about constructing the 'correct' implicatures. In addition, of course, we might also wonder whether there can ever be any 'correct' implicatures. In the second example, the linguistic structure at least allows her/him a choice of only two possibilities. In addition it is hardly likely that the addressee in this second example will conclude that I am lying because I do not know precisely where Margaret is or that I should not give any reply to his question because I do not know this. If I were to say

(6)   I don't know.

I would certainly abide by the CP, but I might also be interpreted as answering brusquely rather than being honest. If I were to utter (6), I would at least preface it with an formulaic, ritualised EPM such as 'sorry':

(7)   Sorry, I don't know.

Uttering (5) at least indicates that I do know that there are two possibilities, and by saying so, I hope to have answered the question at least partially. We might, on the other hand, say that (5) and (7) would be uttered under different conditions, (5) under the condition that I do at least know of the two possibilities and (7) under the condition that I have not the faintest idea where she is. By using the formulaic EPM, I am applying a strategy for reproducing the cooperative nature of the social interaction, i.e. not threatening the co-participant's or my own face, and am consequently seen to be indulging in at least cooperative behaviour.

My decision of whether to reply with (5), (6) or (7) is determined by the knowledge that, in the context of

a. a departmental party, in the framework of the activities of an academic institution,
b. the shared knowledge that Margaret lives in Geneva,
c. the way in which my colleague and I generally interact on a day-to-day basis at our workplace, etc.,

my interactant will have no difficulty in deriving a set of assumptions which will maintain the cooperative nature of the social interaction. I would, after all, be rather shocked if s/he responded to (5) with an utterance like (8):

(8) That's no good to me. I want to know exactly where she is.

or to (7) with an utterance like (9):

(9) 'Sorry'? You're not sorry at all that she's not here, are you?

The problem is simple. If we follow the Gricean CP, there is no way of knowing not only *how* the addressee will derive the implicature, but even *what* implicature or implicatures s/he is likely to derive. We are, after all, *both* jointly responsible for maintaining the equilibrium of social relationships. Even though I must ultimately take responsibility for my own utterances, I constantly have to monitor what has been said, what might be said and what the salient features of the inter-actional context are, in particular the factors of shared knowledge. I have to be prepared to carry out forms of repair work, and I can expect my interlocutors to be as prepared as I am to do the same. In any social interaction I have to monitor what ongoing power relationships hold between myself and my interlocutors, since all human interaction involves degrees of power, sometimes fairly institutionalised and pre-dictable but at other times shifting and unpredictable. If politeness is seen as facework, then, it does not rest in individual utterances alone, but is a constantly negotiable commodity throughout instances of verbal practice. My analysis of 'politeness as facework' is to see it as constantly reconstructed and renegotiated politic behaviour, but however we judge appropriateness in the context of the hypothetical situation under discussion, the Gricean CP is simply too static to allow us to account for these judgements.

There is a very extensive literature on the CP, but for our purposes it is important to mention some other potential weaknesses of the the-ory that have led to revisions, redevelopments and alternative models of cognitive inferencing. Even if we disregard the points made above, the first criticism concerns the number of maxims that are required to set up a 'universal' theory of cooperation in conversation. The three major models of politeness have taken Grice at his word in developing

supplementary maxims or principles to account for linguistic politeness. Can we do away with some of the maxims, conflate them in any
way, or will we have to extend the number available and, if so, to the
tune of how many?

On the surface, Grice's CP almost reads like a set of rational injunc-
tions on how to be a good rhetorician, and although it might have
validity for western cultures, there is no guarantee that the maxims
are equally valid in different cultural settings. Keenan (1971) showed
convincingly that the kinds of postulates set up by Grice do not necessarily hold in Malagasy culture. Her conclusion was that, at the very
least, the individual maxims will need to be adapted to other cultural
conditions in order to account for what is to be taken as cooperative
verbal behaviour outside the western world. In this sense Keenan's critique of Grice's CP is similar to Ide's critique of Brown and Levinson's
model of politeness – the CP is eurocentric. Approaches to the study of
politeness which are based on Grice, like Lakoff's, Leech's and Brown
and Levinson's models, are thus open to the same types of criticism as
Grice himself.

The examples given above show that the Gricean model never gives
an explicit account of how implicatures are derived. At the very least,
we should know how a co-participant in the verbal interaction arrives
at the implicatures s/he arrives at. But we should also know what then
happens if the implicature (or set of implicatures) is not that which
was 'intended' by the speaker (see examples (8) and (9)). The assumption
appears to be that the co-participant will simply be able to reconstruct
the intended meaning, but we have no way of knowing on what basis
this is done, or what happens if s/he gets it 'wrong'.

The major criticism of Gricean pragmatics has come from Relevance
Theory (RT), which goes at least part of the way towards rectifying
many of the problems mentioned above.[3] In the following section I
shall sketch out some of the important features of RT and indicate
how it might be used as a theory for deriving inferences in politeness
research.

SPERBER AND WILSON'S RELEVANCE THEORY

Relevance Theory (RT) is a theory of communication and cognition
rather than a model of pragmatics, although its beginnings can be located in a dissatisfaction with the Gricean model of cooperation and
with the semiotic explanation of communication in terms of language
as a code model. Although Sperber and Wilson do not deny that human

language is a semiotic code and that a certain amount of the code theory of communication may be accepted,[4] they vehemently deny that only a code model can account for how human beings communicate more or less successfully. What is missing in semiotic accounts of communication is the role played by cognition (knowledge) and the nature of inferencing processes. The idea that any human communication can be 'perfect' is rejected by Sperber and Wilson. Successful communication is a question of degrees of success rather than a binary distinction between success or lack of success.

Sperber and Wilson admit that the Gricean model of cooperation is a step in the right direction, but they raise many of the points of criticism dealt with in the previous section. Above all, they argue that, to be a model of cooperation, the maxims should be derivable from one overriding axiom of communication, which they locate in the Gricean Maxim of Relation. As we have seen, this maxim determines that utterance B should in some sense be relevant to utterance A, the problematic phrase here being 'in some sense'. 'In what sense?' is precisely the question that they put. In an early paper Sperber and Wilson show that all the remaining Gricean maxims, and possibly many more such as those suggested by Lakoff and Leech for politeness, are derivable from an axiom of relevance (Wilson and Sperber 1978).

In Sperber and Wilson's terms any utterance within a discourse is a stimulus[5] which alters the cognitive environment of the hearer(s). In making the utterance, the speaker goes on record as having done something which is ostensively manifest to his hearer(s) and which alters the context within which the speaker and the hearer(s) are interacting socially. We can translate this principle into the axioms of emergent network theory by saying that every utterance bears at least one value. Since the utterance is thus on record, it has been carried out with a communicative rather than a merely informative intent and is thus said to be mutually manifest to all the participants.[6] The task of the hearers is to derive at least one value for themselves from the utterance.

Two facts can be deduced from all of this. Firstly, an utterance is assumed to come with *a guarantee of optimal relevance*, i.e. the addressee will always assume that the speaker has done everything in her/his power to produce an utterance which can give rise to what Sperber and Wilson call 'contextual effects'. By this they mean that the assumptions which can be derived from the utterance will significantly alter the speaker's and addressee's mutual cognitive context, i.e. their shared knowledge of that part of the ongoing social and discursive practice. It is up to the addressee to infer the most relevant information (in emergent network terms the most salient value) which the speaker's utterance conveys, i.e. most relevant to the addressee, or what the addressee can reasonably assume to have been the most relevant information intended by the speaker.

Now, it is clear that the addressee may gain little or no 'new' knowledge from the utterance, in which case, even though one must assume that the speaker has done her/his best to utter something optimally relevant, it will remain low on a scale of relevance for the addressee. Alternatively, the addressee may have had to expend so much processing effort to arrive at the contextual effects that the effort may not have been worth the increment in mutually shared knowledge.

Relevance, therefore, is not a black-and-white property of utterances – either the utterance was relevant or it was not – but a sliding scale which may differ from speaker to addressee, from one addressee to the next and from one context to another. Relevance can also be negotiated from one conversational turn to the next. Sperber and Wilson give very detailed examples of how addressees use utterances directed at them to infer information which was not encoded in those utterances. One major principle in RT is that no utterance can ever be fully determined with respect to its meaning. Rather, what happens is this: the addressee will filter out the propositional content from the utterance, then use information from the context of the utterance and her/his own knowledge and knowledge that can be presumed to be shared with the speaker to enrich the proposition by creating inferred assumptions. Depending on the degree to which contextual effects can be generated in this way and depending on the amount of time and effort expended in inferring those assumptions, the utterance reaches a level of relevance for the addressee, i.e. it has a certain value.

Let me illustrate how this happens by returning to the example of the departmental party given in the last section. If A asks me (4):

(4)   Where's Margaret this evening?

and I give (7) as my response:

(7)   Sorry, I don't know.

A must assume my response to be optimally relevant.[7] The proposition that A will interpret from (7) is:

(10)   <RJW does not know where Margaret is this evening>

If A genuinely wanted to know Margaret's whereabouts, then my response does not add much to A's ongoing knowledge and will be low on a scale of relevance although it did not take A much processing effort to derive this inference. However, let us assume that A has every reason to believe that I generally do know about Margaret's whereabouts. Then, based on a supplementary assumption made by A:

(11)   <RJW generally does know where Margaret is>

s/he can derive a number of additional assumptions:

(12)   <On the basis of (11) RJW does know where Margaret is>
(13)a. <If (12), then RJW is lying and knows where Margaret is>
    b. <If (12), then RJW doesn't want to tell me where Margaret is>
(14)   <If (13a) and/or (13b), then RJW doesn't want me to know where Margaret is>
(15)a. <If (14), then RJW is being uncooperative and his utterance is interpretable as a face-threat to me.>
    b. <If (14), then RJW doesn't want me to know that he knows where Margaret is> etc.

The list of potential assumptions that A could make is almost endless, but Sperber and Wilson suggest that A will stop at that assumption which will have given her/him new contextual effects.

In our example, the interesting point is that my utterance of the formulaic EPM (Expression of Procedural Meaning) *sorry* is meant to prevent the addressee from going beyond (13) or (14), although no one can of course guarantee that this will not happen. Having generated the first proposition (10), A will also have generated (probably concurrently) the proposition (16):

(16)   <RJW is sorry about something>

The close contiguity between (10) and (16) will lead to the logical deduction in (17):

(17)   <RJW is sorry that he doesn't know where Margaret is>

In addition, therefore, uttering 'sorry' might prevent the deduction of assumptions (12) to (15).

At this point we have reentered the theory of politic behaviour as facework. Had I simply given response (6) with no 'sorry' and assuming that I also share with A the knowledge that I generally do know about Margaret's whereabouts, to have uttered (6) could have given rise to a whole set of assumptions that I would rather A did not make about me, including the possible assumption that I am being rude, abrupt, uncooperative, impolite, etc. Uttering *sorry* could also equally well have been an expression of genuine regret that I am not able to provide A with the information s/he wants. If this topic in the interaction continues, the ambiguity of *sorry* will probably be resolved. But left at this point, A is free to interpret my utterance either as a stalling strategy or as a genuine expression of regret. Even at the level of this simple exchange of question–response the Brown and Levinson model is not able to help out, since I could have intended my utterance to have been interpreted either way, and A is totally free to derive whatever new information may enrich her/his cognitive environment.

We can see from the example that, in accordance with RT, the participants in social interaction are socially constrained to react to utterances in one way or another, and this is one of the axiomatic principles of the theory of emergent networks. Relevance is assessed in terms of the assumption(s) which can be accessed by processes of inference. The greater the contextual effects are for the hearer(s) by processing the utterance and the less cognitive effort has been invested by them in doing so, the greater will be the relevance of the utterance. In free verbal interaction, it is therefore up to the speaker to see to it that the other participants in the interaction expend as little effort as possible in inferring the most relevant information. The context of an utterance may be seen as the set of assumptions inferred by the participants from the previous discourse, the information made manifest in the immediate physical and social environment of the discourse and the set of assumptions anticipated from the upcoming discourse.

One major problem with RT is that it rarely, if ever, concerns itself with stretches of natural verbal interaction (cf. Watts 1997b and note 3). Nevertheless, it provides an extremely powerful interpretative apparatus, and it can be used to illustrate that no model of linguistic politeness can do without some account of how we reach the kinds of assumptions that we do in ongoing linguistic interaction without considering questions such as the shared cognitive environment of the interactants and the processes of inferencing that are necessary to make sense of what is said. The analysis of naturally occurring verbal interaction carried out in chapter 9 is therefore an effort to locate instances of linguistic politeness within politic behaviour by making practical use of the powerful mechanisms of RT.

RT can help us to break out of the limits of Gricean rationality in which we are constantly measuring what we say against the possible reactions of the addressee. This does not of course mean that RT does not have its own very strong element of rational decision making, but at least it is on the level of the addressee that it should be applied, and at least it allows the constant negotiation and renegotiation of meanings to be seen as a continuous process in verbal interaction. Above all, RT can help us to break free from the idea that politeness is simply a matter of face-threat avoidance or mitigation whilst not abandoning the idea of face altogether. As an instrument of micro-level analysis of verbal interaction it is a much underrated theory, and I shall endeavour to correct that impression by using it here.

POWER AND THE EXERCISE OF POWER

Before we turn to an analysis of extracts from naturally occurring verbal interaction in chapter 9, we need to deal briefly with the final piece of the theoretical jigsaw puzzle presented in this book, namely the notion of power and the term 'exercise of power'. In Watts (1991) a range of theories on how power should be conceptualised are discussed, and since 1990 three important book-length publications have appeared applying notions of power to verbal interaction, Wartenberg (1990), Ng and Bradac (1993) and Diamond (1996). In addition, Bourdieu's work has repeatedly stressed the significance of what he calls 'symbolic power' (see the discussion in chapter 6).

For Bourdieu and his associates 'symbolic power' relies on a prior concept of 'power' residing in notions of institutional dominance. Bourdieu and Passeron (1990: 4) see symbolic power as 'every power which manages to impose meanings and to impose them as legitimate by concealing the power relations which are the basis of its force'. So the power that imposes meanings can be read as the discursive practices which lead to the objectified social structures in accordance with which an individual's habitus is formed and through which s/he develops an intuitive 'feel for the game'. Since these meanings are taken to be legitimate, they conceal the real source of power. Bourdieu's notion of power is thus similar to what Ng and Bradac have called 'power over'. In terms of network theory, 'power over' is held by complex, institutionalised *latent* networks such as school, family, local and national government, in some instances the church, financial institutions, etc.

In Watts (1991), however, the focus is on observing and analysing how emergent networks arise in ongoing social practice, which involves participants in verbal interaction in the potential exercise of power. Power is thus akin to Ng and Bradac's concept of 'power to'. In emergent networks the participants might bring to an instance of social practice different measures of potential 'power over' thus providing them with distinct advantages in terms of freedom of action, and this can often lead to a struggle over the perceived rights to acquire 'power to'.

For the analysis in chapter 9 I shall retain the concept of power as I presented it in Watts (1991):

> An individual A possesses power if s/he has the freedom of action to achieve the goals s/he has set her/himself, regardless of whether or not this involves the potential to impose A's will on others to carry out actions that are in A's interests. (1991: 60)

This implies that an interactant 'has' power in social practice if the goals s/he has set for the interaction are achievable. But this does not imply that that interactant will necessarily use her/his freedom of action to reach those goals, nor that some other interactant(s) might not resist the attempt to do so. Possessing power does not mean using that power, nor does it mean employing force to achieve ends which are not perceived by others as being in their interest.

In the development of an emergent network, therefore, the notion of 'exercise of power' is much more significant. In Watts (1991) it was defined as follows:

> A exercises power over B when A affects B in a manner contrary to B's initially perceived interests, regardless of whether B later comes to accept the desirability of A's actions. (1991: 62)

If B does not 'come to accept the desirability of A's actions, the exercise of power involves opposition and coercion. If B does come to accept the desirability of A's actions, the exercise of power is akin to persuasion.

Let us see how this works by returning to the short extract taken from the *Panorama* programme presented in chapter 1, part of which was repeated in this chapter:

(1)

¹E: are you now willing to discuss uneconomic pits\	
S:	... we're not prepared to go along to the National

²E:	you're not/ **sorry** if I interrupt you .. there\ y/ I- I/ let me just remind you that –
S: Coal Board\ and start –	:er: .. :er:

³E:
S: .. are you going to let me answer the question\ you put a question\ for god's sake let me answer\

Scargill has been invited to the studio to participate in the interview with the moderator after the film sequence about miners returning to work during the miners' strike in 1984–5 has been shown. The media, in particular television, form an institutionalised set of latent networks which has 'power over' the shaping of public opinion on current issues of public interest. They can, in other words, impose meanings on an audience which are taken as legitimate and in doing so, they can conceal the sources of that power. By accepting the invitation to be interviewed on BBC 1 Scargill also accepts this form of 'power over'. Despite the fact that, by virtue of being the president of the National Union of Mineworkers, Scargill also 'possesses' power within a set of institutionalised latent networks, he is unlikely to be able to exercise any of it unless he is given the freedom to do so by the moderator.

Knowing that this is the case and knowing the legitimacy of the public opinion-forming institution of television, Scargill will be prepared to oppose attempts to exercise power over him by the moderator and will attempt to exercise power himself, i.e. to acquire 'power to'. The moderator's question *are you now willing to discuss uneconomic pits?* gives the floor to Scargill, but it contains a set of assumptions which Scargill is likely, in the circumstances, to interpret as face-threatening, e.g.

(18) <you were previously not willing to discuss uneconomic pits>
(19) <the issue is only about uneconomic pits>
(20) <there are uneconomic pits>
(21) <'now' refers to the present point in time, i.e. after having seen the documentary on the miners' hardships and the fact that they are returning to work>

To accept these points would be tantamount to accepting defeat, so Scargill pauses before he begins his response. Although the first clause in his utterance does not seem to address the question, he is interrupted before he can go any further.

Now, part of the politic behaviour of an interview, even though we can expect opposing points of view to be aired, is that an interviewee is given the freedom of action to develop her/his ideas and, if necessary, to justify her/himself in the response given to a question. Emery's interruption is an exercise of power in that he affects Scargill in a manner contrary to Scargill's initially perceived interests. Emery is institutionally in possession of power over Scargill, but he has still violated the politic behaviour in force in a live BBC television interview. The production of the EPM *sorry*, the use of the lexeme *interrupt* and his increased stuttering and false starts are evidence that he is aware of this fact. He then tries to issue a warning to Scargill which includes two EPMs frequently associated with politeness, *[let me] [just] remind you that*. In the first instance, it is unclear what he wants to remind Scargill of. Secondly, he seems to be merely compounding the previous violation of politic behaviour by issuing the warning. Quite apart from this, however, the use of *let me V* and *just* are immediately interpretable as unnecessary attempts at politeness and open up a negative evaluation of trying to misuse his latent power over Scargill. The latter, however, has overlapped this utterance to question whether he is going to be allowed to respond, thereby challenging Emery's position as the interviewer and attempting to exercise power over him.

The struggle over the exercise of power in emergent networks is thus linked inextricably to perceptions of (im)politeness$_1$ and to the maintenance and violation of politic behaviour. In this chapter I have clarified the ways in which Relevance Theory can be used in accounting for the ways in which EPMs that have traditionally been said to encode politeness are processed either as part of the expected politic behaviour of the social interaction or as instances of politeness. I have also shown how social practice in action involves participants in emergent networks through which power is negotiated. We expect to see linguistic expressions of politeness intricately tied up with the exercise of power, and we are now in a position to look at stretches of naturally occurring verbal interaction to assess the validity of these claims in chapter 9.

9 Politic behaviour and politeness in discourse

In chapter 8 I argued that a Gricean approach to the analysis of politeness in discursive practice was insufficient to provide an explanation for interactants' ability to perceive (im)politeness$_1$ against the background of politic behaviour. The option chosen in chapter 8 was to suggest the application of Relevance Theory as a method of accounting for the possible inferences that might lead to the classification of ongoing utterances as (im)polite. I pointed out, however, that RT is a theory of cognition and communication and was not originally designed to track the chain of inferred assumptions made by participants in discursive practice.[1] In this chapter, I wish to show that it can nevertheless be used as a method of analysis of ongoing discourse.

I also demonstrated in chapter 8 how (im)politeness$_1$ is intimately connected with the exercise of power, by reanalysing part of the extract presented in chapter 1 from the BBC television programme *Panorama*, which revealed a conflict between the moderator, Fred Emery, and the leader of the National Union of Mineworkers in the early 1980s, Arthur Scargill. In this chapter I shall analyse two longer extracts of naturally occurring verbal interaction in an attempt to show how certain linguistic expressions might be open to interpretation either as realisations of politic behaviour or as realisations of (im)politeness$_1$.

The range of linguistic expressions presented in chapter 7 will play an important role in this analysis precisely because, as expressions of procedural meaning, they are always latently open to the attribution of politeness$_1$. They are not, I argue, inherently polite expressions. Their function in the verbal interaction is to provide clues to the addressee(s) concerning the value that should be placed on the propositions conveyed by the utterances and what inferencing procedures should be applied. Hence, to return to House and Kasper's terminology, although 'consultative devices', 'play-downs', 'politeness markers', 'hedges', 'understaters', 'downtoners', 'committers', 'forewarnings' and the like are not inherently polite linguistic structures, they are nevertheless important clues to interpret whether the interactant remains within the scope of politic behaviour or violates it either by not uttering the EPM when expected or by uttering the EPM when not expected.

The two extracts from verbal interaction that will be examined have been taken from naturally occurring socio-communicative verbal interaction and represent examples of social practice. As might be expected with such data, the lexemes *polite* or *impolite* are very rarely if ever used to classify an interactant's behaviour explicitly, and there are therefore very few examples of expressive (im)politeness[1]. Nevertheless there are clear indications in the extracts that participants might have interpreted certain aspects of linguistic practice in this way.

CONFRONTATIONAL DISCOURSE

The first extract is taken from a BBC *Panorama* programme immediately prior to the 1997 General Election in Britain in which the leader of the Labour Party and, according to the public opinion polls, the future Prime Minister, Tony Blair, is being interviewed by the *Panorama* moderator David Dimbleby:

(1)

[1]D: Mr Blair\ in this election\ you're asking the electorate to put their trust in you\ the new Blair\ isn't
  B:

[2]D: there a problem that there's an old Blair who believed in quite different things\ which makes it rather
  B:

[3]D: difficult for people to trust the new one\
  B: no\ I don't agree at all\ I mean\ we have been through a big

[4]D:
  B: process of change and modernisation of the Labour Party\ that is absolutely true\ but it has been a

[5]D:
  B: process of change that I think has been well worth undertaking\ and .. as you probably know\

[6]D:
  B: . throughout my time in the Labour Party\ I've wanted to move the Labour Party on from positions\ in

[7]D:
  B: order to get the proper modernised Labour Party that we have today\ New Labour is very much what I

[8]D: but did you believe in Old Labour\
  B: believe in\ it's very much my own creation\   I believed in the values

⁹D:　　　　　　　　　　　　　no\ did you believe in what they stood for\ did you believe in CND\ did you
　B:　of the Labour Party\ yes\

¹⁰D:　believe in union power not being curtailed\ did you believe in nationalisation\ no privatisation\
　B:　　　　　　　　　　　　　　　　　　　　　　　　　　　　　　　　　　　　there are

¹¹D:
　B:　a whole series of policy decisions that I adopted\ along with the rest of the Labour Party\ but the very

¹²D:　　　　　　　　　　　　　　　　　　　　　　　　　　　　　　　　　　I know
　B:　process of modernisation\ has been the very process that I have undertaken in the Labour Party\

¹³D:　that\ but have you abandoned/ did you believe what you said you believed in the eighties\
　B:　　　　　　　　　　　　　　　　　　　　　　　　　　　　　　　look\ of

¹⁴D:
　B:　course we always believed in the idea of a more just and more fair society\ and the Labour Party

¹⁵D:
　B:　believed for a long period of time\ that the way to do that was\ for example\ greater nationalisation\

¹⁶D:
　B:　was for example\ simply more increased state spending\ the whole process of modernisation David\

¹⁷D:
　B:　has been to take the Labour Party away from that\ to keep true to its principles\ but put those

¹⁸D:　　　　　　　　　　　　　　　　　so all that was wrong\
　B:　principles properly in a modern setting\　　　　　　　　no\ I don't say all that was wrong\ I

¹⁹D:
　B:　simply say what is important is to apply those principles to the modern world\ look\ .. John Major

²⁰D:
　B:　stood in the 1970s on a platform of Scottish devolution\ Margaret Thatcher was the person that closed

²¹D:
　B:　more grammar schools than anyone else\ she was a member of Ted Heath's government you know\

²²D:　　　　　　　　　　　it pales into insignificance compared with what you stood for in '83 and '87\
　B:　times move on\　　　　　　　　　　　　　　　　　　　　　　　　no\ I don't

²³D:
　B:　think it does\ actually\ but in any event\ let me say to you\ that my whole time within the Labour

²⁴D:
　B:　Party/ let us just be realistic about this\ from the moment that I came into the Labour Party\ I've

²⁵D:
　B:　argued that it had to change and modernise and update itself\ I was the person who\ when I was the

²⁶D:
　B:　Treasury spokesman for the Labour Party\ was arguing that we had to stand up for the rights of small

²⁷D:
　B:　investors\ I was the person who\ when I got into the Shadow Cabinet\ that withdrew our support for

28 D:
   B: the closed shop it's held in the past\ I was the Shadow Home Secretary that was the person\ that said

29 D:
   B: Labour had to tighten up its stance on law and order\ that we had to stand up for the rights of the

30 D:
   B: citizen against the criminal\ I was the person that argued the case for the changes in the union

31 D: and you were the person\ as a barrister\ who dealt with trade union affairs\ who sat on a
   B: relationship\ –

32 D: select committee\ and who opposed every root and branch\ every detail of the Conservative
   B:

33 D: government's attempts to reform/ to even make the most modest reforms\ in trade union law\
   B: David\

34 D:
   B: those were in the days when people thought\ that the best way to look at collective bargaining

35 D:
   B: arrangements\ between employer and employee\ was not to have a legal framework\ we changed that\

36 D: no\ but hang
   B: and let me say something to you\ I'm proud of the changes that the Labour Party has made\

37 D: on\ I'm asking you about what happened before\ you may be proud of what you've done now\ that
   B:

38 D: implies you're ashamed of what happened before\   but was your instinct right
   B: I'm not ashamed of it at all\

39 D: when\ . for instance\ . you talked about the Tories as people with hobnail boots\ ready to trample over
   B:

40 D: the rights of trade unionists\ I mean\ is that something you'd defend saying now\
   B:

41 D: did you mean to say it\
   B: look\ at that time people thought\ that the best way to have an industrial

42 D:
   B: relations framework\ was to get the law out of it\ that changed\ I was one of those people that changed

43 D: the Conservative Party were in the van on this\ they decided it was
   B: that position of the Labour Party\ –

44 D: right to have a framework\ –
   B: if I could just finish this ...

Before embarking on an analysis of the extract, we first need to establish the lines taken by the participants, the faces which they may believe they have been assigned or which they might wish to be assigned to them by the general public and by one another, and the politic behaviour that is likely to determine the discourse behaviour of the two participants.

The communicative situation is public in that both participants know that they have a lot to lose in the eyes of the television audience if they do not put up a good show. Evidence of this awareness can be given from a number of points in the extract. Blair takes the line that he assumes the general public expects him to take, i.e. to present the revitalised Labour Party as New Labour rather than Old Labour, but at the same time to take care not to frighten off traditional Labour voters by suggesting that Labour's former policies were wrong. To do this, he tries not to mention former policies at all but to present the achievements of the New Labour Party in the immediate past and the present as being his own personal responsibility. The face that he would like to present and that he would like the television audience to endorse is that of a charismatic leader who has almost single-handedly led the Labour Party into a fast-changing modern world, in which Labour's former policies have simply been overtaken.

Dimbleby, on the other hand, knows that this will be Blair's major line, and from the very outset of the interview he proceeds to subvert it by not allowing Blair to present only 'the new Blair' and to conveniently forget 'the old Blair'. If Dimbleby succeeds in carrying this line through during the interview, he knows that the change from Old Labour and the 'old Blair' to New Labour and the 'new Blair' could be interpreted in the eyes of the television audience as mere opportunism on Blair's part in order to gain power. Blair might then lose a number of potential voters, although in all probability not enough to make him lose the election. Dimbleby's position is thus one of potential power, which he can exercise to the detriment of Blair. In fact, the politic behaviour of a television interview in a political affairs programme such as *Panorama* gives the moderator quite extensive latent power to adversely effect the face of the interviewee. This is even the case if the interviewee has a greater degree of potential power over the moderator by virtue of holding high political office, which Blair, note, does not yet hold! On the other hand, for a politician to put up a poor showing in the eyes of the general public could seriously damage either the effective uptake and acceptance of her/his policies or her/his chances in the event of an election. So Dimbleby can be seen to have more potential power at the beginning of the interview than Blair.

The verbal interaction thus bears all the hallmarks of conflictual discourse in which both Blair and Dimbleby have a lot to lose. Dimbleby is constrained to take the line of a firm, but superficially deferential participant, while Blair is constrained to take the line of a potential charismatic leader looking for votes from the general public. Dimbleby might lose members of his audience and Blair might lose voters. In addition, Dimbleby is constrained to make the programme entertaining for the general public, and he can do this only if he adopts an oppositional stance towards Blair, regardless of what his own personal political leanings might be. These aspects of the overall situation will characterise the expected politic behaviour of the interview and will be instrumental in leading us to identify possible examples of linguistic (im)politeness$_1$.

Consider the first two turns in scores 1–8:

(2)

[1]D:	**Mr Blair**\ in this election\ you're asking the electorate to put their trust in you\ the new Blair**isn't**
	POLITIC
	BEHAVIOUR
B:	

[2]D:	**there a problem that there's an old Blair who believed in quite different things**\ which makes it
	POTENTIALLY OPEN TO INTERPRETATION AS LINGUISTIC POLITENESS
B:	

[3]D:	rather difficult for people to trust the new one\
B:	**no**\ **I don't agree at all**\ **I mean**\ we have been through
	NEGATIVE EVALUATION 'CAJOLER'[2]
	OF 'POLITE' UTTERANCE POLITIC BEHAVIOUR
	ATTEMPT TO RESTORE HARMONY

[4]D:	
B:	a big process of change and modernisation of the Labour Party\ that is absolutely true\ but it has been

[5]D:	
B:	a process of change that I think has been well worth undertaking\ and .. **as you probably know**\
	DEFERENTIAL POLITIC BEHAVIOUR
	CARRYING OUT POSITIVE
	FACEWORK

[6]D:	
B:	throughout my time in the Labour Party\ I've wanted to move the Labour Party on from positions\ in

[7]D:	
B:	order to get the proper modernised Labour Party that we have today\ New Labour is very much what I

[8]D:	
B:	believe in\ it's very much my own creation\

Dimbleby opens the interview with a formal term of address which the politic behaviour of a television interview of this kind would demand. I have explicitly indicated this by giving the relevant linguistic structure in bold face and placing an interpretative commentary immediately below it in the score. It may well be the case that Dimbleby is on first-name terms with Blair, but the seriousness of the subject (an imminent General Election), Blair's position as the leader of the opposition party and the relative formality of the programme demand that first-name address be avoided here. Dimbleby's first question – *Isn't there a problem that there's an old Blair who believed in quite different things, which makes it rather difficult to trust the new one?* – could have been put differently and still have stayed within the bounds of politic behaviour – *There's a problem that there's an old Blair who believed in quite different things. Doesn't this make it rather difficult to trust the new one?* Since the question is in excess of what is minimally required, it is open to interpretation as polite.

How does Blair react to the question and how might he have inferred the embedded statement that there is a problem concerning the 'old Blair'? Note that Blair's reaction is an emphatic denial, *No, I don't agree at all.* The negative response particle *no* could be interpreted as a response to the inferred *yes–no* question *Doesn't this make it rather difficult to trust the new one?* But what does Blair not agree with? In Dimbleby's utterance there is no *explicit* statement of opinion. On the assumption that Blair expects the kind of conflict outlined above, the following inferential steps can be proposed:

(3) <D is asking whether I agree with p>
(4) <p = there is a problem x & x = there's an old Blair>
(5) <D believes p>
(6) <since D did not state p, D is paying with politeness>

Blair's reaction to D's thinly disguised statement that the fact that there is an old Blair will make it difficult for people to trust the new one shows that he has given the 'polite' utterance a negative evaluation. In Blair's full response to Dimbleby's question he produces the two phrases *I think* and *as you probably know.* The first of these is easily interpreted as referential rather than a hedge, but the second is a concession to Dimbleby, which has the effect of boosting the moderator's face. But it is not interpretable as polite.

The following five turns in scores 8–13 reveal a considerable amount of face-threatening from Dimbleby to Blair without much effort at mitigation:

(7)

[8] D:	**but** did you believe in Old Labour\
B:	I believed in the values

[9] D:	**no** \ did you believe in what they stood for\ did you believe in CND\ did you
	CONTRADICTION
	NON-POLITIC BEHAVIOUR
	= IMPOLITE
B:	of the Labour Party\ yes\

[10] D:	believe in union power not being curtailed\ did you believe in nationalisation\ no privatisation\
B:	there are

[11] D:	
B:	a whole series of policy decisions that I adopted\ along with the rest of the Labour Party\ but the very

[12] D:	**I know**
	REJECTION
	OF BLAIR'S POINT
	NON-POLITIC
	= IMPOLITE
B:	process of modernisation\ has been the very process that I have undertaken in the Labour Party\

[13] D:	**that** \ **but** have you abandoned/ did you believe what you said you believed in the eighties\
	CONTRADICTION
B:	

Dimbleby's *but* in score 8 effectively rejects Blair's turn as an adequate response to his first question, which he then reformulates as an explicit *yes–no* question, *did you believe in Old Labour?* Blair's response can, arguably, be taken as adequate, *I believed in the values of the Labour Party*, but Dimbleby rejects it with no attempt to mitigate the rejection and then proceeds to ask Blair whether he believed in what they stood for. Is what the Labour Party stood for not equivalent to the values of the Labour Party that Blair claims he believed in, particularly when we then hear Dimbleby exemplify those values? Dimbleby thus violates the politic behaviour in operation in the interaction, although Blair shows no signs that he has interpreted Dimbleby in this way. Dimbleby's behaviour is thus open to interpretation as impolite. Blair's reaction is to try to redirect the audience's attention to the modernisation of the Labour Party and his leading part in that process in the hope of avoiding any comparison between Old and New Labour and an old and a new Blair. In score 12 Dimbleby does not allow Blair to develop his turn further, by latching on a dismissive utterance *I know that* at the first available transition relevance place.[3] The politic behaviour of a television interview does not sanction interruption by the interviewer, particularly not if it is simply to dismiss the relevance of the interviewee's response. The utterance is thus open to interpretation as impolite.

How does Blair react to Dimbleby here? Is there any sign that he may have inferred impoliteness? Consider the following section of the interview in scores 13–22:

(8)

¹³D:

B: **look \ of**
                                                                                                         'CAJOLER'
                                                                                                POLITIC BEHAVIOUR
                                                                                          ATTEMPT TO RESTORE HARMONY

¹⁴D:

B: **course** we always believed in the idea of a more just and more fair society\ and the Labour Party
    COMMITTER
    POLITIC BEHAVIOUR
    FACEWORK

¹⁵D:

B: believed for a long period of time\ that the way to do that was\ for example\ greater nationalisation\

¹⁶D:

B: was for example**simply** more increased state spending\ the **whole** process of modernisation **David**\
              DOWNTONER   INTENSIFIER   DEMEANING
          POLITIC BEHAVIOUR   POLITIC BEHAVIOUR   POLITIC BEHAVIOUR
                        ←ATTEMPT TO RESTORE HARMONY→

¹⁷D:

B: has been to take the Labour Party away from that\ to keep true to its principles\ but put those

¹⁸D: **so all that was wrong**
                                            NEGATIVE FACEWORK
                                    POTENTIALLY IMPOLITE BEHAVIOUR
B: principles properly in a modern setting\   no\ I don't say all that was wrong\ I

¹⁹D:

B: **simply** say what is important is to apply those principles to the modern world\ **look**\ .. John Major
    DOWNTONER   'CAJOLER'
    POLITIC BEHAVIOUR   POLITIC BEHAVIOUR
                                                                ATTEMPT TO RESTORE HARMONY

²⁰D:

B: stood in the 1970s on a platform of Scottish devolution\ Margaret Thatcher was the person that closed

²¹D:

B: more grammar schools than anyone else\ she was a member of Ted Heath's government **you know**\
                                                                      POLITIC BEHAVIOUR
                                                                  APPEAL FOR COMMON GROUND

²²D: **it pales into insignificance compared with what you stood for in '83 and '87**\
                        BLATANT INSULT
                    NON-POLITIC BEHAVIOUR
                    POTENTIALLY IMPOLITE
B: times move on\

Blair's *look* at the beginning of his first turn in score 13 is one of the
class of gambits that Edmondson (1977) calls *cajolers*. It is an EPM which
is used to 'increase, establish or restore harmony between the interlocutors' (House and Kasper 1981: 168). The inferences that Dimbleby
may derive are:

(9)   <Blair perceives a disharmony in the interaction>
(10)   <Blair wishes to restore harmony>
(11)   <Blair requests that I focus on what he is about to say>

The disharmony arises through Blair's interpretation of Dimbleby's previous turn as not abiding by the necessary politic behaviour, i.e. as
being impolite, although Blair does not say explicitly that this is how
he has interpreted Dimbleby's behaviour.

My interpretation is strengthened by the fact that during his turn
Blair uses a number of EPMs to guide the process of inferencing by
Dimbleby. He follows the cajoler with a further EPM, *of course*, which
can be interpreted as a committer (House and Kasper 1981), committing both himself and Dimbleby to the positive truth value of the following propositions. The use of the downtoner[4] *simply* modifies the impact of the expression *more increased state spending*, encouraging the
following inferences by Dimbleby:

(12)   <Blair does not believe in more increased state spending>
(13)a. <Those who believe in more increased state spending are providing a simple
         solution>
    b. <Blair believes (13a)>
(14)a. <The simple solution is not the correct solution>
    b. <Blair believes (14a)>

Finally, the adjective *whole*, which could be omitted without altering
the truth value of the proposition and may therefore be understood
as an EPM, is an intensifier which is meant to underscore the overall validity of that part of the proposition to which it is attached,
i.e. *the process of modernisation*, and to forestall possible misunderstanding. These EPMs are what Blair perceives as necessary to restore the
'harmony' in the interaction. They are elements of politic behaviour
contributing to relational work, but are not interpretable as politeness.
An added attempt to restore the harmony of the discourse situation is
the first-name term of address *David*, which contrasts markedly with
Dimbleby's *Mr Blair* at the beginning of the interview.

Blair's attempts to restore harmony are rejected by Dimbleby's conclusion in score 18 that the previous policies mentioned by Blair were
wrong. Again the utterance is interpretable as impolite, and once again
we have evidence that this is how Blair sees it in the way in which he

reacts to Dimbleby's statement in the following score. We again have the downtoner EPM *simply* and the cajoler EPM *look* in an effort to restore the politic behaviour of the interview. After illustrating how Conservative politicians have also changed their stance on specific issues, he then appeals to a common understanding that times have changed through the EPM *you know*. Dimbleby's response takes the form of an outright face-threat to Blair, *it pales into insignificance compared with what you stood for in '83 and '87*, which is again latched onto Blair's utterance at a potential transition relevance place and represents an attempt to prevent him from continuing.

The first turn by Blair in scores 22–31 below represents a further attempt by him to reestablish the politic behaviour of the interview situation, thus displaying a perception of Dimbleby's face-threat as having been unnecessary and bordering on the impolite:

(15)

[22] D:	
B:	no\ I don't

[23] D:	
B:	think it does**actually** \ **but in any event**\ let me say to you\ that my whole time within the Labour
	DOWNGRADER REJECTION OF D'S PROPOSITION
	POLITIC BEHAVIOUR EVALUATION OF D'S PROP.
	FACE SAVING AS IMPOLITE

[24] D:	
B:	Party/**let us just be realistic about this**\ from the moment that I came into the Labour Party\ I've
	APPEAL TO D
	CLAIMING COMMON GROUND
	FACEWORK + DOWNTONER
	OPEN TO A POLITE INTERPRETATION

[25] D:	
B:	argued that it had to change and modernise and update itself\ I was the person who\ when I was the

[26] D:	
B:	Treasury spokesman for the Labour Party\ was arguing that we had to stand up for the rights of small

[27] D:	
B:	investors\ I was the person who\ when I got into the Shadow Cabinet\ that withdrew our support for

[28] D:	
B:	the closed shop it's held in the past\ I was the Shadow Home Secretary that was the person\ that said

[29] D:	
B:	Labour had to tighten up its stance on law and order\ that we had to stand up for the rights of the

[30] D:	
B:	citizen against the criminal\ I was the person that argued the case for the changes in the union

³¹D:	**and you were the person**\ as a barrister\ who dealt with trade union affairs\ who sat on a
	INTERRUPTION
	OPEN TO INTERPRETATION
	AS IMPOLITE
B:	relationship\ –
³²D:	select committee\ and who opposed every root and branch\ every detail of the Conservative
B:	
³³D:	government's attempts to reform/ to even make the most modest reforms\ in trade union law\

The EPM *actually* serves the function of downgrading the impact of Dimbleby's utterance rather than Blair's denial. This is followed by an EPM *but* signalling an upcoming proposition which will stand in contrast to Dimbleby's evaluation. Blair adds to this the EPM *in any event*, which indicates that the following inferences should be made:

(16) <the proposition(s) that follow(s) is/are true regardless of the truth value of the previous proposition>

(17) <Blair rejects the validity of my proposition in the context of the present argument>

(18) <following on from (15) and (16), Blair considers my proposition to be a face threat beyond the limits of the politic behaviour operative in this situation>

(19) <following on from (17), Blair considers my utterance impolite>

Blair then proceeds to produce an utterance of the type 'Let me do X' – with the pitch pattern shown in example (100) of chapter 7, which is *not* open to a polite interpretation, but has almost the illocutionary force of a warning. In other words he seems to have taken up the redefinition of the politic behaviour in this particular televised political interview as conflictual. Such a procedure might, on the other hand, damage his political face and lose a number of votes, so he follows it almost immediately with a second utterance of the 'Let us/me do X' type with the pitch pattern given in example (101) of chapter 7. Is this second 'Let us/me do X' structure absolutely necessary at this point? Note that it also contains the hedge *just*, which House and Kasper (1981) classify as a downtoner with the force of modulating the impact of his proposition. It is in excess of what is necessary here and is thus open to a polite interpretation, particularly as it comes so soon after the first 'Let me do X' structure. The inclusive *us* is also an appeal to Dimbleby to restore the politic behaviour of the interview situation.

Dimbleby's response is to intervene in Blair's turn and, using the same parallel structure as that used by Blair (e.g. *I was the person*) but throwing it back at Blair with the pronoun *you* (e.g. *you were the person*), he proceeds to utter three propositions which counter Blair's argument:

(20) <you were the person who dealt with trade union affairs>
(21) <you were the person who sat on a select committee>
(22) <you were the person who opposed the Conservative government's attempts to reform union law>

What makes the accusation worse is the implication that, since Blair was a barrister, he should have known better:

(23) <you did all this although you were a barrister>

Dimbleby's verbal behaviour here represents a blatant intervention and thus a violation of Blair's speaking rights (cf. Watts 1991: 136–40). It is an interruption and is open to interpretation as impolite.

The final section of the extract reveals an increasing amount of frustration on Blair's part, culminating in a polite utterance which is interpretable only as a criticism of Dimbleby's behaviour:

(24)

33D:
B: **David**
DEMEANING
POLITIC BEHAVIOUR
ATTEMPT TO RESTORE HARMONY
OPEN TO INTERPRETATION AS PATRONISING

34 D:
B: those were in the days when people thought\\ that the best way to look at collective bargaining

35D:
B: arrangements\\ between employer and employee\\ was not to have a legal framework\\ we changed that\\

36D: **no\\but hang**
CONTRADICTION + FOREWARNING
POLITIC BEHAVIOUR
FACEWORK
B: and let me say something to you\\ I'm proud of the changes that the Labour Party has made\\

37D: **on**\\ I'm asking you about what happened before\\ you may be proud of what you've done now\\ that
B:

38D: implies you're ashamed of what happened before\\ but was your instinct right
B: I'm not ashamed of it at all\\

39D: when\\ . for instance\\ . you talked about the Tories as people with hobnail boots\\ ready to trample over
B:

40D: the rights of trade unionists**I mean**\\ is that something you'd defend saying now\\ did you mean to
'CAJOLER'
POLITIC BEHAVIOUR
SOFTENING UPCOMING FACE-THREAT
B:

[41]D: say it\
   B: **look**\ at that time people thought\ that the best way to have an industrial relations framework\
                 'CAJOLER'
                 POLITIC BEHAVIOUR
                 APPEAL TO ALLOW HIS POINT OF VIEW

[42] D:
   B: was to get the law out of it\ that changed\ I was one of those people that changed that position of the

[43]D: **the Conservative Party were in the van on this**\ they decided it was right to have a
                 INTERRUPTION
                 CONTRADICTION
             OPEN TO INTERPRETATION AS IMPOLITE
   B: Labour Party\ –

[44]D: framework\ –
   B: **if I could just finish this** ...
                 SEMI-FORMULAIC UTTERANCE IN EXCESS OF POLITIC BEHAVIOUR
                 OPEN TO INTERPRETATION AS POLITE
                 EVALUATION OF D'S BEHAVIOUR AS IMPOLITE

In the face of Dimbleby's attack, Blair again resorts to the strategy of addressing him by his first name, *David*, in an attempt to reinstate the politic behaviour of the interview. The danger here is that the strategy could easily backfire, in that the television audience might infer that Blair is taking up a patronising position with respect to Dimbleby. They will, after all, be aware that Blair is not in a position of power in an interview in a political affairs programme.

Blair then tries yet again to redirect the interview so that he can focus on the changes that have taken place in the Labour Party and the prominent position he has had in effecting those changes, i.e. he would like the television audience to focus on New, rather than Old, Labour (and by extension on the new rather than the old Blair). He makes one assertion in score 35, which allows Dimbleby a further point of attack, namely *we changed that*. The proposition leads to the following set of possible assumptions:

(25)a. <Blair's 'we' refers to the Labour Party>
   b. <Blair's 'we' refers to the present leadership of the Labour Party>
(26)a. <Blair's 'that' refers to the legal framework for collective bargaining arrangements between employers and employees>
   b. <Blair's 'that' refers to the Labour Party's attitudes concerning the legal framework for collective bargaining between employers and employees>
(27) <If (26a), Blair is lying since the Labour Party were not governing the country when that legal framework was changed>
(28) <If (26b), then either (29a), (29b) or (29c)>

(29)a. <The Labour Party has not changed its attitude towards that legal framework>
   b. <The Labour Party has changed its attitude towards that legal framework>
   c. <The Labour Party leadership has changed its attitude towards that legal framework>
(30) <If (29b), either (31) or (32)>
(31) <The Labour Party leadership has caused the Labour Party to change its attitude>
(32) <The Labour Party leadership would like us to believe the truth of (31)>

The statement is thus multiply ambiguous, a fact which leads Dimbleby to counter Blair's tack with the EPM *no*, and then to insert a further EPM, *hang on*, which is effectively a forewarning, or a meta-comment on what will probably be interpretable as an FTA. I have interpreted these moves as politic behaviour since Dimbleby has a right, as the interviewer, to return to his question, which he does, *I'm asking you about what happened before.* He then follows it with the FTA, *You may be proud of what you've done now. That implies you're ashamed of what happened before.* An FTA in the conflictual discursive framework of a political interview is hardly interpretable as impolite behaviour.

In Dimbleby's turn in scores 38–41 he reminds Blair of some of the negative comments he had made about the Conservative Party when the legislation was pushed through parliament, and in doing so he resorts to the 'cajoler' *I mean* in an attempt to restore some degree of harmony in the interview situation. His real intention, however, is to focus on the ambiguity in Blair's statement *we changed that.* Blair's *look* in score 41 is an appeal to Dimbleby to allow him to justify the change in attitude of the Labour Party, but he is interrupted by Dimbleby in score 43, a move which is clearly open to interpretation as impolite. What he does is to refer to assumption (26a) above, thereby implying that Blair is lying about who pushed through the legal framework to regulate collective bargaining between employers and employees. This is not lost on Blair, who interrupts him in his turn. The interruption itself is interpretable as impolite, and Blair needs to cover his tracks. But instead of simply saying *Sorry, but I want to finish what I was saying*, he indulges in an utterance which is a variant of the structural type 'Could I do X?' represented in example (74) in chapter 7 – *If I could just finish.* The utterance is more than would be required in this situation and is open to interpretation as polite, but the point of the 'polite' utterance is to support his interruption of Dimbleby rather than to atone for his violation of the politic behaviour. Politeness here is thus used as a means of attack.

In general, given the kind of confrontational discourse that we can expect in this kind of political interview, we would not expect

politeness to play a role at all, and, indeed, potential linguistic politeness is in evidence at only three points during this part of the interview. Impoliteness, on the other hand, is interpretable at six points
in the extract. The majority of linguistic expressions which would
frequently be described in the literature as realisations of linguistic
politeness are a direct or indirect result of the politic behaviour in
operation during this discourse type. In the following section I shall
take a look at another form of public discourse, this time with a focus
on cooperative rather than confrontational interaction.

PUBLIC, COOPERATIVE DISCOURSE

In this section, I shall examine an open-line phone-in programme
which I have glossed in the title of this section as 'public, cooperative discourse'. In chapter 5 I argued that 'the line that listeners can
assume the moderator to be taking in . . . phone-in programme[s] is
that of a friendly, sometimes jovial, sometimes serious but, apart from
his voice, physically distant friend, giving sympathy and advice where
it appears to be needed, joking with the participants and sometimes
even teasing them' (p. 126). In general, therefore, phone-in programmes
constitute cooperative forms of discourse, although there are notable
exceptions in which moderators seem to make it their business to engage in confrontation with callers and even indulge in insulting them.
Because such programmes are broadcast to live radio audiences, the
discourse takes place in the public domain.

The face loaned to the moderator by the audience includes the
following attributes: a friendly attitude towards the caller, which is
displayed by being helpful, sympathetic and not argumentative; humour (including the freedom to tease the caller); knowledge about
local events, issues and characters, etc. The public face that the moderator will attribute to the caller must be largely positive, although it
may contain negative features in which the moderator, rather than the
caller, has a lot to lose if s/he does not manage the interaction skilfully.
In forms of public discourse, participants have a great deal of face to
lose and they need to handle matters delicately. In the Dimbleby/Blair
interview both the participants and the audience were nevertheless expecting confrontation; in an open-line phone-in programme (at least
of the type presented here) this is not the case. The following extract
is taken from a local radio open-line phone-in programme from Radio
Manchester, recorded in 1984.

(33)

¹H:	Mrs Sack\ hello Mrs Sack\
S:	**hello \ erm: I'm ringing**/ :erm: a- a talk by a health inspector\ on your

²H:	
S:	programme\ a couple of days ago\ .. he was talking about infected/ meat being sold for humans\

³H:	oh yes
S:	instead of being processed for pet food\ :erm: he described- he described the case wh- where

⁴H:	
S:	the meat/ it was from a factory\ and then it had:er:/ covered in dirt\ sawdust\ transported in

⁵H:	yes\ it's a fairly famous case\ it's been going on – I think
S:	unrefrigerated vans\ etcetera etcetera\ and I – yeah

⁶H:	the guys have got sent to prison**haven't they**\ or something\
S:	mm y- yes\ that was in this morning's paper\

⁷H:	yeah 2.2 **well** I- I never made a tin of pet
S:	**but** what I'm ringing about is this\ what goes into pet food\

⁸H:	food\ I don't know\ I- I would imagine –
S:	<@no@>:er: **I mean**\ if this is the kind of stuff that goes into pet

⁹H:	.. **you're saying that** if it/ that you object to the idea\
S:	food\ 1.2 it shouldn't even go into pet food\

¹⁰H:	that if it's unfit for human consumption\ it is therefore assumed to be fit for pets' consumption\
S:	. yes I/

¹¹H:	**if it's unfit \ it's unfit is what you're saying**\
S:	unfit :erm: if it's unfit\ it's unfit\ I'm not talking about scraps and things like that\

¹²H:	
S:	I'm talking about •hhh• that b/ that's infected by drugs/ had drugs injected in the animal\:erm:

¹³H:	mm
S:	sawdust\ all that kind of stuff\ I'm not saying that :er: other stuff shouldn't go into pet food\ meat by-

¹⁴H:	
S:	products and things like that\ providing it's clean\ I'm not saying that\ •hhh• it's **just** the- the fact that

¹⁵H:	mm
S:	it was just taken for granted\ that because this was so horrible\ it was . in inverted commas\ 'only fit

¹⁶H:	yes\ I'm not :er: veterin<GARBLED SYLLABLES > or whatever it is qualified\ **but is it not**
S:	for pet food'\

¹⁷H:	**true**\ that :er: animals of various types can tolerate certain kinds\ of what we would regard as
S:	

¹⁸H:	dangerous:er: substances for us\
S:	**yes I know \ but** I don't see why they should :er: tolerate sawdust\

¹⁹H:	
S:	and nails\:er: or whatever it was\ •hhh• but there was also the other point\ that wha/ that- that the fact

²⁰H: mm   **oh yes** \ that's **very frightening**
S: that the food factory even had stuff of that quality on their premises\

²¹H: **indeed** \ and- and somehow the- these **villains** got hold of it\ and- and were able to put into tins for
S:

²²H: pets\ **is there any evidence that they actually did that**\   **I mean** \ **surely**\ I- I've
S: 1.4 ●hhh● er: .. no\

²³H: opened tins of pet food for our cat –   and it looks fine\ **I'm sure** there's no nails and-
S: and it looks all right\ yeah\ yes\

²⁴H: and sawdust and whatever in it\
S: I don't know whether this is the kind of stuff that- that's sold\ sort of

²⁵H: yeah\   **I quite agree**\
S: loose mince stuff or not\ but anyway\ if it's so ˋbad   1.3 it- it shouldn't be sold at all\

²⁶H: **I quite agree with you** \ **I quite agree with you** \ **particularly**/ **I mean**\ I would have thought that- that
S:

²⁷H: the/ there must be a- a- an institutional standards organisation\ that makes sure that really noxious
S:

²⁸H: things don't get into tins for pet food\ and how would they sell it to- to pet owners anyway\ they
S:

²⁹H: would surely defeat themselves\ they'd get a horrible reputation\ as soon as you open the tin\ it would
S:

³⁰H: be a most terrible pong\ **wouldn't it**\
S: I know\ but the- there're so many additives\ I mean- I mean for

³¹H: 1.4 in order to persuade the cat/
S: instance\ why do they have to put colouring into tins of pet food\

³²H: the animal to eat it\ **I suppose** \ **isn't it**\
S: **ah but** / **well** if the animal is anything like mine\ then/ **well**\ it would eat

³³H: yeah\
S: anything\ and i- it- it- it's/ I think it's for the owner\ to make it look better for- :er: for the owners to

³⁴H: yeah\ **Mrs Sack** \ **can I ask you very gently** \ you're not **sort of** :er: one of those people who's
S: see\

³⁵H: totally over the top on the subject of animals\ **are you**\   mm
S: **not at all** \ **not at all** \ **not at all** \ our dog always goes into

³⁶H: **f- forgive me for asking the question** \ **but** you m/ you recognise <@ that
S: **kennels when we go away** \ **not at all**\

³⁷H: there are such people\ don't you\ @>   the –   ... **I mean**\ the thing that sometimes/ the/
S: oh ye\ <@ I recognise that\ @> **no no**\ no no\

³⁸H: bothers me\ **and I'm deliberately trying to provoke you a little bit**\ is that- that sometimes people
S: <@@@@>

³⁹ H: feed to:: pets\ and sometimes to animals\ food that is in fact perfectly good\ and could be used for
S:

⁴⁰ H: starving human beings\   but what
S: **not at all** \ I don- I don't ●hhhe● **I don't do anything like that**\ I'm/ I :er: –

⁴¹ H: do you think of people who do that\ I mean an awful amount of s- solid protein\ which could be used/
S:

⁴² H: **I mean**\ let's think of Ethiopia\ there are thousands and thousands of people starving in Ethiopia\ and
S: yes\

⁴³ H: they badly need protein\ meanwhile people in the western half of the world are feeding it to animals\
S:

⁴⁴ H:
S: **I think it's very bad** \ **I think it's v- I think it's very bad** \ **but** at the same time\:erm: I do read of/ I f:/

⁴⁵ H:
S: I think that I often read of people **sort of** leaving lots of money to animals\ and all the rest of it\:erm:

⁴⁶ H:
S: sometimes one hears (0.6) people say\ 'oh why don't we do this\ why don't they go and/ out and look

⁴⁷ H:
S: after humans\ why don't they do this that and the other'\ but the/ this is apart from pet food\ I reckon

⁴⁸ H:
S: that people\ especially if they live alone\ are entitled to have something of/ some creature of their own

⁴⁹ H: **I could- I couldn't agree with you more Mrs Sack** \ **I couldn't agree with you**
S: to give their love to\ of their own\

⁵⁰ H: **more** \ I think it just depe/ it's a matter of balance\ **isn't it**\ it- it depends on what you use to feed them
S:

⁵¹ H: on\ and how much money you- you actually u- use for them\ because in the end of the day it's a- it's a
S:

⁵² H: question of balance\ as so many questions are\ **Mrs Sack** \ **thank you very much for joining in**\
S:

In the opening sequence of this call Mrs Sack does not address the moderator as *Mr Hatch*, or *Dick*, or *Richard*, after returning his greeting but inserts a filled pause and then launches straight into her topic. This does not allow the moderator to ask after her wellbeing, which is an optional side sequence moderators often choose to insert before launching into the topic of the call. By preventing him from controlling how the interaction should continue, Mrs Sack effectively, but unwittingly, exercises power over him. In this sense her behaviour is open to interpretation as impolite, which might lead to a possible adverse effect on the development of the emergent network. Let's see how the interaction develops through the first few turns:

(34)

¹H:	Mrs Sack\ hello Mrs Sack\
	POLITIC BEHAVIOUR
S:	hello \ **erm: I'm ringing**/ :erm: a- a talk by a health inspector\ on your
	POLITIC BEHAVIOUR + NON-POLITIC BEHAVIOUR
	OPEN TO INTERPRETATION AS IMPOLITE

²H:	
S:	programme\ a couple of days ago\ .. he was talking about infected/ meat being sold for humans\

³H:	oh yes
S:	instead of being processed for pet food\ :erm: he described- he described the case wh- where

⁴H:	
S:	the meat/ it was from a factory\ and then it had :er:/ covered in dirt\ sawdust\ transported in

⁵H:	**yes**\ **it's a fairly famous case**\ it's been going on – I think
	INTERRUPTION
	OPEN TO INTERPRETATION AS IMPOLITE
S:	unrefrigerated vans\ etcetera etcetera\ and I – yeah

⁶H:	the guys have got sent to prison**haven't they**\ or something\
	POLITIC BEHAVIOUR
S:	mm y- yes\ that was in this morning's paper\
	INTERRUPTION
	OPEN TO INTERPRETATION AS IMPOLITE
	EVIDENCE THAT SHE HAS INTERPRETED H'S INTERRUPTION AS IMPOLITE?

⁷H:	yeah
S:	**but** what I'm ringing about is this\ what goes into pet food\
	CONTRADICTION
	FURTHER EVIDENCE OF INTERPRETATION OF H'S INTERRUPTION AS IMPOLITE

In Mrs Sack's first turn in score 1 she begins to state the reason for her call, but breaks off and refers to a health inspector who had talked a few days prior to the present open-line programme about *infected meat being sold for humans* instead of being used for pet food. For Mrs Sack this information forms the background to what she really wants to ask, which is not uttered until her turn in score 7, *what goes into pet food?* For Hatch, and I would suggest for other listeners to the programme, the following inferences can be derived from Mrs Sack's first two turns:

(35) <Mrs Sack is referring to a talk by a health inspector>
(36) <The health inspector was talking about infected meat being sold to humans>
(37) <The meat was covered in dirt and sawdust>
(38) <The meat was transported in unrefrigerated vans>
(39) <In the health inspector's opinion, the meat should have been processed for pet food>
(40) <(36) was an assumption made by the health inspector>
(41) <(37)–(39) are critical comments & Mrs Sack agrees with those comments>
(42) <On the basis of (41) Mrs Sack agrees with (39)>
(43) <Mrs Sack is of the same opinion as the health inspector>
(44) <Mrs Sack wants to discuss the issue of infected meat being sold to humans>

Hatch's uptake of what he assumes on the basis of (35)–(44) to be the topic of the call is thus a consequence of the most relevant information he has been able to derive, and the tag question *haven't they* is a politic move to induce Mrs Sack to continue to develop the topic further.

Her reaction in score 6, however, is evidence that these are not the assumptions she intended him and the radio audience to infer. Her intervention in Hatch's turn displays a certain amount of impatience. She admits that the information about the people responsible for the scandal having been sent to prison was in that day's morning paper, so she complies with Hatch's appeal for cooperation, only to contradict this line of reasoning in the very next part of her utterance. Now, if it is reasonable to assume that inferences (35)–(44) are the most relevant ones to make in the circumstances, her intervention and subsequent contradiction are open to interpretation as impolite. What we have here, then, is a classical case of misunderstanding. The statement of her topic in score 7 results in a very long pause of 2.2 seconds by Hatch.

The stage is thus set for a verbal interaction in which confrontation could become the dominant discursive mode. If this happens, the line that Hatch is expected to adopt by the audience is in danger and might result in possible loss of face for Hatch and the producer of the programme. We can therefore expect to see a very delicate handling of the politic behaviour in this radio phone-in programme to prevent face-loss from happening.

Let us look at the continuation of the interaction from score 7 to score 16:

(45)

⁷H:	2.2 **well** I- I never made a tin of pet
	POLITIC BEHAVIOUR
	OPEN TO POSSIBLE INTERPRETATION AS IMPOLITE BEHAVIOUR
S:	

⁸H:	food\ I don't know\ I- I would imagine –
S:	<@no@>:er: **I mean**\ if this is the kind of stuff that goes into pet
	REJECTION 'CAJOLER'
	POLITIC BEHAVIOUR – ATTEMPT TO RESTORE HARMONY

⁹H:	.. **you're saying that** if it/ that you object to the idea\
	POLITIC BEHAVIOUR
	SUPPORTIVE FACEWORK
S:	food\ 1.2 it shouldn't even go into pet food\

¹⁰H:	that if it's unfit for human consumption\ it is therefore assumed to be fit for pets' consumption\
S:	. yes I/

¹¹H: **if it's unfit \ it's unfit is what you're saying**
                                    POLITIC BEHAVIOUR

                                    SUPPORTIVE FACEWORK

S: unfit :erm: if it's unfit\ it's unfit\ I'm not talking about scraps and things like that\

¹²H:

S: I'm talking about ●hhh● that b/ that's infected by drugs/ had drugs injected in the animal\:erm:

¹³H: mm

S: sawdust\ all that kind of stuff\ I'm not saying that :er: other stuff shouldn't go into pet food\ meat by-

¹⁴H:

S: products and things like that\providing it's clean\I'm not saying that\●hhh● it's **just** the- the fact that
                                                                              DOWNTONER

                                                                              POLITIC BEHAVIOUR

¹⁵H: mm

S: it was just taken for granted\ that because this was so horrible\ it was. in inverted commas\ 'only fit

¹⁶H:

S: for pet food'\

Hatch's flippant remark in score 7 after the 2.2 second silence is prefaced by the EPM *well*, in order to avoid any claim by Mrs Sack that it is not relevant to her question. In effect it signals that the remark should be taken anything but seriously. Recall that the line taken by a phone-in moderator does allow her/him to tease the caller. So we can assume at this point that Hatch is attempting to repair the misunderstanding created by Mrs Sack's confused statement of what her topic is. In this sense it can be taken as an adjustment to the politic behaviour of the verbal interaction. At the same time, however, it could be interpreted by Mrs Sack as a joke made at her expense. If that were the case, what appears to be an attempt to restore the harmony of the relationship could easily be interpreted as impoliteness by Mrs Sack. Do we have any evidence that she has interpreted it in this way?

Evidence is provided in score 8 where she interrupts Hatch with a rejection of the line he has taken at this point (*no*). She does so laughingly, indicating that although she has seen the joke, she does not approve of his flippancy. She follows this with a filled pause (*er*) and the EPM *I mean* in an attempt to restore harmony to the interaction. This is a politic move indicating to Hatch that she did not really intend him to answer the question and focusing him on her real intention in the upcoming utterance. Why, then, did she put the question in the first place?

Her attempt to clarify the topic of her call leads to the following simple inference by Hatch:

(46) <The caller believes that meat which is infected, covered in dirt and sawdust and has
been transported in unrefrigerated vans should not go into pet food>

The problem is that, apart from her claim that the health inspector
said that it should have been processed for pet food, no mention has
been made of anyone claiming that the kind of meat she has described
is actually used in the making of pet food.

At this point, Hatch changes his tone and rephrases what he interprets her as saying at the beginning of his turn in score 9, *you're saying
that . . .* , and concluding the turn with the same phrase *. . . is what
you're saying*. Rephrasing her point of view is a politic move to allow
the wider listening audience to relate to Mrs Sack's opinion and also
to give her an opportunity of carrying the topic further. So it provides
her with supportive facework. The problem is that agreeing on what
the topic actually is has already taken up a great deal of programme
time. Throughout her long turn in score 11 to score 16 she elaborates
on her point of view and finally states her objection, i.e. that the health
inspector had simply assumed that if the meat was unfit for human
consumption, it was fit for pet food.

From score 16 to score 18, Hatch adopts a contradictory stance to Mrs
Sack in order to provoke the kind of argument that might interest his
audience. In order to do this he disclaims any veterinary knowledge
and invites Mrs Sack to accept the truth of the statement that certain
types of animal can tolerate what we might regard as dangerous for
human beings. The politic behaviour of an argument in the public
domain would have enabled him to do this with a statement such as
but surely it's true that . . . . Putting it in the form of a negative question
(*but is it not true that . . .*) is thus in excess of what is required and
invites the interpretation of politeness.

(47)

[16]H:	yes\ I'm not :er: veterin<GARBLED SYLLABLES > or whatever it is qualified\ **but is it not**
	IN EXCESS OF NECESSARY POLITIC BEHAVIOUR
	OPEN TO INTERPRETATION AS POLITE
S:	

[17]H:	**true**\ that :er: animals of various types can tolerate certain kinds\ of what we would regard as
S:	

[18]H:	dangerous :er: substances for us\
S:	**yes I know** \ **but** I don't see why they should :er: tolerate sawdust\
	POLITIC BEHAVIOUR
	INTERPRETABLE AS SUPPORTIVE FACEWORK PRIOR TO THE CONTRADICTION THAT FOLLOWS

¹⁹H:	
S:	and nails\:er: or whatever it was\ •hhh• but there was also the other point\ that wha/ that- that the fact

²⁰H:	mm **oh yes** \ that's **very frightening**
	SUPPORTIVE FACEWORK SUPPORTIVE FACEWORK
S:	that the food factory even had stuff of that quality on their premises\

²¹H:	**indeed** \ and- and somehow the- these **villains** got hold of it\ and- and were able to put into tins for
	SUPPORTIVE FACEWORK
S:	

²²H:	pets**is there any evidence that they actually did that**\
	POLITIC BEHAVIOUR
S:	

In scores 20–21 he makes three moves that can be interpreted as giving face to Mrs Sack. He agrees with her point of view (*oh yes*), he attributes to her and acquiesces in the opinion that the fact that the food factory had such food on their premises is *very frightening indeed*. He also concurs in what he considers to be her interpretation of the perpetrators, namely as *villains*.

During the following six turns in scores 22–25, Hatch unsuccessfully tries to draw Mrs Sack into a discussion on the quality of pet food, at the conclusion of which she simply returns to her previous statement that unwanted substances (which she has by now extended to include nails and drugs injected into the animals) should not be put into pet food. I shall forego a detailed discussion of this sequence and move on to the way the interaction continues in scores 25–34:

(48)

²⁵H:	**I quite agree**\
	POLITIC BEHAVIOUR
S:	

²⁶H:	**I quite agree with you** \ **I quite agree with you** \ particularly/ **I mean**\ I would have thought that-
	POLITIC BEHAVIOUR IN EXCESS OF WHAT IS NECESSARY 'CAJOLER'
	OPEN TO INTERPRETATION AS POLITE POLITIC BEHAVIOUR
	ATTEMPT TO RESTORE HARMONY TO THE INTERACTION
S:	

²⁷H:	that the/ there must be a- a- an institutional standards organisation\ that makes sure that really
S:	

²⁸H:	noxious things don't get into tins for pet food\ and how would they sell it to- to pet owners anyway\
S:	

²⁹H:	they would surely defeat themselves\ they'd get a horrible reputation\ as soon as you open the tin\ it
S:	

³⁰H:	would be a most terrible pong**wouldn't it**\\
	POLITIC BEHAVIOUR
	INVITING AGREEMENT BY THE ADDRESSEE
	SUPPORTIVE FACEWORK
S:	I know\\ but the- there're so many additives\\ I mean- I mean for
³¹H:	1.4 in order to persuade the cat/
S:	instance\\ why do they have to put colouring into tins of pet food\\
³²H:	the animal to eat it**I suppose** \\ **isn't it**\\
	HEDGE
	POLITIC BEHAVIOUR
	DEFERRING TO HER KNOWLEDGE OF PET FOOD
	SUPPORTIVE FACEWORK
S:	**ah but** / **well** if the animal is anything like mine\\ then/ **well**\\ it would eat
	NON-POLITIC BEHAVIOUR + SOFTENER
	CONTRADICTION FACEWORK
³³H:	yeah\\
S:	anything\\ and i- it- it- it's/ I think it's for the owner\\ to make it look better for- :er: for the owners to
³⁴H:	
S:	see\\

In scores 25–26 Hatch overdoes the politic move of agreeing with Mrs Sack. The first utterance is clearly part of the politic behaviour of a phone-in programme, but repeating the phrase *I agree* twice and adding the intensifier *quite* turns what would normally go unnoticed as politic behaviour into potential politeness. But if Hatch cannot get his interlocutor to move away from her simple insistence that substances such as those she has mentioned should not go into tins of pet food, why does he need to display his agreement in quite the way he does?

Almost immediately after this sequence of agreement signals he uses the EPM *I mean* in another politic attempt to shift the argument onto a different level, i.e. that of stating that there must be a control institution to make sure of the quality of pet food put into tins. He backs up his argument by suggesting that, if this were not so, every tin of pet food the owner opened would stink. However, instead of taking up this aspect of the argument, Mrs Sack introduces the 'disreputable' fact that colouring is also added to pet food. Hatch parries this and defers to her knowledge of pet food by uttering the hedge *I suppose* and following it with a tag question, *isn't it*. Rather than criticise her introduction of this extra 'foreign' material in pet food, he chooses to display politic behaviour.

The core of the whole interaction follows immediately after this sequence. By this time in the interaction, the moderator, Hatch, has been at pains to shift Mrs Sack away from her obsession with what might be put into pet food. He has tried to move the discussion to wider issues, has attempted to introduce a note of conflict into the discourse, has tried teasing her, but all to no avail. In addition, the interaction has taken up quite a lot of time that might more profitably have been used to talk to other callers. He is therefore in the difficult position of not knowing how to provoke Mrs Sack into entering an argument, nor of knowing how to bring the call to an end.

After Mrs Sack's turn in score 34 he could have commented on her opinion that colouring is put into pet food for the benefit of the owners rather than the pets, thanked her for joining the programme and moved into a preclosing sequence to end the interaction. He makes the mistake of choosing the alternative option, i.e. of making one final attempt to provoke Mrs Sack into discussion. To do this, he chooses a face-threatening tactic, which he then needs to mitigate through appropriate politic/polite behaviour:

(49)

³⁴H: yeah\ **Mrs Sack \ can I ask you very gently** \ you're not **sort of** :er: one of those people who's
      POLITIC BEHAVIOUR   POLITIC BEHAVIOUR IN   HEDGE
                     EXCESS OF WHAT WOULD   POLITIC BEHAVIOUR
                        BE REQUIRED   FACEWORK
                        FACEWORK
             OPEN TO INTERPRETATION AS POLITE
  S:

³⁴H: totally over the top on the subject of animals\ **are you**\   mm
                       POLITIC BEHAVIOUR
                  INTERPRETABLE AS POLITE
  S: **not at all \ not at all \ not at all \ our dog always goes into**
                      EVIDENCE OF OFFENCE
            CLASSIFICATION OF H'S UTTERANCE AS IMPOLITE

³⁶H: **f- forgive me for asking the question \ but** you m/ you recognise <@ that
                FACEWORK   JUSTIFICATION
             POLITE BEHAVIOUR
  S: **kennels when we go away \ not at all**\
      JUSTIFICATION   EVIDENCE OF OFFENCE

³⁷H: there are such people\ don't you\ @>   the –
  S: oh yes\ <@ I recognise that\ @> **no no \ no no**\
                   EVIDENCE OF OFFENCE

The first utterance by Hatch in score 34 is recognition of the point made at the end of Mrs Sack's prior turn. In the second utterance Hatch changes footing and addresses her formally, as he has done throughout the interaction in accordance with the politic behaviour expected in a radio phone-in programme. It prefaces a question which includes the phrase *very gently*, functioning here as an understater. The question would have been appropriate to the politic behaviour of the situation, so that *very gently* allows it to be potentially interpreted as politeness payment. He follows this with a face-threat enquiring whether she is one of those people who are over the top on the subject of animals. Now, since he intends to commit the FTA anyway in order to provoke her into an argument, he does not need to include the hedge *sort of*, just as he didn't need to include the adverb phrase *very gently* in introducing his question. In doing so, however, he also opens up this utterance to a polite interpretation.

At this point we need to consider whether Brown and Levinson's explanation of face-threat mitigation as positive or negative politeness might not provide an explanation for why Hatch structures his turn in the way he does. We have here a perfect example of an FTA to Mrs Sack's positive face, for which Hatch has chosen to use Brown and Levinson's strategy 6 ('Avoid disagreement')(see chapter 4, p. 89). The deliberate way in which Hatch structures his turn provides evidence that he has chosen this strategy rationally, since 'the hedges . . . serve to avoid a precise communication of [Hatch's] attitude' (Brown and Levinson 1987: 117). But would it not have been enough for Hatch to have said something like the following:

(50) Can I ask you whether you're one of those people who are over the top on the subject of animals?

in which the semi-formulaic EPM of the structural type 'Can I do X?' is used? It is, admittedly, a little blunter, but since Hatch intends to commit the FTA anyway, it at least maintains the politic behaviour required of a moderator in a radio phone-in programme. If Hatch had wanted to soften the blow further, he could have added either *very gently* or *sort of*, as in (51a and b):

(51)a. Can I ask you very gently whether you're one of those people who are over the top on the subject of animals?
  b. Can I ask you whether you're sort of one of those people who are over the top on the subject of animals?

But to add both hedges, to place the hesitation marker *er* immediately after *sort of* and to formulate the utterance as a statement followed by the tag question *are you?* invites the following set of inferences:

(52) <Hatch is about to ask me a question>
(53) <The question is marked [by *very gently*] as a difficult question to put>
(54) <Given (53), the question is likely to be an FTA>
(55) <Hatch has made the statement (56)>
(56) <You are not one of those people who are over the top on the subject of animals>

(57) <The predicate *one of those people who are over the top on the subject of animals* is
        marked by the hedge *sort of*>
(58) <Given (57) Hatch masks what his real opinion of the proposition p is>
(59) <The FTA is the proposition p>
(60) <p = I am over the top on the subject of animals>
(61) <Hatch believes p>
(62) <Hatch is asking me to deny (60)>

Hence, what Mrs Sack is asked to deny does not correspond to what
she can infer Hatch to believe.

A Brown–Levinsonian explanation of this positive politeness strategy
thus leads to potential conflict rather than to real FTA mitigation. To
explain politeness, particularly 'positive politeness' (to use Brown and
Levinson's terminology), as face-threat mitigation invites the question
as to why the speaker needs to commit a face-threat in the first place.
To overdo the amount of payment for committing the FTA, i.e. to go beyond politic behaviour and produce utterances which are interpretable
as polite, is equivalent to the speaker's admitting that s/he believes the
content of the FTA! It is, in other words, a way of intensifying the FTA
rather than mitigating it.

Mrs Sack's response to Hatch in scores 35–36 is strong evidence of
the fact that she has interpreted Hatch in precisely this way. The turn
consists of four vehement denials of the implied claim that she is
over the top on the subject of animals (*not at all*) and one justification
for this denial in the statement that *our dog always goes into kennels
when we go away*. Hatch's politeness payment has thus been evaluated
negatively by Mrs Sack, leading Hatch to cover his tracks in score 36
by asking forgiveness for having asked the question. In effect, however,
the minimal politic behaviour that would be required here is:

(63) You recognise that there are such people don't you?

so that the formulation *forgive me for asking the question* is again extra
politeness payment and (63) is used as a justification for asking it
in the first place. The laughter accompanying the embedded clause
that there are such people and the tag question *don't you?* are evidence
of an attempt to restore a modicum of interpersonal harmony to the
interaction. Mrs Sack responds to his laughter, but she still vehemently
denies any inferred allegation that she is 'over the top on the subject
of animals' (witness the two occurrences of *no* in score 37, which are
repeated immediately afterwards).

The remainder of the interaction represents an attempt by Hatch to
justify his provocative FTA to Mrs Sack, which he verbalises explicitly

in score 38 (*and I'm deliberately trying to provoke you a little bit*), and Mrs Sack's continued interpretation of the points Hatch is making as being a personal criticism of her own behaviour with respect to animals:

(64)

³⁷H:	... **I mean**\ the thing that sometimes/ the/
	APPEALER
	POLITIC BEHAVIOUR
	ATTEMPT TO RESTORE HARMONY
S:	

³⁸H:	bothers me**and I'm deliberately trying to provoke you a little bit**\ is that- that sometimes people
	JOKING
	POLITIC BEHAVIOUR
	FACEWORK
S:	<@@@@>

³⁹H:	feed to:: pets\ and sometimes to animals\ food that is in fact perfectly good\ and could be used for
S:	

⁴⁰H:	starving human beings\ but what
S:	**not at all** \ I don- I don't •hhhe• **I don't do anything like that**\ I'm/ I :er: –
	DENIAL OF SUPPOSED ACCUSATION JUSTIFICATION
	EVALUATION OF H'S UTTERANCE AS IMPOLITE

⁴¹H:	do you think of people who do that\ I mean an awful amount of s- solid protein\ which could be used/
S:	

⁴²H:	**I mean**\ let's think of Ethiopia\ there are thousands and thousands of people starving in Ethiopia\ and
	APPEALER
	POLITIC BEHAVIOUR
	ATTEMPT TO RESTORE HARMONY
S:	yes\

⁴³H:	they badly need protein\ meanwhile people in the western half of the world are feeding it to animals\
S:	

⁴⁴H:	
S:	I think it's very bad\ I think it's v- I think it's very bad\ but at the same time\:erm: I do read of/ I f:/

⁴⁵H:	
S:	I think that I often read of people **sort of** leaving lots of money to animals\ and all the rest of it\:erm:
	HEDGE
	POLITIC BEHAVIOUR

⁴⁶H:	
S:	sometimes one hears (0.6) people say\ 'oh why don't we do this\ why don't they go and/ out and look

⁴⁷H:	
S:	after humans\ why don't they do this that and the other'\ but the/ this is apart from pet food\ I reckon

⁴⁸H:	
S:	that people\ especially if they live alone\ are entitled to have something of/ some creature of their own

⁴⁹H:	**I could- I couldn't agree with you more Mrs Sack \ I couldn't agree with you**
	POLITIC BEHAVIOUR
	MITIGATION OF FACE-THREAT
S:	to give their love to\ of their own\
⁵⁰H:	**more** \ I think it just depe/ it's a matter of balance\ isn't it\ it- it depends on what you use to feed them
S:	
⁵¹H:	on\ and how much money you- you actually u- use for them\ because in the end of the day it's a- it's a
S:	
⁵²H:	question of balance\ as so many questions are**Mrs Sack \ thank you very much for joining in**\
	STANDARD POLITIC BEHAVIOUR
S:	

Hatch begins his turn in score 37 with the appealer *I mean* in an attempt to restore harmony to the interaction and to specify the real topic that he wishes to discuss, namely why it is that people feed their animals with what could be used to overcome starvation in other parts of the world (in this instance Ethiopia). He repeats the appealer in score 42 after Mrs Sack has misinterpreted his statements to imply that she is one of those who sometimes feed to pets 'food that is in fact perfectly good and could be used for starving human beings'. On the other hand, given the vehemence of her denials in score 35, it is clear that she is likely to interpret any further critical statements by Hatch as being an implied criticism of herself (cf. her reaction in score 40, *not at all, I don't do anything like that*).

In scores 42–43 Hatch appears to have achieved his goal of getting Mrs Sack to focus on the starvation in Ethiopia which might be alleviated by transferring some of the meat which is turned into pet food to feed starving human beings. She acquiesces in this assessment in score 44 only to divert attention away from pet food and onto people who bequeath large sums of money to their pets instead of giving it to help the fight against starvation. It transpires that she supports such people in their freedom to do this on the grounds that they have a right to have *some creature of their own to give their love to*. Either she does not see any need to shift away from the subject of pets to that of starving human beings, or she deliberately takes up a stance which conflicts with Hatch's. Hatch is therefore left with no alternative but to terminate the interaction without entering into a closing sequence where both interactants would normally exchange EPMs expressing leavetaking. This is a rather face-threatening thing to do in a phone-in programme, so he is constrained to mitigate the FTA by expressing his (probably feigned) agreement with Mrs Sack in score 49. His final two utterances lie within the framework of politic behaviour in this type of interaction.

We can see from the analysis of this extract that public cooperative discourse involves the need for one or the other of the participants, usually the moderator, to indulge in a certain amount of facework. This can frequently take her/him beyond politic behaviour so that utterances are open to interpretation as polite. The difficulty is to decide whether the interlocutor interprets the polite behaviour positively or negatively, since, in the event of a negative interpretation, what started off as cooperative discourse can be transformed into conflictual discourse. In the interaction between Hatch and Mrs Sack, it should have become clear that whatever Hatch says is liable to be interpreted by Mrs Sack as personal criticism. This has an effect on the kind of face we, as the radio audience, are likely to assign to Mrs Sack. In all probability this will be negative, so that we are not put out by the somewhat abrupt way in which Hatch finally terminates the interaction.

CONCLUSION

The two extracts from naturally occurring verbal interaction analysed in this chapter are not meant in any way to be representative of the kinds of discursive practices that can be found in either public or private verbal interaction. They were chosen precisely because polite behaviour is not generally expected to occur as a salient form of communication within them. In both instances we saw that the exercise of power is closely tied up with politic behaviour which is either contravened or exceeded, i.e. with verbal behaviour open to a first-order interpretation as impolite or polite. On the other hand, in no instance did we encounter the lexemes *polite* or *impolite* used by the participants themselves. In certain cases (particularly in the radio phone-in programme) we saw that what is interpretable as polite behaviour may indeed be connected with facework. The problem is that such facework is often evaluated negatively, since, often, all it does is highlight the face-threat itself.

The principal difficulty in operationalising this conceptualisation of politic and polite behaviour so that we can use the concepts to analyse stretches of verbal interaction and observe the ways in which power is exercised in the development of emergent networks lies in the notion of politic behaviour itself. As we saw in previous chapters, politic behaviour is closely associated with the various kinds of habitus each of us forms in order to perform adequately in instances of social practice.

The habitus also relies on what is perceived to be the objectified social structures which enter into different forms of verbal interaction. For example, in a political interview broadcast on television we would expect there to be a degree of confrontation between interviewer and interviewee, particularly when the interview is made during an election campaign. In political discourse in general, we would expect there to be a degree of face-threatening activity sanctioned by the type of social practice engaged in. But it is only our feel for what is acceptable in such a situation, i.e. how such situations are socially reproduced, that will allow us to perceive a participant's behaviour as appropriate. In fact, we tend to notice the appropriate politic behaviour only when it is violated.

Such violations can, of course, lead to changes in the way in which we view the politic behaviour of a form of social practice and thereby alter the habitus we have learnt to adopt. For example, radio phone-in programmes at the beginning of the twenty-first century are very different in many ways from what they were in the 1980s. Several phone-in moderators deliberately construct their programmes in such a way as to insult their callers, to belittle them, to argue with them openly, etc. Callers know that they will be involved in this kind of discourse, and yet they still ring in and participate. Confrontational discourse has thus become part of the politic behaviour of radio phone-in interaction. This presents a further problem for a theory of politeness that equates politeness with the mitigation of face-threatening (cf. the Brown and Levinson model), since face-threatening itself has become the appropriate form of politic behaviour, in such programmes.

In earlier chapters we have looked at extracts from family discourse. We saw that it is not normally associated with the production of polite language. Nevertheless, certain utterances are still open to polite interpretation precisely because of the delicate balance of power relations during the interaction and the need in close-knit networks to achieve interpersonal equilibrium in the development of emergent networks. Every instance of an emergent network in family discourse contributes towards the successful reproduction of the latent family network. This does not mean that the discursive practices within a family never lead to a redistribution of power and to significant changes within the family structure. Of course they do, otherwise how would we explain the socialisation of family members from children to adolescents to young adults to mature adults forming their own nuclear families?

In every verbal interaction power is latently present and may be exercised at any moment during the ongoing social practice. This will necessitate changes in the politic behaviour valid for the interaction type, and changes will frequently involve certain utterances being evaluated as polite and others as impolite. The evaluation need not always be positive, as we saw in the radio phone-in programme. I submit that this way of conceptualising politic behaviour allows us to grasp how polite and impolite interpretations of verbal behaviour arise in the cut and thrust of verbal interaction, and it has been the purpose of this chapter to illustrate the kind of fine-grained analysis that will enable the researcher to spot instances of (im)politeness$_1$. In the final chapter of this book I shall show how the approach to politeness presented here is capable of accounting for the historical and cultural relativity of notions of politeness in all human societies, and I shall take stock of what this radical departure from theories of linguistic politeness might mean in the future study of politeness phenomena.

10 Politic behaviour and politeness within a theory of social practice

EMPIRICAL WORK ON LINGUISTIC POLITENESS

As we saw in chapter 4, work carried out on linguistic politeness following the reprint of Brown and Levinson's work in 1987 can be grouped roughly into five categories: 1. work criticising aspects of the Brown and Levinson model (much of which we dealt with in that chapter); 2. empirical work on particular types of speech activity (the most common of these being requests, apologies, compliments and thanks); 3. cross-cultural work assessing the ways in which two or more cultures differ in their realisations of politeness; 4. the application of politeness models, mainly Brown and Levinson's, to data in other disciplines; 5. sporadic attempts to suggest alternative lines of enquiry into the phenomenon of linguistic politeness. If we had to categorise the present book, it would appear in category 5, but I shall argue in this final chapter that it represents a serious, radical alternative to current theories on the market.

Empirical work on linguistic politeness in categories 2, 3 and 4 makes up the bulk of material since 1987, and much of it has appeared in journals such as the *Journal of Pragmatics*, *Multilingua*, the *International Journal of the Sociology of Language*, *Language and Society*, etc. It covers such areas as developmental and cognitive psychology, psychotherapy, business and management studies, language teaching, gender studies, law, etc., and the vast majority of this work deals with possible practical applications of politeness theory to the research concerns of these subjects. In doing so, however, Brown and Levinson is far and away the most commonly used model, and I argued in chapter 4 that one major reason for its preponderance is that it appears to provide a sufficiently stable basis on which 'normal science' in the sense of Kuhn (1962) can be carried out. This assumption needs to be challenged before I return to a review of the model presented in this book.

There are two major criticisms that can be applied to most of the current empirical investigations being carried out in linguistic politeness using the Brown and Levinson model. The first is the assumption that the puzzle as to what politeness *is* has been solved simply by relating it to facework. The second is the nature not only of the Brown and Levinson model but also of most other models in the field (cf. the discussion in Eelen 2001). One empirical investigation after another simply accepts the assumption that speakers use strategies of positive or negative politeness when they are faced with the need to mitigate the force of a projected face-threatening act to their interlocutors. The strategies themselves turn out to be a very heterogeneous selection of possible linguistic expressions, all or most of which are not restricted to the field of politeness, i.e. they are not 'inherently polite', as we saw in chapter 7. So, if it can be postulated that the act a speaker/writer intends to carry out is liable to damage the face of her/his interlocutor, the researcher can classify the linguistic expression used to avoid, mitigate, soften, etc. the offence as 'polite'.

But what about the interlocutor? If s/he is still offended, was the utterance 'polite'? And what about a situation in which the speaker would be quite within her/his rights to be absolutely blunt towards the interlocutor, i.e. to commit a 'bald on-record FTA', but chooses instead to 'soften' it in some way, intending the interlocutor to infer that this was a deliberate strategy? Is the utterance then 'polite', and if it is interpreted as such, how will it be evaluated? In this situation, if the speaker chooses a linguistic expression that might be interpreted as 'polite' but aggressive, is it aggressive because the expression is a 'polite' expression or is it not simply because the expression itself is out of place in the situation, i.e. it is perceptually salient?

In most empirical work these questions are never asked and the reactions of addressees are generally taken for granted. The reason is not hard to find. The Brown and Levinson model provides a powerful way of predicting how speakers choose linguistic expressions in the event that they are likely to threaten the interlocutor's face. But it assumes that the speaker must know in advance of her/his utterance *that* an FTA is imminent in order to choose a strategy. It also assumes that the speaker (and for the discussion of written discourse, e.g. in literature, business correspondence, etc., the writer) has time to choose from amongst the strategies available to her/him the one which is most appropriate to the situation.[1] The more familiar the situation is to her/him, the more automatic the choice of strategy. But in that case we are confronted with conventional, ritualised utterances that need no great effort on the part of the speaker to produce. In the terminology of this book, we are dealing here with instances of politic behaviour, i.e. linguistic expressions that are *expected* by both the speaker and the interlocutor. Can we therefore still maintain in this case that we are dealing with linguistic politeness?

The principal problem with current theories of politeness, in particular Brown and Levinson's model, and at the same time the major reason for the lack of any substantial progress in empirical work based on it, is the status of those theories as quasi-objective descriptions and/or explanations of an abstract term, 'politeness'/'impoliteness'. This term is derived from an adjective attributing a subjectively or inter-subjectively negotiated quality 'polite' or 'impolite' to social acts carried out by an individual. It is a consequence of the ways in which individual participants in a verbal interaction perceive those acts. Not only are the qualifications of social acts as 'polite' or 'impolite' highly subjective and a matter for discursive dispute, but the acts themselves may be evaluated negatively, positively, neutrally, etc. For some, saying that an utterance is polite is attributing a positive quality to that utterance and thereby to the person who uttered it. For others, saying that an utterance is polite may well entail feelings of insecurity and mistrust. Did the speaker really mean what s/he said or is there reason to believe that the utterance was insincerely made? No model of politeness currently on the market can account for these very real perceptions of (im)polite behaviour if politeness is elevated to the status of an objective concept in human interaction, universally valid across cultures. In 'objective' theories of politeness, the concept has become the lynchpin in attempting to describe or even to explain the linguistic structures which instantiate it. In the following section I shall review the radically new approach to (im)politeness presented in this book and carry the argument further.

A NEW APPROACH TO AN OLD PROBLEM

We began the book by considering how we would characterise polite behaviour in general and polite language usage in particular. We were not concerned to set up an abstract model to account for polite behaviour in chapter 1, but merely to say what everyday expressions we might use to define how we, personally, understand the terms 'politeness' and 'polite language'. In doing so, it became clear that each individual's subjective classification of her/his own social behaviour or that of another as 'polite' may, but certainly *need* not, correspond to another individual's classification. In other words, we suggested that not everyone agrees about what constitutes polite language usage.

We also saw that most of us are far more likely to recognise and comment on impolite than on polite behaviour and that there is likely to be more overlap in our subjective assessments of impoliteness. Evaluations of polite linguistic behaviour, when and if they occur at all in the course of verbal interaction, range across a continuum from positive to negative. (Im)politeness, therefore, is a disputed term in the English language over which participants in verbal interaction may struggle. A speaker might use a linguistic expression which s/he intends to be heard as more than is necessary to uphold the levels of linguistic behaviour appropriate to the discursive situation, i.e. as polite, but the hearer may not interpret the utterance in the way it is intended to be interpreted. Alternatively, s/he may very well assign the correct interpretation but derive a set of inferences from it that display a negative evaluation. The speaker may be *paying* with politeness for devious reasons that give the hearer reason to doubt the sincerity of the utterance.

From the very beginning of this book, my focus has been on first-order (im)politeness, or what I have called (im)politeness$_1$. Theories of politeness and empirical work using those theories in the extensive and ever burgeoning literature on linguistic politeness rarely if ever consider the discursive nature of (im)politeness$_1$. They do not consider instances of dispute in verbal practice over whether or not a linguistic expression is intended to be heard (im)politely and what effects that might have on the social networking that emerges through verbal interaction. Emergent networks, as we saw in chapter 6, are where power is exercised, and if (im)politeness$_1$ is a disputed term, we can expect it to be linked in interesting ways to power. With notable exceptions, however,[2] this is rarely the focus of work in linguistic politeness.

In chapter 2 we focused attention on the historical and intercultural relativity of notions of politeness within western Europe, a relativity which emerges when we trace the development of linguistic politeness back over a longer period of time. Tracing that development is equivalent to tracing the development of (im)politeness$_1$ – at least in western Europe. In the final section of chapter 2 I showed how notions of (im)politeness$_1$ are intimately tied up with determining what is and what is not 'standard English'. The debate over 'standard English' in Britain has always been a dispute over the dominant linguistic ideology of what Bourdieu calls 'the legitimate language' (cf. Milroy and Milroy 1991, Watts 1999b) and involves very blatant examples of the exercise of power (cf. Smith 1984). The use of the term 'politeness' as a yardstick to define 'standard English' may well have given way to alternative notions in the late twentieth century, notably 'educatedness' (cf. Watts 2002), but this use of the term is evidence of both the extreme volatility of (im)politeness₁ in Britain and the relationship between that notion and the exercise of power.

Even the terms 'polite' and 'impolite' themselves may vary in perceptions of (im)politeness₁ among speakers of English. In chapter 1 we saw that terms like 'rude', 'standoffish', 'haughty', 'courteous', 'discourteous', etc. might be just as readily used to refer to perceived instances of (im)politeness₁. We also took a brief look at terms in other languages that appear to be used in roughly equivalent ways to those in English, and discovered that these share the volatility of the English lexemes and are likewise the subject of discursive struggle.

Chapters 3 and 4 focused attention on some of the best-known theoretical approaches to linguistic politeness in the literature and dealt with criticisms of those approaches which have been made over the years. It was pointed out, however, that the approaches all represent an *objectification* of the notion of politeness in that it is seen as a universal concept valid in all human cultures rather than a discursively disputed term. Raising the term '(im)politeness' to the status of a theoretical concept in linguistic pragmatics and sociolinguistics shifts the concern with politeness phenomena away from *individuals* and the everyday social acts they are involved in and places it above or beyond those individuals at what Eelen calls a 'supra-individual social level'. It creates a theoretical second-order concept of (im)politeness₂. In doing so, however, it places social structures beyond the individuals involved in social interaction. This, in turn, logically entails that social structures are in some sense preexistent factual entities.

However, much of the criticism levelled at models of linguistic politeness, particularly at Brown and Levinson's model, does *not* question the validity of objectifying (im)politeness in this way in the first place. It seems to be more concerned with countering an ideological perspective toward social structure that is perceived as deriving from a western mindset about the nature of social scientific theorising. In chapter 4 I showed how scholars from other, non-western traditions have accused Brown and Levinson of 'eurocentricity'. Now, while I sympathise with the concerns of these scholars – any charge of ethnocentricity in scientific endeavour should be taken seriously – it does not alter the fact that (im)politeness₂ continues to be seen as independent of those who actually use linguistic expressions in ways which they intend to be interpreted as impolite or polite and those who may interpret them and evaluate them as such. In virtually all the models of linguistic politeness on the market, (im)politeness₂ has become a set of strategies available to speakers to enable them to achieve certain communicative goals whilst retaining interpersonal harmony, enhancing feelings of comity and goodwill, showing the requisite levels of cooperation, etc.

But what about the ways in which addressees process those linguistic expressions which are deemed 'polite' in accordance with a model of (im)politeness$_2$? What about the short-term effects on the ways in which the verbal interaction might proceed and the long-term effects of the interpersonal relationships among the participants? As we saw in the examples from verbal interaction analysed in chapter 9, most of the time neither speakers nor addressees are even aware that an utterance is 'polite'. As politeness researchers analysing interactions after the event in accordance with a theory of (im)politeness$_2$ we will want to classify utterances *as* polite. But if the theory does not square with the intuitions of the participants themselves, are we justified in doing so?

Throughout this book, I have argued that we need to consider a radically new way of looking at linguistic politeness. In effect, we need to return to the level of (im)politeness$_1$ and to find ways of looking at linguistic politeness as part of what happens in an interactional exchange. In chapter 6 I argued that verbal interaction involves speakers and addressees working together 'to create some form of common understanding among themselves, even if it is the common understanding that they do not and can never agree'. An utterance made by a speaker and directed at an addressee is a social act, and an addressee deriving a set of inferences from that utterance to enable her/him to respond in some way is carrying out another kind of social act. But both acts are essential to socio-communicative verbal interaction, and both acts are embedded in the ongoing emergent development of an interpersonal relationship. The goal of a theory of linguistic politeness which takes (im)politeness$_1$ as its starting point should not be to explain *why* speakers say what they say and to predict the possible effects of utterances on addressees. It should aim to explain *how* all the interactants engaged in an ongoing verbal interaction negotiate the development of emergent networks and evaluate their own position and the positions of others within those networks. (Im)politeness then becomes part of the discursive social practice through which we create, reproduce and change our social worlds. It becomes part of a theory of social practice.

Hence, in this final chapter I shall run through some of the problems which confront us in carrying out this radical reorientation of politeness theory. The major problem is how the model can relate the notion of (im)politeness$_1$ with facework and politic behaviour. We argued in chapter 5 that politeness was not necessarily coterminous with face-work, despite the fact that most present-day researchers into linguistic politeness seem to think that it is. How does the conceptualisation of (im)politeness presented in this book stand in relation to the notion of face? The term that I have introduced to mediate between facework and politeness, politic behaviour, might be felt to function merely as a substitute for politeness. In other words, it might be argued that all I have done is to shift the weight off politeness onto a third term, which effectively covers every aspect of verbal behaviour that has previously been labelled 'polite'. A rereading of chapter 6 should be enough to dispel this idea, but I shall address it in some detail in the following section.

POLITIC BEHAVIOUR, FACEWORK AND (IM)POLITENESS REVISITED

The controversial concept in the theory of (im)politeness which I have presented in this book is without doubt *politic behaviour*. If it should turn out that politic behaviour is merely what other researchers have termed politeness, the concept itself becomes vacuous and the theory superfluous. If it can be shown that politic behaviour is not what others have termed politeness, then the theory stands and remains open to challenge.

The theory of social practice hinges on the assumption that the ways in which human beings carry out the social acts that make up instances of interaction depend on the prior histories of those who are engaging in the interaction. Recall Bourdieu's equation given in chapter 6:

$$[(habitus)(capital)] + field = practice$$

in which practice is the product of the objectified social structures of the field and the habitus and forms of capital of the participants. Among the objectified social structures of the field are institution-alised forms of behaviour, rights and obligations of the individuals interacting within that field and the power structures that form part of the field. Practice therefore depends on the amount of knowledge about those objectified structures that the individual has internalised as part of her/his habitus.

Specific modes of behaviour have become canonical as part of the objectified structures of the field and, as I pointed out in chapter 1, they represent reproductions of discursive formats that have become institutionalised as expectable behaviour for interaction. Such modes of behaviour, linguistic or non-linguistic, can be considered as appropriate to an interactive event, and since they are within the social constraints operating within the field, they are generally non-salient. It is these modes of appropriate behaviour, linguistic or otherwise, that I wish to call *politic behaviour*. Even though we participate in a multitude of different kinds of verbal interaction, we are generally aware of or are able to work out what sort of behaviour is appropriate. We have seen throughout this book that merely by entering and participating in interactions we recreate them, we reproduce them. Hence politic behaviour is that behaviour, linguistic and non-linguistic, which the participants construct as being appropriate to the ongoing social interaction.

To show that politic behaviour is not equivalent to polite behaviour, consider the following example. Imagine that you have booked two tickets to see a play and that they are numbered P51 and P52. Twenty minutes before the play is due to begin you locate row P and move along it to seats 51 and 52 only to find that someone else is already sitting there. What is the appropriate mode of behaviour in this situation? There are of course several options, but the first thing to do is to make it clear to those sitting in seats P51 and P52 that you have booked them on that particular evening and that there must be some mistake. If you say any of the following:

(1)   a. Excuse me. I think you're sitting in our seats.
     b. Excuse me but those are our seats.
     c. I'm sorry. I think there must be some mistake.
     d. I'm sorry, but are you sure you've got the right seats?

I maintain that you open the verbal interaction within the framework of the politic behaviour that can be expected in this type of situation. Are you thereby being polite? Some would say yes and others would simply maintain that there's not much else you *can* say in the situation. Imagine now that you are one of those sitting in seats P51 and P52. Would you consider (1a–d) to be polite utterances? If you are convinced that they really are your seats, you would hardly have expected them to have said:

(2)   Hey! Get out of our seats.

so their behaviour meets with your expectations. It is politic behaviour. If they had said:

(3)   I'm so sorry to bother you, but would you very much mind vacating our seats?

you would be justified in reacting somewhat self-defensively. After all, you are acting on the assumption that they are *your* seats. Utterance

(3) is justified from the point of view of the ticket-holders of seats P51 and P52, but it is beyond what can be expected in the situation and it is likely to be perceived by those sitting in the seats as unnecessarily aggressive – but at the same time polite.

On the assumption that an utterance similar to (1a–d) is made, it is unlikely that those sitting in the seats will apologise and simply vacate them. This would be equivalent to admitting that they knew all along that they were sitting in someone else's seats – although of course this does sometimes happen. What is now likely to ensue is a negotiation sequence in which the people occupying the seats compare their tickets with yours to try to ascertain where the mistake might lie. For example, you or those sitting in P51 and P52 may have missed a capital R printed in the bottom righthand corner of the ticket indicating that the seats are situated on the righthand side of the auditorium. Alternatively, your tickets or those of the people already sitting in P51 and P52 may actually be R51 and R52 but with the extra stroke in the capital letter R printed rather unclearly. This kind of negotiation sequence constitutes politic behaviour. It's what the participants would expect to happen in this situation, and it is not therefore polite.

We can conclude from this discussion that politic behaviour is not equivalent to polite behaviour, although certain utterances that lie within the scope of politic behaviour may indeed be open to interpretation as polite. The introduction of the term *politic behaviour* into the theory is thus not a way of reintroducing an 'objective' concept of politeness through the back door, as it were.

But is there an objective method by which we can predict which forms of behaviour in social practice will be politic? The answer to this question is a clear 'no', since the theory of social practice is not designed to make such predictions. However, although it is not a predictive theory, we may still assume that individuals have acquired fairly similar forms of habitus. They may not possess equal degrees of symbolic capital, but from the nature of the objectified structures of a social field and the habitus individuals have acquired to deal with interaction in that field they may still display a high degree of consensus in agreeing on what is and what is not politic behaviour. The analyses of verbal interaction given in chapter 9 show that the researcher needs to take every instance of social practice on its own merits in postulating the appropriate politic behaviour, and her/his assessments are just as much open to discursive dispute as the term (im)politeness itself.

Let us now turn to the notion of facework. Chapter 5 was devoted to demonstrating that Politeness Theory, i.e. an 'objectified' theory of politeness$_2$, can only be equated to Face Theory if Brown and Levinson's bipartite division of face into positive face and negative face can be upheld. Much of the criticism of their model presented in chapter 4 is aimed at precisely this division, and a return to Goffman's notion of face is suggested. If we accept Goffman's conceptualisation of face, however, we are constrained to accepting that we are attributed face socially in accordance with the line or lines we have adopted for the purposes of the communicative interaction. This leads to two logical conclusions, firstly that we can be assigned different faces on different occasions of verbal interaction and secondly that all social interaction is predicated on individuals' face needs, i.e. that we can never get away from negotiating facework. Some interaction types will allow for facework which aims at damaging or destroying the face which has been attributed to a participant. We saw this very clearly in the short extract from the *Panorama* interview between Fred Emery and Arthur Scargill as well as in David Dimbleby's *Panorama* interview with Tony Blair. If the interaction sanctions the display of face-threatening (aggressive facework), then that form of behaviour is within what can be expected of the polite behaviour of the interaction type. On the other hand, in a situation in which one participant needs to take particular care not to damage another participant's face, e.g. in the extracts from radio open-line phone-in programmes, that participant (very frequently the moderator) will do everything to circumvent face-threatening (supportive facework). This may then involve linguistic behaviour which is open to interpretation as polite.

Polite behaviour (i.e. politeness$_1$) has been presented throughout this book as being behaviour in excess of polite behaviour, which allows for a fair amount of leeway with respect to the disputability of the term '(im)polite'. This is exactly what we want to achieve in a politeness theory that conceptualises politeness as a first-order notion constantly open to discursive dispute in a theory of social practice.

The interconnections between the terms polite behaviour, facework and politeness can be represented by figure 10.1. The oval with the thick border around it represents the totality of forms of social practice, which can be posited as infinite. Although the number of types of verbal interaction in which individual participants may be involved is potentially unlimited, the forms of polite behaviour will still be largely predictable on the basis of the objectified social structures of the field in which the interaction takes place. Aggressive facework lies on the boundaries of the expected polite behaviour for the interaction and is highly unlikely to use linguistic structures that might be open to interpretation as polite. Supportive facework, on the

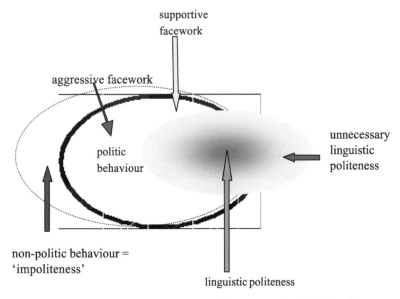

supportive
facework

aggressive facework

politic
behaviour

unnecessary
linguistic
politeness

non-politic behaviour =
'impoliteness'

linguistic politeness

Figure 10.1   Facework, linguistic politeness and politic behaviour

other hand, lies closer to that area in which linguistic behaviour might (but need not) be associated with potentially polite behaviour. Outside the borders of politic behaviour on the left of the diagram we have non-politic verbal behaviour that is not interpretable as sanctioned aggressive facework. We have seen several times throughout the present text that this type of behaviour is almost inevitably interpreted at the first-order level as impolite, rude, brash, etc. The shaded oval in the diagram indicates the degree of dispute there is likely to be over whether verbal structures of politic behaviour are interpretable as polite or not. The closer we get to the centre of this shaded oval, the more likely it will be that the utterance will go beyond the payment that is necessary for politic behaviour. A section of 'polite' behaviour even lies outside the borders of what is politic and, although it is superficially polite, it will almost certainly be evaluated negatively.

Figure 10.1 thus represents diagrammatically the interrelationship between face, politic behaviour and politeness. Presenting (im)politeness$_1$ as a universal aspect of human behaviour is something I have deliberately not done in this book. Is there any way in which theorising politeness as part of a theory of practice can still lay claims to universality? If there is, then we can take this as a starting point to assess how the model might be used empirically. The following section will attempt to do just that.

THE 'UNIVERSAL' NATURE OF THE MODEL AND ITS POSSIBLE PRACTICAL APPLICATIONS

The theory of (im)politeness$_1$ can be conceptualised as part of a theory of social practice. Since social practice is a universal in all forms of social, human existence, a theory of (im)politeness$_1$ must therefore by definition be a universal theory. A counter-argument to this conclusion might be that if a cultural group possesses no way of expressing linguistically what we might express in English by using such terms as 'polite', 'impolite', 'well-mannered', 'rude', 'courteous', 'standoffish', 'aloof', etc. in reference to social acts carried out by its members, then we might well consider social practice to be universal, while excluding (im)politeness$_1$ from this privilege. To do so, however, would amount to the suggestion that there are social groups which do not judge the social acts of their members, i.e. that there are no concepts which are under dispute. This would entail the conclusion that language usage may be free of any moral judgement, a conclusion which is demonstrably not tenable. Hence every social group must have a language variety at its disposal in which a number of lexemes, in their denotative reference, will overlap with English terms referring to the field of (im)politeness$_1$. So (im)politeness$_1$ must be universal.

The status of a model of (im)politeness$_1$, however, is bound to differ from universal models of (im)politeness$_2$. Having objectified the notion of politeness in the latter kind of model, it then becomes necessary to locate those utterances which instantiate the notion across languages and cultures. This immediately leads to the kinds of taxonomy of linguistic structures that we criticised in chapter 7 and effectively prevents us from observing how individuals struggle over the interpretation of those same structures. We may be able to locate cross-cultural differences in linguistic behaviour in accordance with those linguistic structures that appear to refer to the notion of politeness$_2$ in the model. But we will have learnt nothing about how members of the same socio-cultural group struggle over whether a linguistic expression is or is not 'polite' or 'impolite' and what the differential value of that attribution might be. Conceptualising (im)politeness$_1$ as behaviour in excess of (or deliberately not fulfilling) the politic behaviour conventionally required of participants in verbal interaction allows for differential interpretations of the term, it allows for the discursive struggle that is an integral part of the theory of social practice, and it allows the term 'politeness' to be evaluated morally.

How can this conceptualisation of (im)politeness$_1$ be used in empirical research? Chapter 9 represents an attempt to locate those possible points in stretches of naturally occurring verbal interaction that might be open to interpretation as 'polite' or 'impolite'. In some cases participants did not attribute (or did not seem to attribute) that classification to the structures that were looked at. In other cases, however, there is evidence that attributions of politeness or impoliteness can be seen to cooccur with the exercise of power in the ongoing development of an emergent social network. This is an important finding since it links the study of (im)politeness$_1$ with the study of social networking and the ways in which individuals, knowingly or not, exercise power or try to exercise power over others.

If (im)politeness$_1$ is seen as constituting the behavioural frame of (IM)POLITENESS which is latent in all verbal interaction, it should be possible to locate points of dispute and struggle in past exemplars of verbal interaction, many of which are only available in written or printed form. In doing so, we might be able to trace the historical development of linguistic politeness. Similarly the close study of interaction in other socio-cultural groups within the frame of (IM)POLITENESS will lead us to locate points in verbal interaction in which dispute is in evidence and help to clarify the cultural relativity of the term.

In a more practical vein, a closer focus on verbal interaction and the differential attributions of (im)politeness$_1$ by participants might help to raise the sociolinguistic and sociocultural awareness of communicators and provide a more substantial basis on which to aim at more efficient and more effective communication between the members of different socio-cultural groups. This, of course, will rely on an understanding of what the politic behaviour expected in different kinds of verbal interaction might be.

In general, the model presented here can be seen as a contribution to the overall study of human social interaction and the significance of language in that interaction. It should be seen as a contribution to the study of linguistic practice, to the continual attempts by those interested in the study of language and society to get inside the communicating human being and see how s/he functions. A theory of linguistic politeness that sets itself the kinds of aims outlined in this book is, I maintain, a radical departure from the theories of linguistic politeness currently available. My claim is not that it is a 'better' theory. Much still has to be done to find the ways to give an adequate theoretical description of the crucial terms in the theory such as 'face', 'politic behaviour', 'habitus', 'social field', 'symbolic capital' – and of course '(im)politeness' itself. I do claim, however, that the only valid object of a theory of linguistic politeness is not a hypostasised, objectified abstract term 'politeness' but rather the ways in which interactants classify social, verbal acts as realising their own personal conceptualisation of what is 'polite' and what is 'impolite'. (Im)politeness$_1$ is an area of discursive struggle in social practice in every society and in every language. It is that which makes it interesting, and it is that which makes it universal.

Notes

1 Introducing linguistic politeness

1. The transcripts of recorded verbal interaction provided in the text will be presented in the HIAT notation, i.e. reading from left to right as in a musical score (cf. Ehlich 1993; Ehlich and Rehbein 1976, 1979, 1981). Detail will be kept to a minimum so as not to impair the readability of the transcripts. Each line of the 'score' will be numbered as follows:[1]. The termination of a tone group will be represented by the sign \. Intonation contours will generally be omitted, but if required at the end of the tone group they will be indicated in the following way:

   ´: a rising tone
   `: a falling tone
   ^: a rising-falling tone

   In the HIAT notation system overlapping speech is easily interpretable, as the onset of the overlap coincides with the position in the transcript that the current speaker has reached in her/his ongoing turn. Pauses of between 0.2 and 0.5 of a second are represented as follows: . ; those between 0.5 and 0.8 second as .. , and pauses between 0.9 and 1.2 seconds as . . . . Pauses longer that 1.2 seconds will be noted in the transcript with the length given between parentheses, e.g. 1.3. False starts will be indicated by the symbol / and stuttering and/or repetition will be represented by a hyphen following the element repeated. An uncompleted turn is represented by an m-dash, –. Indecipherable speech is represented by a series of question marks placed between angled brackets <???>. Laughter is represented as a series of @ signs placed between angled brackets, and speech accompanied by laughter is represented between angled brackets preceded and followed by @. Accompanying non-linguistic behaviour, wherever it is important as an aid to interpreting 'polite', 'impolite' or 'politic' verbal activity, will be placed in the transcript and represented in small capitals between angled brackets. Filled pauses are represented between colons, e.g. :er:, :eh:. Lengthened vowels are represented by colons. Some chapters will contain intuited examples of linguistic politeness, i.e. examples that are not taken from natural conversation but are fictive exchanges. These will be represented in the conventional way, i.e. not in a HIAT format.

2. It is not unimportant to note that here, too, it is politeness which is focused on, not impoliteness. Although the interest in impoliteness is increasing, as a technical term it is almost entirely missing in the literature.

3. These need not, of course, be exclusively native speakers of English.

4. Sifianou also mentions a second term in Greek, *filotimo*, which she sees as overlapping with *evgenia*. Greek colleagues, however, tend to contradict Sifianou here,

264

saying that *filotimo* implies concepts such as pride and honour, keeping one's word, doing whatever one can to be of use to others. *Filotimo* is felt to be a deeper virtue, whereas *evgenia* is somewhat more superficial.

5. For ease of reading, Rathmayr's Russian and French terms have been translated into English here.

6. Lee-Wong maintains that '[a]s a means–end rationalisation politeness is reduced to pure redressive measures which differs from the Chinese emphasis on ethics and morals. *Limao* is part of normative politeness expected of individuals in any social interaction. Over and above this socially sanctioned code of conduct, individuals may perceive immediate and specific needs – such as the need to orient towards H's positive face and/or the need to use negative politeness as a mitigatory measure to alleviate the imposition' (1999: 25). The term 'negative politeness' refers to Brown and Levinson's distinction between positive and negative face and the politeness strategies addressed to these two types of face as 'positive' and 'negative' politeness. Brown and Levinson's model will be presented and a criticism of it will follow in chapter 4.

7. Fukushima (2000) has criticised the impression conveyed by Japanese authors on politeness that this code of appropriate behaviour is as socially binding as it is made out to be and gives evidence of more 'volitional' than 'discernment' practices in the choice of Japanese politeness[1]. If she is right, then we see the same kind of discursive struggle over the social values of (im)politeness as we have noted for English.

2 Politeness through time and across cultures

1. The term 'mutually shared forms of consideration for others' does not imply that we all carry around in our heads the same set of 'behavioural rules' for interacting in a specific social situation, but rather that in an ongoing interaction we invoke online what we think is the appropriate way to behave in the situation. As long as the other participants do the same, the politic behaviour is renegotiable and reproduced accordingly. The term should not therefore be interpreted to suggest that we have mutually shared knowledge, rather that we react as we imagine others expect us to react, and as long as the others do more or less the same, the politic behaviour is reproduced.

2. There are of course plenty of cultures in which coach travel is completely unknown, although taking one's turn to be served or to acquire something is probably a cultural universal.

3. In several cultures of the world it is an offence to the cook *not* to belch after a good meal. These forms of social behaviour may also, but need not, involve linguistic behaviour.

4. It is also cognate with the Italian *pulire* 'to clean'.

5. Research carried out by Alain Montandon at the Centre de Recherches sur les Littératures Modernes et Contemporaines of the University of Clermont-Ferrand, Jacques Carré at the University of Paris (Sorbonne) and their associates has revealed that the Italian conduct literature of the sixteenth century constituted a hegemonic discourse regulating access to ducal courts based in urban centres in Italy.

6. Della Casa's book might even be considered to represent a form of anti-discourse judging by a comment made by the person for whom it was written, Annibale Rucellai, who claims that Della Casa wrote it 'for fun and to see how our language would bear a style so humble and comical' (Santosuosso 1979: 100). Regardless of Rucellai's comment, however, the book was taken seriously in England.

7. The term was used with respect to 'politeness' by the Earl of Chesterfield in his letters to his son.
8. If we recall the Greek term for 'civilisation', *politizmos*, we can see how close we are to uncovering a hegemonic discourse revolving around an intimate set of terms like 'politeness', 'civilisation', 'innateness', 'politics', 'gentlemen', etc.
9. Cf. the public lectures on elocution offered by Thomas Sheridan or Walker's pronouncing dictionary.

3 Modelling linguistic politeness (I)

1. In the vast majority of cases they have also preferred to focus on politeness rather than impoliteness.
2. This may sound tautologous, but it does highlight the ambiguous nature of scientific endeavour. Try as we might as social scientists, we will never be able to free ourselves from systems of belief, i.e. from ideologies. Claims that science reaches out to find objective explanations of factual data are ultimately ideological, since all data are to a certain extent 'contaminated' by the discursive ideologies of the scientific community itself.
3. Quite apart from the physical impossibility of carrying out such a vast undertaking, the term 'culture' immediately presents us with a whole gamut of virtually insoluble problems, some of which I shall deal with in chapter 6.
4. We need to bear in mind that no attempt to 'explain' politeness as a universal phenomenon of human society will succeed if it does not take into consideration the historical and social relativity of first-order conceptualisations of politeness such as those we looked at in the previous chapter.
5. It is this approach to politeness which Werkhofer (1992) calls 'traditional', as we shall see in the next chapter.
6. The German linguists Porzig and Trier have frequently been accused, not without a certain justification, of 'collaborating' with the racist ideology of Nazi Germany during the 1930s (cf. Helbig 1973).
7. Once again we note that the moral aspect of politeness was also in evidence prior to more modern theories.
8. On the other hand, the pragmatic insistence on upholding the speaker–hearer dichotomy in the interest of raising (im)politeness to the status of a primitive term in politeness theory has effectively blocked the option of focusing on (im)politeness$_1$ by doing away with the distinction altogether.
9. The maxims of the CP will be examined more critically in chapter 8.
10. Publications directly or indirectly inspired by Lakoff's 1975 monograph include Abordonado (1998), Brown (1990), Burstein (1989), Eckert and McConnell-Ginet (1992), Eliasoph (1987), Holmes (1995), Holmes and Stubbe (1997), Holtgraves (1991), Holtgraves and Yang (1990), Johnson and Roen (1992), Johnstone *et al.* (1992), Kamisli and Dogançay (1997), Nakanishi (1998), Rundquist (1992).
11. Hence these rules, too, are normative despite Lakoff's attempt to create a descriptive model of politeness$_2$.
12. Cf. Gu (1990); Haverkate (1984, 1988a, 1988b); Liu (1987); Shu and Wang (1993); Tomoda (1991).
13. Having said this, however, I need to add a cautionary note to the effect that the 'data' are isolated, largely decontextualised examples of language presented through the introspection of the authors. This in itself constitutes a ground for criticism, as we shall see in later chapters.
14. One could of course argue that as we are not dealing with a production model of politeness in the case of Leech this point is invalid.

15. Cf. the recent work by Fukushima (2000), which refutes the impression of a homogenous Japanese culture provided by such researchers as Ide and Matsumoto.
16. See the detailed discussion of Grice's CP in chapter 8.
17. Cf. Arndt and Janney (1983, 1985a, b, 1987) and Janney and Arndt (1992, 1993).
18. Presumably this is written with capital first letters in order to set it off against Grice's Cooperative Principle, Lakoff's Pragmatic Competence and Leech's Politeness Principle.
19. Cf. the situation in the coach station described in the first section of chapter 2.

4 Modelling linguistic politeness (II): Brown and Levinson and their critics

1. In this book I shall reject the simplistic equation Politeness Theory = Face Theory. This does not, of course, deny that the Brown and Levinson model's most basic tenet is that politeness is intimately connected with facework. Facework, however, does not have to use forms of linguistic politeness, and forms of linguistic politeness can also realise clear cases of face damage.
2. I shall argue in chapter 5 that Brown and Levinson's understanding of face is significantly different from Goffman's and leads to different conclusions with respect to the sets of strategies for constructing, regulating and reproducing forms of cooperative social interaction than would a revised version of Goffman's term.
3. Cf. Werkhofer (1992).
4. This is only an apparent exception to the prefacing of the strategy to the FTA since the speaker here has expressed the condition for the exchange prior to the actual exchange (the strategy) in the main clause. S/he could have expressed it the other way round of course: 'Dad, I'll mow the lawn after school tomorrow if you'll help me with my maths homework.'
5. This example also contains some of the previous strategy in which the speaker states the FTA as an instance of a general rule.
6. The debt is stated in the FTA first and the recognition of the debt appears in the promise to buy the hearer a beer. Note that this strategy also has similarities with the positive politeness substrategy of tit for tat (example (14)) and with the substrategy of offer/promise (example (10)). It is not therefore totally clear whether the distinction between positive and negative strategies can ultimately be upheld.
7. The problematic concept here is 'culture', as we shall see in chapter 6.
8. What Gu meant to suggest here is that all forms of linguistic politeness, rather than FTAs themselves, are impolite, since, for Brown and Levinson, the very nature of FTAs *is* that they are inherently impolite.
9. Work by Sifianou (1992a), García (1993, 1999), Glick (1996), Blum-Kulka (1990, 1992) and others has provided evidence supporting this suggestion.
10. Cf. Ide (1992); Ide *et al.* (1992); Mao (1994); Lee-Wong (1999); Gu (1990); Nwoye (1992), etc.
11. At this point we need to exercise extreme caution. Criticism of this kind rests on the assumption that it is possible to divide forms of human society into two categories, 'individualistic' and 'collectivist'. There is evidence to show that this kind of classification does not stand up to close scrutiny.
12. There are two exceptions to this comparison with Chinese face in Nwoye's analysis of Igbo face, namely that in Igbo 'the face is the gateway to the personality' and that 'good/bad fortune is believed to reside in the face, because the face is regarded as a mirror of the entire personality' (1992: 314).
13. It is also noticeable that the researchers are from Asian, Islamic and African cultures. However, at least one European scholar, Anna Wierzbicka, has also

criticised what she calls the 'Anglo-Saxon' focus on distance and the desire not to impose on *alter*'s territory, suggesting that Slavic and Mediterranean cultures accentuate involvement and personal warmth, both attributes of positive face, over and above distance. Although Sifianou still uses Brown and Levinson's approach to politeness to compare English and Greek politeness strategies, her research also displays an overwhelming preference for positive politeness strategies (Sifianou 1992a). It would appear that the Brown and Levinson model is on the retreat to the confines of northwest Europe and North America.

14. There has been criticism of the term 'face' on the grounds that the metaphors used by several cultures refer to other parts of the human body (cf. Strecker 1993) and that it cannot therefore be taken as a universal concept. This ignores the fact that, while some cultures do indeed have no equivalent folk concepts, a much larger and culturally heterogeneous set of cultures do. It also ignores the fact that, although 'face' is not specifically referred to, other parts of the head, e.g. the brow, often are. In addition, it ignores Goffman's point that 'in any society, whenever the physical possibility of spoken interaction arises, it seems that a system of practices, conventions, and procedural rules comes into play which functions as a means of guiding and organizing the flow of messages' (1967 [1955]: 33–4). This kind of criticism simply disregards the metaphorical nature of Goffman's concept and the universal necessity in social interaction for there to be 'an understanding . . . as to when and where it will be permissible to initiate talk, among whom, and by means of what topics of conversation' (1967 [1955]: 34).

15. Of the three terms, *face*, *deference* and *demeanour*, it is demeanour which is most open to cultural variation and which will again enter our discussion of a new approach to politeness in chapter 6 when we discuss Bourdieu's notion of the *habitus*. Goffman admits that, rightly or wrongly, this aspect of an individual's demeanour can lead to the judgement of her/his reliability, suitability as a social interactant, etc. and that it therefore fulfils a diagnostic function in social interaction. At the same time, it is also part of the masking function so commonly in evidence in socially asymmetric interaction, in that it helps to seal *ego* off from a more realistic, penetrating judgement of her/his self.

16. A fourth researcher (Werkhofer 1992) has all but dismantled the theory entirely. Since I shall also argue that Brown and Levinson's model of linguistic politeness is indeed not entirely adequate, Werkhofer's criticisms will be dealt with in more detail in the following section. In chapter 6 an alternative model will be developed. For the moment we shall consider more closely the comments on face made by O'Driscoll and de Kadt.

17. He refers to their interpretation as *B & L face dualism*.

18. O'Driscoll does not discuss whether societies with vertically or horizontally organised social ties correspond to collectivist or indivualistic societies respectively. His examples would lead one to this conclusion, but avoiding the controversial sociological terminology 'collective vs. individualistic society' does not then make the problem disappear. I would prefer to suggest that rather than being an index of one or the other type of social structure, linguistic and non-linguistic politeness is instrumental, at least in part, in actually creating that structure.

19. O'Driscoll has at least introduced a certain amount of social theory into the field of politeness research by making the distinction between strong and weak vertical ties and, more significantly, by making an interesting comparison of politeness with money.

20. Cf. the prepragmatic approaches to politeness presented in chapter 3.

21. There is, in other words, no mention of the complexity of factors involved in any social interaction.

5 Facework and linguistic politeness

1. The term 'Parsonian' is suggested by Eelen to refer to the structuralist–functionalist approach to sociology practised in the 1950s by the American sociologist Talcott Parsons.
2. Cf. the criticisms of the seminal work by Brown and Levinson (1978, 1987) in chapter 4.
3. I hasten to add that it is only 'relatively stable'. Work in psychotherapy shows that our individual conceptualisations of the self can be easily thrown out of balance particularly if the construals made by certain significant interaction partners change unexpectedly.
4. The classical example for this type of institutional organisation is the military.
5. The clearest example that comes to mind here is social interaction within the family.
6. The family gathering in this case took place at my parents' former home in Cornwall in 1985. R refers to me, A to my wife, D to my stepfather and B to my mother.
7. I have not counted A's utterance 'mm' as a full turn, since it is a minimal listener response.

6 A social model of politeness

1. We also noted during chapter 4 that O'Driscoll had made a passing reference to the comparison of politeness and forms of payment.
2. To these five points we can also add that we have to learn how to use linguistic politeness just as we have to learn how to use money.
3. Bourdieu's assessment of ethnomethodology does not take adequately into account the ongoing processual and constructive nature of human interaction, which is the mainstay of ethnomethodological approaches and the underlying principle of Conversation Analysis. Bourdieu has often been criticised for not showing how his theories work in detail in real social practice. Any attempt to make a fine-grained analysis of what individuals are doing in ongoing socio-communicative verbal interaction with CA will reveal the objective nature of the task and the arbitrariness with which Bourdieu simply categorises ethnomethodologically based approaches as being at the subjective end of the spectrum.
4. *The Oxford Latin Dictionary*, edited by P. G. W. Glore (Oxford: Clarendon Press, 1982). Bourdieu's use of the term indicates that he was well aware of its polysemy.
5. I owe this revised formula to the work of one of my graduate students, Babette Neukirchen, who included it in her MA thesis.
6. We will refrain at this point from entering into a discussion on the nature of money, but it should be clear not only that the value of the symbolic resource money can vary considerably but also that it too can become a reified good in its own right.
7. The 'feel' for a situation which an individual can gain and the ways in which s/he reacts accordingly are referred to by Bourdieu as a *habitus* (cf. above). Bourdieu *et al.* (1994: 8) state that '[l]anguage is the most active and elusive part of the cultural heritage', thereby implying that the 'linguistic habitus' is one of the most salient in social interaction and one of the most difficult to change.

8. Henceforth I shall simply refer to 'politic behaviour', as I have done in previous chapters, to refer to aspects of the linguistic habitus, but a more comprehensive understanding of the term would obviously include other, non-linguistic forms of communicative behaviour.

9. At this point we need to exercise extreme caution since e-mail communication is still relatively new (cf. Baron 2001), and not everyone is in agreement about precisely what constitutes its politic behaviour.

10. The phrase *intends to be subscribed to your journal* does, of course, sound non-native, in that one subscribes to a journal rather than being subscribed to it. Perhaps this is the reason why one might have expected a little more than just *please*.

7 Structures of linguistic politeness

1. Ideational meaning is thus more or less the same as Grice's meaning$_n$, or 'natural meaning'.

2. Given that, at the time of writing, she is only eighteen months old, however, she is highly unlikely to be able to attach any meaning to *well*.

3. Cf. e.g. Lakoff (1973b), Svartvik (1980), Owen (1983), Watts (1987), Schiffrin (1987), etc.

4. The reader will note the fact that I am hedging here, the simple reason being that *well* has also managed to escape clear analyses of its procedural meaning.

5. Cf. Thompson and Mulac (1991).

6. In certain languages like German and Dutch, however, pragmaticalised expressions, often referred to as 'particles', are still integrated within sentence structure even though they do not contribute towards the truth value of the proposition in which they appear.

7. This in itself was a process of grammaticalisation.

8. I have deliberately left out any mention of the development of the verb *own* in modern English, as this would have complicated the picture still further.

9. It could of course be argued that this use of *ought* only occurs in non-standard varieties of English, although I would dispute that claim.

10. This example is also dealt with in detail in Hopper and Traugott (1993).

11. Given the utterance in (11), it is, of course, not possible to generate a parenthetical insertion of *you know*, but the sentence-final position is open.

12. Depending of course on whether it is in excess of the politic behaviour or not.

13. This may be one reason why speakers of English who omit such expressions are generally felt to be speaking inappropriately, whereas speakers of Japanese, Korean, etc., who do not use linguistic politeness where it should be used or who use inappropriate structures are felt to be speaking ungrammatically.

14. Cf., e.g., Aston (1995); Axia and Baroni (1985); Baroni and Axia (1989); Bates and Silvern (1977); Becker (1988); Becker and Smenner (1986); Chilman (1980); Ervin-Tripp *et al.* (1990); Garton and Pratt (1990); Garvey (1975); Gleason et al. (1984); Gleason and Weintraub (1976); Greif and Gleason (1980); Kwarciak (1991); Power and Shanks (1989); Valtl (1986); Walper and Valtin (1992); Wilhite (1983).

15. The lexeme *please* is only ever placed in a sentence-internal adverbial position when the proposition is framed as a question which invites interpretation as a 'polite' request.

16. This is the case even though the offerer has not had recourse to a semi-formulaic EPM.

17. Not only is it difficult, if not impossible, to talk about 'British English culture' or 'Greek culture' as if they were homogenous sets of cultural behaviour patterns. It also fails to take into account the wide variation of cultural differences

determined by a complex interplay between such social variables as social class, religion, gender, age, ethnicity, profession, social network, etc.

18. In my own bibliography of references on politeness the following all either have the term 'speech act' in their title, are volumes of articles on the subject of speech acts and speech act analysis, or are included in such a volume: Biq (1984); Blum-Kulka (1983); Blum-Kulka and Olshtain (1984); Bustamante Lopez and Murcia (1995); Campbell (1990); Chitoran (1987); Flowerdew (1991); Fraser (1975); García (1996); Gass and Neu (1995); Geis (1995); Haverkate (1984, 1988a, 1994); Held (1992a, b); Holtgraves (1986); Kachru (1994); Koike (1989); Olshtain and Cohen (1983); Olshtain and Weinbach (1987); Wierzbicka (1985); Yli-Jokipii (1994).

19. Work on linguistic modality usually distinguishes between two principal types, *epistemic modality*, in which the speaker bases the expression of possibility, necessity, predictability, etc. on knowledge that she has, either prior to the interaction or through processing information acquired during the interaction, and *deontic modality*, in which the modal force of the proposition emanates from the speaker herself. Deontic modality thus covers modal meanings such as volition, obligation, desire, permission, etc.

20. The modal verbs *may* and *might* could also be used in this type of structure.

21. I assume that by now the reader will automatically substitute *may* for *can* and *might* for *could* to refer to other registers of English. The argument remains exactly the same for both modal verbs.

22. In the first of a series of lectures held at UCLA in autumn 1964, Harvey Sacks deals with precisely the kind of subversion alluded to here. He considers utterances such as 'May I help you?' made on the phone by staff members at an emergency psychiatric hospital to callers requiring help or information as 'composites', i.e. as formulaic utterances which help to construct the interaction in terms of 'help seeker'/'help giver'. The utterance 'May I help you?' is so conventionalised that the unmarked response is 'yes' followed by a statement of the caller's problem. From time to time, however, utterances like 'I don't know' or 'maybe' are given as second pair-parts. This seems to indicate that, although callers are perfectly aware that the utterance by the staff member is highly conventionalised and part of the ritual of the interaction order, they are also capable of interpreting the utterance as a literally meant question. When they do so, of course, their behaviour becomes salient for the staff member, allowing her/him to make significant inferences for the continuation of the call (Sacks 1992: I, 8–11).

23. Blum-Kulka (1987) challenges the claim that there is a direct relationship between indirectness and politeness. She bases this challenge on the assumption that 'in conventional indirectness properties of the utterance play the more dominant role, while in non-conventional indirectness pragmatic context is probably as, if not more, important' (1987: 142). The examples discussed in this section and in previous chapters clearly support Blum-Kulka's insight. Indeed, all the introspected examples in this chapter would need to be heavily contextualised to allow a polite interpretation.

8 Relevance Theory and concepts of power

1. Cf. the discussion in chapters 3 and 4.

2. One further way in which the CP may be violated is that interactants simply do so inadvertently without even realising that one of the maxims has been violated and therefore without intending any pragmatic meaning to be inferred – although, of course, the addressee probably will infer something.

3. One point for which relevance theorists have been criticised concerns their apparent disregard for the social matrix of verbal interaction. For a discussion of these issues see the articles in Jucker (1997).

4. This is an aspect of their theory which has come in for quite a lot of criticism. For the moment, however, I see no reason to deny the semiotic nature of the language system, however we acquire it or use it, and I shall continue to refer to language as a system in these terms.

5. The term 'stimulus' is not to be understood in the way that it is used in the psychological theory of behaviourism. Sperber and Wilson are not invoking the ghost of Watson, Skinner, Osgood or any other behaviourist in support of their theory. It is simply a commonplace that an utterance directed at B by A represents a stimulus to which B is expected to respond in some way or another. Nothing is being said here about any kind of stimulus–response conditioning, since neither Sperber and Wilson nor any other model of discourse or conversation analysis is a learning theory.

6. One of the possible weaknesses of Sperber and Wilson's model is that they simply assume the notion of intention without giving an explicit definition of how this crucial term is to be understood. This is also a feature of most of the work in speech act theory.

7. It is not my intention to put the reader through a brief course in RT in this section, but I should perhaps mention that Sperber and Wilson's major principle is called the Presumption of Optimal Relevance (revised), which they define as follows (Sperber and Wilson 1995: 270):
   Presumption of optimal relevance (revised):
   (a) The ostensive stimulus is relevant enough for it to be worth the addressee's effort to process it.
   (b) The ostensive stimulus is the most relevant one compatible with the communicator's abilities and preferences.

9 Politic behaviour and politeness in discourse

1. For this reason RT can never be used as the basis from which a theory of (im)politeness$_1$ can be developed.

2. The term 'cajoler' was defined in chapter 7 as a linguistic expression to 'help to increase, establish or restore harmony between the interlocutors'.

3. For the term 'turn relevance place', or TRP, see Jefferson (1973) and Watts (1991).

10 Politic behaviour and politeness within a theory of social practice

1. In the case of the written medium, of course, writers certainly do have more time to plan their utterances, but even here, much of what goes by the label 'polite' is conventionalised ritual in conformity with the politic behaviour expected of the interaction.

2. Cf. here the special issue of *Pragmatics* edited in 1999 by Manfred Kienpointner, in which the connection between politeness and power was the explicit focus of attention.

Glossary of terms

activity type: a conventionally recognised type of social activity that is likely to be categorised in similar ways by social members.

adjacency pair: a single sequence of utterances by different speakers in which the first utterance constrains the second in some way.

algorithmic rules: rules set in algebraic notation for use in computing.

alter: the Latin word for 'other' referring to other persons involved in social interaction beyond the *ego*.

appealers: linguistic expressions which try to elicit some hearer confirmation and are characterised by rising intonation patterns.

boosters: linguistic expressions enhancing the force of the illocution in some way.

capital: the incorporation of resources, which become part of the individual's habitus.

classificatory politeness₁: comments made either by outsiders to the interaction or by the participants themselves, which classify behaviour as '(im)polite'.

competence: a person's unconscious knowledge of the rules underlying her/his language.

connotative meaning: a personal or emotional association evoked by a lexical item that helps to create an individual speaker's meaning.

conversational floor: the metaphorical space available to speakers to produce a turn or turns at talk.

conversational implicatures: those aspects of meaning which are not conveyed explicitly in linguistic form, but must be derived from the context of the utterance.

denotative meaning: the meaning carried by a lexical item that creates a connection between the lexeme itself and some entity in the 'outside world'.

discernment: recognising the appropriate features of the ongoing social interaction and choosing socially appropriate strategies of interaction.

discourse marker: a linguistic expression used to create semantic and/or pragmatic cohesion between different parts of the overall discourse.

discursive format: the generally accepted form, both in terms of linguistic and non-linguistic structure, in which verbal interaction is expected to be conducted.

discursive/discourse practices: the different forms of activity carried out in verbal interaction.

discursive struggle: disagreement among participants in verbal interaction about what a term means personally for each of those participants.

downtoners: a linguistic expression that 'modulates the impact' of the speaker's utterance.

ego: the Latin word for 'I', referring to the central perception every individual has of her/himself in social interaction.

emergent network: a network of social links between individuals set up in the course of socio-communicative interaction.

exercise of power: A exercises power over B when A affects B in a manner contrary to B's initially perceived interests, regardless of whether B later comes to accept the desirability of A's actions.

expression of procedural meaning (EPM): a linguistic or paralinguistic expression that is focused on instructing the addressee how to process the propositional content of the utterance.

expressive politeness₁: the explicit production of polite behaviour.

face-threatening acts (FTAs): any act, verbal or non-verbal, which threatens the way in which an individual sees her/himself or would like to be seen by others (taken from the metaphorical expression 'face', as in 'to lose face', 'face-saving', etc.).

facework: efforts made by the participants in verbal interaction to preserve their own face and the face of others.

first-order (im)politeness ((im)politeness₁): the ways in which (im)polite behaviour is evaluated and commented on by lay members of a language community.

footing: the stance that a participant adopts towards other participants in verbal interaction.

formulaic, ritualised utterances: highly conventionalised utterances, containing linguistic expressions that are used in ritualised forms of verbal interaction.

generative grammar/generative theories of language: grammars and theories of language which aim to define the set of all and only the grammatically well-formed sentences in a language, and containing rules which will produce a potentially infinite set of such sentences.

grammaticalisation: a process through which lexical, denotationally meaningful elements in a language are transformed by successive generations of speakers into morphologically dependent linguistic elements in the grammatical system of that language.

habitus: the set of dispositions to behave in a manner which is appropriate to the social structures objectified by an individual through her/his experience of social interaction.

hedge: a linguistic expression that enables the speaker to avoid being too direct in her/his utterance.

hegemonic discourse: ruling, authoritative discourse.

honorific: a grammatical form used to express the social status of the participants in verbal interaction, including levels of politeness or respect.

ideational meaning: the meaning conveyed conventionally by the way in which messages are put together for transmission, i.e. by their logical structure.

illocutionary act: the act that a speaker carries out in an utterance.

illocutionary force: the intended act carried by an utterance, which may differ from the actual illocutionary act itself.

implicature: an implication or suggestion deduced from the form of an utterance. *Conversational implicature:* implicatures derived by making use of the maxims of the Cooperative Principle. *Conventional implicature:* implications attached by convention to the linguistic structure of an utterance.

incident: an occurrence which appears to break normally accepted standards of behaviour.

inclusive first-person-plural pronoun: a first-person-plural pronoun which includes as its referent both the speaker and the addressee.

indirect utterance/speech act: an utterance/speech act which does not correspond directly to its communicative purpose.

inference: a deduction made by an addressee concerning the assumed intended meaning expressed by a speaker's utterance.

inferencing: the process by which addressees can deduce inferences.

interaction order: the types of social behaviour which take place at certain sequentially ordered points in the interaction.

interpersonal meaning: the meaning of the social link created between speaker and addressee through directing an utterance at her/him.

latent network: the network of social relationships between individuals which each individual assumes to be potentially active.

linguistic relativity: a theory of language which maintains that the distinctions encoded in one language are not found in another language.

line: 'a pattern of verbal and nonverbal acts by which he [sic!] expresses his view of the situation and through this his evaluation of the participants, especially himself' (Goffman 1956).

macro-level description: a description of data which focuses primarily on the overall picture and only secondarily on the details of that picture.

marked: that which occurs less frequently and thus appears unusual and salient.

marketplace: the locus of a struggle over various kinds of capital.

maximal relevance (see *optimal relevance*)

member: the member of a speech community or a social group or a social network.

metapragmatic politeness$_1$: the evaluation of the nature and significance of politeness/ impoliteness produced by oneself or others.

metapragmatic talk: talk about talk or talk about other people's general behaviour.

micro-level description: a description of data which starts at the small details and works outwards towards an overall picture.

objectified social structures: aspects of social behaviour that an individual raises to the status of 'objective' structures by virtue of repeated experience of similar behaviour and observing other people's experience of that behaviour.

on-record: making it explicitly clear to the addressee(s) what the speaker's intention in an utterance is.

off-record: concealing what the speaker's intention in an utterance is such that the addressee(s) needs to infer that intention.

optimal relevance: the addressee assumes that the speaker has done everything in her/his power to produce an utterance which can give rise to 'contextual effects'.

normative: that which pertains to a norm or set of norms.

Parsonian: pertaining to the theories and methods of the American structuralist sociologist Talcott Parsons in the 1950s and 1960s.

politic behaviour: that behaviour, linguistic and non-linguistic, which the participants construct as being appropriate to the ongoing social interaction.

power: the freedom of action to achieve one's goals, regardless of whether or not this involves the potential to impose one's will on others to carry out actions that are in one's interests.

power over: power that appears to be latently invested in complex, institutionalised networks such as school, family, local and national government, in some instances the church, financial institutions.

power to: power that is acquired by interactants at the expense of other interactants in emergent networks.

pragmatics: the branch of linguistic study which concerns itself with the meaning of expressions as and when these are used in verbal interaction.

pragmaticalisation: the process by which the propositional content of linguistic expressions is bleached to such an extent that they no longer contribute to the truth value of a proposition but begin to function as markers indicating procedural meaning in verbal interaction.

preclosing move: a move in a conversation immediately prior to those moves which are made to close off the overall conversation.

prepragmatic approaches to politeness: the study of linguistic politeness prior to the emergence of linguistic pragmatics in the 1960s.

prescriptive: pertaining to a set of behavioural principles, determined by some 'authority', to prescribe to others which forms of behaviour are 'correct' and which 'incorrect'.

presupposition: an assumption made by a speaker that the addressee shares with her/him knowledge of certain facts that will enable an interpretation of the utterance.

procedural meaning: procedures indicating the manner in which propositional meaning can be derived from an utterance.

production model of politeness: a model of politeness which attempts to explain how and why a speaker produces polite utterances.

propositional meaning: the meaning carried by a propositionally well-formed linguistic expression, cf. *ideational meaning.*

redressive action: some action which is designed to correct a wrong done to another person.

relational work: efforts made by the participants in verbal interaction to be as considerate towards one another as possible.

repair work: efforts made by the participants in verbal interaction to repair any damage that might have been done in previous turns at talk.

salient behaviour: behaviour that is noticeable to others.

second-order (im)politeness ((im)politeness₂): a theoretical term in a universal theory of politeness that refers to forms of social behaviour preserving mutually shared consideration for others.

semantics: the study of meaning as this is encoded in the structures of a language, without the need to have recourse to the context of use of an utterance.

semi-formulaic utterances: conventionalised utterances with linguistic expressions that have been focused through processes of pragmaticalisation to carry out indirect speech acts appropriate to the politic behaviour of a social situation.

semiotic system: a system of signs and their associated meanings.

social fields: arbitrary social organisations of space and time that are the sites of constant struggles over capital.

social institution: a socially established set of laws, customs, practices, etc. which regulates and is subservient to the needs of a community.

social practice: the ongoing behaviour of individuals involved in social interaction.

social resource: a set of qualities enabling an individual to gain a degree of status within a social group.

sociolect: a linguistic variety defined on social rather than geographical grounds.

speech act theory: the theory of language which sees it as composed of acts which speakers carry out in relation to others, those acts being realised in speech.

supportive facework: facework that supports other interactants and hence contributes towards the overall facework of the interaction.

symbolic resource: a set of symbolic qualities enabling an individual to gain a degree of status within a social group.

symbolic power: the ability to use the capital in a specific social field in order to change the social order of the field deliberately but without being perceived to do so.

taxonomic: predominantly concerned with processes of segmentation and classification.

transition relevance place (TRP): an area in a conversation in which a co-participant may legitimately take over the floor from an ongoing speaker and begin a new turn-at-talk.

truth values: the values 'true' or 'false' as applied to the correpondence between the content of an utterance and the state of the world to which it refers.

turn at talk: a stretch of talk in verbal interaction that is ratified by other participants and has a recognisable onset and completion.

truth-conditional meaning: the correspondence between a linguistic expression and the conditions that have to be fulfilled for that expression to represent a true state of affairs.

universality: that which is characteristic of all languages or cultures.

unmarked: that which occurs most frequently and thus appears neutral and normal.

volition: choosing to use certain interactional strategies regardless of the features of the social activity type in which the interactants are involved.

References

Abordonado, V. 1998, *The Effect of Gender on Linguistic Politeness in Written Discourse*, PhD thesis, University of Arizona.

Arndt, H. and Janney, R. 1983, 'The clanger phenomenon: the nondeviant nature of deviant utterances', *International Review of Applied Linguistics* 18: 41–57.

Arndt, H. and Janney, R. 1985a, 'Improving emotive communication: verbal, prosodic, and kinesic conflict avoidance techniques', *Per Linguam* 1: 21–33.

Arndt, H. and Janney, R. 1985b, 'Politeness revisited: cross-modal supportive strategies', *IRAL, International Review of Applied Linguistics in Language Teaching* 23(4): 281–300.

Arndt, H. and Janney, R. 1987, *InterGrammar: Toward an Integrative Model of Verbal, Prosodic and Kinesic Choices in Speech*, Berlin: Mouton de Gruyter.

Arundale, R. 1999, 'An alternative model and ideology of communication for an alternative politeness theory', *Pragmatics* 9: 119–53.

Aston, G. 1995, 'Say "Thank you": some pragmatic constraints in conversational closing', *Applied Linguistics* 16(1): 57–86.

Austin, J. 1962, *How to Do Things with Words*, Cambridge, Mass.: Harvard University Press.

Austin, P. 1990, 'Politeness revisited: the dark side', in Bell, A. and Holmes, J. (eds.), *New Zealand Ways of Speaking English*. Clevedon: Multilingual Matters, pp. 277–93.

Axia, G. and Baroni, M. R. 1985, 'Linguistic politeness at different age levels', *Child Development* 56(4): 918–27.

Bargiela-Chiappini, F. and Harris, S. J. 1996, 'Requests and status in business correspondence', *Journal of Pragmatics* 28: 635–62.

Baron, N. 2001, *Alphabet to Email: How Written English Evolved and Where it's Heading*, London: Routledge.

Baroni, M.-R. and Axia, G. 1989, 'Children's meta-pragmatic abilities and the identification of polite and impolite requests', *First Language* 9(3): 285–97.

Bates, E. and Silvern, L. 1977, 'Social adjustment and politeness in preschoolers', *Journal of Communication* 27(2): 104–11.

Bauman, R. 1981, 'Christ respects no man's person: the plain language of the early quakers and the rhetoric of impoliteness', Sociolinguistic Working Paper 88, University of Texas, Austin, TX.

Baumgartner, A. 1908, *Lehrgang der englischen Sprache: II. Teil: Lesebuch*, 7th edition, Zürich: Orell Füssli.

Bayraktaroğlu, A. 1991, 'Politeness and interactional imbalance', *International Journal of the Sociology of Language* 92: 5–34.

Bayraktaroğlu, A. 1992, 'Disagreement in Turkish trouble-talk', *Text* 12: 317–42.

Bayraktaroğlu, A. 2000, 'A repair mechanism in Turkish conversation: the case of *Estağfurullah*', *Multilingua* 1993: 281–310.

Becker, J. A. and Smenner, P. C. 1986, 'The spontaneous use of "Thank you" by preschoolers as a function of sex, socioeconomic status, and listener status', *Language in Society* 15(4): 537–45.

Becker, M. B. 1988, *Civility and Society in Western Europe, 1300–1600*, Indianapolis: Indiana University Press.

Beebe, L. and Takahashi, T. 1989, ' "Do you have a bag?": social status and patterned variation in second language acquisition', in Gass, S., Madden, C., Preston, D. and Selinker, L. (eds.), *Variation in Second Language Acquisition: Discourse and Pragmatics*, Clevedon: Multilingual Matters, pp. 103–25.

Beinhauer, W. 1930, *Spanische Umgangssprache*, Bonn: Ferd. Dümmlers Verlag.

Bellegarde, Abbé de 1696, *L'art de connaître les hommes*, Paris.

Bellegarde, Abbé de ([1698] 1717), *Reflexions upon the Politeness of Manners*, London.

Bentahila, A. and Davies, E. 1989, 'Culture and language use: a problem for foreign language teaching', *IRAL* 27(2): 99–112.

Bergson, H. 1945, *Discours sur la politesse*, Paris: Editions Colbert.

Bex, A. 1999, 'Representations of English in twentieth-century Britain: Fowler, Gowers and Partridge', in Bex, A. and Watts, R. (eds.), *Standard English: The Widening Debate*, London: Routledge, 89–109.

Biq, Y. 1984, 'Indirect speech acts in Chinese polite expressions', *Journal of the Chinese Teachers Association* 19(3): 1–10.

Blum-Kulka, S. 1982, 'Learning how to say what you mean in a language', *Applied Linguistics* 3: 29–59.

Blum-Kulka, S. 1983, 'Interpreting and performing speech acts in a second language: a cross-cultural study of Hebrew and English', in Wolfson, N. and Judd, E. (eds.), *Sociolinguistics and Language Acquisition*. Rowley: Newbury House, pp. 36–55.

Blum-Kulka, S. 1985, 'Modifiers as indicating devices: same or different?', *Theoretical Linguistics* 12(2/3): 213–29.

Blum-Kulka, S. 1987, 'Indirectness and politeness in requests: same or different?', *Journal of Pragmatics* 11(1): 131–146.

Blum-Kulka, S. 1989, 'Playing it safe: the role of conventionality in indirectness', in Blum-Kulka, S., House, J. and Kasper, G. (eds.), *Cross-cultural Pragmatics: Requests and Apologies*. Norwood, NJ: Ablex, pp. 37–70.

Blum-Kulka, S. 1990, 'You don't touch lettuce with your fingers: parental politeness in family discourse', *Journal of Pragmatics* 14(2): 259–88.

Blum-Kulka, S. 1992, 'The metapragmatics of politeness in Israeli society', in Watts, R. J., Ide, S. and Ehlich, K. (eds.), *Politeness in Language: Studies in its History, Theory and Practice*. Berlin: Mouton de Gruyter, pp. 255–80.

Blum-Kulka, S. 1994, 'Review of *Politeness Phenomena in England and Greece: A Crosscultural Perspective* by Maria Sifianou', *Pragmatics and Cognition* 2(2): 349–56.

Blum-Kulka, S. 1997, 'Discourse pragmatics', in van Dijk, T. A. (ed.), *Discourse as Social Interaction. Discourse Studies: A Multidisciplinary Introduction*, vol. 2. London: Sage, pp. 38–63.

Blum-Kulka, S., Danet, B. and Gerson, R. 1985, 'The language of requesting in Israeli society', in Forgas, J. (ed.), *Language and Social Situation*. New York: Springer, pp. 113–41.

Blum-Kulka, S. and House, J. 1989, 'Cross-cultural and situational variation in requesting behavior', in Blum-Kulka, S., House, J. and Kasper, G. (eds.), *Cross-Cultural Pragmatics: Requests and Apologies*. Norwood, NJ: Ablex, pp. 123–54.

Blum-Kulka, S., House, J. and Kasper, G. (eds.) 1989, *Cross-Cultural Pragmatics: Requests and Apologies*, Norwood, NJ: Ablex.

Blum-Kulka, S. and Kasper, G. (eds.) 1990, 'Politeness', *Journal of Pragmatics* 14.

Blum-Kulka, S. and Olshtain, E. 1984, 'Requests and apologies: a cross-cultural study of speech act realization patterns (CCSARP)', *Applied Linguistics* 5(3): 196–213.

Blum-Kulka, S. and Weizman, E. 1988, 'The inevitability of misunderstandings: discourse ambiguities', *Text* 8: 219–41.

Bourdieu, P. 1977. *Outline of a Theory of Practice*, Cambridge: Cambridge University Press.

Bourdieu, P. 1990. *The Logic of Practice*, Cambridge: Polity Press.

Bourdieu, P. 1991, *Language and Symbolic Power*, edited by J. Thompson and translated by G. Raymond and M. Adamson, Cambridge: Polity Press.

Bourdieu, P. and Passeron, J.-C. 1990 [1977], *Reproduction in Education Society and Culture*, London: Sage.

Bourdieu, P., Passeron, J.-C. and de Saint Martin, M. 1994, *Academic Discourse*, Cambridge: Polity Press.

Boyer, A. 1702, *The English Theophrastus: or, The Manners of the Age*, Ann Arbor: Augustan Reprint Society, 1947.

Braun, F. 1988, *Terms of Address: Problems of Patterns and Usage in Various Languages and Cultures*, Berlin: Mouton de Gruyter.

Brown, P. 1976, 'Women and politeness: a new perspective on language and society', *Review in Anthropology* 3: 240–9.

Brown, P. 1980, 'How and why are women more polite? Some evidence from a Mayan community', in McConnell-Ginet, S., Borker, R. and Furman, N. (eds.), *Women and Language in Literature and Society*. New York: Praeger, pp. 111–36.

Brown, P. 1990, 'Gender, politeness, and confrontation in Tenejapa', *Discourse Processes* 13(1): 123–41.

Brown, P. 1994, 'Gender, politeness, and confrontation in Tenejapa', in Tannen, D. (ed.), *Gender and Conversational Interaction*. New York: Oxford University Press, pp. 144–62.

Brown, P. and Levinson, S. 1978, 'Universals in language usage: politeness phenomena', in Goody, E. (ed.), *Questions and Politeness*, Cambridge: Cambridge University Press, pp. 56–289.

Brown, P. and Levinson, S. 1987, *Politeness: Some Universals in Language Usage*, Cambridge: Cambridge University Press.

Brown, R. 1990, 'Politeness theory: exemplar and exemplary', in Rock, I. (ed.), *The Legacy of Solomon Asch: Essays in Cognition and Social Psychology*, Hillsdale, NJ: Lawrence Erlbaum Associates, Inc., pp. 23–38.

Brown, R. and Gilman, A. 1960, 'The pronouns of power and solidarity', in Sebeok, T. (ed.), *Style in Language*. Cambridge, Mass.: MIT Press, pp. 253–76.

Brown, R. and Gilman, A. 1989, 'Politeness theory and Shakespeare's four major tragedies', *Language in Society* 18(2): 159–212.

Bumke, J. 1986, *Höfische Kultur*, Munich: dtv.

Burstein, J. 1989, 'Politeness strategies and gender expectations', *CUNY Forum: Papers in Linguistics* 14: 31–7.

Bury, E. 1992, 'Civiliser la "personne" ou instituer le "personnage"? Les deux versants de la politesse selon les théoriciens français du XVIIe siècle', in Montandon, A. (ed.), *Etiquette et politesse*, Clermont-Ferrand: Association des Publications de la Faculté des Lettres et Sciences Humaines de Clermont-Ferrand, pp. 125–38.

Bustamante Lopez, I. and Murcia, M. 1995, 'Impositive speech acts in Northern Andean Spanish: a pragmatic description', *Hispania: a Journal Devoted to the Interests of the Teaching of Spanish and Portuguese* 78(4): 885–97.

Callières, F. de. 1972 [1693], *Du bon et du mauvais usage*, Geneva: Slatkine Reprints.

Campbell, K. 1990, 'Explanations in negative messages: more insights from speech act theory', *Journal of Business Communication* 27(4): 357–75.

Carré, J. 1994a, 'Ethique et politesse des élites foncières anglaises (1750–1850)', *QWERTY: Arts, Littératures et Civilisations du Monde Anglophone* 4: 339–45.

Carré, J. 1994b, 'The lady and the poor man; or, the philanthropist's etiquette', in Carré, J. (ed.), *The Crisis of Courtesy: Studies in the Conduct-Book in Britain, 1600–1900*. Leiden: Brill, pp. 157–66.

Carré, J. (ed.) 1994c, *The Crisis of Courtesy: Studies in the Conduct-Book in Britain, 1600–1900*, Leiden: Brill.

Castiglione, B. [1528] 1966, *The Book of the Courtier*, New York: Dutton Everyman (first published 1516).

Chilman, C. 1980, 'Parent satisfactions, concerns and goals for their children', *Family Relations* 29: 339–45.

Chitoran, D. 1987, 'The erosion of the boundaries between theoretical and applied linguistics: evidence from speech act theory', in Tomic, O. and Shuy, R. (eds.), *The Relation of Theoretical and Applied Linguistics*, New York: Plenum Press, pp. 115–38.

Chomsky, N. 1972, *Studies in Semantics in Generative Grammar*, The Hague: Mouton.

Clark, H. 1979, 'Responding to indirect speech acts', *Cognitive Psychology* 11: 430–77.

Clark, H. and Schunk, D. 1975, 'Polite responses to polite requests', *Cognition* 8: 111–43.

Clark, H. and Schunk, D. 1980, 'Understanding what is meant from what is said: a study in conversationally conveyed results', *Journal of Verbal Learning and Verbal Behavior* 14: 56–72.

Clark, H. and Schunk, D. 1981, 'Politeness in requests: a rejoinder to Kemper and Thissen', *Cognition* 9: 311–15.

Cook, H. M. 1997, 'The role of the Japanese *masu* form in caregiver–child conversation', *Journal of Pragmatics* 28(6): 695–718.

Coulmas, F. 1979, 'On the sociolinguistic relevance of routine formulae', *Journal of Pragmatics* 3: 239–66.

Coulmas, F. 1981a, ''Poison to your soul': thanks and apologies contrastively viewed', in Coulmas, F. (ed.), *Conversational Routine*, The Hague: Mouton, pp. 69–93.

Coulmas, F. (ed.) 1981, *Conversational Routine: Explorations in Standardized Communication Situations and Prepatterned Speech*, The Hague: Mouton.

Coulmas, F. 1987, '*Keigo*–Höflichkeit und soziale Bedeutung im Japanischen', *Linguistische Berichte* 107: 44–62.

Coulmas, F. 1992, 'Linguistic etiquette in Japanese society', in Watts, R., Ide, S. and Ehlich, K. (eds.), *Politeness in Language: Studies in its History, Theory and Practice*. Berlin: Mouton de Gruyter, pp. 299–323.

Coupland, N.,Grainger, K. and Coupland, J. 1988, 'Politeness in context: intergenerational issues', *Language in Society* 17(2): 253–62.

Crowley, T. 1989, *The Politics of Discourse: the Standard Language Question and British Cultural Debates*, London: Macmillan.

Crystal, D. and Devey, D. 1969, *Investigating English Style*, London: Longman.

Culpeper, J. 1996, 'Towards an anatomy of impoliteness', *Journal of Pragmatics* 25(3): 349–67.

de Kadt, E. 1992, 'Politeness phenomena in South African Black English', *Pragmatics and Language Learning* 3: 103–116.

de Kadt, E. 1994, 'Towards a model for the study of politeness in Zulu', *South African Journal of African Languages/Suid Afrikaanse Tydskrif vir Afrikatale* 14(3): 103–12.

de Kadt, E. 1995, '"I must be seated to talk to you": taking nonverbal politeness strategies into account', *Pragmatics and Language Learning*. Monograph Series 6.

de Kadt, E. 1998, 'The concept of face and its applicability to the Zulu language', *Journal of Pragmatics* 29: 173–91.

della Casa, G. [1558] 1958, *Galateo*, Harmondsworth: Penguin.

Descartes, R. 1637, *Discours de la méthode*, Amsterdam.

Diamond, J. 1996, *Status and Power in Verbal Interaction*, Amsterdam: Benjamins.

DuFon, M., Kasper, G., Takahashi, S. and Yoshinaga, N. 1994, 'Bibliography on linguistic politeness', *Journal of Pragmatics* 21(5): 527–78.

Dupin, H. 1931, *La courtoisie au Moyen Age*, Paris: Picard.

Eckert, P. and McConnell-Ginet, S. 1992, 'Think practically and look locally: language and gender as community-based practice', *Annual Review of Anthropology* 21: 461–90.

Edmondson, W. 1977, *A Pedagogic Grammar of the English Verb: a Handbook for the German Secondary Teacher of English*, Tübingen: Narr.

Edmondson, W. and House, J. 1982, 'Höflichkeit als Lernziel im Englischunterricht', *Neusprachliche Mitteilungen* 35(4): 218–27.

Eelen, G. 1999, 'Politeness and ideology: a critical review', *Pragmatics* 9(1): 163–73.

Eelen, G. 2001, *A Critique of Politeness Theories*, Manchester: St Jerome.

Ehlich, K. 1992, 'On the historicity of politeness', in Watts, R., Ide, S. and Ehlich, K. (eds.), *Politeness in Language: Studies in its History, Theory and Practice*, Berlin: Mouton de Gruyter, pp. 71–107.

Ehlich, K. 1993, 'HIAT: A transcription system for discourse data', in Edwards, J. and Lampert, M. (eds.), *Talking Data: Transcription and Coding in Discourse Research*, Hillsdale, NJ: Lawrence Erlbaum, pp. 123–48.

Ehlich, K. and Rehbein, J. 1976, 'Halbinterpretative Arbeitstranskriptionen', *Linguistische Berichte* 45: 21–41.

Ehlich, K. and Rehbein, J. 1979, 'Erweiterte halbinterpretative Arbeitstranskriptionen (HIAT 2): Intonation', Linguistische Berichte 59: 51–75.

Ehlich, K. and Rehbein, J. 1981, 'Zur Notierung nonverbaler Kommunikation für diskursive Zwecke (Erweiterte halbinterpretative Arbeitstranskriptionen HIAT 2)', in Winkler, P. (ed.), *Methoden der Analyse von Face-to-Face-Situationen*, Stuttgart: Metzler, pp. 302–329).

Elias, N. 1939, *The History of Manners: the Civilizing Process*, New York: Pantheon, 1978.

Eliasoph, N. 1987, 'Politeness, power, and women's language: rethinking study in language and gender', *Berkeley Journal of Sociology* 32: 79–103.

Ervin-Tripp, S. 1972, 'Sociolinguistic rules of address', in Pride, J. and Holmes, J. (eds.), *Sociolinguistics*. Harmondsworth: Penguin, pp. 225–41.

Ervin-Tripp, S. 1979, 'How to make and to understand a request', in Parret, H. and Sbisa, M. (eds.) *Possibilities and Limitations of Pragmatics: Proceedings of the Conference on Pragmatics, Urbino 1979*. Amsterdam: Benjamins, pp. 195–210.

Ervin-Tripp, S.,Guo, J. and Lampert, M. 1990, 'Politeness and persuasion in children's control acts', *Journal of Pragmatics* 14(2): 307–31.

Faerch, C. and Kasper, G. 1989, 'Internal and external modification in interlanguage request realization', in Blum-Kulka, S., House, J. and Kasper, G. (eds.), *Cross-Cultural Pragmatics: Requests and Apologies*, Norwood, NJ.: Ablex, pp. 221–48.

Faret, N. 1632, *L'honnête homme*, Geneva: Slatkine Reprints, 1970.

Ferguson, C. 1967, 'Root–echo responses in Syrian Arabic politeness formulas', in Stuart, D. (eds.), *Linguistic Studies in Memory of Richard Slade Harrell*. Washington: Georgetown University Press, pp. 35–45.

Ferguson, C. 1983, 'God wishes in Syrian Arabic', *Mediterranean Review* 1: 65–83.

Ferguson, C. 1976, 'The structure and use of politeness formulas', *Language in Society* 5(2): 137–51.

Flowerdew, J. 1991, 'Pragmatic modifications on the "representative" speech act of defining', *Journal of Pragmatics* 15(3): 253–64.

France, P. 1992, *Politeness and its Discontents: Problems in French Classical Culture*, Cambridge: Cambridge University Press.

Fraser, B. 1975, 'Hedged performatives', in Cole, P. and Morgan, J. (eds.), *Syntax and Semantics 3. Speech Acts*, New York: Academic Press, pp. 187–210.

Fraser, B. 1980, 'Conversational mitigation', *Journal of Pragmatics* 4: 341–50.

Fraser, B. 1990, 'Perspectives on politeness', *Journal of Pragmatics* 14(2): 219–36.

Fraser, B. and Nolen, W. 1981, 'The association of deference with linguistic form', *International Journal of the Sociology of Language* 27: 93–111.

Fraser, B., Rintell, E. and Walters, J. 1980, 'An approach to conducting: research on the acquisition of pragmatic competence in a second language', in Larsen-Freeman, D. (ed.), *Discourse Analysis in Second Language Research*, Rowley, MA: Newbury, pp. 75–91.

Fukushima, S. 1990, 'Offers and requests: performance by Japanese learners of English', *World Englishes* 9(3): 317–25.

Fukushima, S. 1996, 'Request strategies in British English and Japanese', *Language Sciences* 18(3/4): 671–88.

Fukushima, S. 2000, *Requests and Culture: Politeness in British English and Japanese*, Bern: Peter Lang.

Galliker, M. and Klein, M. 1993, 'Knigges "Umgangsbuch". Zur Entwicklung der bürgerlichen Kommunikationsregeln', in Sonntag, M. and Jüttemann, G. (eds.), *Individuum und Geschichte. Beiträge zur Diskussion um eine 'Historische Psychologie'*, Heidelberg: Asanger, pp. 74–88.

García, C. 1989, 'Apologizing in English: politeness strategies used by native and non-native speakers', *Multilingua* 8(1): 3–20.

García, C. 1993, 'Making a request and responding to it: a case study of Peruvian Spanish speakers', *Journal of Pragmatics* 19: 127–52.

García, C. 1996, 'Teaching speech act performance: declining an invitation', *Hispania* 79(2): 267–79.

García, C. 1999, 'The three stages of Venezuelan invitations and responses', *Multilingua* 18(4): 391–433.

Garton, A.-F. and Pratt, C. 1990, 'Children's pragmatic judgements of direct and indirect requests', *First Language* 10(28, Pt 1): 51–9.

Garvey, C. 1975, 'Requests and responses in children's speech', *Child Language* 2: 41–61.

Gass, S. and Neu, J. (eds.) 1995, *Speech Acts across Cultures: Challenges to Communication in a Second Language*, New York: Walter de Gruyter.

Geis, M. 1995, *Speech Acts and Conversational Interaction*, New York: Cambridge University Press.

Gleason, J. 1980, 'The acquisition of social speech routines and politeness formulas', in Giles, H., Robinson, W. and Smith, P. (eds.), *Language: Social Psychological Perspectives*, Oxford: Pergamon, pp. 21–7.

Gleason, J., Berko, J., Perlmann, R. and Greif, E. 1984, 'What's the magic word: learning language through politeness routines', *Discourse Processes* 7(4): 493–502.

Gleason, J. and Weintraub, S. 1976, 'The acquisition of routines in child language', *Language in Society* 5: 129–36.

Glick, D. 1996, 'A reappraisal of Brown and Levinson's *Politeness: Some Universals of Language Use*, eighteen years later: review article', *Semiotica* 109(1/2): 141–171.

Gluckmann, M. 1962, *Essays on the Ritual of Social Relations*, Manchester: Manchester University Press.

Goffman, E. 1955, 'On face work: an analysis of ritual elements in social interaction', *Psychiatry* 18: 213–31.

Goffman, E. 1956, 'The nature of deference and demeanor', *American Anthropologist* 58: 473–502.

Goffman, E. 1967, *Interaction Ritual: Essays on Face-to-face Behavior*, Garden City, NY: Anchor Books.

Goffman, E. 1971, *The Presentation of Self in Everyday Life*, Harmondsworth: Penguin.

Goffman, E. 1981, *Forms of Talk*, Oxford: Blackwell.

Goodwin, C. and Heritage, J. 1990, 'Conversation analysis', *Annual Review of Anthropology* 19: 283–307.

Goody, E. (ed.) 1978, *Questions and Politeness: Strategies in Social Interaction*, Cambridge: Cambridge University Press.

Greif, E. and Gleason, J. 1980, 'Hi, thanks and goodbye: more routine information', *Language in Society* 9: 159–66.

Grice, H. 1957, 'Meaning', *The Philosophical Review* 66(3): 377–88.

Grice, H. 1969, 'Utterer's meaning and intentions', *Philosophical Review* 78(2): 147–77.

Grice, H. 1975, 'Logic and conversation', in Cole, P. and Morgan, J. (eds.), *Syntax and Semantics 3. Speech Acts*, New York: Academic Press, pp. 41–58.

Grice, H. 1978, 'Further notes on logic and conversation', in Cole, P. and Morgan, J. (eds.), *Syntax and Semantics 9. Pragmatics*, New York: Academic Press, pp. 113–27.

Grosperrin, J.-P. 1997, 'La politesse des premiers ages: un aspect du primitivisme chrétien sous Louis XIV', in Wild, F. (ed.), *Regards sur le passé dans l'Europe des XVIe et XVIIe siècles*, Berlin: Peter Lang, pp. 397–406.

Gu, Y. 1990, 'Politeness phenomena in modern Chinese', *Journal of Pragmatics* 14(2): 237–57.

Guazzo, Stefano (1574) *La ciuil conuersatione*, Brescia: Appresso Tomaso Bozzola.

Halliday, M. 1973, *Explorations in the Functions of Language*, London: Edward Arnold.

Halliday, M. 1978, *Language as a Social Semiotic: the Social Interpretation of Language and Meaning*, London: Edward Arnold.

Harman, G. 1971, 'Three levels of meaning', in Steinberg, D. and Jakobovits, L. (eds.), *Semantics: an Interdisciplinary Reader*, Cambridge: Cambridge University Press, pp. 66–75.

Haverkate, H. 1979, *Impositive Sentences in Spanish: Theory and Description in Pragmatics*, Amsterdam: Benjamins.

Haverkate, H. 1984, *Speech Acts, Speakers and Hearers: Reference and Referential Strategies in Spanish*, Amsterdam: Benjamins.

Haverkate, H. 1987, 'La cortesía como estrategía conversacional', *Diálogos Hispanicos de Amsterdam* 6: 27–63.

Haverkate, H. 1988a, 'Politeness strategies in verbal interaction: an analysis of directness and indirectness in speech acts', *Semiotica* 71: 59–71.

Haverkate, H. 1988b, 'Toward a typology of politeness strategy in communicative interaction', *Multilingua* 7(4): 385–409.

Haverkate, H. 1990, 'Aspectos semioticos de la cortesía verbal', *Revista de Lingüística Teórica y Aplicada* 28: 27–40.

Haverkate, H. 1991, 'La cortesía verbal: accion, transaccion e interaccion', *Revista Argentina de Linguistica* 7(2): 141–78.

Haverkate, H. 1994a, 'The dialogues of Don Quixote de la Mancha: a pragmalinguistic analysis within the framework of Gricean maxims, speech act theory, and politeness theory', *Poetics: Journal for Empirical Research on Literature, the Media and the Arts* 22(3): 219–41.

Haverkate, H. 1994b, 'Review of *Politeness Phenomena in England and Greece: a Crosscultural Perspective* by Maria Sifianou', *Language in Society* 23(4): 584–87.

Helbig, G. 1973, *Geschichte der neueren Sprachwissenschaft: Unter dem besonderen Aspekt der Grammatik-Theorie*, Munich: Hueber.

Held, G. 1987, 'Danken – semantische, pragmatische und soziokulturelle Aspekte eines höflichen Sprechakts (gezeigt am Beispiel des Französischen)', *Klagenfurter Beiträge zur Sprachwissenschaft* 13–14: 203–27.

Held, G. 1988, 'Osservazioni su strategie verbali di cortesia al servicio del ricevente', in Mauro, T., Gensini, S. and Piemontese, M. (eds.), *Dalla parte del ricevente: percezione, comprensione, interpretazione*, Rome: Bulzoni, pp. 293–303.

Held, G. 1989a, 'Beziehungsarbeit und Konversationsanalyse am Beispiel eines Bittgesprächs', *Folia Linguistica* 23: 405–31.

Held, G. 1989b, 'On the role of maximization in verbal politeness', *Multilingua* 7(4): 167–206.

Held, G. 1991a, 'Möglichkeiten der Entschärfung sozialer Übertretungshandlungen', in Stati, S., Weigand, E. and Hundsnurscher, F. (eds.) *Dialoganalyse III. Teil I.* Tübingen: Niemeyer, pp. 319–39.

Held, G. 1991b, 'Sprechen als Ethnomethode', in Dausendschön-Gay, U., Gülich, E. and Krafft, U. (eds.), *Linguistische Interaktionsanalyse: Beiträge zum 20. Romanistentag 1987*, Tübingen: Niemeyer, pp. 155–69.

Held, G. 1992a, 'Aspekte des Zusammenhangs zwischen Höflichkeit und Sprache in der vorpragmatischen Sprachwissenschaft', *Zeitschrift für Romanische Philologie* 108(1/2): 1–34.

Held, G. 1992b, 'Politeness in linguistic research', in Watts, R., Ide, S. and Ehlich, K. (eds.), *Politeness in Language: Studies in its History, Theory and Practice*, Berlin: Mouton de Gruyter, pp. 131–53.

Held, G. 1995, *Verbale Höflichkeit: Studien zur linguistischen Theorienbildung und empirische Untersuchung zum Sprachverhalten französischer und italienischer Jugendlicher in Bitt- und Danksituationen*, Tübingen: Gunter Narr.

Held, G. 1996, 'Two polite speech acts in contrastive view: aspects of the realization of requesting and thanking in French and Italian', in Hellinger, M. and Ammon, U. (eds.), *Contrastive Sociolinguistics*. Berlin: de Gruyter, pp. 363–84.

Held, G. 1999, 'Submission strategies as an expression of the ideology of politeness: reflections on the verbalization of social power relations', *Pragmatics* 9(1): 21–36.

Hendry, J. 1990, 'To wrap or not to wrap: politeness and penetration in ethnographic enquiry', *Man* 24: 620–35.

Hendry, J. 1992, 'Honorifics as dialect: the expression and manipulation of boundaries', *Multilingua* 11(4): 341–54.

Hendry, J. 1993, *Wrapping Culture: Politeness, Presentation and Power in Japan and Other Societies*, Oxford: Clarendon Press.

Herbert, R. 1990, 'Sex-based differences in compliment behavior', *Language in Society* 19(2): 201–24.

Herbert, R. 1991, 'The sociology of compliment work: an ethnocontrastive study of Polish and English compliments', *Multilingua* 10(4): 381–402.

Herbert, R. and Straight, H. 1989, 'Compliment-rejection versus compliment-avoidance: listener-based versus speaker-based pragmatic strategies', *Language and Communication* 9: 35–47.

Hill, B., Ide, S., Ikuta, S., Kawasaki, A. and Ogino, T. 1986, 'Universals of linguistic politeness: quantitative evidence from Japanese and American English', *Journal of Pragmatics* 10(3): 347–71.

Ho, D. 1976, 'On the concept of face', *American Journal of Sociology* 81(4): 867–84.

Holly, W. 1979, *Imagearbeit in Gesprächen. Zur linguistischen Beschreibung des Beziehungsaspekts*, Tübingen: Niemeyer.

Holmes, J. 1986, 'Functions of *you know* in women's and men's speech', *Language in Society* 15: 1–22.

Holmes, J. 1989a, 'Paying compliments: a sex preferential politeness strategy', *Journal of Pragmatics* 12(4): 445–65.

Holmes, J. 1989b, 'Sex differences and apologies: one aspect of communicative competence', *Applied Linguistics* 10(2): 194–213.

Holmes, J. 1990, 'Apologies in New Zealand English', *Language in Society* 19(2): 155–99.

Holmes, J. 1993, 'New Zealand women are good to talk to: an analysis of politeness strategies in interaction', *Journal of Pragmatics* 20(2): 91–116.

Holmes, J. 1995, *Women, Men and Politeness*, London: Longman.

Holmes, J. and Stubbe, M. 1997, 'Good listeners: gender differences in New Zealand conversation', *Women and Language* 20(2): 7–14.

Holtgraves, T. 1986, 'Language structure in social interaction: perceptions of direct and indirect speech acts and interactants who use them', *Journal of Personality and Social Psychology* 51(2): 305–14.

Holtgraves, T. 1991, 'Interpreting questions and replies: effects of face-threat, question form and gender', *Social Psychology Quarterly* 54: 15–24.

Holtgraves, T. 1992, 'The linguistic realization of face management: implications for language production and comprehension, person perception, and cross-cultural communication', *Social Psychology Quarterly* 55(2): 141–59.

Holtgraves, T. 1997a, 'Politeness and memory for the wording of remarks', *Memory and Cognition* 25(1): 106–16.

Holtgraves, T. 1997b, ' "Yes, but . . .": positive politeness in conversation arguments', *Journal of Language and Social Psychology* 16(2): 222–39.

Holtgraves, T. and Yang, J. 1990, 'Politeness as universal: cross-cultural perceptions of request strategies and inferences based on their use', *Journal of Personality and Social Psychology* 59(4): 719–29.

Hopper, P. and Traugott, E. (1993), *Grammaticalization*, Cambridge: Cambridge University Press.

House, J. 1988, ' "Oh excuse me please . . .": apologizing in a foreign language', in Kettemann, B., Bierbaumer, P., Fill, A. and Karpf, A. (eds.), *Englisch als Zweitsprache*, Tübingen: Narr, pp. 303–27.

House, J. 1989, 'Politeness in English and German: the functions of *please and bitte*', in Blum-Kulka, S., House, J. and Kasper, G. (eds.), *Cross-Cultural Pragmatics: Requests and Apologies*. Norwood, NJ: Ablex, pp. 96–119.

House, J. and Kasper, G. 1981, 'Politeness markers in English and German', in Coulmas, F. (eds.), *Conversational Routine*, The Hague: Mouton, pp. 157–85.

Hu, H. 1944, 'The Chinese concepts of "face"', *American Anthropologist* 46(1): 45–64.

Hymes, D. 1986, 'Discourse: scope without depth', *International Journal of the Sociology of Language* 57: 49–89.

Ide, S. 1982, 'Japanese sociolinguistics: politeness and women's language', *Lingua* 57(2/4): 357–85.

Ide, S. 1989, 'Formal forms and discernment: two neglected aspects of linguistic politeness', *Multilingua* 8(2/3): 223–48.

Ide, S. 1993, 'Linguistic politeness, III: linguistic politeness and universality', *Multilingua* 12(1).

Ide, S., Hori, M., Ikuta, S., Kawasaki, A. and Ogino, T. 1986, 'Sex difference and politeness in Japanese', *International Journal of the Sociology of Language* 58: 25–36.

Ide, S., Hill, B., Cames, Y., Ogino, T. and Kawasaki, A. 1992, 'The concept of politeness: an empirical study of American English and Japanese', in Watts, R., Ide, S. and Ehlich, K. (eds.), *Politeness in Language: Studies in its History, Theory and Practice*, Berlin: Mouton de Gruyter, pp. 281–97.

James, A. 1983, ' "Well" in reporting clauses: meaning and form of a "lexical filler", *Arbeiten aus Anglistik und Amerikanistik* 8(1): 33–40.

Janney, R. and Arndt, H. 1992, 'Intracultural tact versus intercultural tact', in Watts, R., Ide, S. and Ehlich, K. (eds.), *Politeness in Language: Studies in its History, Theory and Practice*, Berlin: Mouton de Gruyter, pp. 21–41.

Janney, R. and Arndt, H. 1993, 'Universality and relativity in cross-cultural politeness research: a historical perspective', *Multilingua* 12(1): 13–50.

Jary, M. 1998, 'Relevance theory and the communication of politeness', *Journal of Pragmatics* 30: 1–19.

Jefferson, G. 1973, 'A case of precision timing in ordinary conversation: overlapped tag-positioned address in closing sequences', *Semiotica* 9: 47–96.

Johnson, D. 1992, 'Compliments and politeness in peer-review texts', *Applied Linguistics* 13(1): 51–71.

Johnson, D. and Roen, D. 1992, 'Complimenting and involvement in peer reviews: gender variation', *Language in Society* 21(1): 27–57.

Johnstone, B., Ferrara, K. and Bean, J. 1992, 'Gender, politeness, and discourse management in same sex and cross-sex opinion-poll interviews', *Journal of Pragmatics* 18(5): 405–30.

Jucker, A. 1988, 'The relevance of politeness', *Multilingua* 7(4): 375–84.

Jucker, A. 1994, 'Review of *Politeness in Language: Studies in Its History, Theory and Practice*, edited by Richard J. Watts, Sachiko Ide, and Konrad Ehlich', *Multilingua* 13(3): 329–34.

Jucker, A. (ed.) 1997, *The Social Dimension of Communication*, special issue of *Multilingua* 16(2/3).

Kachru, Y. 1994, 'Crosscultural speech act research and the classroom', *Pragmatics and Language Learning*, Monograph Series 5: 39–51.

Kakava, C. 1997, 'Review article: *Politeness and the particularities of requests* (Review of Sifianou 1992)', *International Journal of the Sociology of Language* 126: 181–98.

Kamisli, S. and Dogançay, S. A. 1997, 'Gender differences in conveying embarrassing information: examples from Turkish', *Women and Language* 20(2): 25–33.

Kasper, G. 1990, 'Linguistic politeness: current research issues', *Journal of Pragmatics* 14(2): 193–218.

Katriel, T. 1986, *Talking Straight: Dugri speech in Israeli Sabra Culture*, Cambridge: Cambridge University Press.

Keenan, E. C. 1976, 'The universality of conversational postulates', *Language in Society* 5: 67–80.

Ketcham, M. 1985, *Transparent Designs: Reading, Performance, and Form in the Spectator Papers*, Athens, GE: University of Georgia Press.

Khanittanan, W. 1988, 'Some observations on expressing politeness in Thai', *Language Sciences* 10(2): 353–62.

Kienpointner, M. 1997, 'Varieties of rudeness: types and functions of impolite utterances', *Functions of Language* 4(2): 251–87.

Kienpointner, M. 1999, 'Ideologies of politeness', *Pragmatics* special issue 9(1).

Klein, L. 1984, 'The third Earl of Shaftesbury and the progress of politeness', *Eighteenth-Century Studies* 18: 186–214.

Klein, L. 1986, 'Berkeley, Shaftesbury, and the meaning of politeness', *Studies in Eighteenth Century Culture* 16: 57–68.

Klein, L. 1990, 'Politeness in seventeenth century England and France', *Cahiers du Dix-septième: an Interdisciplinary Journal* 4(1): 91–106.

Klein, L. 1992, 'Courtly politesse and civic politeness in France and England', *Halcyon: a Journal of the Humanities* 14: 171–81.

Klein, L. 1994, *Shaftesbury and the Culture of Politeness: Moral Discourse and Cultural Politics in Early Eighteenth-Century England*, Cambridge: Cambridge University Press.

Knapp-Potthoff, A. 1992, 'Secondhand politeness', in Watts, R., Ide, S. and Ehlich, K. (eds.), *Politeness in Language: Studies in its History, Theory and Practice*, Berlin: Mouton de Gruyter, pp. 203–18.

Koike, D. 1989, 'Requests and the role of deixis in politeness', *Journal of Pragmatics* 13(2): 187–202.

Koike, D. 1992, 'Brazilian Portuguese directives and a hierarchy of strategies for politeness', in Koike, D. (ed.), *Romance Linguistics: the Portuguese Context*, Westport, CT: Bergin & Garvey, pp. 121–40.

Koike, D. A. 1994, 'Negation in Spanish and English suggestions and requests: mitigating effects?', *Journal of Pragmatics* 21: 513–26.

Kotthoff, H. 1993, 'Disagreement and concession in disputes: On the context sensitivity of preference structures', *Language in Society* 22(2): 193–216.

Kotthoff, H. 1996, 'Impoliteness and conversational joking: on relational politics', *Folia Linguistica: Acta Societatis Linguisticae Europaeae* 30(3–4): 299–325.

Kuhn, T. 1962, *The Structure of Scientific Revolutions*, Chicago: University of Chicago Press.

Kummer, M. 1992, 'Politeness in Thai', in Watts, R., Ide, I. and Ehlich, K. (eds.), *Politeness in Language: Studies in Its History, Theory and Practice*, Berlin: Mouton de Gruyter, pp. 325–36.

Kwarciak, B. J. 1991. *Cognitive Aspects of the Child's Linguistic Politeness*, Dissertation, Abstracts International, vol. 51 (11–13).

Kwarciak, B. J. 1993, 'The acquisition of linguistic politeness and Brown and Levinson's theory', *Multilingua* 12(1): 51–68.

Labov, W. 1975, *Language in the Inner City: Studies in the Black English Vernacular*, Philadelphia: University of Pennsylvania Press.

Lakoff, R. 1973a, 'The logic of politeness; or minding your p's and q's', *Chicago Linguistics Society* 8: 292–305.

Lakoff, R. 1973b, 'Questionable answers and answerable questions', in Kachru, B. *et al.* (eds.), *Issues in Linguistics: Papers in Honor of Henry and Renée Kahane*, Urbana, Ill.: University of Illinois Press, 453–67.

Lakoff, R. 1975a, *Language and Women's Place*, New York: Harper.

Lakoff, R. 1975b, 'Language theory and the real world', *Language Learning* 25(2): 309–38.

Lakoff, R. 1977, 'What you can do with words: politeness, pragmatics and performatives', in Rogers, P. (ed.), *Proceedings of the Texas Conference on Performatives*, Arlington, VA: Center for Applied Linguistics, pp. 79–105.

Lakoff, R. 1979, 'Stylistic strategies within a grammar of style', in Orasanu, J., Slater, K. and Adler, L. (eds.), *Language, Sex and Gender: Does la différence make a difference?*, New York: The Annals of the New York Academy of Sciences, pp. 53–80.

Lakoff, R. 1989, 'The limits of politeness: therapeutic and courtroom discourse', *Multilingua* 8(2/3): 101–29.

Langford, P. 1989, *A Polite and Commercial People: England 1727–1783*, Oxford: Clarendon Press.

Lavandera, B. 1988, 'The social pragmatics of politeness forms', in Ammon, U., Dittmar, N. and Mattheier, K. (eds.), *Sociolinguistics/Soziolinguistik: an International Handbook of the Science of Language and Society/Ein internationales Handbuch zur Wissenschaft von Sprache und Gesellschaft*, 2 volumes, Berlin: Walter de Gruyter, pp. 1196–205.

Lee-Wong, S.-M. 1994a, 'Imperatives in requests: direct or impolite: observations from Chinese', *Pragmatics* 4(4): 491–515.

Lee-Wong, S.-M. 1994b, 'Qing/Please: a polite or requestive marker? observations from Chinese', *Multilingua* 13(4): 343–60.

Lee-Wong, S.-M. 1999, *Politeness and Face in Chinese Culture*, Frankfurt: Peter Lang.

Leech, G. 1977, *Language and Tact, L.A.U.T. Papers* 46. University of Trier.

Leech, G. 1980, *Explorations in Semantics and Pragmatics*, Amsterdam: Benjamins.

Leech, G. 1983, *Principles of Pragmatics*, London: Longman.

Lerch, E. 1934, *Modalität: Stimmführung und affektische Verkürzung*, Leipzig: Reisland.

Lim, T.-S. 1994, 'Facework and interpersonal relationships', in Ting-Toomey, S. (ed.), *The Challenge of Facework*. Albany NY: University of New York Press, pp. 209–29.

Lim, T.-S. and Bowers, J. 1991, 'Facework: solidarity, approbation, and tact', *Human Communication Research* 17(3): 415–50.

Liu, R. 1987, 'Critical review of Leech's Politeness Principle', *Foreign Language Teaching and Research* 2 (70): 42–6.

Magendie, M. 1970 [1924], *La politesse mondaine et les théories de l'honnêteté en France au XVIIe siècle, de 1600 à 1660*, Geneva: Slatkine Reprints.

Magli, P. 1992, 'Mediocrita e bon ton passionale', in Montandon, A. (ed.), *Etiquette et politesse*. Clermont-Ferrand: Association des Publications de la Faculté des Lettres et Sciences Humaines de Clermont-Ferrand, pp. 43–55.

Manes, J. and Wolfson, N. 1980, 'The compliment as a social strategy', *Papers in Linguistics* 13: 391–410.

Manes, J. and Wolfson, N. 1981, 'The compliment formula', in Coulmas, F. (ed.), *Conversational Routine*. The Hague: Mouton, pp. 115–33.

Mao, L. 1992, 'Invitational discourse and Chinese identity', *Journal of Asian Pacific Communication* 3(1): 70–96.

Mao, L. R. 1994, 'Beyond politeness theory: "face" revisited and renewed', *Journal of Pragmatics* 21(5): 451–86.

Matsumoto, Y. 1988, 'Reexamination of the universality of face: politeness phenomena in Japanese', *Journal of Pragmatics* 12(4): 403–26.

Matsumoto, Y. 1989, 'Politeness and conversational universals – observations from Japanese', *Multilingua* 8(2/3): 207–22.

Matsumoto, Y. 1993, 'Linguistic politeness and cultural style: observations from Japanese', in Clancy, P. (ed.), *Japanese/Korean Linguistics, II*. Stanford, CA: Center for Study of Language and Information, pp. 55–67.

McIntosh, C. 1998, *The Evolution of English Prose, 1700–1800: Style, Politeness, and Print Culture*, Cambridge: Cambridge University Press.

Mead, G. 1934, *Mind, Self and Society from the Standpoint of a Social Behaviorist*, Chicago: University of Chicago.

Milroy, L. 1980, *Language and Social Networks*, Oxford: Blackwell.

Milroy, J. and Milroy, L. 1991, *Authority in Language: Investigating Language Prescription and Standardisation*, 2nd edition, London: Routledge.

Montandon, A. (ed.), 1992. *Etiquette et politesse*. Clermont-Ferrand: Association des Publications de la Faculté des Lettres et Sciences Humaines de Clermont-Ferrand.

Mugglestone, L. 1995, *'Talking Proper': the Rise of Accent as Social Symbol*, Oxford: Clarendon.

Mühlhäusler, P. and Harré, R. 1990, *Pronouns and People: the Linguistic Construction of Social and Personal Identity*, Oxford: Blackwell.

Mursy, A. and Wilson, J. 2001, 'Towards a definition of Egyptian complimenting', *Multilingua* 20(2): 133–54.

Nakanishi, M. 1998, 'Gender enactment on a first date: a Japanese sample', *Women and Language* 21(1): 10–17.

Ng, S. H. and Bradac, J. J. 1993, *Power in Language*, Newbury Park: Sage.

Norton, H. 1900, *A Courtesy Book for Older Girls and Boys*, London.

Nwoye, O. 1989, 'Linguistic politeness in Igbo', *Multilingua* 8(2/3): 249–58.

Nwoye, O. 1992, 'Linguistic politeness and socio-cultural variations of the notion of face', *Journal of Pragmatics* 18(4): 309–28.

O'Driscoll, J. 1996, 'About face: a defence and elaboration of universal dualism', *Journal of Pragmatics* 25(1): 1–32.

Olshtain, E. 1983, 'Apologies across languages', in Blum-Kulka, S., House J. and Kasper, G. (eds.), *Cross-Cultural Pragmatics: Requests and Apologies*. Norwood NJ: Ablex, pp. 155–74.

Olshtain, E. and Cohen, A. 1983, 'Apology: a speech act set', in Wolfson, N. and Judd, E. (eds.), *Sociolinguistics and Language Acquisition*. Rowley: Newbury House: 18–36.

Olshtain, E. and Weinbach, L. 1987, 'Complaints: a study of speech act behavior among native and non-native speakers of Hebrew', in Verschueren, J. and Bertucelli-Papi, M. (eds.), *The Pragmatic Perspective*. Amsterdam: Benjamins, pp. 195–208.

Owen, M. 1983, *Apologies and Remedial Interchanges: a Study of Language Use in Social Interaction*, Berlin: Mouton de Gruyter.

Patrizi, G. 1992, 'Il valore della norma. Etichetta come comunicazione e rappresentazione tra *Cortegiano e Galateo*', in Montandon, A. (ed.), *Etiquette et politesse*. Clermont-Ferrand: Association des Publications de la Faculté des Lettres et Sciences Humaines de Clermont-Ferrand, pp. 33–42.

Penman, R. 1990, 'Facework and politeness: multiple goals in courtroom discourse', *Journal of Language and Social Psychology* 9(1/2): 15–38.

Penman, R. 1994, 'Facework in communication: conceptual and moral challenges', in Ting-Toomey, S. (eds.), *The Challenge of Facework*, Albany NY: University of New York Press, pp. 15–45.

Pocock, J. 1985, *Virtue, Commerce, and History: Essays on Political Thought and History, Chiefly in the Eighteenth Century*, Cambridge: Cambridge University Press.

Potkay, Adam 1994, *The Fate of Eloquence in the Age of Hume*, Ithaca: Cornell University Press.

Power, T. G. and Shanks, J. A. 1989, 'Parents as socializers: maternal and paternal views', *Journal of Youth and Adolescence* 18(2): 203–22.

Quirk, R., Greenbaum, S., Leech, G. and Svartvik, J. 1985, *A Comprehensive Grammar of the English Language*, London: Longman.

Rathmayr, R. 1996a, *Pragmatik der Entschuldigungen. Vergleichende Untersuchung am Beispiel der russischen Sprache und Kultur*, Cologne: Böhlau Verlag.

Rathmayr, R. 1996b, 'Sprachliche Höflichkeit. Am Beispiel expliziter und impliziter Höflichkeit im Russischen', in Girke, W. (ed.), *Slavistische Linguistik 1995*, Munich: Böhlan Verlag, pp. 362–91.

Rathmayr, R. 1999, 'Métadiscours et réalité linguistique: l'exemple de la politesse russe', *Pragmatics* 9(1): 75–95.

Reddy, M. 1979. 'The conduit metaphor: a case of frame conflict in our language about language', in Ortony, A. (ed.), *Metaphor and Thought*, Cambridge: Cambridge University Press, pp. 284–324.

Ross, J. 1970, 'On declarative sentences', in Jacobs, R. and Rosenbaum, R. (eds.), *Readings in English Transformational Grammar*, Waltham, Mass.: Ginn, pp. 222–72.

Rundquist, S. 1992, 'Indirectness: a gender study of flouting Grice's maxims', *Journal of Pragmatics* 18: 431–49.

Sacks, H. 1992, *Lectures on Conversation*, vols. I and II, edited by Gail Jefferson, Oxford: Blackwell.

Santosuosso, A. 1979, *The Bibliography of Giovanni Della Casa: Books, Readers and Critics, 1537–1975*, Florence: L. S. Olschki.

Sarangi, S. and Slembrouck, S. 1991, 'Non-cooperation in communication: a reassessment of Gricean pragmatics', *Journal of Pragmatics* 17: 117–54.

Sbisà, M. 1992, 'Review of *Cross-Cultural Pragmatics: Requests and Apologies* edited by S. Blum-Kulka, J. House and G. Kasper', *Journal of Pragmatics* 17(3): 267–274.

Schiffrin, D. 1987, *Discourse Markers*, Cambridge: Cambridge University Press.

Schmidt, R. 1980, 'Review of Esther Goody, ed., *Questions and Politeness: Strategies in Social Interaction*', *Regional English Language Centre Journal* 11: 100–14.

Searle, J. 1970, *Speech Acts*, Cambridge: Cambridge University Press.

Searle, J. (ed.) 1972, *The Philosophy of Language*, London: Oxford University Press.

Shaftesbury, 3rd Earl of, Anthony Ashley Cooper, 1711, *Characteristics of Men, Manners, Opinions, Times: An Enquiry Concerning Virtue or Merit*, London.

Shibamoto, J. 1985, *Japanese Women's Language*, London: Academic Press.

Shibamoto, J. 1994, 'Review of *Wrapping Culture: Politeness, Presentation, and Power in Japan and Other Societies* by Joy Hendry', *Contemporary Sociology* 23(4): 608.

Shu, D. and Wang H. 1993, 'Complimenting and belittling acts in interpersonal rhetoric and politeness principle', *Waiguoyu, Beijing* 3(85): 7–13.

Sifianou, M. 1992a, *Politeness Phenomena in England and Greece*, Oxford: Clarendon.

Sifianou, M. 1992b, 'The use of diminutives in expressing politeness: Modern Greek versus English', *Journal of Pragmatics* 17: 155–73.

Sifianou, M. 1993, 'Off-record indirectness and the notion of imposition', *Multilingua* 12(1): 69–79.

Sifianou, M. 1995, 'Do we need to be silent to be extremely polite? Silence and FTAs', *International Journal of Applied Linguistics* 5(1): 95–110.

Sifianou, M. 1997a, 'Politeness and off-record indirectness', *International Journal of the Sociology of Language* 126: 163–79.

Sifianou, M. 1997b, 'Silence and politeness', in Jaworski, A. (eds.), *Silence: Interdisciplinary Perspectives*. Berlin: Mouton de Gruyter, pp. 63–84.

Sifianou, M. 1989, 'On the telephone again. Differences in telephone behaviour: England versus Greece', *Language in Society* 18(4): 527–44.

Simmel, G. 1900, *Die Philosophie des Geldes*, Leipzig: Dunker & Humbolt.

Smith, J. 1997, 'Review of Joy Hendry, *Wrapping Culture*', *Language in Society* 26(2): 312–17.

Smith, O. 1984, *The Politics of Language 1791–1819*, Oxford: Clarendon Press.

Snow, C., Perlmann, R., Gleason, J. and Hooshyar, N. 1990, 'Developmental perspectives on politeness: sources of children's knowledge', *Journal of Pragmatics* 14(2): 289–305.

Sperber, D. and Wilson D. 1995, *Relevance: Communication and Cognition*, 2nd edition, Oxford: Blackwell.

Spitzer, L. 1922, *Italienische Umgangssprache*, Bonn: Schröder.

Stalpers, J. 1992, 'Between matter-of-factness and politeness', in Watts, R., Ide, S. and Ehlich, K. (eds.), *Politeness in Language: Studies in its History*. Berlin: Mouton de Gruyter, pp. 219–30.

Steinberg, D. and Jakobovits, L. (eds.) 1970, *Semantics: an Interdisciplinary Reader*, Cambridge: Cambridge University Press, pp. 60–5.

Steppat, M. 1994, 'Social change and gender decorum: Renaissance courtesy', in Carré, J. (ed.), *The Crisis of Courtesy: Studies in the Conduct-Book in Britain, 1600–1900*. Leiden: Brill, pp. 27–40.

Strecker, I. 1993, 'Cultural variations in the concept of "face"', *Multilingua* 12(2): 119–41.

Svartvik, J. 1980, '*Well* in conversation', in Greenbaum, S., Leech, G. and Svartvik, J. (eds.), *Studies in English Linguistics for Randolph Quirk*, London: Longman, 167–77.

Thompson, S. and Mulac, A. 1991, 'The discourse conditions for the use of the complementizer *that* in conversational English', *Journal of Pragmatics* 15(3): 237–51.

Ting-Toomey, S. 1994a, 'Face and facework: Theoretical and research issues', in Ting-Toomey, S. (ed.), *The Challenge of Facework: Cross-Cultural and Interpersonal Issues*. Albany NY: State University of New York Press, pp. 307–40.

Ting-Toomey, S. (ed.) 1994b, *The Challenge of Facework*, Albany NY: University of New York Press.

Tirkkonen-Condit, S. 1996, 'Explicitness vs. implicitness of argumentation: An intercultural comparison', *Multilingua* 15(3): 257–73.

Tomoda, S. 1991, 'Cost and Benefit in Language Use: a Case Study of Sentence Particles in Japanese', Ph.D. thesis, University of Arizona.

Trosborg, Anna 1987 'Apology strategies in natives/nonnatives', *Journal of Pragmatics* 11: 147–67.

Valtl, K. 1986, *Erziehung zur Höflichkeit: Höflichkeit als Wertkonzept der Alltagsinteraktion, als Gegenstand empirischer Forschung in den Humanwissenschaften und als Aufgabe der Erziehung*, Regensburg.

Wartenberg, T. 1991. *The Forms of Power: From Domination to Transformation*, Philadelphia, PA: Temple University Press.

Walper, S. and Valtin, R. 1992, 'Children's understanding of white lies', in Watts, R., Ide, S. and Ehlich, K. (eds.), *Politeness in Language: Studies in its History, Theory and Practice*, Berlin: Mouton de Gruyter, pp. 231– 51.

Watts, R. 1987, 'Relevance in conversational moves: a reappraisal of *well*', *Studia Anglica Posnaniensia* 19: 37–59.

Watts, R. 1989a, 'The perceptual salience of discourse markers in conversation', in Weydt, H. (ed.), *Sprechen mit Partikeln*. Berlin: Walter de Gruyter, 601–20.

Watts, R. 1989b, 'Taking the pitcher to the well: native speakers' perceptions of their use of discourse markers in conversation', *Journal of Pragmatics* 13, 203–37.

Watts, R. 1989c, 'Relevance and relational work: linguistic politeness as politic behavior', *Multilingua* 8(2/3): 131–67.

Watts, R. 1991, *Power in Family Discourse*, Berlin: Mouton de Gruyter.

Watts, R. 1992, 'Linguistic politeness and politic verbal behaviour: reconsidering claims for universality', in Watts, R., Ide, S. and Ehlich, K. (eds.), *Politeness in Language: Studies in its History, Theory and Practice*, Berlin: Mouton de Gruyter, pp. 43–69.

Watts, R. 1994, 'Planning in-service training courses: institutional constraints and non-native EFL teachers' perceptions', *International Journal of Applied Linguistics* 4: 19–56.

Watts, R. 1997a, 'Silence and the acquisition of status in verbal interaction', in Jaworski, A. (ed.), *Silence: Interdisciplinary Perspectives*, Berlin: Mouton de Gruyter, pp. 87–115.

Watts, R. 1997b, 'Relevance theory and verbal interruptions: assessing discourse status', in Jucker, A. H. (ed.), *The Social Dimension of Communication*, special issue of *Multilingua* 16(2/3): 153–86.

Watts, R. 1999a, 'Language and politeness in early eighteenth century Britain', *Pragmatics* 9(1): 5–20.

Watts, R. 1999b, 'The social construction of Standard English: grammar writers as a "discourse community"', in Bex, A. and Watts, R. (eds.), *Standard English: the Widening Debate*, London: Routledge, pp. 40–68.

Watts, R. 2002, 'From polite language to educated language: the re-emergence of an ideology', in Watts, R. and Trudgill, P. (eds.), *Alternative Histories of English*, London: Routledge, 155–72.

Watts, R., Ide, S. and Ehlich, K. 1992a, Introduction, in Watts, R., Ide, S. and Ehlich, K. (eds.), *Politeness in Language: Studies in its History, Theory and Practice*, Berlin: Mouton de Gruyter, pp. 1–17.

Watts, R., Ide, S. and Ehlich, K. (eds.) 1992b, *Politeness in Language: Studies in its History, Theory and Practice*, Berlin: Mouton de Gruyter.

Watts, R. and Trudgill, P. (eds.) 2002, *Alternative Histories of English*, London: Routledge.

Weinrich, H. 1986, *Lügt man im Deutschen, wenn man höflich ist?* Mannheim: Dudenverlag.

Werkhofer, K. 1992, 'Traditional and modern views: the social constitution and the power of politeness', in Watts, R., Ide, S. and Ehlich, K. (eds.), *Politeness in Language: Studies in its History, Theory and Practice*. Berlin: Mouton de Gruyter, pp. 155–99.

Wierzbicka, A. 1985, 'Different cultures, different languages, different speech acts: Polish vs English', *Journal of Pragmatics* 9: 145–78.

Wierzbicka, A. 1991a, *Cross-Cultural Pragmatics: the Semantics of Human Inter-action*, Berlin: Mouton de Gruyter.

Wierzbicka, A. 1991b, 'Japanese key words and core cultural values', *Language in Society* 20: 333–85.

Wildeblood, J. 1965, *The Polite World: a Guide to English Manners and Deportment from the Thirteenth to the Nineteenth Century*, Oxford: Oxford University Press.

Wilhite, M. 1983, 'Children's acquisition of language routines: the end-of-the-meal routine in Cakchiquel', *Language in Society* 12(1): 47–64.

Wilson, D. and Sperber, D. 1978, 'On Grice's theory of conversation', Pragmatics Microfiche 3: 5.

Woodhouse, J. 1994, 'The tradition of Della Casa's Galateo in English', in Carré, J. (eds.), *The Crisis of Courtesy: Studies in the Conduct-Book in Britain, 1600–1900*, Leiden: Brill, pp. 11–23.

Yang, Y.-L. 1988, 'The English pronoun of address: a matter of self-compensation', *Sociolinguistics* 17(2): 157–80.

Yli-Jokipii, H. 1994, *Requests in Professional Discourse: a Cross-Cultural Study of British, American and Finnish Business Writing*, Helsinki: Suomalainen Tiedeakatemia.

Ziff, P. 1971, 'On H. P. Grice's account of meaning', in Steinberg, D. and Jakobovits, L. (eds.), *Semantics: an Interdisciplinary Reader*, Cambridge: Cambridge University Press, pp. 60–5.

Index